Inside the Mind of a Mediator

Strategic Conflict Intervention

ASPEN COURSEBOOK SERIES

Inside the Mind of a Mediator

Strategic Conflict Intervention

LIORA PANIZ

ASPEN PUBLISHING

Cover image credit: iStock.com/wildpixel

To contact Customer Service, e-mail customer.service@aspenpublishing.com, call 1-800-950-5259, or mail correspondence to:

Aspen Publishing
Attn: Order Department
PO Box 990
Frederick, MD 21705

Printed in the United States of America.

1 2 3 4 5 6 7 8 9 0

ISBN 978-1-5438-4953-0

Library of Congress Cataloging-in-Publication Data application is in process.

SUSTAINABLE FORESTRY INITIATIVE Certified Chain of Custody
At Least 10% Certified Forest Content
www.sfiprogram.org
SFI-01028

About Aspen Publishing

Aspen Publishing is a leading provider of educational content and digital learning solutions to law schools in the U.S. and around the world. Aspen provides best-in-class solutions for legal education through authoritative textbooks, written by renowned authors, and breakthrough products such as Connected eBooks, Connected Quizzing, and PracticePerfect.

The Aspen Casebook Series (famously known among law faculty and students as the "red and black" casebooks) encompasses hundreds of highly regarded textbooks in more than eighty disciplines, from large enrollment courses, such as Torts and Contracts to emerging electives such as Sustainability and the Law of Policing. Study aids such as the *Examples & Explanations* and *Glannon Guide* series, both highly popular collections, help law students master complex subject matter.

Major products, programs, and initiatives include:

- **Connected eBooks** are enhanced digital textbooks and study aids that come with a suite of online content and learning tools designed to maximize student success. Designed in collaboration with hundreds of faculty and students, the Connected eBook is a significant leap forward in the legal education learning tools available to students.
- **Connected Quizzing** is an easy-to-use formative assessment tool that tests law students' understanding and provides timely feedback to improve learning outcomes. Delivered through CasebookConnect.com, the learning platform already used by students to access their Aspen casebooks, Connected Quizzing is simple to implement and integrates seamlessly with law school course curricula.
- **PracticePerfect** is a visually engaging, interactive study aid to explain commonly encountered legal doctrines through easy-to-understand animated videos, illustrative examples, and numerous practice questions. Developed by a team of experts, PracticePerfect is the ideal study companion for today's law students.
- The **Aspen Learning Library** enables law schools to provide their students with access to the most popular study aids on the market across all of their courses. Available through an annual subscription, the online library consists of study aids in e-book, audio, and video formats with full text search, note-taking, and highlighting capabilities.
- Aspen's **Digital Bookshelf** is an institutional-level online education bookshelf, consolidating everything students and professors need to ensure success. This program ensures that every student has access to affordable course materials from day one.
- **Leading Edge** is a community centered on thinking differently about legal education and putting those thoughts into actionable strategies. At the core of the program is the Leading Edge Conference, an annual gathering of legal education thought leaders looking to pool ideas and identify promising directions of exploration.

For Lynn and Tommy

Summary of Contents

Contents

Part II. Chapters 13

Acknowledgments

To Jordan Jepsen and Aspen Publishing, thank you
for believing in this project and in me.

To Robert, whose unwavering confidence and support made this possible.
Without you, it truly would not be.

To my family and dear friends, who are first to join in on each new
adventure.

To you all — I give my enduring gratitude.

Introduction

Everyone at one time or another is a conflict resolver, from presidents to school teachers, from generals to parents . . .
— *Bernard S. Mayer*

1. The patience of Job . . .
2. The physical endurance of the marathon runner
3. The broken-field dodging abilities of a halfback
4. The guile of Machiavelli
5. The personality-probing skills of a good psychiatrist
6. The confidence-retaining characteristic of [silence]
7. The hide of a rhinoceros
8. The wisdom of Solomon

— *William Simkin*[1]

Long gone are the days of the caveman, when conflict would be resolved by hitting one's adversary on the head with a stick, at the end of which was fastened a point made of bone or stone. This was no doubt effective for creating a winner or last man standing and loser or dead guy. An effective tool for mediating a dispute in which our goal is to foster the spirit of cooperation, and possibly transform the bad relationship into a better one, though? No. No more of the Hatfield and McCoy "lawless and unrelenting family feuds" or "gun-toting vigilantes hell-bent on defending their kinfolk, igniting bitter grudges that would span generations,"[2] killing each other as the means of addressing and resolving conflict. Disappearing are the days of people willing to entrust their case into the hands of those who make the ultimate and final ruling directly affecting their future. Judges and juries are confined to the structure and by the laws of our legal system. Their buck stops at and is stopped by the letter of the law, regardless of what might be better, agreeable, or more equitable for all. On the other hand, mediations exist in a suspended universe where everything is on the table, harnessed only by the expanses of a mediator's imaginative and creative abilities. If one were to trace mediation back

1. William Simkin, *Mediation and the Dynamics of Collective Bargaining*, p. 53.
2. *Hatfields and McCoys*, History.com, A+E Television Networks, LLC.

in history, its appearance in one form or another would be found in nearly every early society including during Biblical times, where the benefits of helping people work out their disputes is evidenced throughout the timeline of humanity, and its necessity and effectiveness is proven repeatedly. There is no version of human interaction and no position therein that unequivocally will not benefit from deepened conflict intervention skills. All one needs to consider is the last time added insight didn't prove useful. Let's just go ahead and call mediation timeless, as are disputes and an eternal propensity toward them, and understand the eventualities of that knowledge for those of us choosing to become mediators: job security.

In the context of conflict resolution, for which litigation has, in modern times, been the vehicle, mediation is becoming the preferred dispute intervention apparatus. In other words, there's a new kid in town. Litigation is often associated with terms such as *adversarial, combative, aggressive, relentless,* and *uncompromising.* Its nature is a zero-sum game where the only two options are win or lose, the latter of which might have negative consequences. In courtrooms, attorneys tailor and construct arguments and support to build cases against opposing parties to demonstrate who is right and who must be wrong, the end goal of which is to defeat and win. This is antithetical to the role of a mediator, which therefore requires training of a different nature. A mediator is a neutral third party—molding the room toward cooperation, compromise, and possibly settlement—not advocating for one side over the other, but instead for both sides to find resolution and agreeable settlement together. Attorney arguments are geared toward identifying, offering, and operating within the context of solutions based on legal outcomes. This precludes focus on the significance of nonlegal outcomes, including what lies at the heart of mediation—consideration of creative, nonmonetary solutions not necessarily defined by the legal system. I often wonder why it is we persist in dubbing alternative dispute resolution mechanisms as alternatives when they are so integral to a system that should strive to create a process for which all levels provide outcomes geared toward balance, participation, and inclusion. One need only look at the ever-increasing traffic jams in the courts, the overwhelming costs of litigation, the lack of control disputants have in court over the outcome of their case, and the confines of the legal system within which the judge and jury operate, to understand. Collectively, these elements greatly affect the way in which we manage disputes. As a result, even more people and institutions are turning to mediation, thereby creating the need for more trained mediators.

Although it is important to learn the process, that which is included in any job description, and the accompanying expectations, the conversation changes when it turns to looking into the qualities of a great mediator or, for example, a great litigator. What sets them apart from the rest when they have all read the same books and are equally trained? That gap, so vividly tangible when one is witness to it, is in the way that they think. It is not only the questions they ask the disputant or the witness, for example, but in the thought process that brought them to asking those questions in the first place. It is the mind-boggling, shockingly savvy line, invisible to everyone else, that somehow they manage to connect from one idea to the next that settles the case, solves the murder, and leaves everyone's mouths agape. Learning how to think in the right direction, and sometimes in the wrong direction, is key. Budding mediators and those interested in deepening their conflict intervention and resolution skills can be taught how to think like a mediator, which is the path to understanding and excellence in conflict intervention.

As a mediator, one must understand how to use skills discretely as well as conjointly, including how to identify which skill to use, how they change form when paired with each other, and how they can be layered. Learning how to resolve conflicts and to perform mediations is not only about garnering information, for example, but also about identifying and interacting with that information while its various components interact with each other. Without understanding that a piece of information such as a disputant's vague response can subsequently be used to deduce a Conflict Handling Mode, combined with the knowledge of what to do with it once it has been successfully identified, what is the point of receiving the information and being aware of Conflict Handling Modes in the first place? The answer is none. There is no point in receiving information simply for the sake of receiving it when one is actually expected to perform a practical application that necessitates a high degree of mastery. Skillfully twisting and turning to meet the needs of disputant(s) and their specific mediation at any given moment – on the fly and with no time to think before you go, go, go – is essential. The nature of skills is interconnected, and acting with a deep and wide understanding of those skills, with any and all at the ready, is imperative to being an effective and fully rounded mediator. To that end, this book constructs facilitated conflict intervention with progressively interlocking strategic management approaches that apply a set of skills in varying ways for purposes specific to differing elements of the process.

A momentary but intensely direct deep dive into the role of the mediator takes us straight to the heart of the concept of a helper. The neutral third party sits squarely outside the conflict, with ideas that nimbly and fluidly bend, curve, flex, and press words, feelings, understandings, impressions, thoughts, and ideas of the strangers sitting in front of them. No doubt you now have visions of an all-powerful magician, robes billowing, beard blowing in the wind created by the wand he is brandishing and waving around; great! That's exactly right. Well, not really, but that was fun! Now back to mediation. I once overheard a discussion of Ishmael, of Herman Melville's *Moby Dick*, in which he was described as a point of entry into the story, a cipher, and a vessel for other people's information, devoid of his own. He sits between the story and the reader and becomes a lens through which the narrative, information, ideas, concerns, and conflict pass. Sound familiar? It should, because that description could easily be exchanged with that of a mediator, the difference being that the mediator's job description is expanded by the incorporation and utilization of the mediation skills discussed in the chapters to come. Call me internuncio, intermediary, or intercessor; interloper, conciliator, or mediator – all are one and the same.

One thing we know as a certainty is that every disputant is different, as are the details of their dispute. They have needs ranging from coddling on one end of the spectrum to virtual verbal combat on the other, and assuredly all mediations require mediators to take different steps to settle the case. Oh, did I say steps just now? My mistake. What I meant to say was that assuredly all mediations require mediators to tackle different giant mountain-sized hurdles that we have to jump over, dig under, or bulldoze directly through. At this point I'll spare the reader and refrain from launching into my rendition of Aretha Franklin's "Ain't No Mountain High Enough," but you get the idea. On my completion of graduate school, my aunt gifted me a notebook. The cover read:

Being a mediator is easy
It's like riding a bike
Except the bike is on fire
You're on fire
Everything is on fire

I laughed. A month or so later I observed a mediation with a retired judge mediator, and I had the notebook with me. (The entire mediation was in caucus, a fact I knew before my arrival, and our client would not be present that day.) He picked it up, read it, laughed a lot, and then abruptly stopped and handed it back to me. Six weeks and a half-dozen or so mediations later, I understood his clipped mood change. So, when I was approached to mediate for two horribly feuding students of the same drama teacher who simply could not be in the same place at the same time as each other anymore without explosive outcomes, I agreed and braced. "I think it will be a good idea for us to have a sleepover. We will all be in our pajamas, sitting on the floor with pillows everywhere, and really talk. With you there as our mediator." I won't lie, somewhere between sleepover, floor, and pillows, I began checking in with myself to make sure I wasn't completely hallucinating. "Sure, no problem," I heard myself say. With my painted smile, controlled nod, and fully packed toolbelt, I said, "Definitely, absolutely. I think that's a great idea. Very innovative." (There was no doubt that they both felt unheard, would need apologies, and would need to be validated, so a little immediate validation from me would only help nudge us in the right direction. It's never too early to begin laying the groundwork as a mediator.) Emotions were already incredibly high for these two, and I knew that they were only going to increase. This might sound like an insanely wild beginning to a mediation story, and it is, but it is just one of many. More important, it is also an example of the benefit of being prepared for anything that can and most certainly will be thrown at you.

What happens when two people perceive the same event differently? Whose perception of that event is "true"? Their truth represents the ultimate truth.[3] So, Ms. Mediator, what do you do? Disputant A is insisting that he bought the brand new, cherry red, fast-as-lightning sportscar with his personal funds, and Disputant B is equally insistent that he was the one who purchased the vehicle, and he did so with funds from his personal account. Two people, two stories, one event, and one option to resolve their conflict: settlement. Now get to work.

3. Daniel Broderick, MD, ESQ.

NOTE TO THE READER

Although the specific terms *negotiator* and *negotiation* are used infrequently throughout this book, this should not be mistaken for exclusions of concepts. During a mediation, the interaction process between disputants is that of negotiating, usually for the purpose of finding mutually agreeable settlement terms. Mediators apply skills to assist in this negotiation process, negotiating with and on behalf of all parties in an effort to reach a successfully mediated agreement.

part I

Prefatory Information

Ms. Shi v. Ms. Vito

Below are the details of the *Ms. Shi vs. Ms. Vito* fact pattern that will be referenced in various ways throughout the book to highlight different aspects of the conflict intervention and resolution process.

BACKGROUND INFORMATION

Here Are the Facts

There is a fig tree on Ms. Shi's property, the bulk of which is growing over a fence and onto Ms. Vito's property, depositing much of its fruit onto Ms. Vito's yard and immediately around and into her pool. Ms. Vito's daughter recently slipped on a fig, falling and breaking her wrist. When Ms. Vito confronted Ms. Shi about the accident, Ms. Shi refused to do anything about the tree. Ms. Vito is demanding that Ms. Shi pay for her daughter's medical bills, for removal of the tree, and for reimbursement for three years of yard and pool and pool equipment maintenance and repairs directly due to the dropped figs.

The Positions

Ms. Shi

Ms. Shi states that the tree is staying no matter what, and she is refusing to pay for any of Ms. Vito's property damages, her daughter's medical expenses, or any form of tree maintenance service.

Ms. Vito

Ms. Vito is demanding that the fig tree and its roots be removed and that she be compensated $100,000 for property damages, and $75,000 for her daughter's medical bills.

How They Ended Up in Mediation

Ms. Shi and Ms. Vito, sisters-in-law and next-door neighbors, have arrived in mediation due to their inability to come to a resolution on the issue of the location of Ms. Shi's tree and the responsibility for the damages, both past and continuing, to Ms. Vito's property, as well as the medical expenses related to her daughter's injury. The constant fighting over these circumstances combined with elevated emotions (details to follow) have resulted in each party seeking legal counsel and initiating legal proceedings; but their family members have jointly succeeded in persuading Ms. Shi and Ms. Vito to attend mediation first. The fighting has gone on for three years, and this is the last stop before litigation. For the sake of their family and any chance at repairing their relationship, finding resolution in mediation would be their best option. The parties, however, are superficially presenting as extremely reluctant and doubtful of the possibility that they will agree to anything in mediation. This surface-level posturing will reveal itself to have layers, the dismantling of which will become critical in the conflict intervention and possible resolution process.

The Interests

Ms. Shi

Ms. Shi cares deeply about the safety of her fig tree, which carries with it the memory and success of her fig business that enabled her to buy her beautiful home and travel the world with her family, the lovely birds she so enjoys watching in the tree, and the incredible shade the tree provides. She clearly has a deeply emotional attachment to the tree, as evidenced by her emotionally driven responses to seemingly rational issues that could have mutually agreeable, collaborative resolutions.

Ms. Shi was under the impression that the previous business relationship she had with Ms. Vito was perfectly fine, and in fact an excellent deal for Ms. Shi, with their workload evenly distributed, until Ms. Vito decided one day to terminate the partnership and the business, turning Ms. Shi's life upside down and creating significant financial issues. Ms. Shi continues to feel betrayed and bewildered by Ms. Vito's actions in ending the business relationship in the manner that she did, believing that:

1. Ms. Shi acted with extreme generosity in agreeing to a 51%/49% partnership with Ms. Vito, when their financial contributions were actually 70%/30%.
2. If and when additional funds were required for the business, Ms. Shi alone provided the necessary funding.
3. Ms. Shi retained her position with the employer where she worked prior to beginning the company with Ms. Vito, at the same time as she worked for her fig company to continue to support her family and their business, as their income could vary from season to season.

a. Ms. Shi's position with her prior employer has always required that she work on the weekends, be available after 5:00 p.m. daily, and travel for work (it is through her work trips that Ms. Shi was able to bring her family along).

i. It is only with the additional funds that came to her from the fig company that she was able to enhance what she could afford without it. This included extended family vacations and a larger home in a better neighborhood next door to her sister-in-law.

4. Ms. Shi also felt that the ownership distribution was very generous to Ms. Vito in light of the facts that:

a. Ms. Vito took two-hour-long lunches every day.

b. Ms. Vito spent a great deal of her time at the office on personal phone calls.

c. Ms. Vito had frequent personal visitors that resulted in additional outings during business hours.

d. Ms. Vito's responsibilities to the company ended when she left the office at 5:00 p.m., Monday through Friday only.

Ms. Vito

Ms. Vito has structural damage caused by the tree's roots, and she has twice replaced pool filters that became clogged due to the dropped figs, which have also brought rodents. She has made extra payments to both the gardener and for pool maintenance relating specifically to issues caused by the tree's roots and the dropped figs. Her daughter suffered a broken wrist after slipping on the fruit. Additionally, due to the height and weight of the branches hanging onto her property, neither she nor her gardener is able to do the maintenance themselves, so it is necessary to hire an outside company. After dozens of pleas and attempts at discussions that have all been met with dismissal and no accountability, acknowledgment, or resolution from Ms. Shi, Ms. Vito is now additionally furious that her daughter has suffered a bad injury.

Their History

They were previously in a business relationship lasting 11 years that ended in a sudden split at the behest of Ms. Vito. The business partnership failed and was terminated because Ms. Vito felt that Ms. Shi was not "pulling her weight," not doing her share of the work, but still taking 51% of the profits. Whereas Ms. Shi went to the office once every other week, spending only one to three hours on average per day, Ms. Vito was in the office five days a week working full eight-hour days. Ms. Shi took her family on numerous vacations, but Ms. Vito felt "chained to her desk" and could never once find the time to travel with her family. On the occasion that Ms. Vito asked if Ms. Shi could cover for her in order to take a family vacation, Ms. Shi declined with a curt "No." Although the business portion of their relationship ended, a familial relationship remained, as they were then and continue to be sisters-in-law and neighbors.

Ms. Shi's 51% ownership position reflected her larger initial investment in the business. Ms. Shi contributed 70% of the initial startup funds, to Ms. Vito's 30% contribution.

MEDIATION BEGINS

In Their Own Words (exchanged during the brief, introductory Joint Session)

Ms. Shi

She does not see the big deal with "a little fruit on the ground." She believes that it is the responsibility of Ms. Vito to stop her own daughters from running around their pool area and to teach them how to be more careful. She grew up taking care of herself, never had a single thing handed to her in her entire life, has had to work for everything she has ever gotten, and has raised her own child the same way. Why should Ms. Vito's daughters be treated any differently? She thinks it is ridiculous that they are not capable of either being more cautious around the tree or doing a little bit of manual labor and picking up the fruit themselves. There is no way she is going to contribute to the raising of a couple of spoiled brats by paying for someone to come in and do a job they should be doing themselves. She feels that Ms. Vito's gardener could just clean up the dropped figs also. She wants to keep the tree because it reminds her of their previous business, a fig jam company, that helped her afford her house and travels with her husband and son. Additionally, she absolutely loves to see all the birds who frequent the tree, as she fancies herself a bird watcher and spends quite a bit of time "birding." She also thoroughly enjoys the shade that the tree provides.

Ms. Vito

She is consistently having to clean up huge amounts of dropped fruit from the fig tree, which brings rodents. She has had to replace her pool filter twice because of clogging due to the figs. In addition, there has been structural damage to her home from the roots of the tree. Her two daughters, Ms. Shi's nieces, have slipped on figs more than once. Ms. Vito has asked Ms. Shi dozens of times to get the tree trimmed or taken out completely, but to no avail. Enough is enough now that her eldest daughter slipped on a fig and broke her wrist, but Ms. Shi still refuses to acknowledge that there is a problem or to take any responsibility for it. She did not even call or visit to see how her niece was feeling after being injured. Ms. Vito will not accept a penny less than her demand of $100,000 for property damages and $75,000 for her daughter's medical bills.

Information Provided to the Mediator in Caucus by Both Parties

Ms. Vito

Although she feels deeply hurt by Ms. Shi's actions and attitude, and is furious and presenting as unwilling to compromise about anything at the moment, Ms.

Vito acknowledges that she actually has mixed feelings about the tree, even though it appears that she wants it removed completely. It does remind her of the bad times during their partnership, but it also reminds her of a business she was able to develop and build from the ground up. Furthermore, she does not choose to harm plants or trees. She is willing to hear options to remedy the issue of the tree without removing or killing it. This, however, is *only* if Ms. Shi does the *right thing* by paying for her daughter's medical bills, as well as for her property damages.

Ms. Vito is willing to show Ms. Shi the estimates she received from the tree trimmer, who can also address the damages from the tree's root system. However, she feels that she has been pushed to her limit, so even doing that, which would allow the tree to remain, feels like she is going out of her way to do something for Ms. Shi. Ms. Vito is not feeling particularly inclined to extend herself, especially because Ms. Shi could not even be bothered to offer a kind word to her niece or ask how she was doing after her injury, let alone come forward to cover the expenses. Ms. Vito is now in a defensive mode in protecting her daughter, who feels that Ms. Shi cares nothing about her.

Ms. Vito has produced receipts and statements reflecting her expenditures thus far, for property damages and her daughter's medical expenses ($43,000 property damages and $25,000 medical), but she feels they do not properly reflect her family's pain and suffering. Therefore, her demand exceeds the simple totals of those expenses, which she feels is totally appropriate and acceptable.

Ms. Vito also admitted that she sort of likes the birds, they are pretty, and she finds their chirping to be soothing; however, the location of the feeder is problematic and that needs to be addressed immediately because it brings the birds to the side of the tree that causes bird excrement to land all over her outdoor furniture, and rats are so attracted to the food, are everywhere, and have damaged the wiring of her pool equipment. If left unmanaged, these issues will continue to worsen.

Ms. Shi

Ms. Shi admits that she is angry at herself for the way she has handled this situation, but she did not know how to control herself, or to communicate in any other way, and then it was too late—she and Ms. Vito were already in this pattern. She disclosed that she has struggled with anger management, impulse control, and feelings of being threatened that have caused her to lash out ever since she was a child. She attributes this to her upbringing, which consisted of an incredibly strict, abusive father, and a mother who became an alcoholic to escape the abuse. When Ms. Shi was 15, her mother took her own life, and Ms. Shi has blamed herself ever since for not being strong enough to protect her mother. There was little love shown in her family and communication was kept to an extreme minimum; needs or feelings were never discussed. Conversing with anyone outside of her nuclear family about anything that was going on inside their home was punishable with a beating from her father. She began working to support herself at the age of 17, and has been taking care of herself ever since. She:

1. Does not know how to be vulnerable and discuss her feelings.
2. Interprets almost everything she hears as a threat that she meets in kind.

3. Rarely is able to craft sentences that reflect what she is actually trying to say.
4. Does not know how to give people the opportunity to express or explain themselves.
5. Has no idea how to fix a situation like this that has unraveled in a way that she never intended.

Ms. Vito is not privy to any of Ms. Shi's childhood experiences or trauma, as she keeps that part of her life a secret. Ms. Shi is deeply hurt that Ms. Vito could ever think that she does not care about her own niece's well-being, yet she realizes that her actions have contributed to their current situation.

Ms. Shi is under the impression that something she cares deeply about, the fig tree, is being threatened by Ms. Vito, and is incensed that Ms. Vito would even dare threaten to have it removed, knowing that it is representative of their former business together and brings the birds she loves to watch.

Ms. Shi recognizes that she is trapped by her own behavior and the only way she knows how to communicate, but she cannot see a way to change it. She feels attacked and threatened by Ms. Vito's demands for monetary compensation, which in turn cause her to be more defensive.

Interests and Positions Ms. Vito and Ms. Shi Share in Common

Deep down, both Ms. Vito and Ms. Shi would like to work things out, rebuild their relationship, and be on better terms with each other. Neither wants to be in a fight, and both regret that their interactions have become so heated and aggressive. There is no reason to think that this presently contentious relationship cannot be changed with open and honest communication through the guided assistance of a mediator and appropriate information explaining true intentions. A tree should absolutely not be causing damage to any person or property, let alone to their relationship.

ADR Advocates

ADR Advocates® is a new program that will provide a designated Advocate for interested parties during mediation. The discussion of an Advocate through the program will take place during the scheduling of the mediation. An appointed Advocate will:

1. Be a source of individualized support.
2. Address all questions and provide answers.
3. Discuss concerns.
4. Provide opinions.
5. Assist in development of approaches and strategies.

All Advocates are trained mediators, and specialists in various categories of conflicts will be available. The benefits of a personal Advocate have been immediately apparent during the initial introduction of *ADR Advocates*®, as evidenced by the increase in effective party interactions, confidence developed out of additional personalized support, and increased creativity of settlement options.

DURING MEDIATION EXERCISES

At the request of each disputant, mediation exercises can be conducted with or without an Advocate, to be discussed with participants after they have reviewed their respective roles. Whether the mediation exercise is conducted in class or as a homework assignment, if a disputant chooses to have an Advocate present, additional participants will be required. If the mediation exercise takes place during class, participants in the role of Advocate will have varying degrees of mediation training. If the mediation exercise is a homework assignment:

1. Students may work together outside of class, alternating between roles, including that of Advocate.

2. The mediator may rotate between the roles during the mediation in a variation of caucus, during which time the mediator could switch into the role of Advocate.
3. Simply find a participant willing to play the role of Advocate and provide that participant with general guidance.

prefatory information 3

Before, During, After: A Mediator's Internal Dialogue

1. **Are you purposefully listening and effectively managing the information you are receiving?**
2. **Are you asking probing questions?**
   a. Is there a mutual understanding of the issue(s)?
   b. Are you giving the parties their *day in court* and an opportunity to fully express in their own words why they believe they are there?
   c. Are you making sure they feel validated and heard, that their feelings and voice matter (at the very least to you, the mediator), and that regardless of anything else, they are not made to feel foolish?
      i. For example, while they are expressing their feelings.
   d. Did you allow them to work through their emotions, possibly assisting them along the way?
      i. This can also be useful in helping them process their emotional turmoil to reach a point of logic and reason, which can then enable a discussion of possible settlement options.
   e. Have you asked what they need to move past this issue and reach resolution today?
   f. When they make demands, are you asking HOW the opposing party is supposed to perform the request?
      i. Asking for their advice about it?
         1. How can that happen?
         2. What are the options?
         3. Would the asking party be able to do the same if the situation were reversed?
   g. Have you noticed that the disputants are not working together?
      i. You know that they must cooperate in some fashion to reach a mutually agreeable settlement.

3. **Are you identifying disputant needs?**
    a. And continuing to do so while the mediation progresses as those needs might evolve?
4. **Are you empathizing by putting yourself into each disputant's shoes to truly understand what they require? What the mediation requires?**
5. **Have you adequately probed beyond the surface-level conversation in an effort to reach the disputants' interests and needs below what they are currently presenting?**
6. **Is disputant emotional involvement and reaction getting in the way of logical conversation?**
7. **Are you utilizing the correct Mediation Style as dictated by the disputants and the conflict: Evaluative, Facilitative, Transformative?**
8. **Are you flowing among Mediation Styles appropriately and as needed?**
9. **Are you approaching each disputant correctly according to their Communication Style?**
    a. Do you notice any difficulties with communication skills?
    b. If you noticed the disputants struggling with verbal skills, have you asked what would make them more comfortable?
    c. Have you considered communicating in a way other than verbally?
    d. Did you suggest that they write down their questions and responses?
    e. Are you allowing them time to think after your questions?
10. **Can you identify the disputants' Conflict Handling Modes?**
    a. Are you using a Conflict Handling Mode that mirrors theirs, one that has opposing characteristics, or a combination of modes?
11. **Have you identified the disputants' desired mediation end goals?**
    a. Do they have the same end goals?
    b. Are their end goals other than a settlement agreement?
12. **Are you considering monetary as well as nonmonetary settlement options?**
13. **Are you continually checking in with yourself and your neutrality?**
    a. Are you making sure YOU are completely clear about what's going on?
        i. Timeline, facts, demands, and proposals.
    b. Do you need to take a moment to think and collect yourself and your thoughts?
    c. Are you remaining neutral?

part II

Chapters

chapter 1

Conflict

"The significant problems of our time cannot be solved by the same level of thinking that created them."

—Albert Einstein

A Shifting Perspective on Conflict

A new perspective on conflict, what can be gained from conflict, how to manipulate conflict, and how to use conflict advantageously to reshape the landscape of conflict intervention.

What if conflict is not a misunderstanding or miscommunication, a fight or a battle, but instead it is an opportunity? Perhaps it is an opportunity for discussion, growth, new understanding, repaired relationships, and to a more extreme degree, shifting power positions, shifting alliances, power grabs, and a move into a dominant position. The idea is to think differently and creatively about conflict. If the mediator can do so, perhaps the disputants can also, and mediation should be reflective of that. Using *conflict as opportunity* as an overarching theme and premise has the possibility and strength to change everything. The mediator can realign expression to meet intention and alter the interpretation of messages, as well. The mediator can change attitudes and responses to questions and answers. What about redefining the purpose behind asking questions? Questions no longer need be seen as imposing, aggressive, or interrogatory, but rather as searches for information to become more compassionate and to seek out avenues toward cooperative solutions.

Conflict is not inherently bad, despite commonly held beliefs that it is. Instead, it is our *reactions* to conflict that determine its impact on those involved. Conflict is a difference of understanding or opinion, and what happens next turns the tide. The manner in which people respond to the initial conflict dictates the development of circumstances that often lead to the need for conflict intervention such as mediation. Somewhere along the way, the understanding of conflict became distorted by the inclusion of the subsequent reactions of the parties, combining an initial disagreement with the responses that created resulting negative, aggressive, and fearful attitudes toward conflict. By separating the response to the conflict from the actual disagreement or conflict itself and by re-creating the understanding of conflict to manage and harness reactions, it becomes possible to remind disputants that a difference of opinion or interpretation is not necessarily problematic, but can be a healthy component of communication and of learning how other people think and process information. Experiences color our understanding and interpretation of events, so the more access we have to different viewpoints, the more our thought processes can be broadened. The exchange of differing ideas without agreement increases our exposure to the way people think. Collective agreement is not required to coexist or to defuse conflict, and differences do not automatically lead to discord or hostility. We do not exist in a vacuum exclusively with people who understand, process information, and respond in the exact same manner as we do. Because of this, the preferable choice is to learn how to interact, collaborate, and effectively communicate with others.

CONFLICT REFRAMED

Identifying an originating conflict, as separated from the subsequent responses to it, is the first imperative reframe that the mediator must provide. At this point, it becomes possible for disputants to hear each other's differing side of the conflict, while disagreeing with it. Was Aristotle correct when he stated, "It is the mark of an educated mind to be able to entertain a thought without accepting it"?

As a mediator, part of the responsibility is to facilitate cooperative communication among disputants, which often necessitates discussing a shifted and reframed perspective on conflict. One of the reasons this is so important is that conflict is experienced differently through the personal and individualized lens of context, causing potentially vastly incompatible interpretations of the same event. When disputants are presenting divergent interpretations, it is not only the fighting, blaming, arguing, or destructive behavior that can stand between resolution and a breakdown of the mediation process—one word may suffice. Being ready at any given moment to reframe a potentially destructive statement is imperative. It is the mediator's job to shift that unsuccessful behavior, turning it into behavior that will be constructive toward a cooperative resolution. The mediator will constantly be reframing opinions and positions that will inevitably be shrouded in reaction and not necessarily reflective of a disputant's true interests. Reframing is and will become an extremely important tool at a mediator's disposal. When the manner in which people respond to the initial conflict dictates what happens next, and what might or might not turn the tide from smooth sailing to rough waters, reframe the understanding of conflict.

FLASH CHALLENGE

Understanding the Idea of Conflict vs. Reactions to Conflict

1. Discuss a conflict or misunderstanding that you are currently engaged in, large or small. Separate the responses to it from the initial disagreement itself—the moment you can pinpoint when the responses and reactions became the defining measure.
2. Write a detailed description of the initial discussion or misunderstanding that led to the situation you're currently in without including any responses to it.
3. Now write a detailed description of the responses to the initial discussion or misunderstanding without any personal emotion or judgment.
4. Write a detailed description of how you believe it could have been handled differently by all parties involved.
5. Can you identify an initial healthy exchange of differing but respected ideas during the course of the discussion or misunderstanding?
6. Identify your opinion of the exact moment the discussion or misunderstanding turned from a healthy discussion of differing opinions into a problematic situation with misbehaving parties.
7. Discuss a plan of action, or mediation, to lead all parties out of the current situation, and toward a safe place where the exchange of differing ideas is encouraged and respected.
    a. Include the way(s) you would explain and teach the other parties about this concept of coexistence of differing and conflicting ideas.

As it has been historically defined and understood by disputants, conflict is difficult enough without also resulting in disputants feeling the need to fight, jockey for position and power, and generally behave aggressively to determine that they are respected and heard. This is symptomatic of and responsive to the often-complicated web that is woven by the whorl of human experiences. Responses might manifest swiftly and immediately after the initiation of a conflict or might take time to present and be accompanied by unintended consequences and ramifications. However, guiding disputants toward combining their shifted understanding of the nature of conflict with appropriate engagement can transform their conflict into a cooperative interaction with effective communication. Mediators and conflict interventionists (all persons who assist those in conflict, including but not limited to mediators) should strive to help disputants understand that they can focus on the conflict only and not that they also must simultaneously fight for survival amongst and against each other. The nature of a conflict is that it is rarely limited to that which meets the eye; so with that in mind, the job of the mediator or conflict interventionist will also be to address more than what disputants are presenting. The goal is to halt the interaction from rising to an extreme level to give parties an improved chance at achieving beneficial and effective conflict resolution.

CONFLICT THROUGH THE LENS OF TRAUMA

"Trauma is a devastating emotional response to brutally painful experiences that threaten safety."[1]

While a shifted perspective of conflict presents an opportunity for effective communication rather than a duel requiring swords immediately poised, conflict is still mostly perceived by disputants in exactly that fashion—with those swords sharpened to the hilt. Therefore, although trauma often exists as a result of the conflict itself, it is with a very high degree of certainty that the trauma exists as the result of immediate and continuing aggressive responses to it. A traumatic effect on disputants embroiled in conflict is that they feel and act like hostages. They may experience the conflict as trauma-producing and feel that they are being held hostage by both the conflict and opposing disputant(s), victimized and forced into a process against their will. Their experience is real, active trauma. It is possible that they might become so desperate that when they find themselves put into conflict situations, they are willing, able, and prepared to say anything to extricate themselves. A mediator must enter into a dispute resolution process bearing that in mind.

While working to shift conflict perspectives, it is essential to approach the conflict as being potentially traumatic for the disputant(s), whose responses might in turn include fight, flight, or freeze. It is crucial for the mediator to listen in a way that enables them to discern a disputant's relative trauma point (severity of

1. Crisis Text Line, "Trauma in America," *Mental Health* (Jan. 7, 2021), www.crisistextline.org.

their trauma) in the context of the conflict and to evaluate the degree to which the trauma is affecting that disputant's behavior and ability to engage in the mediation. The identification of that point will contribute to the mediator's ability to discern which Mediation Style(s) to use, to determine which Conflict Handling Mode(s) and Communication Style(s) the disputant uses, and which they should then utilize in turn. Developing an empathetic and trusting relationship, asking questions to encourage the disputants to fully and clearly express themselves, and probing beneath any surface-level posturing can culminate in the mediator's ability to successfully assist disputants with effective communication and improved strength, validity, and longevity of any settlement agreement.

Recall that we have deconstructed and reconstructed the understanding of conflict. By treating conflict as traumatizing, the mediator opens another avenue of options for managing the dispute, the disputants, and the mediation. Although this reconstructed concept of conflict is necessary to use as a tool to share with disputants for the process of conflict resolution to progress and for current trauma to be mitigated, the disputants are still entering the mediation with the commonly accepted understanding of conflict with trauma responses attached to it. It is in the shifting perspective of conflict that trauma is addressed, validated, and then released in a way that does not stop the disputant from interacting clearly and rationally in mediation. Reactions to trauma span the gamut, inclusive of highly emotional responses as well as those that are entirely devoid of emotion and are part and parcel of conflict and therefore a conflict intervention process. The mediator should not get caught in the trap of a fundamental misinterpretation of traumatic responses as always hyperemotional; they are not. Regardless, the use of Mediation Styles and identification and management of Conflict Handling Modes, in concert with other mediation skills, will be effective in mediating disputes whether or not they are overtly emotional.

chapter 2

Mediation Styles

What, When, and How: One Size Does Not Fit All

WHAT IS MEDIATION?

Mediation is a guided negotiation process during which a mediator, who is an impartial neutral party, provides facilitative, assistive (not determinative) conflict intervention support to parties or disputants who are involved in a dispute and have up to that point been unable to find a mutually agreeable resolution on their own. Unlike in other forms of conflict intervention, disputants in mediation remain active, decision-making participants during the entirety of the mediator-guided negotiation process, including the eventual outcome, be it a mutually agreed-upon settlement agreement or impasse.

WHY MEDIATION?

Choosing mediation avoids pursuing or continuing with courtroom proceedings. Whether the mediation is court mandated or not, with the benefit of a trained and skilled conflict interventionist, mediation has the capacity to reach resolution for all parties. Mediation empowers disputants to retain control of their dispute, to be active participants in the intervention and resolution process, and to reach settlement without court intervention. There are commonly accepted phases of a mediation:

1. Mediator's opening statement and signing of paperwork.
2. Disputant statements and mediator collecting information.
3. Negotiations in joint session, caucus, or a combination of both.
4. Settlement opportunities, proposals, discussions, decisions.

It is important to keep in mind, though, that with the exception of the first phase, the trajectory of any mediation is subject to the facts of the case, the disputants, and frankly and often times, the way the wind blows–as is the case when human emotions are involved.

WHAT DOES A MEDIATOR DO?

A mediator uses guided conflict intervention strategies and techniques to facilitate productive and resolution-oriented conversation between parties who are in conflict. As a neutral party with an impartial position (commonly referred to as a neutral third party), a mediator steps in to assist parties who have tried unsuccessfully to resolve their conflict independently, or who wish to attempt resolution by means other than the beginning or continuation of litigation. The following overview of the mediation process outlines the general arc that a mediation follows.

AN OVERVIEW OF THE MEDIATION PROCESS

"Always talk about the nature of mediation, confidentiality, and an icebreaker usually doesn't hurt."

—Mr. Smith, Professional Mediator Interview, 2018

Mediations can be difficult and emotional, so a clever anecdote followed by mediator strategies can help the parties feel that the events that brought them to mediation need not cause them additional embarrassment in front of a mediator. Mistakes have been made, those parts of the past can be left there, and a new plan of action to move forward will be formed.

1. Provide any necessary initial and immediate statements to the disputants, as well as ground rules regarding appropriate and inappropriate behavior during the mediation.
2. Move into mediator opening statement.
    a. With all parties agreeing to be in the same room (joint session), if possible.
    b. If parties do not agree to joint session, the mediation will be performed with parties in separate rooms (caucus), with the mediator providing the same opening statement to each disputant and moving back and forth among caucused parties (shuttle mediation).
    c. The opening statement will define mediation and the role of the mediator. It will state very clearly that the mediator is present as a neutral third party to help and facilitate the mediation process and not as a decision-maker. The opening statement will also confirm the confidentiality afforded by mediation, its voluntary nature of participation (even if mediation is court ordered, there is no requirement to reach settlement), and the neutrality of the mediator. Ground rules such as not interrupting each other, even with corrections or questions, will also be provided, as well as the direction to disputants to take notes and wait until it is their turn to speak. Each party will absolutely be given the opportunity to

present their thoughts and to explain why, from their point of view, *we are here today*. They will also be given time to state collective mediation goals.

d. The parties should then be asked if they fully understand everything that has been explained to them in the opening statement and if they have any questions or concerns, which the mediator will promptly address.

3. Moving forward, all disputants, the mediator, and anyone else in the room will sign the agreement to mediate and confidentiality paperwork.

a. With confidentiality (and privilege) being a core principle of mediation, the mediator should explain to parties the way confidentiality works in:

i. Mediation overall

ii. Joint session

iii. Caucus

Confidentiality extends not only to the mediator, but to all participants to the mediation as well, including those who are not directly involved in the dispute but are privy to mediation proceedings.

i. All conversations that transpire during mediation are considered to be for the purposes of reaching resolution, including new information and potential settlement offers, and are protected by confidentiality. That means that if, for example, the case does not settle in mediation, nothing that was discussed during that mediation can be used anywhere else, including in court. Even in the circumstances when parties intended their mediation outcomes to be other than resolution, confidentiality remains. This confidentiality shield allows parties to participate fully and freely in their attempts to vigorously pursue a resolution (or otherwise) with disclosures, creative settlement suggestions, and monetary offers for the express purpose of a *mediated* settlement agreement, without concern that should their mediation end in impasse, they will be forced to adhere in court to those very same disclosures, creative settlement suggestions, and monetary offers.

ii. During joint session with all parties to the mediation present, there are no additional confidentiality steps the mediator would need to take.

iii. During caucus, however, the mediator should consider each disputant's room as equally private and confidential. The mediator must not disclose any information from one room to the next without the explicit permission of the disputant to whom the information belongs.

Regardless of where the conversation is taking place, in joint session or caucus, disputants must feel that their often private and personal disclosures are confidential with the mediator and within the mediation.

Reference A, B: **The California Rules of Court:** *See pp. 39-42.*
Reference C: **The Uniform Mediation Act:** *See p. 43.*
Reference D: **Model Standards of Conduct for Mediators:** *See p. 45.*
Reference E: **The Alternative Dispute Resolution Act of 1998:** *See p. 46.*

4. Invite the individual who brought the case forward to begin, for no other reason than that is generally the standard operating procedure for a mediation, and we have to start somewhere.
5. Each party will be given their *day in court*—the opportunity to describe why they feel they are all in mediation that day, what they see as the issue(s), and anything additionally they would like to discuss.
   a. If any emotions rise to the surface at this point, the mediator should immediately pivot, reframe, and redirect to fully address and validate those emotions. For many disputants, mediation is the first time they are being heard and their feelings on these matters treated with dignity and respect, so it is crucial that they feel it from the mediator and eventually, if possible, from the opposing party. In addressing emotions as separate from the problem, it is possible to move beyond them to a place of logic and rationale, where creative problem-solving and solution-oriented brainstorming can take place.
6. The mediator's application of learned mediation skills to guide the disputants toward settlement as the negotiation process takes place.
   a. If the mediator has no knowledge of the case or the disputants prior to entering the mediation, there is a possibility that they may learn of a conflict of interest that must be disclosed to the parties, resulting either in the mediator's self-removal from the case or the mediation progressing forward.
   b. The mediator may also decide that they are not comfortable moving forward mediating the case and should therefore choose to remove themself.
7. Entering the resolution phase of the mediation where brainstorming, collaboration, and problem-solving may take place with the goal of settlement (or alternate disputant mediation goal) at the forefront.
8. If settlement is the overall goal, two distinct paths might emerge. One is specific settlement discussion as the focus and where the collective effort lies; and the other is the focus on working through emotions, building trust, and digging below surface-level posturing to reach true interests and needs in the process of discovering settlement options.

9. Either:
   a. Sign, seal, and deliver a mutually agreeable or "live-with-able" settlement agreement.
   b. Achieve mediation goals other than traditional settlement.
   c. Conclude the mediation in impasse.

MEDIATION STYLES

Evaluative, Transformative, and Facilitative mediation styles govern the manner in which a mediation is conducted. The nature of a conflict and the relationship between parties combine to determine the appropriate applicability of each style. They inform a mediator's thought processes and behavior, as well as the range of a mediator's interactions with parties, the extent of which shifts dynamically depending on the style. Although the level of that dynamic involvement might be equal across these styles, the practical application of each changes the landscape entirely. Although frequently considered by definition to have a graduating range of mediator involvement that is inversely proportionate to party self-determination, that is not necessarily the case, nor is it necessarily the entire picture. That range begins with the Facilitative style having the least amount of participation from the mediator and the greatest level of party self-determination, continues through the Transformative style where the mediator's involvement is progressively increased and party self-determination is decreased, and ends with the Evaluative style where mediator participation is at its greatest and party self-determination is at its least. Mediation styles in action determine their differentiation above and beyond the (sometimes) blurred lines of their definitions. For example, it has been argued that Facilitative mediation produces the highest degree of party self-determination by virtue of the manner in which this particular style is practiced. However, with a firm grasp on the purpose mediation serves and understanding the appropriate application of each style, as well as the widespread and varying forms of conflict intervention, a conflict interventionist practicing any style of mediation—Facilitative, Transformative, or Evaluative—will produce an equal degree of party self-determination, thereby supporting its position as a fundamental and inarguable tenet of the mediation process.

Some mediators limit themselves to one style by specializing in either Evaluative, Facilitative, or Transformative mediations. It is exponentially more beneficial, though, to mediate a cross-section of conflicts and to work on honing the skills necessary to be best prepared for any situation the mediator might encounter, especially taking into consideration the fluidity of mediation, which requires a certain amount of flexibility in mediation styles. Therefore, when a Transformative approach is not working, the mediator is able to pivot across mediation styles to an Evaluative style, for example, as an alternate option. Mediators will likely not find success in guiding a mediation toward settlement by focusing on disputant emotions when what is necessary is discussing how a judge might act in court, including the potential ruling that a larger monetary responsibility might be required should the case not settle in mediation. When halfway through the mediation it becomes apparent that the disputants need a different approach, the mediator must be able to discern that a change in style is necessary and provide it successfully.

Evaluative Mediation

The Evaluative style is traditionally considered to be primarily merits-based with cost-benefit analyses, applied without components traditionally ascribed to the Facilitative or Transformative styles, including the discussion of any emotional components, rehabilitation of relationships, or attention to possible interests below the surface. During an Evaluative mediation, the mediator will:

1. Make assessments.
2. Provide opinions.
3. Challenge parties on the facts and figures they are presenting in their case.
4. Question the parties' demands when they seem inappropriate or require justification.
5. Offer their view of the strength of a case, what it might look like for a disputant in court, and what the best avenue of resolution might be.

It is not a requirement that mediators be subject-matter experts to use an Evaluative style. It is their application of reason and logic and the use of categorizing and balancing techniques to weigh merits of options, strengths and weaknesses of a case, and validity of claims and demands that produces the requisite evaluation. A comparison of mediation against litigation will very likely appear in an Evaluative mediation, although it is not exclusive to this style and not unlikely to appear in other mediation styles as well. (See Appendix, "Mediation vs. Litigation.") In a mediator interview, the question was posed, "How do you ground parties regarding success outside the mediation process, and how do you address their best alternative to a negotiated agreement (BATNA)?" The reply was that the mediator encourages the parties to be realistic by discussing holes and weaknesses in their case, and by working together to recognize the reality of the whole path, not merely looking at potential verdicts through the lens of their optimistic overconfidence, for example. "We ought to be able to come to a resolution based on a cost-benefit analysis. . . . If you settle today you won't have this hanging over you anymore. . . . Think about what value that has" (Mr. Smith, Professional Mediator Interview, 2018).

If the mediator has identified the mediation to be Evaluative and the parties are already in caucus, the decision might be made to turn directly to either the disputant or their attorney to ask them to plead their case, taking you through it step by step. This is where the gloves might come off for the mediator to provide a hard dose of reality. It is more likely that an Evaluative mediation will primarily boil down to who pays what to whom, and be driven by numbers and facts.

During a mediation, a seasoned mediator conducting the mediation in caucus turned to the attorney representing one of the parties and challenged him to present his case:

Attorney: Well, we are not going to agree to anything less than an equally shared split, with half going to each party. If that doesn't work for them, we are fully prepared and ready to proceed to trial.

Mediator: And I'm assuming you've discussed the details of this case with your clients, including the fully outlined and detailed will, which leaves your clients absolutely nothing, as well as the offer from the opposing party, which includes sharing partially with your client, which, again, is outside the parameters of the will and simply a gesture of acknowledgment of familial history.

Attorney: Yup. My client is fully informed, we've discussed it, and I know what a strong case we have. I have advised to agree to half or nothing, and that is our plan. We have discussed the strategy we will proceed with should we move forward with trial, and I have informed them that it is really a winner.

Mediator: Have you litigated many of these cases?

Attorney: Actually this will be my first, but that doesn't matter. The facts are the facts and it's a winner!

Mediator: And have you been before this particular judge before?

Attorney: No.

Mediator: Well, I have 30 years of experience in this area, and I have been before this judge on more than one occasion, so I am going to respectfully disagree with your analysis of the strength of your case. However, you seem very confident in your position, so why don't you present your case to me. Right here and now. Lay it out for us, and I will respond based on the way the law would and how this judge has in the past.

Based on the preceding conversation, what followed was exactly what one would imagine. The attorney began to present his case, and the mediator responded with counterpoints and factual blocks to every point and attempted "home run" the attorney pitched. The mediator questioned the details of the case, the historical relationship of the disputants, their believability, the interaction between the law and the attorney's logic, and what a judge's ruling might look like weighed against the offer that his clients were receiving in the mediation. At the conclusion of the interaction between the mediator and the attorney, the disputants were convinced that the offer they had on the mediation table would be far superior to anything they might receive in court. However, and of course, they wanted more. The mediator, now having solidified the fact that the case would settle in mediation one way or another, went to work and shuttled himself out of that room and into the next. His evaluation process unfolded in each room and in response to every statement and offer, which resulted in an agreement that was acceptable to all. Had it not been for the mediator's ability to perform an Evaluative mediation, the end result would most likely have been impasse and moving on to a courtroom setting. Although the Evaluative style is not appropriate for all mediations and all disputants (as the case is for any mediation style), being adept at evaluating and interacting with parties in this manner can serve some situations very well and can earn the respect of the parties and attorneys present.

The Evaluative style has been a hot-button and controversial issue among mediators (as it might not always reflect the identity of mediation being a disputant-driven process), but it could be rising to the surface as a possible path to reaching communities that have traditionally shunned the practice of mediation. It has become progressively more apparent that the idea of a mediator who keeps their input entirely separate from the parties' conflict is not necessarily what disputants are looking for. Parties are interested less in a referee who facilitates only, and more in a mediator or third party of any kind who brings expertise, experience, opinions, and creativity to the conflict. In addition to the elevated level of assistance, participation, and contribution parties seek, mediators who invest themselves and present as caring about a case and its outcome are found to be substantially more appealing and appropriate. Although the traditional definition of *neutral* has resulted in questioning and suspicion of the Evaluative style among some mediators and conflict interventionists, disputants continue to prove their interest in the style by requesting this form of intervention at an increasing rate. Balance, however, is key when applying the Evaluative style. Effective incorporation of evaluations of the case and disputant positions with possible settlement option ideas, or alternative conflict intervention more accurately aligned with the goals of the parties, might serve those evaluations (and the disputants) best. Too much emphasis on one or the other could result in displeased disputants who become even less willing to collaborate, cooperate, or make possibly necessary concessions between and among each other. One element of the Evaluative style that enables it to be applicable and appropriate across a wider spectrum of disputants and disputes is that it can be applied with varying degrees of intensity by the mediator—this spectrum of intensity being less singularly focused on case analysis and less direct on one end and more focused on case analysis with a more direct approach to evaluating on the other. Keeping in mind the increasing number of disputants who prefer a neutral third party who is more involved than simply as a disengaged facilitator, being able to offer an evaluation of a case without it being perceived as a series of aggressive and domineering directives might be an answer to their call. Conversely, for disputants who require a mediator and mediation style to either match their own more aggressive and direct Conflict Handling Mode (CHM) or Communication Style or who would benefit from a more direct conversation about the reality of their circumstances, the Evaluative style could easily be modified to meet these needs.

FLASH CHALLENGE QUESTIONS

Hint for Flash Challenge Questions 1-3: Imagine a disputant who is overly confident in her mostly unsupported position. She is expressing wildly unrealistic settlement demands and demonstrating an inadequate comprehension of the true benefit she would stand to achieve should she resolve her case in mediation rather than progressing to litigation.

Flash Challenge Question #1:

1. Does an Evaluative style automatically mean a singularly case analysis approach devoid of elements such as emotional components, rehabilitation of relationships, or attention to possible interests below the surface?
2. Is it possible to mediate applying the Evaluative style at varying levels of intensity?

Hint: Consider how your approach might change if the same disputant were emotionally fragile and their behavior was in fact a defense mechanism to protect their hurt feelings.

Your answers should reflect both Hint scenario variations.

   a. If so, might certain levels of intensity be *more* beneficial? Discuss when and how.
   b. If so, might certain levels of intensity be *less* beneficial? Discuss when and how.
   c. If so, could (and should) certain levels of intensity be less controversial in nature due to their possibly more muted tones and strengths? Discuss.
      i. For example, the same message expressed, but delivered differently.
   d. If not, why not? Discuss.

Flash Challenge Question #2:

1. What, if any, are potential pitfalls of an Evaluative style that a mediator should be wary of? Discuss.
2. What, if any, are the actions or strategies a mediator can take to ensure that they do not fall victim to the aforementioned (potential) pitfalls? Discuss.
   a. Should certain types of actions or statements always be avoided?

Flash Challenge Question #3:

1. Are the potential settlement options derived from using an Evaluative style generally narrower and more singular in scope? Discuss.
2. If so, which types of possible settlement opportunities are excluded by virtue of utilization of this style?

Facilitative Mediation

In a Facilitative mediation, the mediator acts strictly in the capacity of assisting and supporting disputants in their communications with each other, including guidance toward the clarification of misunderstandings or misinterpretations that might occur, and ensuring that disputants adhere to predetermined ground rules. While the mediator maintains control over the process, this does not include determining discussion content and if and how the mediation settles. The mediator will refrain from making suggestions, providing evaluative or opinion-based input, or dictating the direction of the conversation. It is not a prerequisite for mediators using the facilitative style to be expressly versed in the particular topics involved in a conflict. Therefore, it is logical for a mediator to engage with the disputants in a manner that positions those disputants at the forefront of their own discussions, with the mediator as the communication and mediation guide only.

For some mediators, the use of the Facilitative style would only be appropriate when parties are:

1. More amicable and receptive to each other.
2. Capable of communicating more efficiently and effectively.
3. Knowledgeable about the subject area of their conflict.
4. Willing and able either to reach settlement or to make the conscious and informed decision to move forward with a different form of conflict resolution.

However, a mediation with disputants characterized in this manner is not a requirement for the application of the Facilitative style. The style choice could be a result of a request from the parties, the general preference of the mediator, or a strategic approach based on the mediator's assessment of the conflict and its participants, with potential for fluidity of styles.

FLASH CHALLENGE QUESTIONS

Hint for Flash Challenge Questions 4-6: Imagine that the disputants specifically requested the Facilitative style, a mutual request based on their individual previous experiences with both the Evaluative and Transformative mediation styles. Their goal is to reach settlement in mediation.

Flash Challenge Question #4: Is it possible for a mediator who is engaging in a mediation utilizing a Facilitative style *only* to ensure that there is:

1. Fairness
2. Respect
3. Forward momentum
4. Actual progress

in the mediation process if parties are not accomplishing any of the above on their own? Discuss.

Flash Challenge Question #5: If a mediation has reached an impasse using a facilitative style, should that be an indicator to a mediator to switch styles? Discuss.

Flash Challenge Question #6: What if the parties specifically ask a mediator for more help and intervention during a Facilitative mediation? Can and should the mediator provide it even if it goes against their belief that all mediations should be conducted in a Facilitative manner? Discuss.

Transformative Mediation

If the mediator has identified the mediation as Transformative in nature, then it would be appropriate to expect to find that the disputants had a relationship prior to entering the mediation process and will have a relationship in some capacity, even if only in the past, upon its conclusion. The goal of Transformative mediation is not only to work through the current dispute, but also to build and design a framework of "what to do when . . . , how to avoid . . . , and how to work on the relationship and build each other up" that works for them, feels good, and is beneficial within their relationship and as individuals. The mediator's job goes beyond facilitating negotiation and communication, evaluating a case, or working through the dispute. It is also to help repair and possibly reshape the relationship, which often necessitates more of a focus on the emotional components connected to the dispute. Some mediators believe that a Transformative approach to mediation is one that should always be employed, regardless of the level of relationship between the parties. In other words, by virtue of being involved in a conflict situation, disputants have entered into a form of relationship with each other that satisfies the "relationship" characteristic of the Transformative style.

During the Transformative Process

1. Discern where disputants get stuck in their interactions during the conflict, resulting in the need for mediator assistance, and determine how to get unstuck.
2. Examine the disputants' conflict interaction, including their Conflict Handling Modes (see Chapter 4, "Conflict Handling Modes") and Communication Styles (see Chapter 3, "Communication Styles").
3. If disputants are triggering each other, the cycle of ineffective conflict management is perpetuated unless and until those triggers are properly identified and addressed (see Chapter 3).
4. Identify the precise balance of equal and sometimes opposite interaction approach(es) required for disputants to effectively communicate with each other.
   a. The disputants might be locked in a pattern that will not change unless they shift the manner in which they interact.
   b. The mediator can work with the parties to develop a new pattern of interaction.
5. Look for, target, and discuss what locks disputants into their conflict pattern. Included are:
   a. Pride.
   b. Ego.
   c. Fear.
   d. Insecurities.
   e. Inability to evolve with and within the conflict pattern.
   f. The conflict pattern itself.

g. Conflict pattern triggers:
   i. Who will love me now?
   ii. Will I ever be with anyone again?
   iii. Identities created by their participation in the conflict pattern.
   iv. Whole being is attacked or called into question.
   v. Who will I be without this pattern—will I matter?

6. Find the objective and subjective perspectives within the conflict pattern, such as shifting attitudes from obligation and dread to one of choice and preference; for example, "I choose to go with you to visit your family as an opportunity to show my support for you and dedication to this relationship, rather than as an obligatory action associated with the relationship."

If disputants in a Transformative mediation are mired in a repetitive pattern of recirculating unproductive conversations or are met by the possibility of impasse at every turn, or both, a mediator might consider shifting the mediation away from using previously unsuccessful surface-level approaches. When treating a symptom falls short, set it aside and investigate potential root causes that have contributed to the existence of the conflict in the first place. This can be done by targeting deeper underlying issues and concerns beneath superficial posturing that may have developed as a result of the preexisting relationship. Addressing subsurface layers can remove those potentially problematic obstacles that might be interfering with the successful resolution of the conflict. Approaching disputants holistically by being consciously inclusive of these as yet unaddressed aspects of the conflict could lead disputants through repetitive conflict patterns or impasse and into settlement. The mediator's approach might also be to encourage parties to discuss:

1. Their concept of the origination of the conflict.
2. The emotions they have been feeling since its inception.
3. The changed course of their relationship with each other.
4. Their desired outcome for their relationship after a resolution to the conflict has been reached.
5. Suggested strategies to accomplish their relationship goal(s).
6. Fundamental communication issues that might have contributed to the conflict.

If communication is ineffective, it can create a ripple effect from perceived, although perhaps unintentional, disrespect between parties with an existing relationship that can lead to a dispute requiring conflict intervention. With ineffective communication as the culprit and after investigating below the surface, if the mediator can determine that the disrespect was unintentional, then reaching an awareness and acceptance that the conflict never should have escalated as it did is the goal of a shift to effective communication. The desired outcome of the shift to effective communication would be to bring to light that the escalation only occurred as a result of quick-fire responses in perceived kind to an originally misinterpreted and unintended offense. *Taking a beat* (see Chapter 10, "Managing Impasse") could have then and will likely now be a pivotal element to restoring the relationship to a functional and conflict-free state. Asking for clarity of intent and clearer explanation of statements is not always easy and might require additional steps to address the extra layers built into a Transformative mediation, but it should be attempted whenever appropriate, as it is an avenue that could lead to settlement.

During a Transformative mediation, many mediators believe that it is more advantageous to keep the disputants together in joint session. However, to immediately conclude that parties should automatically be kept in joint session by sheer virtue of the mediation being Transformative might be shortsighted by not addressing the specifics of each dispute. In fact, *especially* in the case of Transformative mediations, where emotions often run the highest and most volatile, and situations are the most layered and complicated, it only makes sense to move the parties into caucus to wade through potentially inflammatory statements and emotional outbursts before bringing them back together into joint session. This precludes potential destruction of a relationship and derailment of a mediation by isolating and keeping exclusively within caucus the emotionally fueled and triggered responses that are not necessarily reflective of true interests and would not be productive in joint session. Doing so in caucus could enable a subsequent joint session that leads to resolution and restoration of the relationship. Immediate decisions to be in joint session or caucus can be uninformed at best and detrimental to the parties and their mediation at worst.

FLASH CHALLENGE QUESTIONS

Hint for Flash Challenge Question #7: The case concerns a fight that erupted at a party taking place in Disputant A's home. Disputant A and Disputant B are strangers—the party was for profit where tickets were sold online to the general public—and there are no insurance companies involved. There is no indication that the two will ever cross paths again.

Flash Challenge Question #7: Are there certain types of cases (nature of the conflict) that are not served well by a Transformative style?

GENERAL BENEFITS OF CAUCUS

Relevant for all Mediation Styles

1. Disputants have the opportunity to express their emotions privately with only the mediator present, therefore without the risk of inflaming any other disputant and potentially derailing the mediation. They can get angry, yell,

curse, and make negative remarks about another party. The mediator will allow them to express themselves freely to work through their emotions sufficiently. This expression of emotions often paves the way for rationale and logic, so that the mediator can then find success in bringing the disputants to an emotionally level place where potential cooperative settlement options can be explored.

2. Aggressive and inflammatory statements can be reframed before they are heard by another party and potentially cause damage to the mediation.
3. The mediator can use the separation of caucus as a tool to encourage disputants to disclose additional information that they might otherwise feel uncomfortable disclosing in front of another party.
   a. Disputants may reach a place of safety and security more quickly, and therefore feel freer to discuss real issues and interests below their surface-level posturing.
   b. The pressure of speaking in front of an opposing party can affect answers.
   c. Regarding an issue of safety, at the very least, the mediator must be told the absolute truth.
4. Conversation can be easier when disputants are not concerned with how they might come across or be interpreted by another party.
5. Disputants might feel more comfortable letting down their guard and becoming emotional, thereby opening the door for the mediator to reach the crux of the issues that would be otherwise unattainable.
   a. This can, of course, consequently place the mediation on the path to resolution and settlement.
6. Caucus is nonnegotiable with even the slightest of safety concerns regarding one or both of the disputants' abilities to control themselves.
7. It can be treated as a way for the mediator to touch base with disputants. During joint session, if the mediator at any time feels that either party is hesitant, they should caucus immediately even if just to quickly and specifically discuss that hesitancy in private. The mediation can then proceed back in joint session or remain in caucus.

GENERAL BENEFITS OF JOINT SESSION

Relevant for all Mediation Styles

1. All parties have an opportunity to hear what everyone has to say without any points, tone, or intent potentially lost or diluted when messages are relayed back and forth by the mediator practicing shuttle mediation during caucus.

2. Disputants may hear statements from each other with an emotional component that they might not have realized was there.
   a. Pain is often masked by anger, but that mask may come off when disputants in a preexisting relationship come face to face. It is during this interaction that underlying emotions, those other than anger, can be identified and expressed.
3. All parties are hearing the exact same information at the exact same time.
4. The parties can work jointly to brainstorm cooperative settlement options.
   a. Creative activities such as brainstorming, where all parties can contribute and work together and be inspired by each other's ideas can drive a mediation into settlement.
5. The parties can ask each other questions directly, gaining immediate clarity.
6. Apologies in person rather than through a mediator go a long way.

FLASH CHALLENGE

Mediation Styles: Transformative, Evaluative, Facilitative

1. Based on the conflicts listed below, with only the superficial information provided, identify which Mediation Style you would use to mediate the case:
   a. Transformative
   b. Evaluative
   c. Facilitative
      i. Strangers who got into a car accident.
      ii. Neighbors disputing over a parking spot.
      iii. Family members fighting over property.
      iv. An individual and an insurance company.
      v. A cooperative couple going through a divorce.
      vi. A cooperative couple, with children, going through a divorce.
      vii. Close siblings dividing up assets left to them by their parents.
      viii. A fiercely feuding divorced couple in need of a custody arrangement.
      ix. A father and son, furious at each other, fighting over their family business.
      x. A small-town shoe store and their local longtime customer.
      xi. A man identified to you as abusive and as an ex-partner.
      xii. Two corporations posturing and jockeying for power.
2. Based on the brief descriptions above, can you identify an automatic opportunity in which a combination of styles could be beneficial? Discuss.
3. Based on the brief descriptions above, discuss how you would use caucus, joint session, or both.

DISCUSSING MEDIATION STYLES

In conversations about Mediation Styles, there is often a clear line between those who support the Facilitative and Transformative approaches as the way to mediate conflicts and those who support using only the Evaluative style as the way to mediate (see Chapter 5, "Maintaining Neutrality"). The conversation, however, is larger than simply the banter of opinions from those in the conflict management community. This has become more and more evident as mediation proceeds into modern times with the need to tackle modern issues and conflicts becoming increasingly urgent. The conversation must also include the varied and often complicated disputant interests and needs specifically with regard to resolution. The way in which mediators manage a mediation must be a direct result of the way in which the parties prefer to find resolution. For example, if contentious parties in a particular mediation are strangers heading into it and will be strangers coming out of it, and their only goal is to hammer out the numbers that will bring resolution to the case without forcing them into litigation, then a mediator should choose to approach the case with an Evaluative style. Why would they even attempt Facilitative or Transformative approaches when the circumstances and wishes of the parties do not support any of the characteristics of either of those styles? The answer is that they should not. Forcing particular styles onto parties for the sake of "that is what mediation is all about" or "mediation means . . ." is not only inappropriate, but it disregards another of the most foundational tenets of mediation, which is that both the process and the outcomes are driven, controlled, and dictated by the disputants and the disputants only. As conflict interventionists, we are there to provide the vehicle through which party needs can be met, to offer the type of help and support disputants have expressed needing, including to surmise their needs based on their behaviors, and to bring to the table experience, skills, and third-party abilities that disputants themselves cannot provide.

FLASH CHALLENGE QUESTIONS

Flash Challenge Question #8:

1. At what point can and should a mediator put the needs of the parties above her own style preferences and ideas about "what mediation is or should be"? Discuss.
2. Should this even be a necessary question? Discuss.

Ms. Shi v. Ms. Vito

A Look into Mediation Styles

For the most part, this would be a Transformative and Facilitative mediation because of past history and expected future continuation of the relationship. Ms. Shi and Ms. Vito are not strangers, and they are currently struggling with their communication, necessitating a facilitator to assist them while allowing them the space to work only with each other. However, due to the aggressive position Ms. Shi has adopted toward Ms. Vito's daughter's injuries and the distribution of responsibility for the tree's cleanup, the mediator may consider also using an Evaluative approach. The purpose here of switching styles would be to assist Ms. Vito in viewing the strengths and weaknesses of her case from the perspective of what she might be facing should the case be taken to court. Based on the facts of the case, the current extremely ineffective communication between the parties, and their heightened emotional states, caucus will likely be an effective tool to provide a protected space where inflammatory or aggressive statements and emotional outbursts are prevented from reaching the other party. A combination of caucus and joint sessions might be considered to:

1. Validate the disputants' emotions.
2. Let disputants feel and actually be heard.
3. Reach interests below surface-level posturing (both in common and conflicting).
4. Give disputants their day in court.
5. Reframe, redirect, and pivot to keep disputants on track.
6. Maintain focus on the mediable and negotiable issues.
7. Move them past their initially presented conflicting positions.

This combination can also help when parties begin to shift their focus away from the conflict and potential resolution options and onto assigning the fault they each believe lies with the other. Caucus can be used to correct such derailment before continuing in joint session.

Initial Approach

As a Transformative mediation in which there will be an effort to preserve the relationship between the disputants, the initial approach even before addressing the current conflict will be for the mediator to establish the baseline of the relationship: what it has been in the past, where it is now, and what it could be in the future. An additional aspect of the relationship to consider is that there will very likely be spillover onto the other members of their family, causing tensions, rifts, and the taking of sides, making it unpleasant and uncomfortable for all. To address the conflict without losing sight of its impact on the relationship and of the relationship on the conflict, the Transformative and Facilitative approaches will likely address the broader aspects of the relationship and its connection to the conflict, whereas the Evaluative style might be applied toward present conflict elements, at least at the outset. At this initial phase, the disputants are expressing positional bargaining and negotiating styles that are competitive, aggressive, and adversarial, which are not beneficial to a Transformative mediation – nor to either of the other two mediation styles, for that matter. The goal of using a combination of mediation styles at different times and for various reasons is to address and move the disputants beyond their highly charged, negative emotions so they are willing and able to effectively communicate with each other. The willingness to express their underlying interests and needs beneath the aggressive positions currently being presented may follow as well.

Reference A: The California Rules of Court

Division 9. Evidence Affected or Excluded by Extrinsic Policies: Chapter 2. Mediation [115-1129]

1119. Except as otherwise provided in this chapter:

(a) No evidence of anything said or any admission made for the purpose of, in the course of, or pursuant to, a mediation or a mediation consultation is admissible or subject to discovery, and disclosure of the evidence shall not be compelled, in any arbitration, administrative adjudication, civil action, or other noncriminal proceeding in which, pursuant to law, testimony can be compelled to be given.

(b) No writing, as defined in Section 250, that is prepared for the purpose of, in the course of, or pursuant to, a mediation or a mediation consultation, is admissible or subject to discovery, and disclosure of the writing shall not be compelled, in any arbitration, administrative adjudication, civil action, or other noncriminal proceeding in which, pursuant to law, testimony can be compelled to be given.

(c) All communications, negotiations, or settlement discussions by and between participants in the course of a mediation or a mediation consultation shall remain confidential.

(Added by Stats. 1997, Ch. 772, Sec. 3. Effective January 1, 1998.)

1120. (a) Evidence otherwise admissible or subject to discovery outside of a mediation or a mediation consultation shall not be or become inadmissible or protected from disclosure solely by reason of its introduction or use in a mediation or a mediation consultation.

(b) This chapter does not limit any of the following:

(1) The admissibility of an agreement to mediate a dispute.

(2) The effect of an agreement not to take a default or an agreement to extend the time within which to act or refrain from acting in a pending civil action.

(3) Disclosure of the mere fact that a mediator has served, is serving, will serve, or was contacted about serving as a mediator in a dispute.

(4) The admissibility of declarations of disclosure required by Sections 2104 and 2105 of the Family Code, even if prepared for the purpose of, in the course of, or pursuant to, a mediation or a mediation consultation.

(Amended by Stats. 2017, Ch. 60, Sec. 1. (SB 217) Effective January 1, 2018.)

1121. Neither a mediator nor anyone else may submit to a court or other adjudicative body, and a court or other adjudicative body may not consider, any report, assessment, evaluation, recommendation, or finding of any kind by the mediator concerning a mediation conducted by the mediator, other than a report that is mandated by court rule or other law and that states only whether an agreement was reached, unless all parties to the mediation expressly agree otherwise in writing, or orally in accordance with Section 1118.

(Added by Stats. 1997, Ch. 772, Sec. 3. Effective January 1, 1998.)

1122. (a) A communication or a writing, as defined in Section 250, that is made or prepared for the purpose of, or in the course of, or pursuant to, a mediation or a mediation consultation, is not made inadmissible, or protected from disclosure, by provisions of this chapter if any of the following conditions are satisfied:

(1) All persons who conduct or otherwise participate in the mediation expressly agree in writing, or orally in accordance with Section 1118, to disclosure of the communication, document, or writing.

(2) The communication, document, or writing was prepared by or on behalf of fewer than all the mediation participants, those participants expressly agree in writing, or orally in accordance with Section 1118, to its disclosure, and the communication, document, or writing does not disclose anything said or done or any admission made in the course of the mediation.

(3) The communication, document, or writing is related to an attorney's compliance with the requirements described in Section 1129 and does not disclose anything said or done or any admission made in the course of the mediation, in which case the communication, document, or writing may be used in an attorney disciplinary proceeding to determine whether the attorney has complied with Section 1129.

(b) For purposes of subdivision (a), if the neutral person who conducts a mediation expressly agrees to disclosure, that agreement also binds any other person described in subdivision (b) of Section 1115.

(Amended by Stats. 2018, Ch. 350, Sec. 1. (SB 954) Effective January 1, 2019.)

1123. A written settlement agreement prepared in the course of, or pursuant to, a mediation, is not made inadmissible, or protected from disclosure, by provisions of this chapter if the agreement is signed by the settling parties and any of the following conditions are satisfied:

(a) The agreement provides that it is admissible or subject to disclosure, or words to that effect.

(b) The agreement provides that it is enforceable or binding or words to that effect.

(c) All parties to the agreement expressly agree in writing, or orally in accordance with Section 1118, to its disclosure.

(d) The agreement is used to show fraud, duress, or illegality that is relevant to an issue in dispute.

(Added by Stats. 1997, Ch. 772, Sec. 3. Effective January 1, 1998.)

1124. An oral agreement made in the course of, or pursuant to, a mediation is not made inadmissible, or protected from disclosure, by the provisions of this chapter if any of the following conditions are satisfied:

(a) The agreement is in accordance with Section 1118.

(b) The agreement is in accordance with subdivisions (a), (b), and (d) of Section 1118, and all parties to the agreement expressly agree, in writing or orally in accordance with Section 1118, to disclosure of the agreement.

(c) The agreement is in accordance with subdivisions (a), (b), and (d) of Section 1118, and the agreement is used to show fraud, duress, or illegality that is relevant to an issue in dispute.

(Added by Stats. 1997, Ch. 772, Sec. 3. Effective January 1, 1998.)

1125. (a) For purposes of confidentiality under this chapter, a mediation ends when any one of the following conditions is satisfied:

(1) The parties execute a written settlement agreement that fully resolves the dispute.

(2) An oral agreement that fully resolves the dispute is reached in accordance with Section 1118.

(3) The mediator provides the mediation participants with a writing signed by the mediator that states that the mediation is terminated, or words to that effect, which shall be consistent with Section 1121.

(4) A party provides the mediator and the other mediation participants with a writing stating that the mediation is terminated, or words to that effect, which shall be consistent with Section 1121. In a mediation involving more than two parties, the mediation may continue as to the remaining parties or be terminated in accordance with this section.

(5) For 10 calendar days, there is no communication between the mediator and any of the parties to the mediation relating to the dispute. The mediator and the parties may shorten or extend this time by agreement.

(b) For purposes of confidentiality under this chapter, if a mediation partially resolves a dispute, mediation ends when either of the following conditions is satisfied:

(1) The parties execute a written settlement agreement that partially resolves the dispute.

(2) An oral agreement that partially resolves the dispute is reached in accordance with Section 1118.

(c) This section does not preclude a party from ending a mediation without reaching an agreement. This section does not otherwise affect the extent to which a party may terminate a mediation.

(Added by Stats. 1997, Ch. 772, Sec. 3. Effective January 1, 1998.)

1126. Anything said, any admission made, or any writing that is inadmissible, protected from disclosure, and confidential under this chapter before a mediation ends, shall remain inadmissible, protected from disclosure, and confidential to the same extent after the mediation ends.

(Added by Stats. 1997, Ch. 772, Sec. 3. Effective January 1, 1998.)

1127. If a person subpoenas or otherwise seeks to compel a mediator to testify or produce a writing, as defined in Section 250, and the court or other adjudicative body determines that the testimony or writing is inadmissible under this chapter, or protected from disclosure under this chapter, the court or adjudicative body making the determination shall award reasonable attorney's fees and costs to the mediator against the person seeking the testimony or writing.

(Added by Stats. 1997, Ch. 772, Sec. 3. Effective January 1, 1998.)

1128. Any reference to a mediation during any subsequent trial is an irregularity in the proceedings of the trial for the purposes of Section 657 of the Code of Civil Procedure. Any reference to a mediation during any other subsequent noncriminal proceeding is grounds for vacating or modifying the decision in that proceeding, in whole or in part, and granting a new or further hearing on all or part of the issues, if the reference materially affected the substantial rights of the party requesting relief.

(Added by Stats. 1997, Ch. 772, Sec. 3. Effective January 1, 1998.)

Reference B: The California Rules of Court

Division 6 Witnesses: Chapter 1. Competency [703.5]

703.5 No person presiding at any judicial or quasi-judicial proceeding, and no arbitrator or mediator, shall be competent to testify, in any subsequent civil proceeding, as to any statement, conduct, decision, or ruling, occurring at or in conjunction with the prior proceeding, except as to a statement or conduct that could (a) give rise to civil or criminal contempt, (b) constitute a crime, (c) be the subject of investigation by the State Bar or Commission on Judicial Performance, or (d) give rise to disqualification proceedings under paragraph (1) or (6) of subdivision (a) of Section 170.1 of the Code of Civil Procedure. However, this section does not apply to a mediator with regard to any mediation under Chapter 11 (commencing with Section 3160) of Part 2 of Division 8 of the Family Code.

(Amended by Stats. 1994, Ch. 1269, Sec. 7. Effective January 1, 1995.)

Reference C: The Uniform Mediation Act

Section 4. Privilege Against Disclosure; Admissibility; Discovery

(a) Except as otherwise provided in Section 6, a mediation communication is privileged as provided in subsection (b) and is not subject to discovery or admissible in evidence in a proceeding unless waived or precluded as provided by Section 5.

(b) In a proceeding, the following privileges apply:

(1) A mediation party may refuse to disclose, and may prevent any other person from disclosing, a mediation communication.

(2) A mediator may refuse to disclose a mediation communication, and may prevent any other person from disclosing a mediation communication of the mediator.

(3) A nonparty participant may refuse to disclose, and may prevent any other person from disclosing, a mediation communication of the nonparty participant.

(c) Evidence or information that is otherwise admissible or subject to discovery does not become inadmissible or protected from discovery solely by reason of its disclosure or use in a mediation.

Legislative Note: The Act does not supersede existing state statutes that make mediators incompetent to testify, or that provide for costs and attorney fees to mediators who are wrongfully subpoenaed. See, e.g., Cal. Evid. Code Section 703.5 (West 1994).

Section 5. Waiver and Preclusion of Privilege

(a) A privilege under Section 4 may be waived in a record or orally during a proceeding if it is expressly waived by all parties to the mediation and:

(1) in the case of the privilege of a mediator, it is expressly waived by the mediator; and

(2) in the case of the privilege of a nonparty participant, it is expressly waived by the nonparty participant.

(b) A person that discloses or makes a representation about a mediation communication which prejudices another person in a proceeding is precluded from asserting a privilege under Section 4, but only to the extent necessary for the person prejudiced to respond to the representation or disclosure.

(c) A person that intentionally uses a mediation to plan, attempt to commit or commit a crime, or to conceal an ongoing crime or ongoing criminal activity is precluded from asserting a privilege under Section 4.

Section 6. Exceptions to Privilege

(a) There is no privilege under Section 4 for a mediation communication that is:

(1) in an agreement evidenced by a record signed by all parties to the agreement;

(2) available to the public under or made during a session of a mediation which is open, or is required by law to be open, to the public;

(3) a threat or statement of a plan to inflict bodily injury or commit a crime of violence;

(4) intentionally used to plan a crime, attempt to commit or commit a crime, or to conceal an ongoing crime or ongoing criminal activity;

(5) sought or offered to prove or disprove a claim or complaint of professional misconduct or malpractice filed against a mediator;

(6) except as otherwise provide in subsection (c), sought or offered to prove or disprove a claim or complaint of professional misconduct or malpractice filed against a mediation party, nonparty, or representative of a party based on conduct occurring during a mediation; or

(7) sought or offered to prove or disprove abuse, neglect, abandonment, or exploitation in a proceeding in which a child or adult protective services agency is a party, unless the

[Alternative A: [State to insert, for example, child or adult protection] case is referred by a court to mediation and a public agency participates.]

[Alternative B: public agency participates in the [State to insert, for example, child or adult protection] mediation.]

(b) There is no privilege under Section 4 if a court, administrative agency, or arbitrator finds, after a hearing in camera, that the party seeking discovery or the proponent of the evidence has shown that the evidence is not otherwise available, that there is a need for the evidence that substantially outweighs the interest in protecting confidentiality, and that the mediation communication is sought or offered in:

(1) a court proceeding involving a felony [or misdemeanor]; or

(2) except as otherwise provided in subsection (c), a proceeding to prove a claim to rescind or reform or a defense to avoid liability on a contract arising out of the mediation.

(c) A mediator may not be compelled to provide evidence of a mediation communication referred to in subsection (a)(6) or (b)(2).

(d) If a mediation communication is not privileged under subsection (a) or (b), only the portion of the communication necessary for the application of the exception from nondisclosure may be admitted. Admission of evidence under subsection (a) or (b) does not render the evidence, or any other mediation communication, discoverable or admissible for any other purpose.

Legislative Note: If the enacting state does not have an open records act, the following language to paragraph (2) of subsection (a) needs to be deleted: "available to the public under [insert statutory reference to open records act] or".

Section 7. Prohibited Mediator Reports

(a) Except as required in subsection (b), a mediator may not make a report, assessment, evaluation, recommendation, finding, or other communication regarding a mediation to a court, administrative agency, or other authority that may make a ruling on the dispute that is the subject of the mediation.

(b) A mediator may disclose:

(1) whether the mediation occurred or has terminated, whether a settlement was reached, and attendance;

(2) a mediation communication as permitted under Section 6: or

(3) a mediation communication evidencing abuse, neglect, abandonment, or exploitation of an individual to a public agency responsible for protecting individuals against such mistreatment.

(c) A communication made in violation of subsection (a) may not be considered by a court, administrative agency, or arbitrator.

Section 8. Confidentiality

Unless subject to the [insert statutory reference to open meetings act and open records act], mediation communications are confidential to the extent agreed by the parties or provided by other law or rule of this State.

Reference D: Model Standards of Conduct for Mediators

Standard V. Confidentiality

A. A mediator shall maintain the confidentiality of all information obtained by the mediator in mediation, unless otherwise agreed to by the parties or required by applicable law.

1. If the parties to a mediation agree that the mediator may disclose information obtained during the mediation, the mediator may do so.

2. A mediator should not communicate to any non-participant information about how the parties acted in the mediation. A mediator may report, if required, whether parties appeared at a scheduled mediation and whether or not the parties reached a resolution.

3. If a mediator participates in teaching, research or evaluation of mediation, the mediator should protect the anonymity of the parties and abide by their reasonable expectations regarding confidentiality.

B. A mediator who meets with any persons in private session during a mediation shall not convey directly or indirectly to any other person, any information that was obtained during that private session without the consent of the disclosing person.

C. A mediator shall promote understanding among the parties of the extent to which the parties will maintain confidentiality of information they obtain in a mediation.

D. Depending on the circumstance of a mediation, the parties may have varying expectations regarding confidentiality that a mediator should address. The parties may make their own rules with respect to confidentiality, or the accepted practice of an individual mediator or institution may dictate a particular set of expectations.

Reference E: The Alternative Dispute Resolution Act of 1998

Section 652. of title 28, United States Code, is amended to read as follows:

Sec. 652. Jurisdiction

(d) Confidentiality Provisions—Until such time as rules are adopted under chapter 131 of this title providing for the confidentiality of alternative dispute resolution processes under this chapter, each district court shall, by local rule adopted under section 2071(a), provide for the confidentiality of the alternative dispute resolution processes and to prohibit disclosure of confidential dispute resolution communications.

chapter 3

Communication Styles

"When attitudes are hostile, facts are unconvincing."
—*Dr. Haim Ginott*

MEDIATION AND COMMUNICATION: THE MEDIATOR AS A COMMUNICATION EXPERT

Communication success or failure is the deciding factor that stands between a disagreement or misunderstanding escalating to the level of a mediation-worthy conflict—or not. Communication Styles, the ways in which disputants communicate with each other, determine how they interact while presenting and responding to information. The interplay of Communication Styles dictates the trajectory of a mediation and whether it concludes in impasse or in a mediated settlement agreement. Communicating effectively does not mean knowing every answer, being a particularly talented or professional communicator, being a mind reader, or immediately understanding what someone else is saying—that would be unrealistic. What it does mean, however, is engaging in a process and manner that results in communication successfully leading to a desired end goal. In the same way that a reference librarian knows how and where to find information that can solve unanswered questions, mediators and conflict interventionists have to be able to determine and then effectually interact with disputants' varying Communication Styles to assist them in reaching their conflict resolution goal, in whatever form that may be. To maneuver around and through the multitude of obstacles that emerge from the inner workings of the human psyche, and when a disputant is both the obstacle *and* the solution, a mediator must manage their Communication Styles. This will make navigating in the right direction, identifying, accessing, and receiving correct and necessary information to continue guiding (tugging, pulling, pushing, and corralling) the disputants and the mediation a substantially more realistic possibility.

Being versed in communication and its styles is both a necessity and a requirement when participating in a field that relies upon communication.

The immense and supportable importance placed on communication is not exclusively centralized around disputant interactions with each other. A mediator's ability to engage in, guide, and lead effective communication is the tip of the spear, and that which stands between the process and a beneficial outcome. Effective communication encompasses Communication Style changes and tailored strategies to best suit the uniqueness that all conflict situations and disputants bring with them. It should not necessarily be mistaken for communication that is identified as particularly cooperative or lacking animosity. As long as the goal remains the focus with continuous forward momentum toward it, the communication process to get there can take many forms, and what might be unacceptable and unmanageable to some disputants will not be interpreted the same way by others. When the layers of details are stripped away, conflict can be boiled down to:

1. A fundamental inability for parties to communicate properly and effectively as their means of understanding each other.
2. Expressing personal interests and needs in an inappropriate manner.
3. Ineffective discussion of personal interests and needs (1 and 2), leading to an inability to understand how to correctly interact, resulting in possible mutually agreeable solutions remaining out of reach.

When communication is ineffective, the likelihood of conflict engagement resulting in agreeable solutions rests on a wing and a prayer. Conflict and communication are intertwined and dependent on one another. It can be argued that conflict does not exist without communication, as the manner in which interests and needs are communicated in conjunction with the way *reactions* to those interests and needs are expressed are the impetus for whether or not an interaction becomes escalated to that of a conflict destined for mediation intervention in the first place. For example, two people get into a car accident, one of them rear-ending the other. Both parties emerge from their cars, immediately check to make sure everyone involved in the accident is uninjured and not in need of medical attention, and proceed to exchange insurance information as the party who rear-ended the other apologizes for their action, which was, of course, an accident—as pointed out by the driver of the car that was hit. A handshake and a wave conclude the interaction, and all parties leave the scene having behaved appropriately based on what the nature of the situation necessitated. However, this interaction could have gone horribly wrong in more ways than there are pages in this book. One possible scenario resulting from ineffective communication might be a malicious transformation born out of misinterpreted, manipulated, and weaponized statements. The responsibility of a mediator is to ensure that such a scenario is not provided the opportunity to erupt and that communication is used toward effective and constructive ends, whether those ends be resolution, deeper understanding, the ability to have clear expression and understanding, something in between, or a combination of them all.

The Proper Use of Communication Can Lead To:

1. Improvement in problem-solving and conflict resolution.
2. Overcoming incorrect assumptions and misinterpretations.

3. Identifying beneath-the-surface needs and interests.
4. Removing superfluous verbal and emotional outbursts stemming from needs not (yet) being met.

Each of these benefits contributes to an unparalleled improvement in conflict engagement, resolution, and the mediation process.

FLASH CHALLENGE

The Power of Communication

1. Based on your understanding and any additional insight you might have, what is your definition of communication?
2. How can communication be helpful?
    a. Provide examples.
3. How can communication be harmful?
    a. Provide examples.
4. How can harmful communication be transformed into helpful communication?
    a. Create a dialogue example of communication that starts out as harmful but is shifted into being helpful.
5. Provide two global examples of conflicts that could be beneficially affected by currently harmful communication being shifted into helpful communication.
    a. Discuss how the current communication is harmful.
    b. Discuss what needs to be added to or removed from the currently harmful communication to shift it to being helpful.
    c. Discuss your creative ideas for how that shift could happen.
    d. What would the shift sound like?
        i. Create a dialogue leading us from harmful to helpful communication.
    e. Discuss the impact helpful communication could have on the conflicts, the impacted countries, and the citizens.
        i. Current impacts.
        ii. Future impacts.
6. Who should be involved in shifting the communication?

IDENTIFYING DISPUTANT COMMUNICATION STYLES AND PREFERRED METHODS OF COMMUNICATION

Words should always be chosen wisely and their impact given deep consideration as it can be an exercise in futility to unsay what has already been said.

There is a natural extension of the above statement to mediations, especially when disputants are strangers with no foundation for understanding each other's Communication Style or *language*. Even if the disputants are not strangers, their understanding of each other's Communication Styles, and their ability to communicate effectively and efficiently with each other may be doubtful. Learning to speak the same language, or at least to absorb enough of one another's language to maximize cross-comprehension is not something that generally happens naturally. This can require considerable effort and guidance, and for the vast majority, this skill has not yet been developed. This is, of course, where a mediator can begin functioning as a *translator*, explaining, reframing, empathizing, and searching below the surface for clarification to assist the disputants and facilitate effective communication. In many cases, there is no substantial difference between two people who actually speak different languages and two people whose differing Communication Styles create different languages. These differences can be severe and impactful on the mediation process itself, as well as affecting the likelihood of reaching settlement.

There is a noticeable overlap between Communication Styles and learning styles, and rightfully so. What is the purpose of communication if not to convey messages with the intention for the listener to understand, absorb, and incorporate that information into their responses, actions, and perception of the speaker—all of which also happen to largely contribute to the learning process. Communication Styles and learning styles are intertwined and must be approached in that manner, as one and the same and all integral to a holistic approach. The more comprehensively mediators understand the disputants with whom they work, the better equipped they are to provide help and produce results that match disputants' needs. By identifying and understanding disputant Communication Styles, mediators and conflict interventionists are able to adapt their own Communication Style to match or complement disputants' styles to ensure the best possible scenario for the transfer of information between and among parties. This should lead to the clearest level of understanding and absorption possible.

COMMUNICATION STYLES

1. **Verbal**
   a. Verbal communication is not restricted to a disputant using his voice to convey a message, but it is also the manner in which he conveys that message because the way words are both used and received matters. All too often, communication is thought about as an informational one-way street—that street belonging to the person speaking; however, equally if not more important, it is the way the information is received. Although the way a person interprets a message is not completely within our control, making efforts to ensure that the message is clear, reflective of true intentions, and potentially followed by questions to double- and triple-check that clarity certainly is. In mediation, disputants cannot say anything they like in any manner they like, without regard for the potential

consequences of their message in its reception by an opposing party; quite the opposite, in fact.

b. *Mediator intervention*

   i. Disputants should be encouraged to make it their duty to take every step possible to ensure that their words are completely and fully understood in exactly the way intended. Those steps include expressing their point(s) until clearly understood by explaining themselves in detail, asking if an opposing party has any questions about what they are saying, and possibly reframing or changing their tone in case the message is misinterpreted. Other parties may shut down and enter *defense mode*—a position in which they feel the need to be on the defensive—if they interpret an aggressive or accusatory tone. If disputants have entered *defense mode* it is highly unlikely that they will be able to listen to the message with any ability to hear it clearly. The mediator will need to defuse this position before additional progress can be made by asking parties to reiterate what they believe they are hearing to ensure that the messages match, as they may be unaware that they have not understood or been understood accurately.

c. When a disputant struggles with oral delivery of a message, verbal communication can include written communication as well.

d. *Mediator intervention*

   i. If the mediator identifies that disputants are struggling to express their message orally, a strategy could be to suggest that they write down what they wish to say. This can become the manner in which they will consistently communicate, providing all of their questions and responses in written form. It can also be an exercise to assist the disputants in clarifying their thoughts and the way they compose their message prior to delivering it orally. The written message can be read to an opposing party by the disputant who wrote it, or it can be read by the mediator either in caucus or in joint session. These decisions can be made by the disputant and the mediator together, taking into consideration factors such as comfort level, emotional atmosphere of the mediation, relationship between the parties, or nature of the conflict.

2. **Nonverbal**

   a. For anyone who has ever attempted to communicate with someone speaking a language different from their own, nonverbal cues and other aspects of the communication process become immediately necessary; for example, pointing to a desired location on a map as a question, and then a point in a particular direction as the answer. A smile can immediately relax and express a message to someone who does not understand what is being said but is desperately attempting to identify tone. Pointing at oneself and stating your name transcends most language barriers, and holding one's hands up in the air has become a universal symbol for nonthreatening posture and sometimes indicates "I'm here to help."

b. Disputants who feel more comfortable and rely on a nonverbal Communication Style may be found:

   i. Shrugging their shoulders in response to a variety of questions

      1. Shoulder-shrugging has different meanings and can be confusing without verbal attachment or clarification. The best strategy when interacting with a disputant who responds to questions and statements in this manner is to ask them to explain their action in words. If the party has a hard time verbally expressing their nonverbal action, the mediator may prompt them with questions for them to simply answer or as a suggested opening for their explanation.

   ii. Sighing

      1. The simple act of inhaling and exhaling, but with gusto, is often interpreted (and intentionally utilized) as a sign of annoyance, irritation, frustration, aggravation, and disrespect. Such strong sighs are often used to demonstrate feelings such as:

         a) This is a waste of my time.

         b) You are moving too slowly for me, and I already knew all of that information.

         c) I am better than you.

         d) I do not have respect for what you are saying.

         e) I do not want to wait until you are finished speaking because what I have to say is more important than what you have to say.

      2. Sighs of a softer variety can indicate resignation, sadness, and disappointment.

   iii. Using facial expressions to display feelings

      1. Facial expressions (eye rolling, head shaking, pursed lips, grimacing, etc.) by one disputant while another is speaking can be extremely triggering, offending, and distracting. These expressions can have undesirable repercussions.

   iv. Gesturing

      1. As with all nonverbal communication, there are common and cultural differences that can exacerbate the misinterpretations of gestures.

         a) Cultural differences and gestures that may be misinterpreted include:

            i. Pointing

            ii. Winking

            iii. Thumbs-up

            iv. OK sign

            v. Touching one's own face

2. Suffice it to say, when in conflict, it is even more important to be mindful and careful with making gestures as well as interpreting gestures made by others.

3. *Mediator intervention*

   a) The preferred method of management is first to identify that the gesture actually transpired, and then to seek clarity on its intent and meaning. At that point the explanation may be sufficient to keep the mediation on track. If not, the mediator may need to intervene with caucus, reframing, or reminding the parties that liking each other is not a prerequisite to conflict intervention and mediation, but behaving in a respectful manner to each other is.

c. *Mediator intervention*

   i. If the mediator identifies that a disputant is having difficulty controlling their nonverbal communication, or chooses not to exercise control, there might be a decision to move the mediation into caucus. However, if the mediator finds it preferable to attempt continuing the mediation in joint session, the disputant can be given an opportunity to acknowledge their behavior, including offering an apology. This decision should be based on the disputant's offending behavior and their verbal response(s).

   ii. There is often more truth in nonverbal than verbal communication—think about professional poker players who devote time and energy to controlling, camouflaging, or eliminating their *tells*. With this in mind, it behooves a mediator to pay close attention to a disputant's nonverbal communication because it might be possible to decipher true intent without any verbal assistance.

3. **Time to process**

   a. For some disputants, processing information and making decisions quickly is comfortable and preferable. They make instant decisions, are confident in their responses, and find comfort in fast-paced communication. Interacting with an opposing party who processes information more slowly can be frustrating and interpreted as an intentional delaying tactic.

   b. For other disputants, time to process is a requirement. They need time to process the information they are receiving, to connect to the mediation, to figure out their feelings and emotions, and to decide how to respond to statements from an opposing party. While this is a requirement that satisfies one disputant's need, it can simultaneously have a different effect on other disputants and the mediation.

   c. *Mediator intervention*

      i. For disputants who require time to process to engage properly and fully in the mediation, the mediator will need to ensure that they are given the time they need. It might be beneficial to the disputants and the outcome of the mediation to work in caucus. This will allow disputants to process in their individually necessary ways both comfortably and privately without the pressure of another party watching them, possibly making rude remarks, and avoiding any additional misunderstandings. It will also allow the mediator to work separately with the parties as they process information. In other words, for parties who require time to process, the mediator could become a sounding block or support system, reminding them that they can take the time they need and not feel pressured. For disputants who process more quickly, the mediator might be operating more in the role of firefighter, dousing the flames of aggravation and irritation as they perceive this time to process as ridiculous, unnecessary, or a manipulation tactic. Keeping parties calm and encouraging an understanding of what each needs is a baseline job requirement when attempting to keep a mediation on track.

ii. Unless all parties either process in the same way or completely understand and accept one another's differences (Wouldn't that be nice!), the mediator will be continually explaining and reframing both the need for extra time to process, as well as statements that might be tinged with annoyance, discourtesy, or offensive commentary from a quicker paced responder whose patience has waned.

4. **Direct**

a. Direct approaches ask questions, make statements, or provide answers that are to the point. Direct approaches to questions and statements from a disputant or a mediator can lead to only one of two possible outcomes. The first outcome is that a disputant interprets the directness as aggressive, disrespectful, and offensive. Direct communicators are often referred to as having no filter, shooting from the hip, being a bull in a china shop, and calling it as they see it. Although there is nothing wrong with being honest and having confidence in opinions and statements, problems do arise when direct statements or questions come at the expense of the feelings of the person on the receiving end. The second outcome is that a direct statement or question cuts through the extraneous noise that all too often accompanies conflicts, making it difficult to remain focused on the actual issues. Being direct can draw the focus in the room to the heart of an issue and force the conversation to be exclusively about that. Sometimes being direct is the only way to cut through the chatter, especially when emotions are elevated, and an everything-but-the-kitchen-sink situation is unfolding.

b. *Mediator intervention*

i. If it is the mediator, the disputants, or all of the participants communicating with this direct approach, situational considerations should be factored into the decision to engage in this manner. The consequences of being direct can be deeply impactful and severe, and whether it is to the betterment or detriment of the process should be measured. Additionally, even if it was concluded that a direct approach should be taken, it would be surprising if communicating only in that manner would prove to be the wisest course of action. Weaving together the direct and indirect approaches when appropriate might be a better choice. This could be accomplished by using a direct approach followed by a softer, more indirect explanation of the direct statement or question. The mediator can assist the parties in deciding how to approach each other either right away or after they are met with less than desirable responses or reactions to their statements by discussing the costs and benefits of a direct versus indirect approach, and how each can be accomplished. A possible role play between the mediator and disputants individually could help the parties in understanding the difference between the two Communication Styles and how to recognize and engage in them. Depending on the relationship between the parties and their attitudes toward each other, the mediator might even consider recommending that the parties engage in this same exercise with one another to receive feedback about how their words are perceived. It could be extremely helpful for the parties to have an opportunity for introspection, as well as to understand the impact their words are having on someone else, whether they realize and intend it or not.

5. **Indirect**

a. Indirect approaches are questions, statements, or answers that are not directly to the point. An Indirect approach can also result in one of two outcomes. The first is a confusing and unfocused question or statement that gets lost in translation. Not only might the message be buried or missed completely, but it can also be incredibly frustrating for a direct communicator to interact with an indirect communicator, as it might lead them to feel that they are getting nowhere. Conversely, an indirect communicator might be equally frustrated while attempting to interact with a direct communicator, as they could feel continually misunderstood, pressured to act faster, and that an opposing party is not taking the proper amount of time to give them and the conflict the respect that they believe is necessary and deserved. The second outcome of an indirect approach is a delivery that has an element of finesse added to refine a direct approach.

b. *Mediator intervention*

i. Indirect communicators might be encouraged to restructure their message to be closer to their point for the purpose of staving off confusion or misunderstanding by providing less that a listener must sift through.

ii. Consider the finesse added for refinement to be a reframed direct approach that carries the originally intended message, but that has been rewrapped from a garbage bag tied with duct tape into a package with shiny wrapping paper and an elegant silk bow. A finessed message may also purposefully take more time to reach a central point when considering sensitive feelings. By engaging in further conversation and open-ended questions to provoke deeper discussions and possibly assist listeners in realizing a particular point on their own, an element that previously evoked anger or hurt might now have that power removed.

FLASH CHALLENGE

Direct vs. Indirect Communication Styles

Part A

1. Compose a total of five sentences on three different topics.
   a. The sentences can be questions, statements, or a combination of both.
2. First, write the sentences in the style of Direct Communication.
3. Next, rewrite the sentences in the style of Indirect Communication.
   a. The structure of your sentences might change and additional sentences could be required to deliver your message.
4. List some of the differences you incorporated into each sentence to identify it as Direct versus Indirect.
5. Are your Indirect sentences longer or were additional sentences required?
   a. If so, explain.

Part B

1. Deliver both your Direct and Indirect sentences to two people.
2. After each sentence, stop and ask them how they felt about the sentence.
   a. Did they find it offensively direct?
   b. Did they find it confusingly or unnecessarily indirect?
   c. Did they respond well to it?
      i. If not, how would they have preferred it?
   d. Record their answers, including changes, if any, they would have preferred in each sentence.
   e. Do their responses follow any sort of pattern based on the content of the sentence(s)?
      i. As your sentences should vary in nature, a pattern might emerge grouping category of approach with category of content. For example, if the sentences that you created are of a personal nature, and it is established that the participants prefer an Indirect approach consistently, then the emerging pattern is a connection between content of a personal nature and their preference for an Indirect approach. If the sentences are of a professional nature and it is established that the participants prefer a Direct approach consistently, then the emerging pattern is a connection between content of a professional nature and their preference for a Direct approach.

3. Based on their answers, can you determine an overall preferred method of communication: Direct or Indirect?
   a. Possibly a combination of both given the content and context?
4. Are you more comfortable delivering Direct or Indirect sentences? Explain.
   a. If you are comfortable with both, explain when, why, and how Direct versus Indirect styles can or should be used.
5. Do your speaking and listening Communication Styles match? In other words, do you prefer to receive information in an Indirect manner, but speak with a more Direct approach? Or vice versa? Or are they the same? Explain.
6. Based on the responses you received to the delivery of your sentences, has this exercise encouraged you to change or combine your Communication Styles in the future?

6. **Visual**
   a. Disputants who communicate visually generally prefer the addition of a written or graphic component. They tend to have difficulty turning words into concepts and grasping the entire picture of a set of circumstances described to them verbally only.
   b. Traits of a Visual communicator:
      i. Confusion when there are many details.
      ii. Speaking rapidly.
      iii. Interrupting.
      iv. Asking for pictures or graphics.
      v. Taking notes or drawing.
      vi. Asking for details to be written down.
   c. *Mediator intervention*
      i. A mediator may decide to format the details of a case or the various aspects of a proposed settlement offer into a list so that elements can be separated, discussed in greater detail individually from the rest of the items on the list, and compared and contrasted. The more complex a situation, the more beneficial the inclusion of a graphic component can be for parties in general, and for visual communicators specifically. Graphs or drawings can provide clarity or further illustrate a point, such as the drawing of the location of a structure, elements within it, or proximity.
7. **Auditory/Cognitive**
   a. Auditory or Cognitive communicators place a heavy emphasis on listening. For them, hearing the words is their pathway to comprehension, so they generally require different and possibly additional explanations, prefer in-depth conversations, and might ask questions about details that

others might not even notice. They could also require the use of repetition to feel comfortable with information presented and confident in their understanding of it.

b. Traits of an Auditory or Cognitive communicator:
   i. Enjoy and require extensive conversation.
   ii. Curious for additional information.
   iii. Tend not to interrupt.
   iv. Detail oriented.

c. *Mediator intervention*
   i. The mediator should be prepared to engage with this disputant in a manner that focuses on further explanation of details and circumstances. This communication will likely require the mediator to reiterate what has already been said and to devise additional ways to provide clarification of subjects being discussed. Not all disputants immediately understand in the same way. For example, when hearing the words "round and bouncy," not all will immediately conclude that the object of the discussion is a ball.
   ii. The mediator should remain aware of the Auditory or Cognitive communicator's potential uncertainty in conclusions drawn from the presented information. Therefore, the mediator should continuously inquire to determine whether or not these communicators have a clear and correct grasp of the material.

8. **Emotional**

a. Disputants who are driven by emotions and whose Communication Style in any given moment is determined by their emotional state can be exceedingly difficult to communicate with. This style is often devoid of the incorporation of critical facts that are required to gain proper perspective. Emotional communicators have an intense focus on their feelings about the conflict and how they have been personally affected (more severely than anyone else), rather than on contextual information and working toward solution options.

b. Traits of an Emotional communicator:
   i. Can become anxious in conflict or tense situations and cease to communicate effectively or at all.
      1. This is problematic during a mediation process that relies on parties communicating with each other, or at the very least, with the mediator.
   ii. Might require additional mental and emotional support.
   iii. Fearful of making decisions.
   iv. Searching for connections.
   v. Overly sensitive and quick to take offense.
   vi. May be singularly focused on their feelings.

c. *Mediator intervention*

i. The mediator might employ a strategy of allowing the disputants to work through their emotions with encouragement to "get them out." Because some of these points might be interpreted as rude or inflammatory by another party, this might be a conversation best conducted in caucus. The mediator should listen carefully and respectfully, being prepared to provide support, understanding, and comfort as needed and appropriate and to ask questions and make statements intentionally to demonstrate to disputants that they are being heard and that what they are saying matters. Regardless of how irrelevant to the conflict the mediator might find the disputant's feelings, they must allow the party the time to work through their emotional state.

ii. The mediator could also attempt to take a leadership position for an emotional communicator. A slightly stronger guiding hand, while remaining respectful, might assist the disputant to feel safer and eventually able to find confidence and strength on their own. A mediator should aim for a strategic balance between this stronger approach and ensuring that the party remains involved and engaged. Striking the right balance could accomplish shifting the disputant from emotion-led feelings and decisions to acting and making decisions thoughtfully, logically, and rationally.

9. **Passive**

a. Passive communicators do not express their needs or feelings, and often refrain from responding during hurtful situations. Instead, they might allow themselves to be taken advantage of or treated unfairly.

b. Without expression of feelings or responses from the passive communicator, misunderstanding and frustration on the part of an opposing party often ensue.

c. Traits of a Passive communicator:

i. Soft-spoken.

ii. Lack of or poor eye contact.

iii. Non-self-advocating.

iv. Allowing others to infringe on their rights.

v. Allowing others to take advantage.

d. *Mediator intervention*

i. In managing parties who are Passive communicators, the mediator should take extra care to ask them to respond directly to questions and statements in ways other than "I'm fine," "It's fine," "I don't care," or "Whatever they want." The mediator might choose to encourage disputants to express their feelings differently, as those replies might not be truthful or completely reflective of their interests and needs. This process might require moving the mediation into caucus with additional time spent on helping the disputants feel comfortable expressing themselves. Creative communication exercises should also be considered, such as role-playing the conversation with the mediator, whom the party might perceive as safer, or having the Passive communicator write a note with a more forthcoming and less passive reply to be delivered to an opposing party. Each of these options could help a mediation to reach a resolution that incorporates the Passive communicator's true interests rather than being determined by their passive style of permitting others' needs to be met in place of their own.

ii. The mediator could consider using a lead-by-example communication strategy to simultaneously demonstrate a leadership position of strength and guidance and to provide support and encouragement for the disputant who is a Passive communicator. It is possible that this disputant will begin to emulate the mediator's behavior and find their own voice to express their true interests and needs once they recognize that following the mediator's lead and communicating similarly could be beneficial. For the mediator, this is a strategy comparable to one that might be used when working with an Emotional communicator.

10. **Aggressive**

a. Aggressive communicators often behave in a manner that is not reflective of a desire to incorporate opposing positions or the feelings, interests, and needs of other parties into a solution-oriented conversation. They might violate the rights of others by being verbally abusive to further their own interests.

b. Traits of an Aggressive communicator:

i. Strong eye contact.

ii. Use of criticism, sarcasm, humiliation, and domination.

iii. Frequent interruptions and failure to listen to others.

iv. Easily frustrated by parties presenting positions different from their own.

v. Speaking in a loud, overbearing manner.

vi. Demanding.

c. *Mediator intervention*

i. An Aggressive communicator is easy to identify and hard to miss. It is common for this Communication Style to cause problems during mediation even if all parties communicate in this same manner – the only thing worse than being with one Aggressive communicator is being with two! In joint session, a mediator might find it difficult to manage parties who are communicating aggressively, as one of the characteristics of the style is to respond rapidly without filtering messages to ensure that they are productive. It could prove wise for a mediator to move these parties into caucus to continue the mediation. This will provide the mediator the opportunity to reframe messages between parties, excluding anything inflammatory, rude, detrimental, inappropriate, or unacceptable. It will also permit the mediator to speak to the parties individually, encouraging them to interact without their aggressive style. As the mediator is not personally involved in the conflict, it is possible that a disputant might be able to curtail their aggression when no other party is present. This could help the mediator reach information that is below their surface-level Communication Style and find options that had thus far been blocked by the aggressive exterior.

ii. The mediator's own behavior and Communication Style when interacting with an Aggressive communicator will depend on whether the mediator decides to mirror or balance that style. If the mediator chooses to mirror the disputant's style, the resulting aggressive attitude will not be directed at the disputant, but rather toward the conflict, with a fierce dedication to resolution and putting the conflict behind them. If the mediator balances the Aggressive style, they will behave with empathy, patience, and a continual focus on the conflict and solution options regardless of how the disputant acts and where they might attempt to drive the conversation. This does not mean that the mediator should ignore feelings expressed by the disputant, but rather that the mediator will acknowledge and reframe those feelings that have an aggressive bent and search for creative ways to incorporate the disputant's interests and needs into possible solution options. It can prove challenging for the mediator to remain poised when a disputant directs aggressive behavior toward them, but in those situations the mediator can remind the disputant that they should reciprocate the respect they are being shown and also that:

1. The mediator is not an adversary.
2. The mediator has not been in any manner a party to the conflict.
3. Their aggressive attitude might in fact be getting in the way of seeing all solution possibilities clearly and through a forward-looking lens.
4. Regardless of how aggressive and angry they are and regardless of how much they resent being in mediation, the singular purpose of the mediator is to assist in the process of finding a solution to the conflict that not only puts an end to it, but also results in an outcome that proves beneficial to them.
5. Their aggressive attitude might be getting in the way of seeing all solution possibilities clearly and through a forward-looking lens.

11. **Passive-aggressive**

   a. Passive-aggressive communicators might present as passive in their communicating style when, in actuality, they are likely building anger and internal resentment that will not remain repressed. The identification and management of the layered complications of one Communication Style hidden underneath another are integral to the multifaceted task of mediation. This will require the mediator to approach with a dual strategy of tending to a passive communicator and an aggressive communicator consecutively or even simultaneously. Passive-aggressive messages and actions have the ability to cut deeper and wider with longer lasting impact than most messages delivered in a direct or even traditionally indirect fashion. Still hidden resentment and its responses generally do not take forms customarily presented by aggressive outbursts, but will likely be indirect, buried within statements or questions that appear to be related to a completely different topic. The listener might not realize until an inopportune moment that this is not the case. For example, imagine what might happen if a mediation reaches all the way to settlement discussions only for one disputant to realize that what they interpreted as a compliment at an earlier point was actually meant as a condescending remark demeaning their intellect. Such a realization could not only immediately halt any additional discussions, but it could propel the entire mediation to impasse. This Communication Style is what is referred to as a *doozy*.

   b. Traits of a Passive-aggressive communicator:

      i. Pouting.

      ii. Muttering under the breath.

      iii. Using body language in inappropriate and purposefully rude ways.

      iv. Giving the silent treatment.

      v. Expecting others to know what they did wrong while being unwilling to provide an explanation.

      vi. Creating false rumors or details to make someone else look bad and themself look better, or even just "for the fun of it."

      vii. Presenting as cooperative and collaborative, when behind the scenes playing a much different game, which might include:

         1. Sabotage.

         2. Building a separate and increasingly damaging case.

         3. Pretending to negotiate in good faith, only to refuse settlement and cause a mediation to end in impasse—the true goal all along.

   c. *Mediator intervention*

      i. The mediator will need to pay very close attention to the manner in which disputants ask and answer questions, make statements, emote, and express body language, because identifying a passive-aggressive communicator is not always an easy task. The mediator will go from a micro to a macro approach by shifting from discussing conflict details and possible settlement options to comparisons between mediation and litigation, BATNA (Best Alternative to a Negotiated Agreement) and WATNA (Worst Alternative to a Negotiated Agreement), and potential creative mediated outcomes as differentiated from court rulings. The micro approach requires engaging with the Passive-aggressive Communication Style presented in response to any conflict discussion; however, the macro approach will focus on the general benefit of settling in mediation as the disputant's best interest, devoid of mention of either the conflict or the parties. By shifting to this macro approach dedicated to the benefits of the process, there is no need or opportunity for the disputant's Passive-aggressive Communication Style to be part of the equation. Focusing the attention on what could happen by not settling in mediation might encourage the disputant to begin interacting in a way that will allow them to reach their best interest – settling in mediation. A dose of reality has been known to go a long way in producing disputants whose intentions and actions shift to those of parties who wish for and intend to settle in mediation.

12. **Assertive**

  a. The Assertive Communication Style sits at the intersection between open, forthcoming communication and consideration of listening parties. An Assertive communicator represents themself, their needs, and their interests in a way that does not trample on or disrespect the needs and interests of anyone else. In fact, there is usually a conscious effort made to bring balance to a conversation where all voices are heard, addressed, and involved in the decision-making process.

  b. More often than not, an Assertive communicator understands the benefit of speaking from a place of "I," which removes blame from a statement or question by controlling the focus of the message and keeping it squarely representative of the speaker: "I feel upset" as opposed to "You upset me," for example. The Assertive style aims to express and incorporate rather than blame and divide.

  c. Traits of an Assertive communicator:

    i. Listening without interrupting.
    ii. Clearly stating interests and needs.
    iii. Incorporating interests and needs of others.
    iv. Standing up for personal rights.
    v. Maintaining good eye contact.
    vi. Using "I" descriptive statements instead of "you" blaming statements.

d. *Mediator intervention*

i. Assertive communicators tend to be expressive communicators as well, so the mediator should take advantage of a disputant who is capable of and willing to be this communicative to learn as many facts, interests, needs, and intentions as possible. This gathered wealth of information will then be at the mediator's disposal for potential use during the mediation. The Assertive Communication Style can produce conversations that feel comfortable and familiar almost immediately, making it easier to build rapport. The mediator should lean into this characteristic and use it as a foundation to develop a trusting relationship. This can lead to a disputant's willingness to be open to new and creative settlement ideas at the suggestion or encouragement of the mediator.

ii. Short of thanking a disputant for communicating in this manner (I jest, but only partially), a mediator might choose to encourage a disputant who is not communicating in this manner in response to one who is to recognize the differences and benefits of the Assertive style. The mediator could consider providing a few sentences as examples for a disputant to see the style differences, and to highlight the immense benefit of a Communication Style that is:

1. Self-advocating.

2. Respectful.

3. Inclusive.

4. Encouraging to all parties to present their positions and interests.

13. **Adult Attachment**

a. Adult Attachment styles are pivotal in shaping the development of relationships and directly affect the way adults interact. These styles do not necessarily present on their own, but are foundational building blocks and often a driving force by which a Communication Style is developed and expressed. Awareness of Attachment styles provides deeper understanding of why disputants behave the way they do, with insight into intentions, feelings, behaviors, and interplay with conflict in general. They are the internal mechanisms that fire immediately when conflict arises, the external manifestation of which is expressed through a Communication Style. In conflict situations, they can become intensified and add additional layers to that style.

i. Insecure Attachment

1. Includes Anxious and Avoidant Styles

a) Anxious

i. Feelings driven.

ii. Emotions used as weapons, often with embellished positions of victimization.

iii. Focus on the worst possible outcome and real or imagined position as victim.

iv. Difficulty seeing beyond their stated position in the conflict to begin forward-thinking conversations that include solution options.

v. Misinterpretation of situations due to the effects of personal triggers that shape their understanding of present circumstances.

vi. Frequent overreactions resulting from triggers.

b) Avoidant

i. Fact and logic driven.

ii. Preference to create distance from a conflict and those involved.

iii. Preference to avoid engagement in collaborative resolution conversation that attempts to address all interests and needs.

iv. Association of emotion with weakness, their own as well as those of an opposing disputant, leading to a refusal to acknowledge any emotion or emotional distress. This could intensify feelings of anger from an opposing party who might rightfully interpret such behavior as dismissive of their interests, needs, and experiences within the conflict.

v. More likely that difficult or painful memories and triggers remain in the past and do not become involved in current situations by coloring them in ways that might be incorrect.

2. Quick to anger.

3. Manipulative to reach their desired goals.

4. Might engage in hostile and inappropriate behavior to get attention.

5. Difficulty communicating effectively and appropriately in general, and expressing their needs and interests specifically.

6. Can shut down when faced with a difficult situation, question, statement, or feeling.

7. More likely to refuse the concept of being on the same side with an opposing party and working together against the conflict. They might instead prefer to remain separate, apart, and against an opposing party.

8. Less inclined toward mutually beneficial solution suggestions as possible settlement options, preferring to win.

ii. Secure Attachment

1. More likely to engage respectfully in conflict situations.

2. Tend to be more trusting and interested in having a functional relationship.
3. More likely to prefer cooperative, collaborative, and mutually agreeable conflict intervention approaches and solutions.
4. Capable of taking responsibility for a wrongdoing and apologizing when necessary and appropriate.
5. More likely to communicate with ease and effectiveness.
6. More likely to embrace the concept of being on the same side with an opposing party and working together against the conflict.

b. *Mediator intervention*

i. Fifty percent of people interact with a Secure attachment style and 50 percent of people interact with an Insecure style,[1] creating a strong possibility that both styles will present during a mediation. Accordingly, a mediator will benefit from understanding those styles, how to manage the differences, and how to recognize their impact on disputants during conflict intervention. The mediator should work with a targeted strategic approach by identifying a problematic attachment style and addressing it. For example, if a disputant is quick to anger, manipulative in reaching their goals, or exhibits hostile or inappropriate behavior, the mediator should move the parties into caucus. Once there, the behavior will either cease as a result of caucus separating the disputants from one another or it will persist, regardless of the separation, in which case the mediator will need to address the problematic behavior. Another reason to caucus might be to privately help a disputant to realize that they are being triggered by past experiences rather than appropriately interpreting present circumstances. This could be a brief caucus if the misinterpretation is resolved. When, for example, a disputant is less inclined toward mutually agreeable solution suggestions as possible settlement options, a mediator could reframe the options exclusively in terms of their benefit for that disputant, thereby shifting the focus away from their jointly beneficial nature.

14. **Stress Responses**

a. Stress responses are the emergency systems the body instinctively employs when it senses danger and shifts into protection and preservation mode. These responses, known as *fight or flight responses,* can become activated unintentionally by the body's release of hormones that take over physical and mental faculties to dictate behavior. Feelings of loss of control that are often caused by conflict situations can trigger stress responses and induce panic. It can be difficult for a disputant to manage this physical

1. Kirk, Isabel B., "Conflict styles," in *The SAGE Encyclopedia of Marriage, Family, and Couples Counseling* (2017), at 2.

reaction, creating an impediment for a mediator to continue with the process in that moment. Stress responses generally require a full stop to a mediation and a pivot to allow attention and care to be focused directly on the response to mitigate, move through, and move beyond. The autonomic defense reactions are:

i. Fight: Remain and deal with a threat.
ii. Flight: Flee to safety.
iii. Freeze: Reactive/attentive immobility.

These responses may present themselves unexpectedly within any Communication Style. Consider a disputant who suddenly becomes overwhelmed by a particular topic of conversation, promptly shuts down, and proceeds to avoid discussing it any further. That would be a freeze response. Would it be surprising to find out that this disputant engages with a Direct Communication Style and a Secure Attachment Style?

b. *Mediator intervention*

i. Neglecting to address stress responses might exacerbate a disputant's current state. Rather than attempting to press onward with mediation discussions, once the mediator recognizes such a response, they might have no choice but to shift the focus and interrupt the proceedings at this point. If a disputant's flight response was engaged in reaction to a statement made by an opposing party, causing them to flee the room in tears, for example, then this behavior will need to be addressed for the mediation to proceed. Managing stress responses is dependent on what disputants present, but a mediator might be able to determine a connection to specific content or a delivery system that could be causing the response. A mediator's approach cannot be one size fits all, but included in their strategy should always be:

   1. To devote attention directly to the response.
   2. To create a calm space for the triggered disputant, possibly in private away from any other parties. This calm space should include reassurance that they are in a judgment-free environment. If the disputant expresses embarrassment or regret over their stress response, the mediator should confirm that the only issue to be concerned with is working through that response without being distracted by any additional feelings.
   3. To target what caused the response.
   4. To identify their needs and to help them move forward with the mediation.

ii. If the mediation is amicable or one with developed empathy, the disputant(s) and the mediator could work together to intervene before there are additional occurrences. Otherwise, the mediator could decide to caucus to prevent further stress responses that might have been triggered by an opposing party by reframing or removing inflammatory statements.

1. A benefit of an amicable mediation in such circumstances is the teamwork and deepened empathy developed by an opposing party willing to participate in helping the disputant exhibiting the stress response work through it. That would go a long way toward the mediator's ability to bring the parties together, instead of remaining pitted against each other, and to work jointly against the conflict in the direction of mutually agreeable and creative settlement options.

iii. The mediator might find it necessary and beneficial to create conversations and new perspectives that enable this disputant to view their position differently without feeling any loss of control. The mediator might then be able to shift the disputant's current position and focus to an action- and solution-oriented position by using:

1. Reframing.
2. Creative viewpoints.
3. Leadership.
4. Support.
5. Encouragement.
6. A more structured approach with questions that are specific and closed-ended.
7. Detailed solution suggestions to replace vague and loose concepts.

MEDIATOR'S INTERNAL QUESTIONS TO HELP IDENTIFY A DISPUTANT'S COMMUNICATION STYLE

1. Based on what I have witnessed thus far, including statements, questions, responses, and body language, what might be the most successful manner by which this disputant receives information – their Communication Style?
2. What is the best way I can convey information that aligns with their Communication Style?
3. Which forms of communication does this disputant best respond to?
   a. Details.
   b. Broad concepts.
   c. Information that has been reframed to allow little to no room for misinterpretation.
4. Which forms of communication does this disputant respond least favorably to, possibly leading to additional conflicts? The answer to this question does not imply that a mediator will exclude information that falls into this category, as that is not a luxury always available during mediation. However, knowing the answer to this question will allow the mediator to use certain

forms of communication with topics presented differently to offset negative responses and misinterpretations that could follow.

MANAGING COMMUNICATION STYLES

It would be foolish to believe that all parties in a mediation interact with the same Communication Style. If they happen to, count your mediator blessings! It is far more likely, though, that the mediator will be managing different Communication Styles, which could become problematic. When disputants have difficulty recognizing other styles as equally valid as their own, and are locked in the mindset of doing things their way only, they could be creating more conflict. If the mediation is between strangers who will never see or interact with each other after the final resolution to the conflict, addressing their Communication Styles might only be necessary up to the point that, or only so deep as, the mediator can find clarity on the facts of the case and move into solution options. If the mediation is Transformative, working with disputants who are in a preexisting and ongoing relationship, then taking the time to dig into their Communication Styles will be crucial for the disputants, the mediator, the mediation, the ability for settlement to last, and their relationship moving forward. Assisting disputants to comprehensively understand their own and each other's Communication Styles can provide much needed clarity and meaning behind actions and statements. Addressing the possible impacts of those styles will enable an atmosphere of deeper and more accurate understanding, empathy, and collaborative problem-solving. Recognizing that people interact with conflict in divergent ways will create opportunity for various Communication Styles to be validated and work together during the dispute resolution process. Failure to acknowledge, accommodate, and accept different Communication Styles can be a deadbolt in the door labeled impasse. One possible solution is to discuss Communication Style differences as a conversation rather than an argument and as an issue relating strictly and only to Communication Styles, not to the disputants. Remove assumptions, blame, anger, and frustration by identifying the different styles, looking at potential origins of those styles, and then reframing to a mutually agreeable language and ideas. Some disputants need time to process information, whereas others are quick on the draw. This can be addressed by caucusing to keep the quick-drawing disputant occupied while an opposing party has time to process and collect their thoughts. The mediator should emphasize that the need for processing time is genuine and for the purpose of fully thinking about and considering the information the disputant is receiving rather than as a tactic of any sort. This is a good thing, and any other party should view it as such. If the mediation is Transformative, it could prove important to bring the parties together in joint session to address their Communication Styles together and allow the parties to express respect and support for each other. This will help build a foundation for conflict management success in the future.

One important takeaway from a discussion about various Communication Styles is that they can be altered and shifted. They are learned behaviors that can be unlearned and relearned. Disputants should be reminded that it is not out of the ordinary to make mistakes as they work toward adopting new Communication Styles and that they will have the help and support of the mediator as they attempt to communicate differently and more effectively. The mediator will be present to help them get back on track and to provide suggestions for how better to approach each other, as well as consistent reminders that accidental missteps and messages packaged incorrectly are not immediate grounds for attack and blame. There is a benefit to taking a beat and allowing time to self-correct, apologize, provide clarity, explain true intention(s), and then reset and try again. That is where teamwork lies, growth is developed, and change can occur. That change, of course, can produce potential creative and mutually agreeable settlement options that previously did not exist.

A MEDIATION ACTIVITY

Mediation Switcheroo

By allowing participants to "try on" different Communication Styles, this activity creates empathy and an increased understanding of each disputant's Communication Style and corresponding needs. It will provide the opportunity to experience moving in and out of and expanding comfort zones, and to interpret and interact with information from different perspectives. Walking a mile in each other's shoes might help disputants approach conflict differently as they engage with a Communication Style environment new to them and arrive at brand new, creative settlement options.

1. Consider an activity during a mediation where the disputants "try on" each other's Communication Styles. Before that, though, try it out during a Mediation Exercise.
    a. If disputants are unsure of their preferred method of communication, the mediator could engage in a dialogue encouraging them to identify their communication comfort zones—the manner of interaction they are most comfortable with—and how best they interpret, interact with, and respond to that information. For example, the mediator might suggest that disputants compare the way they feel about receiving information in a direct manner, in a more subtle indirect fashion, in caucus, or in joint session.
    b. If the parties remain unsure after a discussion, and the mediator is also unsure, the parties can engage in this exercise to try various other styles on for size. A preferred method will emerge and present itself naturally through trial and error.
2. This exercise contains two different mediator options:
    a. Disputants exchanging Communication Styles, resulting in the continued presence of more than one style, but now switched and used by opposite parties. For example, Disputant A is engaging with an Aggressive style and Disputant B is engaging with an Assertive style. Once the switch occurs, Disputant A will engage with an Assertive style, and Disputant B will engage with an Aggressive style.

b. Collectively using one Communication Style and then shifting to another.
    i. Disputant will describe how they feel and need to approach the conflict (their preferred Communication Style), and then all parties will proceed with engaging in the mediation using that style.
    ii. After each disputant has described their approach, and time has been devoted by all parties to engaging in the conflict in that manner, the disputants will then collectively shift to the approach that is preferred by an opposing disputant and devote the same amount of time to this different Communication Style.

3. In a Transformative mediation, the outcome of this activity might be something that is eventually worked into a settlement agreement to govern future interactions with each other. For example, if Disputant B has a difficult time interacting with Disputant A when they communicate with an Aggressive style, then in future interactions Disputant A will be mindful of that and work to engage in a manner that is less confrontational.

TRIGGERS

There are certain actions, words, or statements that evoke a response to a current situation, a remembered experience, or both. Memories of previous experiences elicited by interpreted similarities with a current event could cause immediate responses that are external manifestations of internal associations. Whereas some responses are warranted based on current circumstances, others might not be if they are responses driven only by a memory. Learning enough about a disputant to identify and avoid realized and potential triggers will prove useful in enabling the mediator to subsequently craft appropriate reframes removing those triggers, and in conjunction with a possible move into caucus, to help the mediation progress.

DEFUSERS: Reframing Triggering Accusatory Statements into Statements of "I"

Accusatory Language	Assertive Language
You're making me angry.	I feel really upset and hurt.
You don't care about me.	I feel lonely and disconnected from you.
You are mean.	I want to be treated with kindness.
You are loud and annoying.	I have a hard time focusing when there is distraction from loud noises.
Stop bossing me around.	I can make my own decision about this.

FLASH CHALLENGE

Triggers to Reframe

1. Reframe the common trigger words listed below. Feel free to use as many descriptive words as you would like in your reframes.

Common Trigger Words

- Argumentative
- Attention-hungry
- Bossy
- Demanding
- Dramatic
- Fussy
- Inflexible
- Stubborn
- Tattletale

2. How would you help shift the interpretation of behavior defined by a trigger word? For example, Disputant A has verbally labeled Disputant B's behavior as defiant. It is clear that Disputant B has been triggered by the use of this word, which will likely result in an additional negative interaction between them. Prior to discussing the triggering incident with Disputant B, a mediator might take the opportunity to engage with Disputant A about exactly which behaviors they are categorizing as defiant, and whether or not those behaviors could, in fact, be the result of completely different intentions. What if being defiant is actually being determined to be heard, confident in a particular position based exclusively on the facts of the case, and reflective of a tone that is an expectation based on a cultural norm different than one's own?
3. How would you help a disputant understand and accept the negative ramifications of defining a particular behavior using trigger words and the resultant improvement by creating and using a reframed version?

TRIGGERS AND CONTEXT

The understanding of fundamental differences derived from diverse cultural norms, socioeconomics, educational backgrounds, familial intergenerational communication constructs, and lifestyles, among other factors, need to be recognized and incorporated to expand the concept of triggers. Each one of these communication influencers independently or collectively could shape the entirety of an understanding behind or connected to words or action. For example, two strangers meet at a party where one asks the other, "What do you do for a living?" Here is the problem: Partygoer A (the question asker) inquired with the intentions of being friendly, meeting a potential new friend, opening a conversation with a new person, showing interest as a desirable quality within a friendship, and behaving in what they have learned to be a socially acceptable manner. However, Partygoer B (the question receiver) did not interpret the question in any of those ways. To them it was intrusive, rude, an opportunity people take to have the question asked back to them so they can brag about what they do for a living, and overstepping boundaries. What Partygoer A did not know prior to asking Partygoer B this question is that in Partygoer B's family, financial matters are extremely personal and not to be discussed, especially with strangers. To Partygoer B, asking such questions is an act of interrogation, hostility, and intrusion. This is never a topic to be asked about when intentions are friendly, as it is also perceived to be a bar by which to measure a person's worth. Conversely, what Partygoer B did not know is that Partygoer A would never even have imagined that the question could be interpreted in any of these ways that engender negative feelings or provoke anything other than a simple answer. Within the context of mediation, it should be clear why this could become problematic, as it stretches beyond simple misinterpretations or miscued replies to the very fabric and foundation of identity. A person's relationship to language and communication is part and parcel of how their interactions and connections are formed and responses are understood by others.

During the mediation process, wherein active disputant participation is a requirement, if the mediator discerns that certain responses are possibly misplaced or misinformed and could interfere with a productive mediation, then the mediator should take steps to mitigate. Three separate actions should follow, likely in caucus.

1. The mediator will assist the listener to identify what caused the triggered response, exactly how they are interpreting the speaker's message, and if their understanding might not be entirely accurate by virtue of a trigger or personalized lens.
2. The mediator will assist the speaker to ensure that their delivery properly reflected their intent by encouraging the speaker to further explain their message.
3. With the gathered information, the mediator will guide the speaker to express their message more clearly and accurately. The mediator will also guide the listener to be aware of their lens and to be receptive to an understanding that triggers and trigger similarities do not necessarily reflect the true light of the intention. Taking a beat will prove its value in this moment (see Chapter 6, "Listening").

FLASH CHALLENGE

What's Your Trigger?

1. Find three people and ask them what their verbal triggers are. Ask them to think about conflict situations they have been in and to recount specific words and/or statements that caused them to become immediately more upset and that elicited strong reactions from them.
2. Make a list of their trigger words.
3. Now make a second list of their trigger words that you have reframed into statements.
4. Deliver those reframed trigger statements to your partner and ask if they feel the same reaction to them or if the reframe has shifted their previous reaction enough so that they would have been able to continue communicating effectively, remaining in control of their emotions.

FLASH CHALLENGE

Communication Dissected: A Conversation Between Family Members

Read the dialogue below and answer the questions that follow.

A Conversation About Communication Between Family Members A and B

A: I've realized, at 51, that I think I'm ready to turn over a new leaf as far as some of my communication skills are concerned. I think I get so excited about what I want that maybe my conversations probably come off as aggressive, and I need to be more willing to hear what everybody else has to say.

B: That's hard because there are a lot of opinions. I think it is in our culture for women. They think they have to fight for their position. After our conversations I go home with a stomachache almost every single time. Certain situations lately are really magnifying our communication breakdown issues. There are a lot of times that it feels unsafe to discuss things in this family. We are just not really talking to each other, we are talking at each other.

A: I think sometimes you are just quiet, and I am more forceful. It is all exuberance, but I know it can seem like I am forcing.

B: I am a little more quiet. I have a tendency to be cautious.

A: I would like it if you would say more.

B: More than likely when I have an issue with someone, it is rare that I fight with them. In my marriage of ten years, I can recall maybe five real fights we have had. Maybe not even that. I was married before, and in that marriage there was a lot of fighting and a lot of pain. I promised that as I came out of my divorce that if I ever married again I would be more cautious and more careful by not mentioning everything that upset me so that fights could be avoided.

A: I think we need to figure out how to have these conversations. Not the actual conversation, but how to have a conversation.

B: You are talking about changing the way we communicate. I would love to change it dramatically. I am relieved that you are saying that maybe what we are doing isn't working, and that you are asking if we can figure out a better way. Yes. I one hundred percent feel the same way.

A: The next time we all get together we need to have a real discussion about some ground rules for our conversations.

B: Yes.

A: Okay, I feel really good. Even though we approach things differently and with different perspectives, the one core thing that we do agree on is that we want the family to stay together. I think the whole idea that we are a unit and we continue to make these decisions together is what defines our family structure.

A Conversation About Communication Between Same Family Member A and Family Member C

C: I do not like conversations that are heavy, but when you are with other adults together in a family, you have to have serious conversations.

A: This is really awkward because I can't figure out the best way sometimes, so I'm just going to jump in. It is about Communication Styles, and I've realized that I think there is something that I want to change about my Communication Style, and I think it's when I tend to get so excited about what I want that I can't hear anything else.

C: You are very stubborn, like you have blinders on, and can see only what you're aiming for and that's what you're going for, whatever it is.

A: I think I am going to try to change that because we do have some big things that we need to communicate about as a family in the next several months and I want to make sure that we are good because in certain conversations you and I have definitely gotten very loud on opposite ends.

C: Yes. You have been way in favor of certain things on one end of the spectrum while I was at the complete opposite end of the spectrum saying no, absolutely not.

A: I really have no hard feelings about anything, and I just want to make sure that we clear the air.

C: I'm good with you now, but there are a few reasons from the past that cause me to have certain feelings now. One of those reasons is that I felt like what everybody else wanted to do was more important than what I wanted to do. When I look back, I wish I would have taken better care of myself and my kids within our family. I wish I would have had the courage to stand up for myself more, but I got overwhelmed. I know myself and I know that if I were back in that living situation again it would be the same thing. That's why I can't allow it and I am so against it even though you're in favor of it.

A: That's fair. I can see that. I think this is a long-standing, deep hurt for you, and I think it could have been handled so much better if we would have been communicating, really listening, and really saying what we needed to say.

C: Now sometimes it just feels awkward when we are all together.

A: Yes. I wonder why it feels awkward.

C: I'm always a little nervous, sometimes to the point of being nauseous. It's hard to get together and to feel like I still matter and that I am still important, because I think when it comes down to it, I don't matter that much, not really. So, it's hard to come into a place where I think I'm going to have equal say because I won't. I won't have an equal voice.

A: Do you think that the communication methods or styles could help you feel like you were more heard?

C: I think so. I don't feel like we're at the point where we can be completely honest.

A: Why not? Why not make it that way? I just think it's time to talk about some of that stuff. Are you thinking I'm nuts?

C: I don't think you're nuts, but I think it's unrealistic. There's a fine line between being honest and being safe, and it can be crossed easily.

A: Bring the fallout. Bring it, because we are never going to make progress until we get through the mess.

C: I'm willing to give it a try, just so you know.

A: Okay, but you're not hopeful?

C: Well, I hate to say it, but no, not really.

A: Part of me says it is easier to just go on like this, separated from each other, to focus on whatever else we are doing individually, and I acknowledge that, but the other part of me is saying no. This is no way to live with your family. This is not what we signed up for.

C: No, this is not what any of us signed up for, so I don't want to continue with what we have now.

A: I don't think it's sustainable.

C: Well, it's stupid. It's separate and it's not what we signed up for.

A: I really and truly believe at my core that if we can't figure this out, nobody is going to want to stick together if we are not communicating effectively. Who wants to stick around? That's way too much work and it's not very much fun. So, I think it is the key to our ultimate, long-term survival as a family unit.

C: I think we are at a crossroads. I think you are one hundred percent right. We are at a crossroads.

A: I'm in a place where I want something different, and what we have been doing hasn't been working, so I'd like to try something different, and I guess the communication is the biggest piece of it.

C: I think so, too.

A: I really and truly believe that if we don't start taking care of our family as a unit now, it's not going to exist for much longer.

1. If you were mediating these conversations, would you use the Evaluative, Transformative, or Facilitative Mediation Style(s)? (See Chapter 2, "Mediation Styles.")

2. These are the Communication Styles present during the conversations:
    a. Direct
    b. Indirect
    c. Emotional
    d. Passive
    e. Aggressive
    f. Passive-aggressive
    g. Newly Assertive (shifting away from communicating with an Aggressive style)
    h. Insecure Adult Attachment issues
    i. Stress Responses
        i. Assign all of the items from the above list to the family members.
        ii. How were you able to make the connections between the items on the list and the family members?
        iii. Provide the specific parts of the dialogue that were indicators to you.
3. Do you believe any of their Communication Styles need to be shifted to accomplish more effective communication and problem-solving?
4. Which Communication Style(s) would you adopt to interact effectively with the parties? Discuss.
    a. Would you switch styles as you converse with the different parties?
5. Which mediation skills might you use to assist in this conversation?
6. Based on the conversations, do you think the family members share the same goals?
7. What are some questions you might ask them?
    a. List your questions in direct response to their statements.
    b. List additional questions that are not necessarily in direct response to their statements, but that might provide answers you feel would be beneficial.
8. If you were mediating this conversation, would you recommend joint session, caucus, or a combination of both? Discuss.
    a. Do you think either joint session or caucus would benefit both parties equally, or one over another? Discuss.
    b. What is the general nature of their attitudes toward each other? Discuss.
    c. Do you think those attitudes may be different below the surface? Discuss.
9. Would you reframe any of their statements?
10. What are some creative communication approaches you might suggest to them?
    a. Role-playing each other's Communication Styles with one another?
    b. Role-playing each other's Communication Styles with the mediator?
    c. Discussing triggers and potential reframes?
    d. Discussing Stress Responses: what leads to them and how it feels while it is happening?
    e. Listening and then repeating back what they believe they heard.

chapter 4

Conflict Handling Modes

Situational Flexibility and Fluidity

Understanding Conflict Handling Modes (CHMs) is instrumental to a mediator's method of conducting a mediation. The way disputants behave during conflict is shaped by their CHM, the manner of their interaction with conflict, each other, new information within the context of the dispute, and willingness to find and entertain reasonable and fair settlement options or other means to achieve mediation goals. Disputants' Communication Styles are a direct result of their CHM, and mediators could be put at a substantial disadvantage by not knowing which style to use, how and when to use it, and which would be the most effective as they attempt to interact appropriately with each CHM. If Disputant A is speaking Greek and Disputant B is communicating through interpretive dance, the mediator had best be prepared to speak Greek to Disputant A and communicate through interpretive dance with Disputant B. Chess master Bobby Fischer said, "I don't believe in psychology. I believe in good moves," but we are going to alter his statement slightly to read, "I don't believe in psychology only. I believe in good moves always." In other words, why waste time and energy in excluding every part of something, in this case psychology, when one could stand to benefit in some way from some part of something? That's a good move. Having at least a baseline understanding of, for example, triggers, hidden meanings, motivations, conflict behaviors, and helpful versus harmful questions and responses will only improve a mediator's ability to resolve conflict effectively and successfully. Good moves are the policy. Learn them in and out, top to bottom, through and through, upside down, right side up, and all across the board.

Mediators should identify CHMs to facilitate communication when disputants are incapable of communicating directly with each other. As outlined by Kenneth W. Thomas and Ralph H. Kilmann in the Thomas-Kilmann Conflict Mode Instrument (TKI), there are five CHMs – Competing, Compromising, Collaborating, Avoiding, and Accommodating[1] – on two axes measuring assertiveness and cooperativeness. Assertiveness is defined as the extent to which the individual attempts to satisfy his or her own concerns, and cooperativeness is defined as the extent to

1. Thomas, Kenneth W., and Ralph H. Kilmann, "Thomas-Kilmann Conflict Mode Instrument Profile and Interpretive Report" (2001).

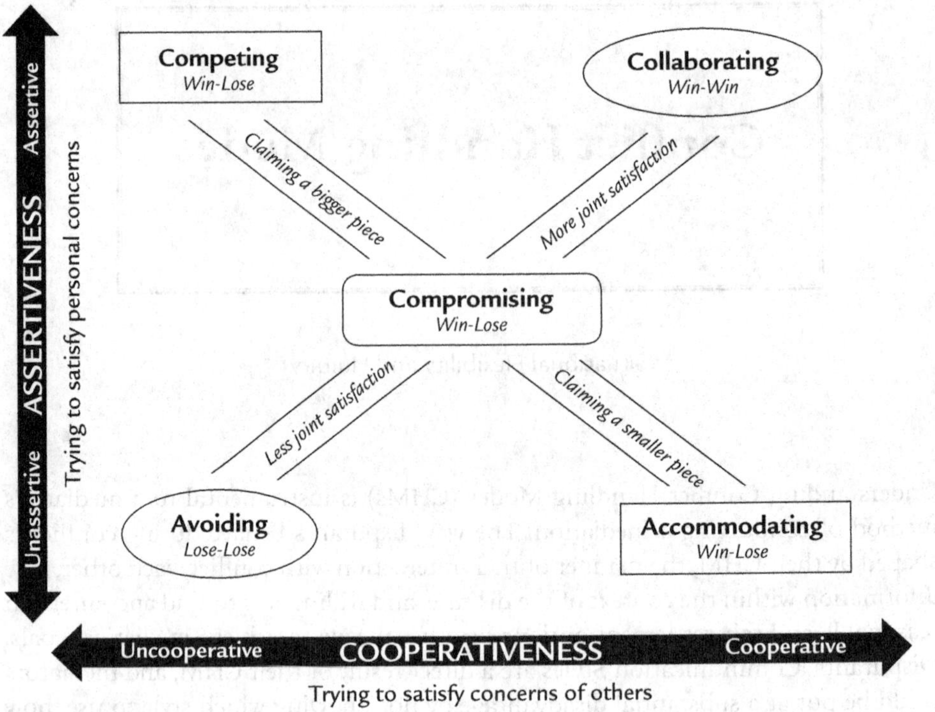

Figure 4-1

Source: Thomas, Kenneth W., *Introduction to Conflict Management Improving Performance Using the TKI* (2002), 4-5, 8-10.

which the individual attempts to satisfy the other person's concerns. These two axes are used to express the five CHMs, as each method of dealing with conflict varies in those two substantial ways. The more assertive someone is, the less interested they are in anyone else's interests. Conversely, the more cooperative someone is, the more concerned they are with the interests of others. One main purpose of the TKI is to identify choices disputants make during conflict intervention so that mediators can deepen their understanding and develop tools to better manage the conflict, with the ultimate goal of directing it onto a more constructive, solution-oriented path. What follows is a discussion of the five CHMs, including a cost-benefit analysis presented in the style of Thomas's notations on the impacts of the various modes.

COMPETING

***Competing** is assertive and uncooperative, a power-oriented mode. When competing, individuals pursue their own concerns at another's expense, using whatever power seems appropriate to win their position. Competing might mean standing up for your own rights, defending a position you believe is correct, or simply trying to win.*[2]

2. Id.

Also identified as Confronting and Dominating, Competing is the most assertive and least cooperative of all the CHMs, with a win at all cost and above all else mentality—pointedly uncooperative. Those who express the Competing mode see only the polarities of right and wrong, good and bad, and winner and loser. They believe that they are wholly justified in their stance, as evidenced by aggressive and unwavering defense of their position, welcoming in those who agree with and support them, and displaying antagonism toward those they perceive to be in opposition. This stance will be personally interpreted as utterly logical, and as logic is the determining factor between right and wrong, so, too, are their positions and their input logical and therefore correct. It should come as no surprise that managing any one of these behaviors on its own can be daunting, let alone their combination, linked together in an order that is in such stark contradiction to the collaborative nature of mediation. In the United States particularly, there is a proclivity toward competing demonstrated, for example, by the overwhelmingly high volume of commission-based companies whose employees have no option but to compete against each other for job security and to achieve success. Also consider the intense focus on children's activities and sports, the vast majority of which are competitive and proclaim winners and losers. Look at the enormous salary paid to professional athletes, which becomes their reward for successfully competing and securing one of a limited number of positions on teams. These inflated paychecks are the direct result of the adoration of fans, that of a reverence often akin to religious fervor. Competition has been rewarded on an epic scale. Further, there are hundreds of competition-based television programs showcasing contestants fighting week after week to be seen as the best, to be called the best, and to win large sums of money. It is strikingly clear that competing to win has become equated with success and self-worth. Baking shows are the latest example of this trend, and when baking becomes a competitive sport, it might be time to take a step back and reevaluate the moral fabric of a society! Being competitive in daily life is a knee-jerk reaction for many people, especially in conflict situations. In this collectively accepted two-sided world, that of winner and loser, those are often the only perceived options when one individual interacts with another. With cooperation as a third option having been disregarded, it is no wonder that so many conflicts become unnecessarily contentious and competitive. The deeply ingrained idea of only two possible outcomes to any scenario is a fundamental hurdle to the mediation process. The concept of a loser and by extrapolation that there will be a winner must be eradicated from the explanation, understanding, and application of the cooperative and collaborative mediation process.

Benefits of the Competing Mode

1. **Leadership**
   a. When strong leadership is necessary either in defense of oneself or on behalf of others (e.g., a whistleblower), a leader has the strength and resolve to step up, guiding the way when no one else is doing so.

2. **Action**
   a. When a quick decision is necessary, the determination associated with a Competing mode enables the ability to take swift action.
3. **Iron fist**
   a. When a specific outcome is critical, compromise is unacceptable and therefore not an option.
   b. Confidence in fighting for what is right, including in an emergency, where safety is a concern, when an unpopular decision is necessary, and when unpopular action must be taken is manifest.
4. **Self-defense**
   a. Willingness to stand up for and protect personal welfare, interests, positions, standpoints, and undeterred by potential challenges or attacks.
5. **No fear**
   a. Willingness, without fear of repercussion, to debate and test one's own, as well as others', assumptions and viewpoints.

An important component of the Competitive mode is that when attempting to apply it in a productive way, disputants should focus on being persuasive by using merits and facts, rather than defending their position with all of their might and pointed vocabulary simply for personal or professional gain. Guiding disputants to believe in and commit to applying this mode beneficially with thoughtful arguments, factual information, clear explanations, shared concerns, and collaborative solution ideas and options is by all accounts an excellent use of the Competing mode. Additionally, receiving the support of those who become swayed to one side over another for the aforementioned reasons rather than from the use of fear or force, results in a deeper level of commitment and dedication to a settlement. Even within the Competing mode, the ties of such a collaborative resolution are unbound with far less ease than those of a resolution that is reached by any other means.

Costs of the Competing Mode

1. **Tense relationships**
   a. One party to the conflict may feel resentful or exploited, possibly leading to retaliation. Even the hint of a competing CHM can instantly put an opposing party on the defensive and shift the entire mood of a mediation.
2. **Intimidation**
   a. Compelled agreement to resolution can lead to lack of important and effective communication and exchange of ideas, causing creative problem-solving, cooperative discussion of ideas, and possible win-win solutions to be overlooked.
3. **Egocentricity**
   a. The drive for power, being right, and winning are paramount at the expense of everything else, with an inability to see when collaborating and shifting stances would be beneficial.

4. **Persuasive influence**
   a. Compulsory or forced decisions result in reduced commitment and support from those who are affected, and alienation of possibly necessary individuals.
5. **Fight club**
   a. Resorting to extreme and excessive methods to reach a desired outcome, potentially resulting in impasse.
6. **Language**
   a. Toxic, disrespectful, demeaning, judgmental, impatient language, and cursing are tools often used when the Competing mode is wielded as a weapon.

The Competing mode is often manifested through negative techniques, the identification and understanding of which benefit disputants and mediators alike as they navigate a mediation involving at least one competitive disputant. There could be varying degrees of dishonesty, especially when expressing interests and goals or even true positions in a disputant's strategic effort to place themself more advantageously within the conflict conversation. In their efforts to undercut and dismantle an opposing party's position, competing disputants might use criticizing and strategically questioning language in their attempts. Additionally, to enforce the greater value of their own position and to create an illusion of validity, competing disputants might employ denials of their own responsibility, accusations, blame, and verbal attacks. Combating and tamping down the use and impact of the negative aspects of the Competing mode are integral to reaching a mutually agreeable resolution.

Mediator Intervention

1. Mediators must endeavor to remember that disputants present at the mediation table frequently exhibit CHMs from one end of the spectrum to the other, often shifting at a moment's notice or manifesting multiple modes at once.
2. Most collaboration directly contradicts the tenets of competition, so begin early to change disputants' mindsets to offset any predisposition toward a Competing mode that might be lurking ruthlessly and mercilessly behind Door Number One.
3. There is no room for competition at the mediation table – no winners and no losers in a collaborative process – and only a collective loss when a mediation cannot be saved from impasse. More often than not, impasse occurs because one or all of the disputants are displaying a Competitive CHM and approaching the mediation with the expectation of a "winner's circle" outcome that offers exclusively everything they want and nothing that the opposing party needs. In mediation, winning is accomplished only when all parties can be active, dignified, and respected participants in the process and collaboration is used to reach the collectively agreed-upon outcome.

a. *Collaboration* in this context refers both to shifting from an assertive to a cooperative CHM, as well as a mediator's ability to manage a disputant's existing assertive CHM in a way that produces a mutually agreed-upon, collaborative mediated solution. To do so, a mediator could switch from joint session into caucus to encourage that disputant who is negotiating competitively and demonstrating no intention to shift or incorporate aspects of cooperative CHMs into their behavior to minimize their overtly assertive mode. Once in caucus, the mediator can reframe inappropriate and inflammatory statements from the competitive disputant before they reach an opposing party. The mediator might choose to interact by mirroring with an equally Competitive mode, and perhaps using an Evaluative mediation style only when interacting with the competitive disputant. Interacting with an equally opposite CHM is an option as well. Even if the disputant does not shift out of Competitive mode, by virtue of the separation afforded by caucus, the mediator has gained the ability to mitigate potentially detrimental ramifications that come along with that particular mode by shifting and reframing messages before relaying any information to another party. The process of finding a collaborative, mediated solution could also benefit from the use of guided questions in the attempt to access interests, needs, and unresolved emotional trauma possibly concealed during joint session by the assertive CHM.

4. The mediator can convince parties that winning is achieved by working on the same side together, moving past the conflict and putting it behind them without the additional time, energy, and money required by litigation.
5. A potential pitfall of competing that should be avoided in the quest to use it as a tool for good is the failure to eschew using blatantly unfair tactics. Even when it becomes possible to win by might through an unmitigated upper hand (verbal tap dancers and fancy movers, we are speaking to you), the mediator should encourage the disputant not to succumb to the temptation. Lying about or exaggerating a position just to win could backfire after a settlement for the current conflict is reached, and in future conflicts that may arise. One of those fancy moves might be to use misdirection, or to bring up everything including the kitchen sink, but this, too, is a faulty line of thinking when considering that the general intention of mediation is to find fair and collaborative outcomes, and a mediated resolution rather than litigation is desired. This is especially true if the mediation is Transformative. The mediator should consider reminding this disputant that a judge would not be as intimidated by an assertive party as an opposing disputant might be.

COMPROMISING

Compromising *is intermediate in both assertiveness and cooperativeness. When compromising, an individual has the objective of finding an expedient, mutually acceptable solution that partially satisfies both parties. Compromising falls on a middle ground between competing and* *accommodating, giving up more than competing but less than accommodating. Likewise, it addresses an issue more directly than avoiding but does not explore it in as much depth as collaborating. Compromising might mean splitting the difference, exchanging concessions, or seeking a quick-ground position.*[3]

Similar to the Collaborating mode, the disputant who is using the Compromising mode, or bargaining, is at the midpoint on both the assertiveness and cooperativeness axes, as they are equally assertive and cooperative. The compromiser tries to find the medium by considering their own needs, as well as the needs of others. Compromisers do try to cooperate, but not at their personal expense only, meaning that all parties forfeit portions of their concerns to reach a mutually agreeable outcome. Unlike with collaboration, a compromiser is generally more interested in finding an easy way out that works for everyone. This generally avoids complexity and instead looks for more superficial options.

Benefits of the Compromising Mode

1. **Pragmatism**
   a. A solution that does not necessarily meet all of the needs of each disputant but is nonetheless mutually agreed-upon and serves as a temporary stopgap for a smaller issue that is getting in the way of larger issues. Agreeing to a compromise on the smaller issue(s), temporarily or not, can allow the mediation to get back on track. If the compromised solution to the smaller issue is in fact temporary, it can be addressed at a later point in the mediation once other more important issues are addressed.
2. **In and out**
   a. A resolution that can be reached and agreed-upon more quickly.
3. **Perceived fairness**
   a. Resolutions are created that aim for disputant perceptions of fairness, rather than exact equivalences that might not necessarily be interpreted as fair.
4. **Preserving the relationship**
   a. Parties shift positions and acquiesce, thereby limiting the amount of damage being done to the relationship or stopping the damage completely.
   b. When competing and a win/lose scenario will cause harm to a relationship, compromising is a way to settle, causing the least amount of undue damage and ensuring that parties walk away feeling the solution is as fair and equal as possible. If at the end of the day, everyone has lost something through compromise, it is a winning day.
   c. When a disputant's mediation goals are other than a mediated settlement agreement, compromising could lead to proper and effective communication, which might actually be the goal. For example, the addition of

3. Id.

a mediator facilitating communication between parties who have been unsuccessful in that regard brings about the realization that their ineffective communication was the conflict, and that the circumstance that resulted in the need for mediation was merely a symptom of that faulty communication. In such a case, the repaired communication would be identified as the true goal of the mediation and a traditional settlement agreement would be unnecessary.

Costs of the Compromising Mode

1. **Unresolved concerns**
   a. When concerns are compromised and issues are not fully resolved, there is residual frustration and the possibility of future flareups remains.
2. **Imperfect solutions**
   a. A mediated agreement reached through the Compromising mode may produce a settlement of lesser quality than one reached through the Collaborating mode.
3. **The last resort**
   a. When time, money, and energy have run out, and BATNA has "Settle today" written all over it, practical matters move to the forefront and compromising to reach settlement becomes the only way out. Original goals may be clearly out of reach or irrational, and a discussion about the even stronger irrationality of those goals should the case go to court might have transpired. This could also lead disputants to realize that they must compromise and settle because they cannot risk the alternative. This does not necessarily mean they are throwing in the towel. Instead, they are beginning the dance of exchanges, gradually tempting the other party to join them, until a settlement is reached. This can, in fact, lead to satisfaction if both parties feel that they have gained in addition to having lost.
4. **The game**
   a. It is possible that time and power are the only factors at play, and the disputant using the Compromising mode does not wish to participate in the back-and-forth, negotiating and competing game anymore. Worn down, they no longer care who wins, the game is no longer appealing, and the outcome is irrelevant, thereafter leaving them open to a poor compromise as the result of conflict and mediation fatigue.

Mediator Intervention

1. Compromising should not be used when there are matters involved that are too important to sacrifice in even the smallest amount. The mediator should not encourage compromise, but should instead work to ensure that the parties retain or receive what is vital to them; Collaborating or Competing would be better CHMs in that scenario. Reserve compromising for matters that are of lesser importance, but still important enough to be meaningful to any disputant within the context of the conflict. Sound strategies would be for the mediator to:

a. Encourage a disputant who cares less about a matter to compromise so that the mediation can move forward, especially in a moment of impasse, and especially if it is a deciding factor between settlement or not.
b. Encourage all sides to compromise on issues back and forth, to slowly move the mediation forward, and to ensure that no side feels they are giving more while another side is giving less. *Fairness* matters to disputants when one is giving in to another during a negotiation about a matter within the larger mediation. Resentment is a difficult hurdle to overcome, so to the degree possible, prevent participating in its buildup.

2. When compromising produces an agreement, it does not always deliver resolution to deeper needs, emotional or otherwise. Although it might result in a settled solution to a dispute, or to components thereof, when disputants make concessions, especially in response to demands, the result could be less than optimal. With underlying problems and dissatisfactions potentially just beneath the surface of a compromise, ill feelings might be bred and deepened by new resentment from a perceived unbalanced compromise added onto the already heavy load of a conflict. Whether this comes to light during or after the mediation, disputants will be paying the price if it is not addressed head-on. A compromise should be for good reason, fair to all from the outset, or equally unfair to create a reverse perception of mutual fairness. Either way, a compromise must be well thought out, discussed, and then discussed again. Unless parties dictate as such and only after being thoroughly discussed with the mediator, compromise should not necessarily be employed automatically. This decision most likely will be determined in caucus, unless the parties have come to an arrangement together before entering mediation, in which case it can be discussed in joint session. The mediator should help the parties create a clear plan of action that outlines and separates important issues from unimportant issues to discover points that are appropriate for compromise and those that are not. It would be foolish and shortsighted for the mediator to encourage compromise on an issue from the "important issues" column simply to settle the case in the easiest possible way, especially if an end in sight rests on resolving one of those issues. Resist the urge to do this, because it will backfire for the disputants who might be interacting with each other after the mediation is over. Additional conflict is a virtual guarantee resulting from discontent relating to an ill-conceived compromise and it stands to reason that there will be negative impacts from the mediator encouraging as well as disputant(s) agreeing to bad settlements. Do not do it! Compromise when it is right and apply other CHMs when more appropriate and advantageous to disputants and to their conflicts.
3. When to compromise
   a. When a resolution, any resolution, is to the benefit of the disputant(s) because:
      i. The BATNA is unacceptable.
      ii. It is the fairest option.
      iii. A relationship would be preserved.

iv. A new relationship would be fostered.
v. All parties would leave the room feeling satisfied about decisions that were made during the mediation and settlement process.
vi. It provides a resolution to a dispute that has become more detrimental, necessitating the termination of involvement by any means, compromise being the shortest and most direct route.

b. When total agreement has proven to be impossible, but a settlement still must be reached. There are aspects to the conflict that are important to all parties, and the only solution is for everyone to begin bending. Creativity will quickly become a mediator's sharpest tool in this moment.
c. When there are larger, more pressing issues involved in the conflict, the path to which is blocked by smaller, less consequential components. Disputants might compromise on the smaller issues or, at the very least, agree to set them aside to waive their interference with the larger ones. Addressing larger issues often has a way of sorting out smaller ones without necessarily spending time, discussion, and negotiating power on them. By moving past the smaller issues to get to the larger ones, the mediation might also be solving the smaller ones in the process or, if not, the mediation can circle back around to them later.

4. Compromising has a strong logical component. When Disputant A is proposing compromises and Disputant B is vehemently against them, sharpen your senses. Compromising involves providing facts to reinforce and explain offers, a desire to find resolution, and a nod to the give-and-take aspect that often leads to settlement. If this is met with outrage and irrational behavior in response, be aware that there is likely an emotional disputant with unresolved issues below the surface, which may or may not even pertain to that conflict and opposing party. If the mediation is in joint session, it would be prudent for the mediator to caucus at this point to preserve Disputant A's compromising behavior while addressing Disputant B's needs and to shift them to a more rational, logical place where the possibility of compromise can be reintroduced. The mediator encourages the compromising and forward-toward-settlement thinking of Disputant A, while simultaneously practicing shuttle mediation and working with Disputant B. There might be points that Disputant A needs Disputant B to know, and certain responses that Disputant B might seek, including validation, an apology, mutual respect, and agreeing to disagree. The mediator can carefully shape the mediation to include what each disputant needs, all the while bearing in mind that the path is there, and Disputant A is on it and waiting, sometimes patiently and sometimes not, for Disputant B to join. However, mediation is often an uneven path, with offshoots and forks abounding, and one or all disputants could easily veer off course. Any time a mediation involves disputants who differ in any of the following areas which singularly or collectively create an incompatibility theme that can be applied to a majority of mediations, the mediator should be prepared to encounter disagreements specifically about compromising:

a. Their CHMs.
b. The way they approach conflict in general.
c. The way they internalize disputes.
d. Levels of emotionality.
e. Thinking versus feeling drives.

Of course, this will likely no longer be the case once the parties have worked through their emotions, have had their "day in court," and addressed any additional needs essential to arriving at the holy grail of rational and logical communication.

FLASH CHALLENGE QUESTION

Flash Challenge Question #1:

What if the dispute involves a power disparity? For example, employer versus employee, more educated versus less educated, or wealthy versus poor. Could the dispute benefit from compromising? Why or why not? Discuss.

Managing Thinkers and Feelers

Thinkers respond to facts and logic, understand the opinions of all parties, create logical alternative solutions, focus on analyzing others, stand firmly in their positions, and are less emotionally driven. *Feelers* are emotionally driven and focused less on rationality and logic. They empathize with interests of other parties and would change themselves before expecting others to do so. Thinkers must allow feelers to express their emotions, to which the response should be validation to ensure feelings of being heard. Logic and reason will have absolutely no impact on a disputant who is lost in emotional turmoil. If a disputant feels attacked and unheard, without addressing their specific needs as a feeler, for example, they might become ultradefensive and dig their heels in more deeply. They might become fixated on how greatly wronged they have been and how unfair it all is. This can become extremely frustrating for a thinker, who believes that they are taking both positions into consideration and providing wholly logical and rational explanations for well-crafted compromises. As we know, perhaps all too well, it is a short jump from frustration to anger and then ultimately to giving up, or in mediation terms, to impasse. The moral of that story is that the balls in the air need to remain there, so consider this your juggling lesson and practice. The mediator must keep the thinker engaged and willing to hang in there until they can move the feeler through their journey from emotional to logical on the path to accepting and interacting with compromise. Accordingly, the settlement ending should include:

1. Consideration of what both parties have expressed.
2. Reiteration of specific language to show that they have been heard and their feelings taken into account and noted.
3. A conclusion with what can be perceived as a fair solution.

Although these inclusions are relevant for a mediated settlement agreement, they are likewise and equally applicable toward mediation end goals that have different parameters.

FLASH CHALLENGE QUESTION

Flash Challenge Question #2

If all disputants are feelers, do you think a Compromising Conflict Handling Mode would be the most effective? If so, explain. If not, which Conflict Handling Mode(s) would you recommend and why?

A Deep(ish) Dive into the Humanistic Approach

A Beneficial Strategy When Formulating Settlement Option Suggestions

The Humanistic Approach (Carl Rogers, Abraham Maslow) relies on a perspective emphasizing the qualities that individualize and distinguish one person from another. Recognizing each person to be a distinct and complete individual will enable the mediator to apply a laser focus on the differentiated specific needs of each disputant to make wise moves using appropriate skills to guide the mediation. Viewing disputants as unique, instead of attempting to categorize them based on their behavior and its causes, helps prevent the mediator from making potentially inaccurate assumptions simply because behavior is reminiscent of "something someone else did at some point for some other reason." Avoiding miscategorization of disputants will help the mediator prevent using incorrect CHMs, providing inappropriate settlement option suggestions, or making incorrect moves on their internal chess board. The mediator should take the time to listen, absorb, and design creative, tailor-made settlement options that fully address the diverse emotional needs and desires of the parties. Settlement agreements should be responsive to the call of the Humanistic Approach by incorporating each disputant's unique requirements, which will produce a resolution reflective of and geared toward individualization rather than generalization. This can help ensure collective satisfaction, mutual agreement, and the staying power of a settlement. An additional component of this approach is that behavior is determined not only by free will, but also by treatment from others, especially whether one feels valued or respected, with nature and nurture as active participating influences. Therefore, it is critical for the mediator to ensure that disputants treat each other appropriately, because inappropriate treatment could lead to an emotional state that precludes effective communication for collaborative work. The Humanistic Approach will lead the mediator to substantially better insights into disputants' behavior, motivations, and needs, which can be layered to produce a larger picture in the hunt for settlement.

COLLABORATING

Collaborating *is both assertive and cooperative. When Collaborating, an individual has the objective of finding an expedient, mutually acceptable solution that partially satisfies all. It involves digging into an issue to identify the underlying concerns of the two individuals and to find an alternative that meets both sets of concerns. Collaborating between two persons might take the form of exploring a disagreement to learn from each other's insights, resolving some condition that would otherwise have them competing for resources, or confronting and trying to find a creative solution to an interpersonal problem.*[4]

At the opposite end of the spectrum from Avoiding, Collaborating includes assertive as well as cooperative qualities, and is high on both the assertiveness and cooperativeness scales. Collaborators, also known as problem-solvers, address their own needs and those of others without compromise or concession. They attempt to understand the mindset of an opposing party so that a win-win outcome can be reached where neither party feels that they are in a losing position. A collaborator will take all sides into consideration and look to underlying problems to find solutions. For collaboration to be successful, parties must be willing to listen to each other's expressed needs and interests, and to exchange ideas based on an understanding of their individual experience within the conflict. Collaborators believe that finding desirable, common ground settlement options that take into consideration and address the needs of all parties leads to the most advantageous outcome. For a mediation to be conducive to a Collaborative mode, certain characteristics are necessary:

1. A baseline agreement that the conflict is a mutual problem and finding a mutual solution option is the way to come to resolution.
   a. "We" should be used instead of "I" as much as possible to reinforce this understanding.
2. A safe and trusting environment.
   a. Disputants must believe that they are collaborating with the same intentions, and that they have their collective best interests in mind.
3. The desire to reach layers beneath superficial-level posturing to work through any emotional upheaval.
4. Interpersonal skills that include functional and effective communication with the same or similar goals.
5. Disputants who are open-minded to each other's creative settlement ideas.
6. A conflict that can or should be mediated, allowing for creative settlement options attained though collaborative discussion and brainstorming.
   a. This should not be a conflict that would be better served if litigated or that is so steeped in emotional turmoil and aggression that collaboration, at least for the moment, is entirely off the table.

4. Id.

Benefits of the Collaborating Mode

1. **Two heads are better than one**
   a. When searching for creative settlement options, particularly when a case is multifaceted, the entire mediation process is best served by input from all parties, and is especially well served by input from parties who are versed in topics that pertain directly to the conflict. For example, in an unlawful detainer dispute in which parties have been unable to pay their rent, resolution options may have veered into discussing working off money owed, and the renter's occupation as a construction foreman could greatly contribute to creative settlement conversations. The more interesting and specific information the mediator can obtain, the greater their creativity can expand, and the farther outside of the box solution options can reach. This will increase the chance of finding new and unique potential settlement agreements that might be acceptable to all parties and will likely surpass any preliminary positions presented independently at the onset of the mediation process.
2. **Schmooze a little**
   a. The best way to learn from another person is to collaborate with them and open a conversation by encouraging an exchange of ideas and expertise. Within this type of interaction lies the possibility of advantageous findings that could lead to unearthed critical information below the surface, impasse breakthrough, and mutually agreeable, new settlement suggestions. There is no expectation of confrontation, argument, or competition, thereby resulting in no need to defend positions or viewpoints through the use of hostile behavior, regardless of incompatibility of statements.
3. **Reinforcing relationships**
   a. By improving relationships, parties are brought together to work in a respectful and honest manner toward conflict resolution.
4. **Deepen the commitment**
   a. When disputants actively participate in creating potential settlement options, especially when they have labored to meet the concerns of everyone involved in the conflict, a natural sense of ownership and pride are formed. By collaborating in the resolution process, which leads to a developed sense of ownership, a deeper commitment to the agreed-upon settlement will be found.

Costs of the Collaborating Mode

1. **Psychological demands**
   a. There are mental and emotional demands required of disputants to work together toward the greater goal of settlement. Parties must be receptive to different perspectives, positions, opinions, and obstacles.
2. **Susceptibility**
   a. Unscrupulous parties could abuse a cooperative disputant's willingness to work together to find a settlement that is the most fair collectively by manipulating that proffered cooperation into a strategy with the

intention of causing the cooperative disputant to accede to an agreement that singularly benefits the unscrupulous party.

3. **It takes time**
   a. Comparatively speaking, collaborating might create a lengthier process than other CHMs. Although working together has its benefits, saving time is not necessarily one of them.
4. **On thin ice**
   a. Divulging truthful and often highly personal information to find potential settlement options that meet the true concerns of all disputants involved in a conflict might inadvertently jeopardize an amicable mediation or add fuel to the fire in a hostile room. For example, if an amicable mediation is at an impasse due to lack of mutually agreeable settlement options, the mediator might begin probing deeper into the conflict and into the experiences of each disputant to access previously undisclosed information. This could lead to creative, mutually agreeable settlement options, but the information disclosed could be inflammatory and cause the mediation to become embroiled in emotional upheaval, resulting in more harm than good. Regardless of whether or not a settlement is reached through this process, the end may not justify the means, as a destroyed relationship and words spoken that can never be taken back could be left hanging in the balance.

Mediator Intervention

Generally speaking, collaborating is a crowd favorite—for a crowd of mediators, that is—when approaching and managing conflict; however, getting to a place of collaboration, where all parties involved are using a Collaborative CHM, is usually a different matter entirely. It takes time to reach mutual disputant willingness and then to work through the collaboration process itself, so it does not serve all mediations and conflicts equally well. For example, with conflict issues that one disputant deems less significant, but that present as extremely important to an opposing party, spending excess time, energy, and goodwill on collaborating and bargaining is less than desirable. A more skillful move on the chess board with the endgame in mind would be to compromise by giving that opposing disputant what they are asking for on this issue of imbalanced importance only. By doing so, what has been accomplished?

FLASH CHALLENGE

You Tell Me!

Come up with an example of giving in to a lesser issue while working through a conflict. (Consider a divorce scenario, if you are stuck.)

1. Why would a disputant make the decision to do this?
2. What can be accomplished in doing so?
3. Which actions would you recommend to a disputant?

a. Does it depend on the conflict, the disputants, and the mediation? If so, discuss examples of which type of conflicts, disputants, and mediations would require each of the following options to realize the benefit of *giving in*:
   i. Agree completely.
   ii. Negotiate, drag it out, and then agree.
   iii. Make it clear that you are doing them a favor by giving them what they want.
   iv. Be reserved when that would not be the norm, to demonstrate a behavioral shift.
   v. **Extra Credit:** Fill in additional options, should you come up with any.

4. Are there any potential drawbacks?

A Note to the Reader

Consider for a moment the amount of stress that sits on the shoulders of a person embroiled in conflict. Maybe you have personal experience feeling this same way. Remember that, whether they realize it or not, and admit it or not, disputants are experiencing some level of trauma that is registered by their bodies. Disputant A could be feeling like a hostage, entirely gripped by fear, dragged into a conflict against their will, and forced into a mediation with unknown and possibly ruinous outcomes. Add to that opposing Disputant B with a Competing CHM who seems hell-bent on winning no matter how hard Disputant A attempts to explain what they believe to be the facts of the conflict, and that they did nothing wrong to Disputant B. Do you think there is any possible way that Disputant A would be able to devote brainpower to thinking about possible out-of-the-box creative settlement options? To divert energy away from defending themself against a Competing mode to think of unique, collaborative resolution options? Likely not. Lacking the contributions of all parties, or at least their willing participation in a mediation to brainstorm settlement options that they find acceptable and that would satisfy their needs, resolution is extraordinarily difficult and potentially out of reach. Without taking steps to move parties into a different emotional position, how can they possibly be expected to comprehend an atmosphere of collaboration, let alone engage in it? If the conflict is important enough to devote the time and energy, then the work to reach collaboration is necessary and worth it. (See Chapter 1, "Conflict," for an extended discussion on trauma.)

> **FLASH CHALLENGE QUESTION**
>
> **Flash Challenge Question #3**
>
> 1. During a Transformative Mediation, could it be a wise decision to encourage disputants in a problematic romantic or business relationship to collaborate with each other?
>   a. If so, why?
>   b. If not, why not?
> 2. Propose strategies that would be beneficial to reaching a collaborative outcome.

How to Collaborate

How can one possibly imagine collaboration to occur if:

1. An honest picture of all concerns is not painted?
2. Past experiences that color the ability to productively engage in the conflict are excluded?
3. There is a failure to identify disputants' underlying concerns?
   a. These concerns may or may not have anything to do with the conflict that is currently being mediated but might still be presenting as obstacles.

Leaping immediately over concerns and to positions can result in a tug of war with positional arguments and disagreements, ending with a winner and a loser. This is innately not collaborative and certainly a tenuous, less than desirable outcome. As noted in most discussions about mediation, if at any time it becomes evident to the mediator that something is brewing other than what is being presented by disputants, or they have become locked into disparate positions, then it would be prudent to separate the disputants' underlying concerns from their positional stances. Identifying underlying concerns can lead the mediator to deep-seated issues that the disputants may be grappling with, without simultaneously addressing the conflict that precipitated the mediation. It is altogether possible that the disputants are not aware of the depth of the effect that a past experience has had on them, and how much it is currently affecting their ability to function cooperatively and collaboratively during the mediation. If the mediator is able to separate out and set aside conflict details to focus on deeper concerns only, disputants might then be able to return to the conflict in a productive, collaborative way that has the possibility of reaching settlement. Clarification of and attention to concerns rather than positions promotes a rotation of the conflict with a new and more accurate mutual understanding of the issues and an opportunity for a collaborative resolution.

When parties are finally able to reach a place where collaboration feels natural, necessary, and desirable for settlement, an understanding of their unity against the conflict has been reached. The idea of satisfying the concerns of all parties in the hunt for a settlement can become integral to the meaning of the word *settlement*, in that, unless it provides mutual satisfaction, it is not, in fact, a settlement at all. As every coach of every team has ever said, "Teamwork makes the dream work!" We mediators could not agree more. If disputants can concur that the direction of the mediation should be toward seeking out the best overall outcome for all parties, then hurdles be damned, because we are in this together—and that is a good position to be in!

AVOIDING

***Avoiding** is unassertive and uncooperative. When avoiding, an individual does not immediately pursue their own concerns or those of the other person. They do not address the conflict. Avoiding might take the form of diplomatically sidestepping an issue, postponing an issue until a better time, or simply withdrawing from a threatening situation.*[5]

"If I sense a conflict heading my way, I run for the bushes and don't come out."
—***Self-described conflict avoider/ostrich***

The disputant who is using the Avoiding mode is low on both the assertiveness and cooperativeness scales. The avoider would generally prefer to be somewhere else entirely instead of dealing with a conflict. A disputant with an Avoiding CHM might have developed an unhealthy relationship with conflict, viewing it as bad, scary, threatening, antagonizing, and deeply traumatizing. In this case, their only recourse when faced with conflict will be to avoid it at any cost to make it disappear as quickly as possible. For an avoider, it would be difficult to believe in or trust certain interactions as viable and productive means to ending a conflict, such as:

1. Mutual communication, or freely and openly expressing and discussing ideas and feelings without judgment or punishment.
2. Listening.
3. Jointly considering options.
4. Approaching and interacting with differences or incompatibilities as a potential learning experience.
5. Giving and receiving validation.

---

5. Id.

Benefits of the Avoiding Mode

1. **To leave or to stay: That is the question**
   a. Avoiding known stressors and anxiety triggers by removing oneself from harmful situations and people when the benefit of leaving outweighs the benefit of staying or when there is no chance of satisfying concerns by engaging in the conflict.
   b. Avoiding specific aspects of a conflict, especially in mediation, by not becoming engaged can prevent escalations in unnecessary defensiveness and positional aggression when taking something personally or feeling attacked.
2. **Time constraints**
   a. When an issue is less important, especially when there are other, more pressing matters, avoiding prevents time and energy being spent on low-priority matters.
   b. When there is not enough time to give a conflict its due in order to come to a reasonable solution option. Matters could become worse if a rushed conversation or rushed problem-solving is attempted when it is neither the correct time nor the correct place.
   c. Allowing for the necessary time to obtain and review additional information that directly or indirectly pertains to the conflict and could have an impact on the decision-making process. Rushing to make a decision or come to a conclusion leads to results that are not optimal, that are generally not the most thought out, and may leave too many stronger, more beneficial options unaddressed or on the cutting-room floor.
3. **Setting up for success**
   a. Provides the time to be less distracted and better prepared to deal with the matter at hand, including a cool-down period to allow for cooler heads to prevail, by taking a beat or counting slowly. A common technique offered by therapists when aiding clients in dealing with anger management issues is to advise them to count to ten. This practice should provide the opportunity to calm down from the surge of anger often caused by conflict and to regain clear thinking for calm and efficient communication to follow. The collective effect is to restrict damage that could result from engaging while angry.
4. **Stay out of it**
   a. If one does not need to be involved, and nobody has asked for help, an avoider will not become involved.
5. **Shifting the focus**
   a. When an issue that is not central to the conflict presents itself, but is actually a defense mechanism or superficial posturing, avoid it. There is no need to waste time and energy, or heap potentially larger problems onto an issue that might not be real. Fighting about a symptom of a problem instead of the problem itself never got anyone out of hot water and is no solution.

6. **Don't take the bait**
   a. Failing to avoid a purposeful smoke screen would be an error in judgment. This failure could be an inadvertent act of cooperation in avoiding the real issue. Additionally, responding to concocted concerns such as questioning and preparing to argue about the color of the shoe choice on Tuesday when it is a blatant attempt to shift the focus away from a central issue such as who paid more toward the mortgage during a divorce mediation should be avoided.

Costs of the Avoiding Mode

1. **It takes two to tango**
   a. In a professional environment that necessitates interaction with co-workers to perform required tasks, avoiding them could inhibit essential behavior.
2. **Intentional or unintentional provocation**
   a. Avoiding can lead to anger and indignation from those whose concerns are being ignored, and who see the avoidance as intentionally dismissive behavior.
3. **A sleeping dog never lies**
   a. It should come as no surprise that what is swept under the rug rarely remains hidden there, and even on the off chance that it does, it has a way of permeating the air, nonetheless. When addressing a conflict is postponed, it can become larger, more layered, more time-consuming, and more complex than it was in its original form, with more disastrous effects than it would have had if it had been addressed at the outset.
4. **Missed opportunities**
   a. Avoiding creates additional or greater issues rather than engaging in a communication process, the latter of which could result in the potential exchange of ideas and information.

Mediator Intervention

1. When a disputant lashes out, it is more often than not about themself or their ability to behave appropriately in conflict situations than it is about the person to whom they are directing their onslaught. There could be blaming, name-calling, accusations, intentionally hurtful comments, overgeneralizations, and a loss of control over their anger, to name a few. Disputants should be able to rely on the mediator to address and defuse any outbursts instead of taking that bait. In this scenario, avoidance will remove a potential new obstacle that could be created if the disputants engage in an additional argument, instead of staying on track toward resolution of the conflict. When suggesting avoidance as a strategic advantage, it would be most beneficial for the mediator to encourage parties to avoid becoming involved in any outbursts that are clearly extraneous to the conflict, as difficult as that might be for those who are not natural avoiders.

2. To assist extreme avoiders from retreating even more deeply into their Avoidant CHM, the mediator can investigate possible causes and contributing factors. These might include a history of abuse (emotional, verbal, physical), bullying, relationships with extreme power imbalance, negative attitudes toward communication, and a general fear of speaking out. Once the mediator has established a baseline for those causes and contributing factors, they can help the disputant identify the possibility that their reticence to participate in the current conflict is being colored by their history, which could be to their detriment. As a solution, the mediator might suggest that the disputant separate the background causes of their Avoidant CHM from their present responses to shed that burden to be able to negotiate in a manner more suited to a successful resolution.
3. A mediation option presented in this book is "Take a beat," which builds in a momentary and intentional act of avoidance by not addressing the conflict directly. This beat can provide the time to manage potential interference that might be barreling toward the mediation as a result of disputants' inadequate impulse control. The opportunity to regain perspective and composure can quite literally stop an impending impasse in its tracks.
4. If avoidance is the strategic choice, it would be prudent to identify that feelings are not being ignored or overlooked, but that there might be a better time and a better way to address the specific issue, neither of which would be in that moment. Make sure all disputants are clear on why avoidance has been chosen so that they do not mistake thoughtful and purposeful avoidance for malicious evasiveness.

FLASH CHALLENGE

Avoiders

1. Interview different people about the way they deal with conflict. Continue interviewing until you find two individuals who use the Avoiding Conflict Handling Mode.
   a. You should discuss with them the definition of the various Conflict Handling Modes, if necessary.
   b. People are generally aware of the way they behave during conflict; if they are not, ask them to describe a recent conflict they were involved in, and try to figure out their Conflict Handling Mode based on the information they provide. If you cannot, move on to someone else.
2. Discuss with them how they used avoidance during past or present conflicts.
   a. Seek details about the conflict, how their Avoiding Conflict Handling Mode presented itself, and what happened as a result.
3. Using the information about the conflict they described to you as the example, work with them to shift out of their avoidance pattern.

a. Design alternate scenarios of what transpired during their conflict, focusing on what could have happened had they interacted utilizing alternate Conflict Handling Modes.

4. Ask them about whether or not the conflict still affects their life.
   a. If it does, how? Discuss.
      i. If it does, reframe how the conflict could have been addressed differently to change the outcome.
5. Discuss the resolution of the conflict, if there was one.
   a. Address other, more collaborative and advantageous settlement options that could have been open to them had they not relied on Avoidance.
6. Based on their comfort level, ask questions about how conflict was handled in their past.
   a. By them, their family members, or those around them.
   b. Is this a pattern of behavior formed over the course of their lifetime?
   c. Might this be a defense mechanism?
7. Ask if they see the benefit of using alternate Conflict Handling Modes.
8. Ask if they see the damage that can be caused by Avoidance.
   a. Of course, Avoidance can be effective, so it is possible that in the scenario presented to you, Avoidance was in fact beneficial and therefore worked in a participant's favor. However, this will not always be the case when using the Avoidance mode.

ACCOMMODATING

Accommodating *is unassertive and cooperative—the opposite of competing. When accommodating, an individual neglects their own concerns to satisfy the concerns of the other person; there is an element of self-sacrifice in this mode. Accommodating might take the form of selfless generosity or charity, obeying another person's order when you would prefer not to or yielding to another's point of view.*[6]

The disputant who is using the Accommodating mode is low on the assertiveness scale and high on the cooperativeness scale. The accommodator does not take care of their own needs, choosing instead to cooperate with and satisfy another party, even to their own detriment. The accommodator focuses on preserving relationships over personal interests. They believe that you catch more flies with honey than with vinegar, which can put them at a distinct disadvantage, especially when interacting with disputants at the opposite end of the spectrum with a Competitive CHM. Awareness of the limitations of the Accommodating mode and knowing

6. Id.

when and when not to accommodate are key to its proper utilization as it can be so quickly and easily manipulated. These inclined peacekeepers are feelers rather than thinkers, are conflict-averse, and can be slower in sorting through information, coming to conclusions, making decisions, and moving to action. When up against a disputant using the Competing mode, who is a thinker and leans in the exact opposite direction of an accommodator, it is clear how an accommodating feeler can be steamrolled. An interaction between these disputants can result in a win/lose scenario, potentially forming a behavioral pattern out of this interaction. However, the formation and repetition of this pattern might be unintentional on the part of a disputant interacting with an accommodator. For example, when choosing a work team in a professional setting, it would be very natural for someone who is not an accommodator to create that team with members who are accommodators. This would ensure a harmonious work environment with team members who do not put up a fight even if and when they are in disagreement, and that the person who is the least accommodating would rise as the leader. If you want something done exactly your way with little or no resistance, building your team with accommodators is the way to go, especially when considering the alternative, which could be a team of competitors.

Benefits of the Accommodating Mode

1. **Stepping back**
   a. Allowing others to take the lead as a show of support and to afford them an opportunity to be heard.
2. **Keeping the peace**
   a. When it is to the benefit of all involved, to preserve harmony and collaboration above chaos and disruption.
3. **Quid pro quo**
   a. Used to build social capital by doing favors with the intent of leveraging them at a later time. Accommodating in matters that are of lesser importance to one disputant can go a long way for another, as is the case with compromising in this same way and for this same reason. Suggesting that a disputant do a little now to get a lot later is a good move on a mediator's internal chessboard of potential strategic options. Doing a lot, when it really does not matter personally, can do even more. Therefore, it is a good idea to differentiate between short-term and long-term goals and determine whether accommodations should be used now or later.
   b. Used as a way of apologizing and repairing previous or current damage.
4. **A better way**
   a. Can cut present losses to minimize future losses in a losing situation.
   b. Can allow for the option of a better solution when one realizes that they are wrong or that another position is stronger and makes more sense. This flexibility can demonstrate being reasonable, paying attention, and the willingness to change with new information and clarification.

Costs of the Accommodating Mode

1. **Capitulation**
   a. Forfeiture through shifting personal positions or interests in favor of another's.
2. **Taking advantage**
   a. An unhealthy pattern of pacifying the needs of others at the cost of one's own can quickly form if Accommodating is overused, becoming a crutch to end conflict situations quickly or to avoid them altogether.
   b. It can become a quick fix to a deleterious relationship with conflict that can be abused by disputants who might take advantage of the situation.
3. **An unhappy customer**
   a. Agreeing to a settlement that is less than desirable, does not fulfill true concerns, and is one-sided.
4. **Obfuscation**
   a. Agreement as a result of insincere accommodation could cause an opposing party to be confused about true intentions by believing the agreement to be sincere, when fact it is not. The end result is a fundamental misunderstanding of true feelings, which can cause setbacks in other areas of the conflict intervention process.
5. **Undue delay**
   a. Agreeing to a settlement offer that is unsustainable because it does not reflect true needs or interests will require discussions and settlements to be undone and redone at a later date.
6. **A ticking time bomb**
   a. Continual acquiescence and disregarded personal needs and concerns may lead to outbursts that are aggressive and detrimental to the mediation process and to a relationship, resulting in possible impasse and the permanent parting of ways.

Mediator Intervention

1. If accommodating disputants continue to give in to opposing parties, it could become beneficial to eventual settlement for the mediator to ensure that the accommodations are on issues that are truly not of any substantial import. This might be during caucus with the accommodating disputant while delving into elements of previous or potential accommodation. Peeling back layers and peering below the surface could help ensure that any settlement reached will be truly representative of all parties' needs and interests and have durable staying power. With such a settlement, and the learned effort it requires, when the mediation concludes and there is no longer a neutral third party present to facilitate communication and conflict intervention, the disputants will be able to replicate their managed interactions to avoid returning to mediation as a result of an inability to identify and appropriately interact with each other's CHMs. One disputant consistently giving up their own interests and needs to acquiesce to another's is a recipe

for resentment, anger, distrust, turmoil, conflicts swept under the rug that will inevitably not remain there, possible eventual retaliation, and a broken relationship.

2. Once the mediator has successfully assisted an accommodating disputant to understand that their current CHM is not effectively serving their best interests, new conflict interaction approach designing, role playing, and discussing potentially more beneficial outcomes that would result from shifting CHMs could all be helpful tools to introduce while edging a disputant even further away from their Accommodating mode. Dissecting scenarios where an accommodating disputant could say "no" instead of "yes," and providing methods to do so, could help allay fear and anxiety while shifting away from accommodating. For example, outlining decisions that are well thought out, rational, logical, and supported by clear information and that take factors important to them into consideration paint a picture of a person who is assertive, thoughtful, and deserving of respect for the decisions they make—a confidence builder. Approaching them in the way they approach situations, slowly and carefully, will speak to them in a language closer to their own. For them, the ideas might be scary at first, but the approach could feel familiar.

EXAMPLE ACCOMMODATING PROBLEM

Potential impasse: Mediation progress comes to a standstill when disputants are being too considerate of one another, with no side willing or able to be assertive enough to make a decision or even offer a solution option due to politeness or fear of rocking the boat.

EXAMPLE ACCOMMODATING SOLUTION

The mediator can step in to provide direction or to help move things along with an assertive position. This guidance to move toward settlement can be in the form of suggestions for how to begin brainstorming, possible questions one disputant might have for another but is reluctant to ask, encouragement to express deeper feelings and emotions, creative solution options, or even a BATNA reality check, should the conflict not be settled in mediation. A move from joint session into caucus could evoke more honest and less accommodating conversations that progress the mediation toward resolution.

FLASH CHALLENGE

Clue

1. Interview three different people about the way they deal with conflict.
   a. You should discuss with them the definition of the various Conflict Handling Modes, if necessary.
   b. People are generally aware of the way they behave during conflict; if they are not, ask them to describe a recent conflict they were involved in and try

> to figure out their Conflict Handling Modes based on the information they provide. If you cannot, move on to someone else.
> 2. Ask them to describe how they used one specific Conflict Handling Mode, or various Conflict Handling Modes, in a recent conflict.
> 3. Did the mode(s) benefit them in the outcome of the conflict? Discuss.
> 4. Did the mode(s) help resolve the conflict? Discuss.
> 5. Could the conflict have come to a better settlement if they had used a different Conflict Handling Mode at any point during their conflict? Discuss.
> 6. Could they identify the Conflict Handling Mode that was being used by an opposing disputant? Was the opposing disputant using more than one mode? Discuss.
> 7. Do they have a favorite or go-to Conflict Handling Mode?
>   a. If yes, which one and why?
>   b. If no, why not?
>   i. Do they recognize a benefit to flowing between modes, shifting to best fit different conflicts or different elements within the same conflict?

3. There is no true answer for "What is the best way to handle conflict?" or in this case, "What is the best CHM?" because conflicts are multidimensional. It is reasonable, therefore, to assume that each of the aforementioned CHMs serves a purpose when used appropriately. A cost-benefit analysis can be applied when considering the use of each CHM, the outcome of which will include a consideration of:
   a. Drawbacks.
   b. Consequences.
   c. Desirable and undesirable outcomes.
   d. The conflict itself.
   e. The parties involved in the conflict.
   f. The relationship between the disputants.
   g. A clear understanding of the specific circumstances that call for the use of each mode.

   Added to this is the concern for the ability to properly use the various CHMs:
   a. Can each mode be used to effectively reach the desired outcome?
   b. Are the parameters of each mode's beneficial qualities clear and manageable?
   c. Are the parameters of each mode's detrimental qualities clear and manageable?
4. The good news is that it is entirely possible to shift a disputant's CHM. The bad news is that the mediator will be facing CHMs that can make mediation, and discussions in general, complicated and difficult. The mediator might experience an intersection of CHMs if and when disputants shift modes in reaction to one another or to different elements of the conflict. If, for

example, there is a disputant who is predominantly an extrovert and thinker, they might be less inclined to use the Collaborating mode, favoring competing or compromising instead. When the mediator begins working toward opening the conversation to look at the benefits of collaboration, it could be helpful to approach this disputant with data and facts that equal and rival their own. Focusing on the benefit that the change in modes could bring them instead of discussing the benefit to the other party, or even possible mutual benefit, will likely be more persuasive and effectively prove to them that they should shift out of one mode and into another.

EXAMPLE OF CONFLICT WITH A FOCUS ON CONFLICT HANDLING MODES

Interview with an Academic Office Manager

Interaction between the Academic Office Manager and the New Administrator:

1. **The New Administrator.** The New Administrator came from a different school culture with a much larger student body and staff with frequent turnover. The new school was much smaller, with teachers who had been on staff for many years and who had formed a familial bond. They were a tight-knit group and were not necessarily welcoming to the New Administrator. The new position included some uncharted territory, as the school was changing certain internal systems, a fact that did not necessarily sit well with some of the tenured staff. The New Administrator was experienced, though in a different climate of teacher interactions and contributions, exhibited a twist on a one-upper attitude by always needing to improve on what other people were saying even when in agreement, and presented a variation of dismissive behavior by making no room for teachers voicing their resistance to some of the changes.
2. **The impending change.** A procedural change was being proposed, and the New Administrator was advising the staff by email. The change was to the manner in which students would be aggregated in an emergency, prior to dismissal to parents or guardians. The previous manner was alphabetically by student last name and the new method would be by class grouping at the time of the emergency.
3. **The concerns about the new system.** It would add a layer of delay for parents to collect their child(ren) by necessitating staff members to identify schedules to locate which classroom the student(s) were in, thereby creating a lengthier exit. In addition, siblings in different classrooms would no longer be together, again creating a need for some parents to have more than one child's schedule located. Those siblings who were comforted by being together during an emergency would now be separated.
4. **Identification of their Conflict Handling Mode.** The CHM used by the New Administrator was Competing. It was identified through the responses

defending the change and restating the position, rather than discussing any of the logical points that were brought up in reaction to the proposed change.

Competing statements:

- "My plan will work better."
- "I've considered all the possibilities, but . . ."
- "The parents can just wait . . ."

For example:

- One reason the New Administrator presented supporting the change was that teachers and students who knew each other would be remaining together as they stayed in the classroom configuration rather than dispersing into alphabetical lines with possibly different teacher monitors.
- The response from teachers who supported remaining in the alphabetical lines for the drills was that the existing system gave them the opportunity to interact with many students on campus, rather than only those in their classrooms. They believed that this would be beneficial to both students and teachers alike.
- The reply from the New Administrator was very simple and dismissive: "My way is better, and so the change will be implemented with the upcoming drill."
- In response to this, there was an attempt to outline as logically as possible the difficulties that would arise, particularly for families with more than one student, and the additional time that would be required to release students from different classrooms. There was a conscious decision not to stray from this logic into what could possibly be the New Administrator's personal need to implement a dramatic change. It became clear that for the New Administrator, this was more about creating avenues of change rather than considering what might simply have been a better and well-tested plan.
- This was met with lack of interest, and no additional discussion of the points. The door was promptly closed, with no further input welcomed.

5. **How to decide which Conflict Handling Mode to use.** Initially, there was an attempt to have the New Administrator explain why the logic detailed in response to the new proposed changes was invalid, with the goal to move forward collaboratively and have discourse about it, even if it involved compromise. Collaboration seemed to be the correct CHM to reach a mutually agreeable conclusion. There was a current relationship, there would be a continued relationship, and it was believed that there was nothing adversarial in this matter. Additionally, keeping in mind the New Administrator's need to earn respect while implementing potentially unwelcomed changes, collaborating would offer a beneficial opportunity to be heard as the new leader, while simultaneously incorporating input from faculty and staff with differing opinions and points of view.
6. **Shifting to a different Conflict Handling Mode.** It became clear that to the New Administrator, the need to make a mark was paramount. Since the New Administrator joined the staff, teachers' responsibilities were made

more burdensome and complicated by additional paperwork, administrative red tape, and new requirements. Instead of engaging in conversation about the points brought forward to prevent the emergency drill change, the New Administrator declined to discuss it any further by labeling this new change "improvements for you" and stating that changing from alphabetical order to classroom groupings would simplify the teachers' duties during the drill. Even though it was this same New Administrator who implemented other changes that required more work for the teachers, the New Administrator was still able to manipulate the description of this drill procedure change by convincing the teachers that the change was made with their best interests in mind. The reality was that the change merely provided an opportunity for the New Administrator to put a stamp on the so-called improvement.

The only option left was to let it go and no longer pursue any attempt to have a logical conversation based on the facts or on the merits of the newly proposed drill change. If there was not a continuing relationship to consider, then there likely would have been additional pursuit to reach a resolution that was mutually beneficial, instead of one-sided. Additionally, if it had been more important to anyone other than the New Administrator, there would have been a need to force a continued conversation.

At first, the Academic Office Manager's decision to shift out of the Collaborating mode was difficult because of a mistaken belief that there was a greater good with common ground that both the Academic Office Manager and the New Administrator would naturally be seeking. As it turned out, that was not the case. Attempting to shift the New Administrator's Competitive mode into a Collaborative mode was going to be impossible. The New Administrator had the decision-making power to implement new procedures, a deeply vested interest in pushing through the change to the existing procedure, and absolutely no desire or need to listen to anyone else's opinion. With that in mind, the Academic Office Manager decided to let it go and move on with an intact relationship. In a conflict with potential effects on a relationship, thorough consideration must be given to exactly how that relationship could be affected by either pushing forward using a particular CHM—or not. In this instance, the preservation of the relationship had to be prioritized, leading to the decision to accept the New Administrator's change and move on.

FLASH CHALLENGE

Do It Yourself!

1. Find and interview three people who fall into any of the following categories: mediator, attorney, employer, therapist, academic administrator, professor. You will ask them to discuss one conflict scenario. Example questions are provided exhibiting the necessary variations for attorney, employer, and therapist. Your questions for the additional professionals on the list can follow

suit, reflecting their appropriate variations. If you do not have access to professionals in those categories, begin posing the questions to other potential participants and see if they can answer them. If they can, great! If not, move on to someone else. Altering, substituting, and adding questions more consistent with different positions is appropriate. Write down all of their answers.

2. Discuss with them the definitions of the different Conflict Handling Modes so they can identify their own, as well as those exhibited by the person(s) with whom they had the interaction.
3. How can you turn their answers into helpful tools for yourself when in future conflict situations as mediator or even as a disputant?
4. What are your takeaways from your interviews? Discuss.
5. In your opinion and based on your interviews, what is most important to learn and understand about Conflict Handling Modes? Discuss.
6. How does identifying and understanding someone's Conflict Handling Mode aid in interacting with them and in the overall dispute intervention and resolution process?
   a. Answer from your perspective as a mediator.
   b. Ask your interviewee to answer from their perspective.

Remember, it is not only about which Conflict Handling Mode the client or disputants are using, but also which Conflict Handling Mode the mediator should select to properly guide and manage them.

Interview with an Attorney

"As an attorney, in your legal experience . . . "

1. How did you know which Conflict Handling Mode to use and when?
   a. Describe the person(s) with whom you were interacting. (Work with the interviewee to develop that description into a character profile of a person using that specific type of Conflict Handling Mode.)
   b. What are the details of the conflict? (Include back history if necessary and appropriate to the conflict.)
2. How did you identify the Conflict Handling Mode of the person(s) with whom you were interacting?
   a. . . . so that you could decide which Conflict Handling Mode to use yourself.
   b. Were there any trigger words and statements that indicated to you which Conflict Handling Mode they were using?
      i. Are there any common trigger words or statements that you have encountered for each Conflict Handling Mode (regardless of whether or not they were used in the scenario being presented)?
   c. Do you have certain "stock" responses?
3. If you realized you were using the wrong Conflict Handling Mode, how did you shift to a new one?
   a. Did you remain calm?
   b. Did you ever panic?
      i. If so, how did you regain your composure?

4. Do you regularly flow between Conflict Handling Modes?
5. Generally, and examples would be great, how do you select which Conflict Handling Mode (s) to use to manage:
   a. Your client(s)
   b. Opposing party(ies)
   c. Witnesses
   d. During depositions
   e. Witness on the stand
   f. Cross-examining a witness on the stand
      i. How did you decide which Conflict Handling Mode to use when, for example, you knew that a witness's fluctuating emotions would require shifting between various modes to properly interact with them, but you also needed to take into consideration the presence of the jury and that only certain, possibly other, Conflict Handling Modes would appeal to them?
         1. Is this potentially contradictory use of Conflict Handling Modes a factor during strategizing? If not, why not?
         2. Were you able to avoid jury disengagement?
         3. Can you provide an example when you had to maintain the jury's engagement and to ensure that they were convinced by your argument when it required a different Conflict Handling Mode from one most appropriate to managing a witness? How did you do it?
   g. Opening statements
   h. Closing statements
6. How do you shift a Conflict Handling Mode when communicating and problem-solving are impossible with the current mode?

Interview with an Employer

Internal conflicts may be between employees, between employee and employer, or company and customer.

1. How did you know which Conflict Handling Mode to use and when?
   a. Describe the person(s) with whom you were interacting.
      i. Work with the interviewee to develop that description into a character profile of a person using that specific type of Conflict Handling Mode.
      ii. If it was between two or more employees, describe each of them.
   b. What are the details of the conflict? Include back history if necessary and appropriate to the conflict.
2. How did you identify the Conflict Handling Mode of the person(s) to whom you were speaking?
   a. ... so that you could decide which Conflict Handling Mode to use yourself.
   b. Were there any trigger words and statements that indicated to you which Conflict Handling Mode they were using?
      i. Are there any common trigger words or statements that you have encountered for each Conflict Handling Mode (regardless of whether or not they were used in the scenario being presented)?
   c. Do you have certain "stock" responses?

3. If you realized you were using the wrong Conflict Handling Mode, how did you shift to a new one?
   a. Did you remain calm?
   b. Did you ever panic? If so, how did you regain your composure?
4. Do you regularly flow between Conflict Handling Modes?
5. How did you use Conflict Handling Modes when you were interacting with employees and clients?
   a. How did you decide which Conflict Handling Mode to use when, for example, you knew that a particular mode was needed to properly interact with the:
      i. Employee: This would be Transformative for you and the employee, the employee and their peer, or both, because unless you fired them, they would continue working with you if the issue was with you, and with other employees if the issue was with another employee.
      ii. Customer: Not necessarily Transformative to begin with, as they are generally strangers, but it might be your ongoing goal to turn all customers into repeat customers, making the goal for all of the interactions Transformative in nature.
   b. Describe your consideration process in how to deal with and appeal to employees and customers.
      i. Did you have to struggle against using a Conflict Handling Mode you would normally use because you knew it would not properly serve your overall purpose?
      ii. Did you perform a cost/benefit analysis: the cost to you of using certain Conflict Handling Modes as opposed to what using other modes could enable you to gain?
         1. The cost/benefit of feuding employees leading to firing or having employees quit?
            a) The time and money it would cost to train new hires.
            b) Employees being out of work with no income.
            c) Lost customers
               i. Loss of income from their purchases
               ii. Loss of free advertising through supportive word of mouth, and the potential shift to negative press?
            d) Which Conflict Handling Mode would exacerbate this situation, and which could defuse it?
               i. Were you (or they) willing or able to shift Conflict Handling Modes to resolve the conflict even if that shift was extremely difficult?
6. How do you shift a Conflict Handling Mode when communicating and problem-solving are impossible with the current mode?

Interview with a Therapist

"In your practice . . ."

1. How did you know which Conflict Handling Mode to use and when?
   a. Describe the person(s) with whom you were interacting.
      i. Work with the interviewee to develop that description into a character profile of a person using that specific type of Conflict Handling Mode.
      ii. If it was between two or more employees, describe each of them.
   b. What are the details of the conflict?
      i. Include back history if necessary and appropriate to the conflict.
2. How did you identify the Conflict Handling Mode of the person(s) to whom you were speaking?
   a. . . . so that you could decide which Conflict Handling Mode to use yourself?
   b. Were there any trigger words and statements that indicated to you which Conflict Handling Mode they were using?
      i. Are there any common trigger words or statements that you have encountered for each Conflict Handling Mode (regardless of whether or not they were used in the scenario being presented)?
   c. Do you have certain "stock" responses?
3. If you realized you were using the wrong Conflict Handling Mode, how did you shift to a new one?
   a. Did you remain calm?
   b. Did you ever panic? If so, how did you regain your composure?
4. Did their Conflict Handling Mode drag the conversation off track and away from any therapy goals set?
   a. What did you do to remain on course?
   b. How did you get back on course?
5. How did you shift their Conflict Handling Mode when:
   a. Communicating during the process was impossible due to their use of a particular mode.
   b. Problem-solving was impossible due to their use of a particular mode.
   c. Are you familiar with Motivational Interviewing?
      i. If so, do you use it to help change behavior?
      ii. If not, what are some other techniques you use?
6. Do you regularly flow between Conflict Handling Modes?
7. Which are the more difficult Conflict Handling Modes to interact with, and which are the easiest?
8. How do you use Conflict Handling Modes when you are interacting with clients?

FLASH CHALLENGE

Identify the Conflict Handling Mode

Statements

1. "Fine, just tell her she can have it. Nobody cares about what I need, like always. She just makes demands and then I have to say 'fine' or else we are stuck in place."
2. "Okay, so you say you need to keep the tree because you love it so much. Can you please describe to me everything you love about it, and why?"
3. "I want exactly the amount I am asking for and I don't care if this goes to litigation. I have plenty of time and money, and if I lose in court, you can count on as many appeals as it takes! I don't care about or believe a word you're saying."
4. "I don't want to say anything else because it will just cause more conflict."
5. "All right, well I guess since you said I could have the couch, you can have the bed even though I am the one who picked it out and you would not even come with me to the store to look at it."

Instructions

1. Find a participant and ask them to assume the role of disputant. Deliver a different one of the above statements and ask them to respond and engage in an ensuing conversation. Perhaps they have experience with similar statements; if they do, invite them to respond genuinely by describing their prior encounter(s). Repeat this with three different participants.
2. Engage as the opposing disputant and respond, allowing a natural conversation to unfold based on the statement you selected.
3. Continue with the conversation as long as necessary to identify their instinctively occurring Conflict Handling Mode.
4. Continue with the conversation past your identification of their Conflict Handling Mode, taking into account any resulting shift in your Conflict Handling Mode.

Assignment

1. Identify the participant's Conflict Handling Mode.
   a. How did you come to your conclusion?
2. How did you proceed with the disputant once you identified their Conflict Handling Mode?
   a. Did the way you managed and approached the conversation change once you identified their Conflict Handling Mode?
      i. If so, how did your approach to them change?
   b. Did you change your Conflict Handling Mode once you identified theirs? Discuss.

3. Which Mediation Style do you think would best suit their Conflict Handling Mode? Discuss. (See Chapter 2, "Mediation Styles.")
4. Extra credit: Find an additional participant and deliver one of the same statements you used above (follow the same Instructions) and answer the assignment questions. Discuss the similarities and the differences.

FLASH CHALLENGE

Take the TKI

1. Take the Thomas-Kilmann Conflict Mode Instrument (TKI) test to find out your own Conflict Handling Mode and TKI Profile.
2. Does your profile change the way you think you should handle conflicts in your life?
   a. If so, how? How is the way you are currently handling conflict out of sync with your profile?
   b. If not, why not? How is your current style of handling conflicts in line with your profile?

FLASH CHALLENGE

Observe and Report

1. Observe a disagreement.
   a. The disagreement can be between parents, siblings, friends, coworkers . . . anyone.
   b. Describe the disagreement including its various elements.
      i. Distinguish between superficial posturing and their individual, as well as collective, needs below the surface.
2. Identify which Conflict Handling Modes are being used.
   a. List all of them.
   b. How were you able to identify each one?
      i. Could you find common trigger words and/or statements that led to an obvious example of the disputant's Conflict Handling Mode? (See Chapter 3, "Communication Styles.")
   c. When was each one used?
      i. For example, were the Conflict Handling Modes used in response to specific types of statements or questions?

ii. For example, were the Conflict Handling Modes used to deflect certain statements or questions?

3. If you were to make Conflict Handling Mode recommendations based on your observations of the disagreement, what would those recommendations be?
   a. Which were helpful?
   b. Which were harmful?
   c. Which should be avoided?
   d. Which should have been used in place of other ones, and how?
4. Extra credit
   a. Discuss creative settlement options you can come up with based on the disagreement you observed.
      i. How did you arrive at these options?
      ii. How would you lead your disputants to them?
      iii. How would you discuss the options with them?
   b. Would you have taken them into caucus?
   c. Discuss the brainstorming process (in caucus or joint session) with each or all disputants.

SHIFTING CONFLICT HANDLING MODES

When it has become clear that a CHM must be shifted, a mediator's purposeful guidance and baseline strategy will be to sow the seeds of thought. Intentionally combining disputant needs and restructured mediator suggestions into indirect, open-ended questions can guide a disputant in a discussion to move them toward embracing the necessary shift from a disruptive or detrimental CHM to one that is more conducive to effective communication and settlement. The strategy is that the disputant will internalize the mediator's questions and create their own original thought recognizing the necessity of a shift.

A shift to an alternative mode should occur when:

1. A CHM is being overused, underused, or is standing in the way of a proper settlement with staying power.
2. A settlement is agreed to as a result of disputants' misuse or manipulation of any of the modes.

The strategies that follow progress from this baseline and include more direct and participatory behavior from the mediator.

The following excerpt is from an interview with a psychologist with an emphasis on shifting a Competing CHM.

Interviewer (I): . . . it is an interesting thought to consider what competing fulfills in a person, because it's not generally to the betterment of conflict interaction, a mediation, or a mediated settlement agreement.

Psychologist (P): Right, it's not helpful at its extreme. There's nothing wrong with some competition, but when it gets to an angry sort of self-absorbed, inability to collaborate, if you're in that zone, it's not at all helpful.

I: Is there anything that you have been able to say or describe to someone with a competing mode in order to get them to see the benefit of collaboration—to shift into a collaboration mode? Or, in your experience, has it been a process of whether or not they can get there on their own?

P: Being there for them to hear their feelings, their frustrations, and even their anger can be helpful to understand what's been triggered. If they feel, for example, put down by someone or that people did not respect them.

I: Do you ask about specific feelings or triggers?

P: No it's not so much that, but more of the fact that I hear that underneath.

I: But do you bring it up to them? Do you have a conversation about it?

P: Sometimes. It depends, but sometimes. Usually I have to get through hearing the anger first.

I: Right. And then have you been the one who's presented the idea or the benefits of collaboration instead of competing? Or do you find that they get there on their own once they let their feelings out?

P: Yes, the latter, although I support it. In some cases I say, you do need to move on with your life because if you stay in this fighting zone it's going to take so long to get out of it, and it takes you away from what you really need to do with your life. In the other cases, the person gets in trouble when he's too combative and competitive, as opposed to more healthy competition, which is important to consider because competing could go either way, right?

I: Yes, there are pros and cons to using each mode, the proper and improper way to use them, and the over- and underusage of each as well. My primary focus is to see what we can distill that can help someone in a neutral third-party position identify a little bit more readily and quickly what they're dealing with. Specifically what type of mode the disputant is presenting because it helps shape the way you then interact with them. It's very helpful information.

P: Well, I think with somebody who's competing, they really need respect, and more importantly to feel respected.

I: So, when you hear somebody defending themself in their position and being argumentative, is that where you go?

P: Somewhat. There's a reason why they're so defensive.

How to Shift a Competing Conflict Handling Mode

1. Ask for clarity, facts, and information rather than using a positional defense.
2. Listen with earnest attention and validate the disputants' words and feelings.

3. If a disputant is using a Competing mode, the mediator's internal alarm should be going off because where there is a Competing mode being presented, there is generally a reason for it. It is highly unusual that a disputant's CHM would be Competing by a choice that is free of perceived necessity, realistic or otherwise. This mode is almost always used for reasons such as insecurity, embarrassment, past trauma, or feeling disrespected and unheard, among others. By addressing their reasons for deeming it necessary to be competitive, the opportunity to move past the Competing mode and into others that make settlement more accessible may present themselves.
   a. If the perceived necessity is unfounded, the ensuing conversation will likely require the utilization of skills such as listening, empathizing, and identifying their true interests and needs below the surface. The need for the application of this particular set of skills results from the emotional components that have become the driving force behind this disputant's CHM.
   b. On the other hand, if the CHM is being used as a direct response to an opposing party's CHM, then the ensuing conversation will likely require addressing the CHMs of all parties to the dispute. Addressing one without addressing the other(s) will not effectively allow for a shift because the need will remain intact.
4. Build a safe space and encourage the competing disputant(s) to search for their own feelings beneath what they are currently presenting. Could there be something from their past that is causing them to behave in this manner that can be addressed and avoided while moving forward?
5. Mirror the words and behavior of the disputant who is using the Competing mode in order to speak their language. In doing so, it may become an option to use this same shared language to begin discussing a mode such as Accommodating, using words and ideas they would respond to, such as by reframing the concept and explanation of Accommodating into one of Competing. Consider using the Competing mode to create a "competition" by suggesting that this disputant try to make the most creative settlement suggestions that address the needs of all parties. Compliments and challenges go far with those who use the Competing mode, such as "That is a tall order, and only an incredibly clever and skilled disputant could do such a thing."
6. Mediators can put themselves into the position of the person that the competing disputant imagines they are superior to and working to defeat. By providing an interaction using a CHM that creates the dynamic that the competing disputant is seeking in response to their Competitive mode, the disputant might receive what will fulfill that need and move out of their competitive state. Feeling dominant over and validated by someone, the mediator in this scenario, could be enough for them to shift out of one CHM and into another that is more conducive to settling the conflict.

7. Weigh the pros and cons of the Competing mode with the disputant, focusing on potentially unappealing repercussions of continuing with this mode, including escalation of the conflict, unnecessarily aggressive reactive behavior, hurt feelings, and destruction of a relationship.
8. Shift emphasis away from positions and posturing, and onto feelings, needs, and what is happening beneath the surface. Stress empathy by putting the shoe on the other foot and addressing how the disputant might feel if the situation were reversed. Encourage questions and clarity over judgment and argument.
9. Focus on the disputant's ability to be creative and lead a settlement options brainstorming session. Find possibilities for mutual gain and highlight that such a solution is in no way a loss but instead a win for all, and most important, a win for them.
10. The following suggestion pertains to nonviolent threats between disputants who are excited and one-upping one another and who have engaged in angry banter that is hollow in nature. If there have been any threatening statements, one can assume that they will be met with defiance, an equal and opposite threat or counterthreat, and retaliation from an opposing disputant. Reframe threats into cautioning. This holds true outside of the mediation room as well, so it is an excellent suggestion to bear in mind. Take a moment to think about a situation you were in where threats were involved, and how quickly the situation escalated immediately thereafter. Now imagine if reframing had been used and the threats avoided. The mediator should reframe disputants' positions away from threats and into cautionary responses based on resultant factual outcomes: realistic causes and effects expressed in a nonthreatening, if/then manner.
    a. For example, in response to a threat of retaliatory behavior, rather than replying with a threat in retort, a disputant may calmly explain that any threats will be met with protective action taken in the form of legal remedies. This statement is a refusal to become engaged in a cycle of threats.
11. See Appendix, "Motivational Interviewing."

How to Shift a Compromising Conflict Handling Mode

1. Shifting the mode of a disputant using a Compromising mode can be complicated. It could be perceived by other parties as the mediator acting outside of the definition of neutrality in order to balance the power toward a party who is overly compromising. (See Chapter 5, "Maintaining Neutrality.") A perceived impartiality might develop when shifting a Compromising CHM, as the mediator is effectively guiding the disputant into a mode in which they will ask for more, fight back, and not automatically accept what they are being offered. For example, there is a distinct difference between shifting Compromising and Competing CHMs. When shifting a Competing CHM, a mediator is not directly affecting a potential settlement outcome.

The shift is isolated to the manner in which the party is negotiating. In some instances, that distinction can be interpreted as blurred lines of impartiality. There is a difference, though, between balancing power in a way that is not impartial and doing so in a way that is. To diminish any perception of impartiality, at the beginning of a mediation, the mediator can describe certain actions they might take that could affect all parties (see Chapter 5). In doing so, an option is created for the mediator to take steps to ameliorate any power imbalance between the disputants and having already disclosed this, it will present as no surprise.

a. For example, in an opening statement, a mediator might explain to the parties that during conflicts with deep emotional components it is not uncommon for those emotions to greatly influence the way in which parties negotiate. Should this situation arise, the mediator can take steps to privately, or collectively, discuss with the parties possibly more effective ways to interact with each other by using different CHMs.
b. During an opening statement, a mediator can disclose that for every settlement option proposed and especially for those that any party considers agreeing to, a review process will ensue, likely in caucus. The mediator will guide the disputants through dissecting the settlement to ensure that they fully understand all of its components.

2. The actions the mediator takes to shift the mode of the compromising disputant can be in the form of activities that do not inherently draw attention to the fact that this disputant is in a less powerful position. For example, taking extra time to discuss what might happen if they settle may shed light on interests or needs not currently being met by the compromise they are considering. If the parties are in caucus, the mediator can ensure that no party feels that more time or attention is being given to any one disputant over another by remaining in each room for the exact same amount of time. The conversations that transpire in each room, however, might differ greatly. If the parties are in joint session during the mediator-led settlement clarification review, they might come to realizations independently about whether or not their interests and needs are actually being met by the proposed settlement being discussed.

FLASH CHALLENGE

From Compromising to the Beyond

1. Using the prompt below from a divorce mediation, design responses that encourage a disputant to shift from a Compromising mode to an alternative CHM.
2. Include the support you would provide for the needed shift.

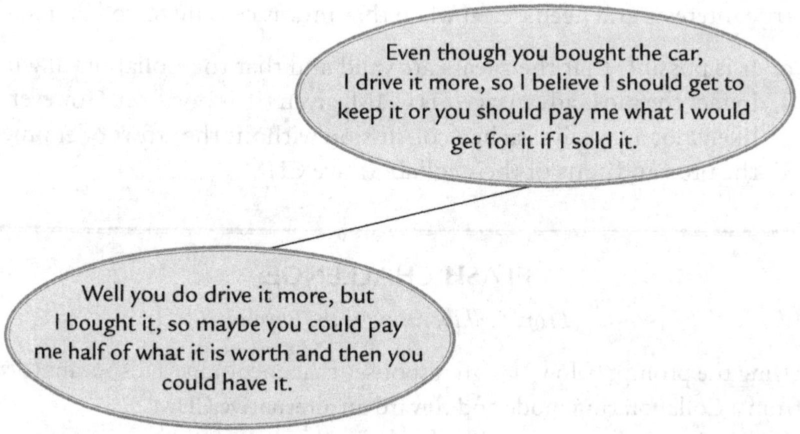

3. Continue the flowchart with your response, followed by a potential response from the disputant until you have filled in at least three bubbles with mediator intervention. Your bubbles should provide alternate perspectives highlighting why a shift away from the Compromising mode could be in the disputant's best interest. The mediator's intervention might also include a shift away from overusing the Compromising mode and into more appropriate usage of the mode.

How to Shift a Collaborating Conflict Handling Mode

1. Sometimes reviewing the reason(s) for a need to shift from a Collaborating mode is enough. A look at those reasons, which could include true needs and concerns not being met and potential manipulation, might sufficiently inspire the collaborating disputant to consider incorporating an alternate mode into their conflict resolution behavior.
2. For a disputant who is accustomed to collaborating, role playing with the mediator acting as a disputant using a more assertive mode could help them become comfortable and confident with the idea of speaking up and standing their ground. This is a shift that would provide a new and different approach for a disputant who has thus far negotiated by considering what is best for all first and foremost, even if their own best interest could be somewhat different.
3. The mediator might also consider discussing the potential consequences that the disputant fears if they were to reduce their collaborative efforts. By identifying those potential consequences, thereby removing the unknown (and the disputant's fears along with it), the mediator could assist them in becoming

confident to be more forthcoming with the positions that represent their true interests and needs, even when that means ceasing to collaborate.

a. It is possible that their fears are valid and that the Collaborating mode is in fact the most advantageous CHM, given their position. However, this is likely not an easily reached conclusion without the effort of enumerating the pros and cons of their collaborative CHM.

FLASH CHALLENGE

From Collaborating to the Beyond

1. Using the prompt below, design responses that encourage a disputant to shift from a Collaborating mode and toward an alternative CHM.
2. Include the support you would provide for the need to shift.

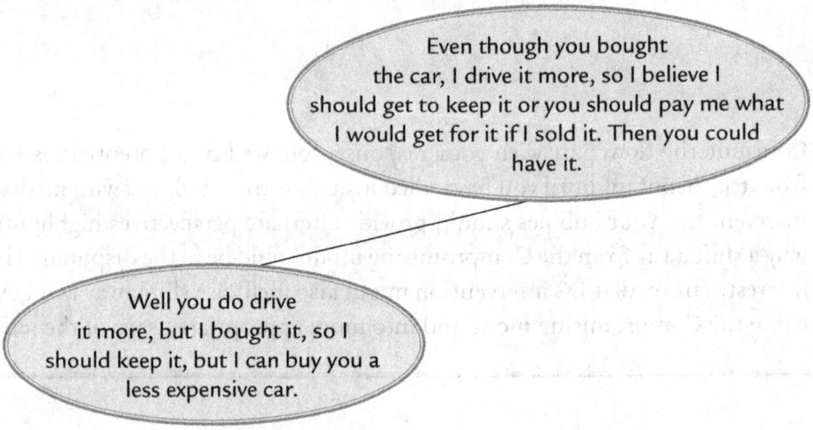

3. Continue the flowchart with your response, followed by a potential response from the disputant until you have filled in at least three bubbles with mediator intervention. Your bubbles should provide alternate perspectives highlighting why a shift away from the Collaborating mode could be in the disputant's best interest. The mediator's intervention might also include a shift away from overusing the Collaborating mode and into more appropriate usage of the mode.

How to Shift an Avoiding Conflict Handling Mode

1. Encourage a discussion that weighs the pros and cons of avoiding the conflict. Discuss what the conflict could turn into and the potential impact(s) if it continues to be avoided rather than addressed presently by engaging in what is required to find a resolution.
2. Create a plan of action to manage the conflict by taking small steps to gently introduce a different CHM approach such as Compromising or Collaborating. Addressing and managing possible fear and anger during this CHM transition process will be key to reaching the desired outcome. As often as is necessary, deliver a consistent and clear reminder about the detrimental impact(s) of avoiding the conflict and the potential benefit(s) of engagement.
3. Engage in a role-play session in caucus with the avoidant disputant so that they can practice new CHMs for engaging with an opposing party. Allowing the disputant to privately experience what it sounds and feels like to use CHMs other than Avoidance will build their confidence in anticipation of attempting a changed mode. This exercise is a practice in nonavoidance and has the potential to reduce the stress and anxiety the disputant might feel when considering other CHMs. The role-play might be one of the first times that the disputant has had the opportunity to express and discuss feelings in a supportive environment, which could become crucial in their willingness to be a collaborative participant in settlement discussions. The mediator should offer encouragement and validation by providing leadership, support, and safety to the disputant as they move into the unfamiliar territory of new CHMs. This will shift the disputants away from their association between conflict and emotional trauma—contributing factors to the development of their Avoidant CHM.
4. Remind all parties to the dispute that in general, most people would prefer to avoid being involved in conflict as much as possible. If they agree, then that is one check for them in the collaboration process—an essential step to reaching settlement. A pat on the back is deserved all around! This could help build collaborative momentum.

FLASH CHALLENGE

From Avoiding to the Beyond

1. Using the prompt below, design responses that encourage a disputant to shift from an Avoiding mode and toward an alternative Conflict Handling Mode.
2. Include the support you would provide for the need to shift.

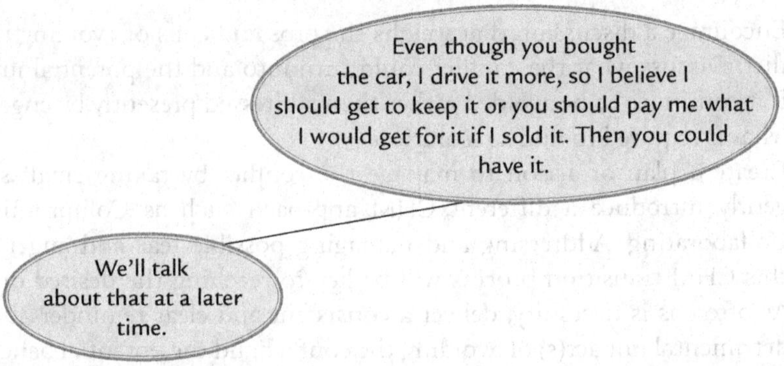

3. Continue the flowchart with your response, followed by a potential response from the disputant until you have filled in at least three bubbles with mediator intervention. Your bubbles should provide alternate perspectives highlighting why a shift away from the Avoiding mode could be in the disputant's best interest. The mediator's intervention might also include a shift away from overusing the Avoiding mode and into more appropriate usage of the mode.

The following excerpt is from an interview with a psychologist with an emphasis on shifting an Accommodating CHM.

I: What about Compromising or Accommodating? I'm sure you've interacted with people who don't stand up for themselves enough and instead give in?

P: Yes, accommodating. That's very common. Often usually too much accommodating, and they're accustomed to doing that because that was the only way they knew to maintain a relationship—always trying to please the other person.

I: How have you been able to identify that somebody is too accommodating or too compromising?

P: Well, usually by the time they come to therapy it's gotten them into some kind of emotional trouble. Either they've been taken advantage of or are very unhappy.

I: And how do you discuss with them shifting out of that mode? Or how do you build them up?

P: Helping them feel safe so that they can be assertive with me, so that they don't have to be accommodating with me. They may not even know what they think and feel.

I: Is the thought process that if they can be less accommodating and more assertive with you, that they could then potentially do that with other people as well, so you're building the skill set?

P: Yes, and even just knowing themselves. When you've been sort of this chameleon, always changing depending on who you're with, you don't really know what you feel and what you want.

I: Interesting. That exact same idea can be applied to somebody in conflict. If they have a history of being totally accommodating and compromising when not in conflict, perhaps they are being that way in the conflict as well. If you separate them from other parties by moving into caucus, you may elicit the information that they do not even totally understand the foundation of the conflict itself, let alone what would truly address their concerns.

P: That's right.

I: How do you begin a conversation with them about actually figuring it out?

P: Because they probably feel threatened in a mediation situation, I would imagine that they try to accommodate others as best they can as a mode of defense. They try to figure out what someone else wants.

I: Yes. The problem then becomes that once they go home or are in a situation where they're totally comfortable, maybe by themselves, they do not remain in an Accommodating mode. They no longer need to be that way, so all of a sudden the settlement that they agreed to by way of accommodating ceases to work for them. This is usually followed by anger and regret and then the settlement falls apart. We have to do whatever we can to avoid that scenario by striving to address true interests and needs during the mediation.

P: Yes, to find out what they might really want.

I: Right.

P: But then they might be afraid that if they insert what they really want, they're going to lose the other person, or the other party, or that they're going to be punished.

I: Any suggestions how a mediator can deal with that? We want to move away from agreements that are consequences of CHMs rather than being representative of addressing disputants' true needs and interests. "Okay, you settled, you agreed, I'm good" should not necessarily be the approach from mediators when one or more parties are clearly overly accommodating. That's not the way it should be done.

P: I think a lot of this is how you listen. With somebody who's just being accommodating, you might suspect that they have other feelings, too, and you can check.

I: Do you think a lot of validation would help? For example, when in caucus, stating, "Does it make you angry, and if it does, it's okay, it's completely confidential here, if you don't want me to say anything I won't, this is a safe space."

P: Well probably it can, but can you really do that as a mediator?

I: Yes, we can. Conversations that take place during caucus are confidential to each room unless otherwise given permission by a disputant.

P: So they have to trust the mediator.

I: Correct . . . that's a whole different chapter . . . building trust in 45 seconds.

(Both laughing.)

P: I think that's a real problem.

I: Yes, it's a tough nut, and so that would be a crucial component of helping someone open up.

P: Absolutely, absolutely.

I: What about helping them understand the intricacies of the conflict? For example, would it or could it be helpful to write out the various components so that they can focus on each separately so that they're not overwhelmed by their fear of conflict or by their need to be accommodating? They can just put those on a shelf and look at what they need to focus on?

P: Could be, could be, even just laying out their choices, and the fact that they have a choice. I think that would be helpful.

I: The goal is to find different ways of helping disputants shift out of overly Accommodating modes, which can be made even trickier since sometimes it has to be done on the quicker side as required by the mediation.

P: I think what you were saying before about a way of simplifying or laying it out clearly almost like a flowchart or something like that. I can see that being helpful for some people. The idea that you do have a choice about how to interact with conflict is really important.

I: That's a really good point. That choice may be something that they haven't experienced before.

P: Yes, they haven't the experience and don't believe in it.

I: That's a good point. That's helpful. Okay, anything else on that mode?

P: Now that was accommodating, and it seems like it's sort of similar in a way to avoiding.

I: Yes, there's definitely overlap there between avoiding and accommodating, that's a good point, because by accommodating you are avoiding speaking up about and revealing actual feelings and needs.

How to Shift an Accommodating Conflict Handling Mode

1. Delving into what lies beneath that which is being superficially presented is crucial when a disputant begins to agree to a settlement that might not be in their best interest. Taking stock of their true concerns, specifically those not being met by a proposed settlement agreement, could enable them to see the benefit of being more assertive. Without attempting to come to a

more balanced agreement, the settlement that is reached could be heavily one-sided and less likely to stand the test of time. Therefore, a mediator may move to caucus with this disputant to engage them in an exercise to become more cognizant of their position in the conflict, their interests, and other potential settlement options.

a. List #1: Make one list separating each part of the conflict that is affecting the disputant who is using the Accommodating mode. Make sure they clearly understand every conflict point on the list.
b. List #2: Make a second list with the points of the proposed settlement agreement separated out in an organized, understandable way. Discuss:
    i. What each point entails.
    ii. The impact of each point on all disputants.
    iii. What will be relinquished, and what will be received.
    iv. Possible short- and long-term ramifications of each point.
c. List #3: Create a third list of new, possible alternative settlement options that aim to be preferrable and that parallel each point on the currently proposed settlement agreement list you just made (List #2 above). Encourage the disputant to work with you to find options that could better suit their true needs and concerns. If their needs are being met by any part of the current settlement agreement, those components can simply be copied over as is to this third list.

2. In caucus, encourage the disputant to discuss the conflict. In doing so, the disputant might begin to express concerns that contradict what they have been agreeing to thus far. Validate not only what they are saying, but that they are opening up and speaking up for themselves. Validating these first steps in shifting away from their Accommodating mode will lay a foundation of confidence for the disputant, as well as support from the mediator, leading to a trusting relationship between the two.
3. In caucus, interact in a role-play with the disputant focusing on points that they have addressed thus far using their Accommodating mode. Ask them to "try on for size" what it would feel like to act in a way other than accommodating. Try, for example, collaborating instead. Encourage creativity in finding options that could satisfy the concerns of all parties involved, instead of sacrificing their own in favor of another's simply to end the conflict.
4. In caucus, ask them directly, "What are you concerned will happen if you don't accommodate but instead bring up your concerns and try to collaborate?" By discussing their fears relating to not accommodating, a new and less frightening perspective can be gained and collaborative strategizing for how to present their concerns could begin. If they are willing to collaboratively strategize with the mediator, they are demonstrating the beginnings of a shift in behavior and mode that can potentially be built on and carried over into their behavior with an opposing party. They are effectively practicing their shift in CHM with the mediator using training wheels before applying it to their interaction with other disputants when the training wheels come off. By being in caucus, the disputant receives the supportive, neutral hand

of the mediator there to assist in making sure they do not fall. This disputant can think about the mediator as a helmet.

5. Discuss how the conflict is affecting them physically, emotionally, and professionally, as well as the impact it is having on their quality of life in general. The point of doing this is to take some of the power out of the conflict and to remind them that they have an element of control over what happens. They do not need to accommodate at all costs just to reach an end to the conflict. It should be possible to find solutions that take into consideration their concerns and end with a resolution that could transform the conflict from current turmoil to future progress.

chapter 5

Maintaining Neutrality

The Role of the Mediator

MEDIATION EXAMPLE

(This Mediation Example includes confidential information for the mediator and for each disputant, respectively, and should only be provided to a participant performing the specific role in Flash Challenge: *Mediate the Case!*)

MEDIATOR NEUTRALITY

During this mediation, the mediator struggled to maintain impartiality due to interpreting the Petitioning Party (Landlord) as:

1. A bad actor.
2. Having behaved in a purposefully harmful manner toward the Responding Party (Tenant) and her young son.
3. Behaving in an insincere and purposefully strategic manner leading up to and during the mediation, designed to cause the Responding Party to leave the residence for no reason other than to receive increased rent from a new tenant, regardless of any harm that would be caused.
4. Having no regard for the consequences of his actions, which he knew would cause a mother and her son to be homeless.

The mediator also identified a power imbalance that manifested in the form of the tenant being bullied by the landlord.

DISPUTANT BACKGROUND INFORMATION

Petitioning Party (Landlord living on premises)

1. Landlord is attempting to evict the Responding Party, his live-in tenant and her young son (Tenant), on the grounds that they:
   a. Use the common area too much.
   b. Do not clean the areas of the house that they use.

c. Eat food that is not theirs.
d. Broke the television.
e. Come and go from the house outside of the *acceptable activity* hours designated in their contract.

2. Landlord is using intimidation by:
   a. Threatening to call immigration if Tenant does not leave, even though she has five months left on her contract, which Landlord freely admits without hesitation.
   b. Threatening that if Tenant does not settle in mediation, which will include vacating the premises immediately, he will "ruin her in court," "win easily," and cause her to "lose everything including the shirt on her back."
3. Confidential Information
   a. When Tenant moved in seven months ago, Landlord was in a financial bind and needed the income stream immediately. Because of that, he offered Tenant a monthly rental agreement at well below market value for a 12-month lease, requiring an extremely minimal security payment. Now, however, his situation has changed, and he is no longer in a difficult financial position. He plans to continue doing whatever it takes to get Tenant to leave so that he can bring in a new tenant for at least twice the amount of the rent payments he is receiving now.
   b. He is not willing to offer or agree to any settlement that involves a monetary payout to Tenant. He also states that he is entitled to keep all of her initial security payment because of the damages he claims that she and her son caused.
   c. Should he not get exactly what he wants, he is perfectly ready and willing to conclude the mediation in impasse and to be heard by a judge. He believes that once he describes Tenant's behavior and how, as an elderly gentleman, he has been taken advantage of and bullied (by Tenant) into accepting an unreasonably low security deposit and unreasonably low monthly rent payments, that he will prevail in court.

Responding Party (Tenant living on premises)

1. Single mother with a six-year-old son who has been renting a room from the Petitioning Party for the past seven months as part of a 12-month lease.
2. Refutes all of Landlord's accusations.
3. Reiterates the intimidation and threats from Landlord, and adds that he has gone so far as to:
   a. Purposefully burn trash in the backyard immediately outside the back door even though he has been informed on multiple occasions that not only is this an illegal practice, but that her son suffers from severe asthma and has had to triple the use of his medicated inhaler since Landlord has begun this offensive action.
   b. Put a padlock on the refrigerator and withhold the key from her.

c. Turn the volume up to full blast on the television at all hours of the day and night when he knows that she homeschools her son and works from home during the day. The loud volume not only causes issues while she attempts to work and while her son does his schooling, but it also keeps them awake during the night.
   i. When they have asked Landlord many times to turn the volume down to a reasonable level or to wear headphones, their requests were met either by being ignored or with responses such as, "My house, my rules. If you don't like it, get out."
4. Confidential Information
   a. It would be impossible for Tenant to move into a new place with her current monthly income. She is living paycheck to paycheck and would have no way of raising enough money for moving costs. Additionally, she was able to secure these accommodations at a very reasonable price, far below that of other rooms she inquired about renting. Landlord did not run her credit when she moved in. If he had, he would have seen troubles in her past that have since been problematic for her. Although these problems were through no fault of her own, instead stemming from being taken advantage of in a past domestic relationship that included her credit cards being stolen and used in amounts that exceeded $80,000, the charges remain on her credit as red flags to any potential landlord. This will certainly be an issue if she has to apply for new accommodations where her credit will likely be checked.

DISPUTANT DEMEANOR

Petitioning Party (Landlord):

1. Is extremely abrasive.
2. Presents as willing to employ any tactics he can possibly think of to get Tenant out of the home.
3. Believes he is completely justified in his behavior, position, and demands by virtue of being the owner of the property.
4. Does not believe that the 12-month term described in the lease agreement they both signed when Tenant moved in matters if he wants her to leave sooner. He believes it is at his discretion and choice—a choice he believes that he is entitled to make whenever he decides to make it.
5. Is threatening and aggressive. He continues to threaten Tenant if she does not move out or if their case does not settle in mediation.
6. Laughs at the prospect of providing her with any financial incentive to move out, feeling extremely confident that a judge will completely side with him.
7. Has no family to speak of.
8. Has decided that he is fed up with everyone around him and those that he sees on television making money from renting to tenants. Now that he is financially

stable, he refuses to be left behind in what he believes should be a financial windfall.

Responding Party (Tenant):

1. Presents as extremely fearful of Landlord and concerned for her safety if she remains in the home.
2. Feels that she has absolutely no choice but to fight to stay in the home.
3. Is very concerned over where she and her son will go if they are forced out of the home and explains that they will likely be homeless for an indeterminate amount of time.
4. She and her son have no additional family to speak of—she has no contact with her son's father.
5. Is crying, as is her son.
6. Has brought a copy of the signed lease agreement that extends for an additional five months.
7. Has also brought pictures of the chained refrigerator and video recordings with audio of the television volume, as well as a list of the intimidating and aggressive statements Landlord has made to her and her son.
8. Does not understand how someone can go from being so warm and welcoming when they first moved in to being so nasty and mean now.
9. Believes that she is an excellent tenant. She always pays her rent on time and she and her son are clean, quiet, and keep to themselves.
10. She and her son have provided help to Landlord whenever he has asked for it in the form of moving furniture, cleaning up the backyard, carrying in his groceries, and running miscellaneous errands for him.

MEDIATOR THOUGHTS

1. What happened to cause this shift from Landlord?
   a. The shift presents as being very sudden.
2. There seems to be more going on than just wanting to make more money.
3. Landlord's insensitivity might be a defense mechanism or masking something else going on.
4. Which behavior is real—the initial nice guy or this person now?
5. What is beneath the surface?
6. What is the reason behind Landlord's particular Conflict Handling Mode (CHM)?
   a. Can it be shifted by an altered perspective, the incorporation of whatever is actually happening beneath his superficial position or empathy for Tenant's situation?
      i. Perhaps he should be extended empathy as well?
      ii. Perhaps he feels that in his past struggles no one ever empathized with him, and now he is taking it out on her?
7. What is Landlord's true Communication Style?

   a. Pay attention to how he responds to mirroring his Aggressive style as well as combating it with an opposite style to determine an appropriate response style.
8. Plan to blend Mediation Styles:
   a. Facilitative, to help them communicate their true needs and concerns with each other.
   b. Transformative, to repair the current relationship and to structure a new one with possible additional components that could be part of a settlement agreement.
   c. Evaluative, to assist Landlord in shedding light on the reality of the merits of his case and on how his position and actions could possibly be perceived and interpreted by a judge within the law (without giving legal advice, of course).
9. Discuss:
   a. BATNA and WATNA with Landlord.
   b. Their signed, binding rental contract.
   c. There is no proof of any bad behavior from Tenant and her son.
   d. Tenant is not making any demands other than to uphold their initial contract and for Landlord to stop his intimidating behavior.
   e. The beneficial aspects of keeping present Tenant (based on their description), including that they are quiet, keep to themselves, are kind, and have proven to be helpful to him in the past.
   f. While Landlord may charge a new tenant more money, their behavior will be unknown.
      i. Less rent money might be the price of safety and peace of mind, which may be well worth it.
   g. Landlord may continue to benefit more and more from having people around the house who are willing to help him as he gets older.
      i. Can calculate how much more money he envisions he will receive from a new tenant and compare it to what he could potentially spend on paid assistance.
         1. If he had to hire people to help him, he would be spending money that he is saving now by receiving the help from Tenant and her son.
         2. May have to realign any illusions about how much of an increase in rent he is likely to receive.
   h. Landlord intimidation and aggressive tactics for which Tenant has proof will not be looked upon kindly by a judge, especially with a child involved, and could result in punishment or financial penalty.
10. Neither party has any family or support to speak of—a point of commonality.
11. Perhaps there are additional chores or activities Tenant and her son would be willing to do to stay in the home and end the conflict.
12. Encourage Tenant to look into housing programs throughout the city and to be put on as many lists as possible so she has options.

13. If Tenant were to leave, how much money would she need if she could find a new living arrangement?
14. If Landlord paid Tenant what she needed to vacate the home, how long would it take him to recoup that money from a new tenant?
15. Review the Mediator Neutrality Checklist (provided later in this chapter).

FLASH CHALLENGE QUESTIONS

Before you mediate the case (Flash Challenge: Mediate the Case! later in this chapter), answer the following Flash Challenge Questions based only on your reading of the preceding Mediation Example.

Flash Challenge Question #1: Considering the facts of this case, how might a mediator's struggle to maintain neutrality affect the way the mediator interacts with the parties and mediate the case?

Flash Challenge Question #2: Are there any elements within this conflict that may cause the mediator to feel compelled to state or reinforce a position? (See "A New Vision of Neutrality" later in this chapter.)

1. Provide your answer(s) in dialogue form.
2. Explain your position and thought process.

Flash Challenge Question #3: Pick three of the enumerated Mediator Thoughts. For each:

1. Discuss and expand.
2. Are there any conclusions you are able to draw?

There are pillars of mediation that bind us, and then there are the binding ties of a promise of effective and appropriate neutrality we as mediators make to the people we serve.
It is in the distinction that we find the definition of our purpose.

As a mediator, conflict interventionist, facilitator, or one who just wants to help when others are in conflict situations, it is important to understand where and how to draw the line between participant or disputant and the external party brought in to assist with conflict intervention. Although that line does not exist in the same place for everyone, and for some it is more of a constantly moving whispered guideline rather than a hard line drawn in the sand, it does exist somewhere and somehow, nonetheless. As individuals who step in to assist others during times of conflict, we must have a firm grasp of the boundaries we designate for ourselves as those that we will not cross, be they steadfast or pliable. To do that, a thorough consideration of various perspectives on the concept, presence, and validity of neutrality is critical.

It is reasonable and appropriate to assume that there will be disputants in conflict attempting a resolution process such as mediation who recognize that they need help and actually want it. The behavior of a mediator who is detached and unwilling to engage can have a negative impact on resolution attempts and leave disputants in the same or worse position than when they entered the room. For mediators to fail to use all of the mediation skills at their disposal or to assist in any way they can is not only unhelpful, but it can be harmful by creating more feelings of frustration and helplessness as the disputants receive no assistance in reaching settlement. Behaving appropriately in the role of mediator is a task of learning to implement conflict resolution skills to assist disputants, while maintaining a position that is unbiased, impartial, even-handed, and balanced. In other words, and as has been stated before, the mediator is on everyone's side, which inherently means not on one side over another, but equidistant between them. Becoming an "inside man" by allowing parties to share the details of their stories and subsequently asking probing questions to reach beneath the surface is not a breach of neutrality. Rather, it is an act of respect to demonstrate the desire to become as informed as possible and to be as helpful as possible in the most honest way available.

Neutrality is a position that exists in an ever-shifting space. As the neutral third party, a mediator seeks, finds, and interprets what a disputant might not—including maneuvering within the thinnest crevices of conflict where the mediator identifies potential opportunities to transform into common ground and settlement options that remain unrealized to those embroiled in dispute. A neutral line can cut through areas of conflict and emotion and stand as a guardian of safe space and protection. Disputants who believe unwaveringly that they are right and that "everyone will agree once they hear my side" might feel that mediation is pointless because "there is no way the conflict can be resolved because there will never be agreement about what happened or who is right, who is wrong, and who is at fault." However, these disputants are not factoring in the possibility of understanding each other without agreeing with each other. To be clear, understanding does not need to equate with acceptance or validation beyond the recognition that another party's position exists for them and will coexist within the context of the mediation process. The acknowledgment of such understanding presents an impetus with enough reason and opportunity for a mediator to begin working on creative solution strategies within their role as a neutral third party, there to assist all parties equally. When there are disputants on opposite ends of a dispute, input from a neutral in the form of questions or suggestions might be heard and interpreted differently than if that information was coming from the disputants themselves. Having a neutral position creates space for conversation where conflict does not lie. A neutral third party can receive information from one disputant and convey it to another in a manner that is devoid of emotion. In that context, that information can affect the other disputant in a new and different way. This delivery from the neutral may allow the disputant to finally hear a message that was otherwise getting lost in the emotional history of the conflict and its disputants. If by their actions mediators can prove continued neutrality and fairness, then disputants might be willing to interact differently with them than with opposing parties. This means that at last, and possibly for the first time, there can be a shift in the way the very same conflict is being addressed and thought about by the very same disputants. It is commonly agreed that when on the inside of a conflict it can be very difficult to see the issues clearly, including understanding true intentions, hearing what an opposing party in the conflict is saying, and judging the validity and propriety, or lack thereof, of one's own actions and behavior. A mediator can step into the very center of a conflict, into the combat zone, and not be swayed in one direction or another, remaining entirely neutral no matter what happens or what is said. The information they receive may be rich with details, impact, and shock value, but their neutrality will remain intact. They will carry and deliver messages, reframes, suggestions, and insight; they will clarify misunderstandings and yet still remain neutral.

One facet of neutrality that can pose difficulty for some disputants is understanding that it does not mean that the mediator will remain silent, refrain from asking questions, or not engage in conversations about their position. For example, if a mediator is using an Evaluative mediation style, they could be perceived by a disputant to be less than neutral. This, however, could not be further from the truth. Asking probing and reflective questions that encourage a disputant to take a hard look at their case and what could happen if they progress to litigation is a fundamental aspect of a mediator attempting to guide parties through the intricacies of their positions and options. As a rule, a mediator should explain to disputants immediately that they are on everyone's side equally, and that it is the job of the mediator to help disputants see the full picture of their situation, their BATNA, their WATNA, and the facts of the case as presented by all parties. If not explained properly, these actions could be misinterpreted as indicative of a mediator favoring one side over another. However, raising concerns, questioning statements disputants make, and discussing potentially unforeseen consequences could become parts of the only barrier to moving to litigation (see Appendix, "Mediation vs. Litigation"). Without making an effort to this effect, can mediators truly say that they have left disputants fully informed?

As a general rule, the neutral role of a mediator is interpreted to mean that the mediator shall:

1. Act in accordance with their third-party, nondisputant position.
2. Neither impede nor encourage any particular settlement decision of the disputants based on personal opinion or interpretation. This pertains to opinions and interpretations of settlement decisions identified by the mediator as being beneficial or detrimental to any or all disputants.

3. Conduct the mediation in a manner reflective of acknowledging the disputant-led nature of the process.
   a. The mediator will defer to party self-determination.
   b. The mediator shall act in a supporting role.
4. Refrain from intervening to alter any perceived or real disputant power imbalance.

This list is based on the belief that a neutral who abides by these rules is more fair, impartial, unbiased, objective, and rational. In actuality, though, the origins of the word *neutral* stem from being neither active, passive, nor disengaged, and the opposite of *neutral* is not *partial* or *partisan*, but actually *involved* or *engaged*.[1] A much better description of the mediator would be unbiased, impartial, even-handed, and balanced, reflected by their equal participation for and with all parties in a mediation. The mediator should endeavor to incorporate foundational tenets of mediation and the role of a mediator, such as the disputant-led nature of the process. Conflict specialists are recognizing that a shift toward and incorporation of a reconstructed description of neutrality is likely more responsive to party preferences.

Although there is no single concept of neutrality that is imposed in its entirety, nor is there a standardized application of consequences or penalties should a mediator not adhere to the ascribed definition of neutrality (conflict of interest issues aside), this chapter presents the ethical standards outlined by the American Arbitration Association, the American Bar Association's Section of Dispute Resolution, the Association for Conflict Resolution in the Model Standards of Conduct for Mediators, the National Conference of Commissioners on Uniform State Laws (NCCUSL) in the Uniform Mediation Act, and the California Rules of Court.

Whether a mediator is mediating a case that has already begun moving through the legal system, that is about to be heard by a judge, is in a private mediation, or is stepping in to assist when a conflict erupts, it is always appropriate to adopt guidelines and to adhere to ethical standards, specifically those surrounding impartiality, fairness, and acting in a balanced manner.

MODEL STANDARDS OF CONDUCT FOR MEDIATORS (2005)

The following are excerpts from the Model Standards of Conduct for Mediators (2005).

> These Standards are designed to serve as fundamental ethical guidelines for persons mediating in all practice contexts. They serve three primary goals: to guide the conduct of mediators; to inform the mediation parties; and to promote public confidence in mediation as a process for resolving disputes.[2]

1. Benjamin, R. D., "The Physics of Mediation: Reflections of Scientific Theory in Professional Mediation Practice," *Mediation Quarterly*, vol. 8, 1990.
2. Model Standards of Conduct for Mediators (2005), "Preamble."

Standard I: Self-determination

A. A mediator shall conduct a mediation based on the principle of party self-determination. Self-determination is the act of coming to a voluntary, uncoerced decision in which each party makes free and informed choices as to process and outcome. Parties may exercise self-determination at any stage of a mediation, including mediator selection, process design, participation in or withdrawal from the process, and outcomes.

1. Although party self-determination for process design is a fundamental principle of mediation practice, a mediator may need to balance such party self-determination with a mediator's duty to conduct a quality process in accordance with these Standards.
2. A mediator cannot personally ensure that each party has made free and informed choices to reach particular decisions, but, where appropriate, a mediator should make the parties aware of the importance of consulting other professionals to help them make informed choices.

B. A mediator shall not undermine party self-determination by any party for reasons such as higher settlement rates, egos, increased fees, or outside pressures from court personnel, program administrators, provider organizations, the media or others.

Standard II: Impartiality

A. A mediator shall decline a mediation if the mediator cannot conduct it in an impartial manner. Impartiality means freedom from favoritism, bias, or prejudice.

B. A mediator shall conduct a mediation in an impartial manner and avoid conduct that gives the appearance of partiality.

1. A mediator should not act with partiality or prejudice based on any participant's personal characteristics, background, values and beliefs, or performance at a mediation, or any other reason.
2. A mediator should neither give nor accept a gift, favor, loan, or other item of value that raises a question as to the mediator's actual or perceived impartiality.
3. A mediator may accept or give de minimis gifts or incidental items or services that are provided to facilitate a mediation or respect cultural norms so long as such practices do not raise questions as to a mediator's actual or perceived impartiality.

C. If at any time a mediator is unable to conduct a mediation in an impartial manner, the mediator shall withdraw.

Standard VI: Quality of the Process

A. A mediator shall conduct a mediation in accordance with these Standards and in a manner that promotes diligence, timeliness, safety, presence of the appropriate participants, party participation, procedural fairness, party competence and mutual respect among all participants.

10. If a party appears to have difficulty comprehending the process, issues, or settlement options, or difficulty participating in a mediation, the mediator should explore the circumstances and potential accommodations, modifications, or adjustments that would make possible the party's capacity to comprehend, participate, and exercise self-determination.

C. If a mediator believes that participants' conduct, including that of the mediator, jeopardizes conducting a mediation consistent with these Standards, a mediator shall take appropriate steps including, if necessary, postponing, withdrawing from, or terminating the mediation.

UNIFORM MEDIATION ACT (2003)

The following are excerpts from the Uniform Mediation Act (2003).

(a) Before accepting a mediation, an individual who is requested to serve as a mediator shall:

(1) make an inquiry that is reasonable under the circumstances to determine whether there are any known facts that a reasonable individual would consider likely to affect the impartiality of the mediator, including a financial or personal interest in the outcome of the mediation and an existing or past relationship with a mediation party or foreseeable participant in the mediation; and

(2) disclose any such known fact to the mediation parties as soon as is practical before accepting a mediation.

(b) If a mediator learns any fact described in subsection (a) (1) after accepting a mediation, the mediator shall disclose it as soon as is practicable.

[(g) A mediator must be impartial, unless after disclosure of the facts required in subsections (a) and (b) to be disclosed, the parties agree otherwise.]

CALIFORNIA RULES OF COURT

The following are excerpts from the California Rules of Court (revised January 1, 2013).

Rule 3.853 Voluntary participation and self-determination

(2) Respect the right of each participant to decide the extent of his or her participation in the mediation, including the right to withdraw from the mediation at any time; and

(3) Refrain from coercing any party to make a decision or to continue to participate in the mediation.

Advisory Committee Comment

Voluntary participation and self-determination are fundamental principles of mediation that apply both to mediations in which the parties voluntarily elect to mediate and to those in which the parties are required to go to mediation in a mandatory court mediation program or by court order. Although the court may order participants to attend mediation, a mediator may not mandate the extent of their participation in the mediation process or coerce any party to settle the case.

After informing the parties of their choices and the consequences of those choices, a mediator can invoke a broad range of approaches to assist the parties in reaching an agreement without offending the principles of voluntary participation and self-determination, including (1) encouraging the parties to continue participating in the mediation when it reasonably appears to the mediator that the possibility of reaching an uncoerced, consensual agreement has not been exhausted and (2) suggesting that a party consider obtaining professional advice (for example, informing an unrepresented party that he or she may consider obtaining legal advice). Conversely, examples of conduct that violate the principles of voluntary participation and self-determination include coercing a party to continue participating in the mediation after the party has told the mediator that he or she wishes to terminate the mediation, providing an opinion or evaluation of the dispute in a coercive manner or over the objection of the parties, using abusive language, and threatening to make a report to the court about a party's conduct at the mediation.

Rule 3.853 amended and renumbered effective January 1, 2007; adopted as rule 1620.3 effective January 1, 2003.

Rule 3.856 Impartiality, conflicts of interest, disclosure, and withdrawal

(a) Impartiality

A mediator must maintain impartiality toward all participants in the mediation process at all times.

(b) Disclosure of matters potentially affecting impartiality

(1) A mediator must make reasonable efforts to keep informed about matters that reasonably could raise a question about his or her ability to conduct the proceedings impartially, and must disclose these matters to the parties. These matters include:

(A) Past, present, and currently expected interests, relationships, and affiliations of a personal, professional, or financial nature;

(2) A mediator's duty to disclose is a continuing obligation, from the inception of the mediation process through its completion. Disclosures required by this rule must be made as soon as practicable after a mediator becomes aware of a matter that must be disclosed. To the extent possible, such disclosures should be made before the first mediation session, but in any event they must be made within the time required by applicable court rules or statutes.

(Subd (b) amended effective January 1, 2007.)

(c) Proceeding if there are no objections or questions concerning impartiality

Except as provided in (f), if, after a mediator makes disclosures, no party objects to the mediator and no participant raises any question or concern about the mediator's ability to conduct the mediation impartially, the mediator may proceed.

(Subd (c) amended effective January 1, 2007.)

(d) Responding to questions or concerns concerning impartiality

If, after a mediator makes disclosures or at any other point in the mediation process, a participant raises a question or concern about the mediator's ability to conduct the mediation impartially, the mediator must address the question or concern with the participants. Except as provided in (f), if, after the question or concern in addresses, no party objects to the mediator, the mediator may proceed.

(Subd (d) amended effective January 1, 2007.)

(f) Circumstances requiring mediator recusal despite party consent

Regardless of the consent of the parties, a mediator either must decline to serve as mediator or, if already serving, must withdraw from the mediation if:

(1) The mediator cannot maintain impartiality toward all participants in the mediation process; or

(2) Proceeding with the mediation would jeopardize the integrity of the court or of the mediation process.

Rule 3.855 amended and renumbered effective January 1, 2007; adopted as rule 1620.5 effective January 1, 2003.

Advisory Committee Comment

Subdivision (b). This subdivision is intended to provide parties with information they need to help them determine whether a mediator can conduct the mediation impartially. A mediator's overarching duty under this subdivision is to make a "reasonable effort" to identify matters that, in the eyes of a reasonable person, could raise a question about the mediator's ability to conduct impartially, and to inform the parties about those matters. What constitutes a "reasonable effort" to identify such matters varies depending on the circumstances, including whether the case is scheduled in advance or received on the spot, and the information about the participants and the subject matter that is provided to the mediator by the court and the parties.

Although (b)(1) specifies interest, relationships, affiliations, and matters that are grounds for disqualification of a judge under Code of Civil Procedure section 170.1, these are only examples of common matters that reasonably could raise a question about a mediator's ability to conduct the mediation impartially and, thus, must be disclosed. The absence of particular interests, relationships, affiliations, and section 170.1 matters does not necessarily mean that there is no matter that could reasonably raise a question about the mediator's ability to conduct the mediation impartially. A mediator must make determinations concerning disclosure on a case-by-case basis, applying the general criteria for disclosure under (b)(1).

Rule 3.857. Quality of mediation process

(b) Procedural Fairness

A mediator must conduct the mediation proceedings in a procedurally fair manner. "Procedural fairness" means a balanced process in which each party is given an opportunity to participate and make uncoerced decisions. A mediator is not obligated to ensure the substantive fairness of an agreement reached by the parties.

Rule 3.857 amended and renumbered effective January 1, 2007; adopted as rule 1620.7 effective January 1, 2003.

Advisory Committee Comment

Subdivision (c). The explanation of the mediation process should include a description of the mediator's style of mediation.

Subdivision (d). Subject to the principles of impartiality and self-determination, and if qualified to do so, a mediator may (1) discuss a party's options, including a range of possible outcomes in an adjudicative process; (2) offer a personal evaluation of or opinion on a set of facts as presented, which should be clearly identified as a personal evaluation or opinion; or (3) communicate the mediator's opinion or view of what the law is or how it applies to the subject of the mediation, provided that the mediator does not also advise any participant about how to adhere to the law or on what position the participant should take in light of that opinion.

One question that frequently arises is whether a mediator's assessment of claims, defenses, or possible litigation outcomes constitutes legal advice or the practice of law. Similar questions may arise when accounting, architecture, construction, counseling, medicine, real estate, or other licensed professions are relevant to a mediation. This rule does not determine what constitutes the practice of law or any other licensed profession. A mediator should be cautious when providing any information or opinion related to any field for which a professional license is required to avoid doing so in a manner that may constitute the practice of a profession for which the mediator is not licensed, or in a manner that may violate the regulations of a profession that the mediator is licensed to practice. A mediator should exercise particular caution when discussing the law with unrepresented parties and should inform such parties that they may seek independent advice from a lawyer.

Note to the Reader

There are ethical standards that are black and white, but there are also standards that are considered gray because they require adapting interpretation and application specific to each case. So, what do we do about the gray? Can we use the black and white to help us manage the gray? Where is the standard that outlines the specific moment party self-determination is breached? Granted that mediators are not permitted to stop disputants from making final decisions to agree to or reject a settlement, a mediator should act to ensure that all parties have at least a firm grasp of the settlement components, which can include a mediator-led discussion of elements of the settlement that might not meet the disputant's interests or needs. Does that blur the line in a necessary way? What about the line of neutrality? When is it crossed? If and when power imbalance precludes equally informed decisions about settlement, does the mediator's act to ensure that parties become equally informed cross that line or does it reasonably reposition it? Is it different for every mediator—based on their intent and specific delivery purpose—and for every disputant—based on their emotional state, case, and ultimate interpretation? With many standards positioned as guidelines and those guidelines requiring informed, thoughtful, and educated decisions by mediators and conflict interventionists, the answers rest on the framework of correct and appropriate choices. Understanding neutrality, mediator intervention, mediation styles, and exactly what individual disputants require, as well as the clear standards that bind mediators and mediation, will enable effective work within these prescribed guidelines.

APPLICATION OF ETHICAL STANDARDS

There are any number of circumstances that arise that could and should give a mediator pause:

1. Considering how best to proceed.
2. Weighing the consequences and ramifications of strategic decisions.
3. How to act in the best interest of:
   a. Disputants.
   b. The specific mediation.
   c. The mediation process overall.
   d. Neutrality.

Responses to the following scenarios and accompanying questions should reflect your understanding and personal interpretation of the excerpted ethical standards presented herein and a wide consideration of neutrality-related topics, such as creating fair and equal mediations (see "Power Imbalance" later in this chapter).

Scenario #1

You are mediating a landlord/tenant dispute. On one side is the landlord who is present, represented, informed about the law, and clearly experienced in such matters. On the other side you have a tenant who is without counsel, has never been in a situation like this before, and has demonstrated that he is uninformed, scared, and intimidated. The mediation is taking place in caucus, and the landlord has just said something to you that makes you pause.

The landlord has informed you that she is aware that the tenant has no idea that the law is on his side and that if they went to court the judge would almost certainly grant him substantially more than what she is offering now. Knowing that the tenant does not realize this, the landlord is planning on using his lack of knowledge to come out on top in the mediation settlement, which she is confident he will sign because he is intimidated and has no experience with the justice system in general.

As you leave her and return to confer with the tenant, you know you need to make a decision about how to proceed.

Questions for Scenario #1

1. Even though the tenant has not brought up counsel or asked you for an opinion, which could open the door for you to advise him to seek legal counsel to ask any questions, do you specifically express that it could be in his best interest to consult an attorney before he agrees to any settlement arrangement?
   a. Would doing so breach your impartiality and neutrality?
2. Do you allow the parties to agree on a settlement that is heavily skewed in favor of the landlord even though you also know that the tenant has the law on his side?
   a. Recall the position that a mediation is not in fact a mediation at all if a settlement is not as fair and balanced as possible with all parties informed and power balanced. Discuss your position.
3. Would speaking up about the imbalanced nature of the settlement breach your impartiality and neutrality?
4. Would not speaking up breach your impartiality and neutrality?
5. Do you find this a situation that needs to be managed at all, or do you simply proceed in the manner that they have chosen, including to settle?
6. How would you manage this situation?
7. If you were to consult any of the above ethical standards, how would they dictate that you proceed?
   a. Model Standards of Conduct for Mediators (2005)
   b. Uniform Mediation Act (2003)
   c. California Rules of Court
8. Do you agree with the positions the ethical standards represent? Why or why not?
   a. Model Standards of Conduct for Mediators 2005
   b. Uniform Mediation Act 2003
   c. California Rules of Court

Scenario #2

You are mediating a case between Disputant A and Disputant B. Disputant B is refusing to even entertain the idea of settlement because they know for sure that the judge will see it their way and that they will win in court. Disputant B is the owner of a small neighborhood restaurant that they have owned and operated for the past 40 years. They came to the United States with nothing and worked tirelessly every day that they have been here, seven days a week, to build a life for themself and their family that is entirely supported and made possible by their beloved restaurant. However, this is an Americans with Disabilities Act case, and you know that the law is not on their side.

Disputant A has never been through the legal system before, there are no "repeat-player" concerns, and they can prove everything they are saying.

You are mediating in caucus, and no matter how many times you have reminded Disputant B that they have the right to seek legal counsel, the answer remains that they have no interest in doing so and there is no need, because "we will win in court." You have worked hard to bring together a settlement that blends monetary and nonmonetary components, and is one that you believe is fair, but more important, it is a substantially more favorable settlement for Disputant B than one they could and most likely would be facing from a court ruling. Unfortunately, try as you might to discuss the comparisons between mediation and litigation, BATNA and WATNA, and possible settlement outcomes, Disputant B will not budge. Even when you try to discuss the importance of the restaurant to the health and well-being of the family and emphasize that they could lose everything as a possible consequence of an adjudicated decision, Disputant B is not swayed by your efforts.

You find yourself feeling desperate about their lack of understanding. You are also becoming increasingly aware that your personal history, which bears strong similarities to their family story, might be affecting your ability to remain as neutral as you should be. While that has only manifested internally for you at this point, Disputant B's unwillingness to hear reason, combined with your desperation and family history, could be beginning to affect your own behavior and decisions.

Questions for Scenario #2

1. According to the ethical standards above, can the mediator advise a disputant about how to adhere to the law or what position they should take when they are unrepresented?
    a. Would it matter if the party knew the law and began to discuss it with the mediator?
    b. Can the mediator suggest that a disputant look up the law right there on their cellphone?
        i. Would this be considered advising parties to seek counsel? Or would this be more akin to giving legal advice?
2. Do you allow yourself to continue on as you have been until Disputant B recognizes what you are attempting to express to them, or until both sides deem an impasse and quit the mediation?
3. Do you take a moment to step out and consult your Mediator Neutrality Checklist?
    a. If you realize that you are not able to maintain your neutrality:
        i. Will you be able to accept their decision about settlement or impasse?
        ii. Will you be able to remove yourself as mediator from the mediation?
4. According to the ethical standards outlined above, are you trampling on Disputant B's right to self-determination if you carry the conversation beyond the information that you have provided thus far?

   a. Are you able to accept that self-determination is a double-edged sword?
   b. Will you be able to remain removed from both disputants' actions as they self-determine?
      i. According to the ethical standards, must you?
5. Do the feelings and actions described thus far depict a mediator who has managed to maintain neutrality in spite of the situation and including their personal history?
6. Is there a tangible line that a mediator should not cross when a party expresses that they will or will not accept a settlement offer, even when pressing on would be in their very best interest?
7. Where is the line between a mediator's role, including doing everything possible to see the best outcome for all parties, and a disputant's ability to make choices even if those choices will bring harm to themself that the mediator sees coming?
   a. Is there a line at all?

Scenario #3: Lightning Round!

1. **Public Safety:** You are mediating a case between a manufacturer of surgical supplies and the daughter of a deceased recipient of one of their products, whose death was a direct result of defective dissolving sutures that were used during surgery. The manufacturer is eager to settle and is willing to pay in the high six figures to keep the detrimental information about the defective sutures confidential and out of the public arena.
   a. Considerations
      i. **Confidentiality**: The confidentiality that mediation and a mediated settlement afford will not expose the defective sutures to the public and will most likely result in additional deaths. The company has made it very clear that they have no intention of making any public announcements, as it is more financially advantageous for them to pay out on an individual and as-needed basis. The confidentiality will also prohibit all parties from discussing any part of the mediation with anyone not directly participating in it; and it also specifically bars any disclosure of a financial settlement agreement, effectively stopping any communication with or guidance for other potential victims.
      ii. **Public Health and Safety:**
         1. Is the issue of public health and safety within the purview of a mediator?
         2. Should a case involving public health and safety be mediated at all if that means it will remain confidential?
      iii. **Proof**: Whether or not the defective sutures will affect anyone else is not in question. They absolutely will and possibly already have, as noted in internal documents and emails confirming the use of the

defective sutures during dozens of previously performed surgical procedures. The documents and emails also confirm that the company's position is to take no action unless an occurrence of harm from use of defective sutures is brought to them, at which point it will be handled in mediation notwithstanding cost of payout(s).

2. **Emotional Joint Session:** You are mediating a case in joint session and as one of the disputants describes their experience, you begin to cry. You did not cry when the other party detailed their story.
3. **Playing Games:** You are mediating a case and as the day progresses it becomes clear that Disputant A is purposefully negotiating in small financial increments to drive up the settlement, simultaneously threatening to refuse to settle and to take the case to court. In caucus with Disputant A, when you asked for an explanation of their negotiation strategy, it was disclosed to you that they were "having fun" seeing how much they could get out of Disputant B. Disputant A went on to disclose to you that they did not care about the numbers—having already met and surpassed their target amount—and would be fine settling at any point and definitely will, as they had no true intention to end up in court. However, currently having fun at Disputant B's expense and getting as much money as possible is their new chosen course of action.

   Meeting with Disputant B in caucus, you are able to see just how much they are suffering under the threat of litigation as well as trying to come up with the money to meet Disputant A's settlement demands. They are visibly upset and are discussing canceling their medical insurance and using the small amount of money set aside for their children's college funds to afford the financial demands of Disputant A. Disputant B continues to ask, "Is this enough?" as they cobble together small amounts of money to negotiate back to Disputant A.

   You know (confidentially) with certainty that all Disputant B has to do is refuse to pay any more money, in which case Disputant A would agree and the case would be settled and over with. However, as you learned about this information in caucus, you are not permitted to disclose any of it. Disputant A is not operating or negotiating in good faith any longer, and Disputant B is unnecessarily suffering an outcome that most likely would become improved and therefore preferable if they did, in fact, go to court.
4. **Winning Streak:** You are mediating a case and before walking in the door you have decided that you will bring the case to a settled agreement no matter what. It would be such a shame for your winning streak of mediated cases reaching settlement to end. Also, you have noticed that mediators working for the same firm as you include their settled cases statistics in their online bios and the firm has an unwritten policy of sending more cases to mediators with the best settlement track records. As it is clear that the higher the number of settled cases, the better, you have also come to realize that those statistics matter to disputants in their consideration of who to hire.

Questions for Scenario #3: Lightning Round!

1. **Public Safety**
   a. Do the considerations change any of your answers to questions posed in Public Health and Safety section?
   b. Would and should a mediator's decision be different depending on whether or not there is irrefutable proof of impending public harm?
   c. Should there be a decision made to hold the manufacturer accountable in a public setting to force them to change their policies on issues such as this one?
      i. Could this also be an important action to use to deter other manufacturers from behaving in the same manner that does not prioritize public health and safety?
         1. Should this be an internal consideration at all for a mediator, or is it completely outside the bounds of the role? Discuss.
            a) Does the idea of a mediator acting with the best interest of the public in mind instead of the parties go against mediation's intention for the mediator to assist parties in finding a settlement that is in their best interests if taking that action results in a mediated outcome that goes against the best interests of one or both parties?
2. **Emotional Joint Session**
   a. Does showing this level of emotion automatically depict the mediator as partial and biased toward that disputant?
   b. Does it matter that the crying happened in response to only one of the disputants?
   c. What would be your answer if the mediator had cried when hearing both parties speak?
   d. Is crying a level of emotion that is fundamentally too great for a mediator to be expressing at any point during a mediation?
      i. Is it indicative that they have become too involved and emotionally invested to be considered a neutral third party any longer?
   e. Is it possible to remain impartial and still express emotion?
   f. Is expressing emotion in mediation appropriate or is emotion expressed in any and all ways inappropriate?
      i. Identify categories of appropriately expressed emotion, if any, as opposed to inappropriately expressed emotion, including your explanations for each.
3. **Playing Games**
   a. Would the mediator be maintaining impartiality and adhering to mediation guidelines if they were to tell Disputant B to stop offering more money?
      i. Because Disputant A has already broken the rules of mediation in that they are not negotiating in good faith, is it then acceptable to advise Disputant B?

   ii. Would it be acceptable to advise Disputant B if Disputant A had not disclosed anything to the mediator and, other than a sense the mediator might have, that Disputant B's true intentions were unclear?

b. Is there a particular way the mediator could encourage or gently lead Disputant B to realize on their own that they could at least try saying "No" to see what happens?
   i. Provide some examples of what the mediator could say to Disputant B.
c. Could the mediator speak to Disputant A, reminding them that their behavior does not adhere to guidelines for acting in good faith and is not appropriate for the mediation process? Could Disputant A be further advised that their behavior and negotiating strategy will not provide for a fair and balanced settlement outcome?
   i. Could Disputant A interpret this action as partial toward Disputant *B*?
   ii. Do you believe it is the mediator's responsibility to step in when there are behaviors and actions taken by parties that do not uphold the values of the mediation process such as negotiating in good faith?
      1. If so, explain.
      2. If not, explain.
   iii. What could the mediator say to Disputant A? What might this conversation sound like? Provide examples.
   iv. Do you believe the responsibility lies with disputants to speak up or to refuse to continue in a mediation if this type of bad faith behavior, or something similar to it, is happening?

4. **Winning Streak**
   a. Is the mediator breaching neutrality if they decide that a mediated settlement is best and work toward it immediately without waiting to form this opinion until after learning about the case and the positions of the parties with regard to their interests?
   b. Should the mediator consult disputants to determine if they desire a mediated settlement agreement?
   c. Is it appropriate for a mediator to always work toward a mediated settlement agreement?
   d. If a disputant informs the mediator that they do not plan to settle in mediation because they believe their case must go to court for reasons other than financial gain, is it appropriate for the mediator to attempt to convince them that settling in mediation is still the best option?
      i. What if their reason to go to court is for financial gain? Is it appropriate for the mediator to attempt to convince them that settling in mediation is still the best option?
   e. Is it appropriate for a firm to incentivize mediators to settle cases?
      i. Does this set a bad precedent that might preclude disputant wishes?
   f. Should the practice of including settlement statistics in mediator bios as a method of advertising stop?

i. If so, why?
ii. If not, why not?

Concluding Questions

1. Is there a consistency to your answers to the above questions for Scenarios 1-3?
2. If not, does that indicate that your answers are being guided by internal cognitive biases?
   a. Which of your answers may indicate cognitive biases?
   b. Which cognitive biases can you detect?
      i. Within yourself?
         1. Once you detected and properly addressed your bias(es), did it cause you to change any of your answers?
         2. If not, discuss.
      ii. Expressed by the parties?
3. How might your answers differ if they were not affected by any biases?
4. Is it acceptable to respond differently depending on the specifics of a situation, or does that automatically imply a lack of impartiality or bias?

POWER IMBALANCE

Deeply ingrained in the discussion of mediator neutrality is the issue of disputant power imbalance. The following discussion points outline various perspectives focusing on whether or not mediator involvement in addressing power imbalance is an act that crosses the line away from neutrality and into partiality and advocacy. For some mediators and conflict interventionists, there are perspectives and corresponding positions that are definitive. However, as this topic evolves and grows in relevance, for others the answers are situationally dependent. Contributing to the framework of this conversation are these questions:

1. Can neutrality and action toward balancing power imbalances coexist?
2. Can neutrality and inaction toward balancing power imbalances coexist?
3. Is a mediator's neutrality defined by this action or inaction?
4. Should balancing power among disputants be intrinsic to the position of neutral?
5. Should balancing power among disputants be definitively excluded from the definition of neutral?
6. Does a neutral's ability to properly mediate depend on whether or not disputant powers are balanced?

The question remains: Can and should power imbalance mitigation be discretionary on the part of the neutral?

DISCUSSION POINTS AND POSITIONS FROM THE CONFLICT INTERVENTION COMMUNITY: MEDIATOR NEUTRALITY WITHIN THE CONTEXT OF POWER IMBALANCE

1. Is it only by the mediator's act of balancing power imbalance(s) that a true mediation is accomplished?
   a. If there is a power imbalance between disputants, and the mediator does nothing, an agreed-upon settlement cannot be fair. This is supported by the claim that a mediation represents a process culminating in a collaborated settlement that takes into consideration collective interests and needs, supported by an equivalent understanding of facts and options among disputants. How, though, can a disputant with less power, skill, knowledge, and understanding really have a seat at that table?
      i. One solution for this particular dilemma is to offer pre-mediation power-balancing sessions with each disputant.[3] During these sessions, the mediator will meet individually with the disputants to assist them in better understanding their position, how they can behave in the mediation, consideration of their options, possible strategy, and the mediation process overall.
         1. During a pre-mediation session, disputants may also be given the opportunity to express and release some of their more volatile frustrations without any other disputant present, thereby causing no harm or detrimental ramifications of words said and statements expressed. Participating in such a session can be helpful later during joint session when tensions may be raised by sheer virtue of the parties being in one another's presence. The theory suggests that the release beforehand might help disputants maintain composure during the mediation, and for disputants to have moved through enough emotion to allow for discussions driven by reason and logic instead.
2. Does addressing and intervening in power imbalance invalidate neutrality? Can a mediator take steps to equalize the distribution of power in a mediation in such a way that they can still be seen as unbiased and as not taking one side over another?
   a. The conversation in response to these questions hovers around the true definition of how a mediator represents neutrality, as well as whether balancing power in and of itself equates to taking one side over another.
   b. Is the mediator instantly no longer neutral the moment they attempt to assist a less powerful disputant in a way that could alter an existing balance of power?

3. Hansen, Silke, "Civil Rights Mediation Oral History Project," The Community Relations Services, Conflict Management Initiatives and University of Colorado Conflict Resolution Consortium, www.civilrightsmediation.org

3. Is the role of mediator upheld and preserved if it is multidimensional, encompassing neutrality and impartiality expressed at different times and in different ways?
    a. If the mediator acts in a way that is outside of the general understanding of neutral, but is still impartial, objective, and fair, then the mediator is still acting in the capacity of the third-party neutral because their behavior is still part of the multidimensional understanding that is mediator neutrality.
4. Should mediators and mediation organizations dedicate more time explaining to disputants:
    a. Mediator neutrality
        i. What is and is not included under the umbrella of neutrality?
            1. This discussion of mediator neutrality should include preparing the disputants for potential engagement from the mediator, who will not necessarily remain silent, but will always remain impartial, balanced, and even-handed.
            2. If the mediator plans to intervene should a power imbalance present itself, that conversation can be included in the introduction of mediation during an opening statement.
    b. Expectations from the mediation process and from the mediator specifically so that actions taken are not at any point misconstrued as biased?
        i. Discussing with disputants at the beginning of mediation that what they can expect from the mediator throughout the process could be beneficial to ensuring that all parties are clear about what is going to happen. This can also avoid any questions about mediator behavior down the line.
        ii. Included in the initial conversation about the mediator's role could be certain activities that the mediator may recommend to address any potential disputant power imbalances. The mediator might choose not to frame it in this way, but laying a foundation of what to expect in front of all parties together in the same room could be an excellent strategy.
        iii. This activity can be presented as a standard operating procedure and protection for all involved parties so that no one can say later that they were not made aware of what they were signing, as would be done for any contract. This is also a power-balancing activity in disguise. (See Chapter 4, "Conflict Handling Modes.")
        iv. For example:
            1. That the mediator may confirm mutually agreed-upon ground rules should the parties begin to act in a way that contradicts them.
            2. That the mediator may work to shift Communication Styles and Conflict Handling Modes (CHMs) that are having detrimental impact on the mediation.

3. That the mediator may detail how their settlement process works and that it may include discussing with each disputant the potential ramifications of what agreeing or not agreeing to the settlement might be for them. This may include eventually dissecting and evaluating each part of a proposed settlement point by point, and not moving on from one point to the next until the mediator is certain that each disputant thoroughly understands exactly what they may or may not be agreeing to.

c. The difference between the theory and practice of mediator neutrality?

i. The transformation between the theory of neutrality and neutrality in practice determines the true definition of neutrality. If not in practice, it is just words on paper that do not account for disputant needs, intricacies of cases, and the nuanced and complicated layers of human interaction and emotion. Therefore, it is after neutrality is put into practice that its true and individualized (to mediators and disputants) definition is formed.

5. Why is there an acceptable difference between a disputant power imbalance in mediation and a party in litigation who can afford a better legal team than their counterpart—a team that creates a power imbalance skewed in their favor?

a. In this situation, does the judge, jury, or legal system have an obligation either to do nothing about this clear power imbalance or to do something to rectify it?

b. Is the judge less than neutral when they ask one party or the other if they understand something?

i. If a settlement agreement is being read into the record, it is procedure for a judge to ask all parties to confirm that they understand the terms.

c. And by the way, should there be a difference in acceptability between the more formal process of litigation and the less formal process of mediation? In the more formal process of litigation, should there be increased acceptability standards making a power imbalance unacceptable even if it would be acceptable in mediation?

i. If so, what steps can and should be taken to rectify power imbalance in litigation?

1. Does this cause issues of legality?

6. If it is outside the bounds of neutrality for mediators to assist in the balancing of power, should disputants have advocates present during mediations to assist with this particular issue? (See Prefatory Information, Chapter 2, "ADR Advocates.")

a. Relieving the mediator of the necessity to consider and act when power imbalance becomes apparent could be beneficial to this part of the neutrality debate.

FLASH CHALLENGE

What Do You Think?

1. Based on the discussion points, discuss your thoughts on mediator neutrality.
   a. What should the definition of neutrality be?
2. Include your thoughts on disputant power imbalances.
   a. What, if anything, should be done about it?
      i. By the mediator?
      ii. By someone other than the mediator?
   b. If you believe nothing should be done, explain your position.

MEDIATOR NEUTRALITY FROM THE PERSPECTIVE OF THE DISPUTANTS

A cross-section of disputants stated that their primary concern was that the mediator should:

1. Be fair.
2. Be honest.
3. Be trustworthy.
4. Not take any side over another.
5. Listen to what they had to say.
6. Genuinely care about helping them.
7. Not act as an uninvolved spectator.

COGNITIVE BIASES

With the intention to provide information and wiggle room for individual creative thinking, concept development, and personal and professional growth, when it comes to cognitive biases this book focuses on definition, effects, and management. This focus is specifically for the purpose of becoming acquainted with both sides of the cognitive bias issue – cognitive biases affecting the mediator and those affecting the disputants – as well as with the goal of proper mediator conduct.

A conversation about cognitive biases and mediation often takes place when discussing disputants' behavior in situations of impasse (see Chapter 10, "Managing Impasse"), or generally during the mediation process. There are cognitive biases that mediators should be aware of, as they could also be affected, which could become problematic for a mediator's ability to maintain neutrality in the proper performance of their role. Naturally, there will be some overlap of cognitive biases that affect disputants as well as mediators, with outcomes that might or might not differ, but are nevertheless inappropriate and need to be properly addressed and managed. In no uncertain terms, a mediator exhibiting any form of bias is a problem; however, with proper identification and understanding, a mediator may be able to move past or set aside a bias and continue in an impartial manner for the duration of a mediation. The argument routinely bounces between two schools of thought:

1. Biases can be removed completely.
2. Biases can never be removed completely and instead require proper management.

COGNITIVE BIASES POSSIBLY AFFECTING MEDIATORS

The Halo Effect

The halo effect[4] occurs when an impression of a person, including their character and their physical appearance, has a direct impact on the way they are treated. For example, a mediator could become biased toward a particular disputant they find believable, attractive, or familiar—the mediator identifies traits or characteristics they share in common with the disputant. The bias could also cause a mediator to find a disputant believable because they find them attractive, for example. In other words, the assessment of one characteristic or trait as favorable or appealing can extend to other characteristics or traits such as truthfulness. This is an error in reasoning and could be indicative of additional errors in reasoning, which is inappropriate for a mediator whose job includes providing rational assistance. A mediator finding a disputant believable and truthful is not innately good or bad; it really does not matter. The problem arises when a mediator begins to act according to their interpretations and biases, in this case based on the halo effect. This also includes negative feelings they might have developed toward a party sitting on the other side of a disputant who has earned their favor. Both sides of this bias are unacceptable and could drastically affect the way in which a mediator behaves toward disputants and performs in their role as an impartial third party.

It can be extremely difficult to remain balanced and supportive of all parties when the mediator has developed a negative impression of a disputant as a result of the halo effect. (As an aside, whether or not the negative impression is an inaccurate result caused by the halo effect or is supported by a disputant's behavior, the mediator must still act in accordance with being bound by resistance to this impression.) Maintaining an awareness that the halo effect could be inappropriately altering their perception of the disputants—a clear obstacle to performing their responsibilities—should cause the mediator to consciously uphold the core values and fundamental tenets of the mediation process by remaining balanced and unbiased toward all parties. The mediator can utilize tools such as these:

1. Reminding themself of their role as a mediator, and the proper behavior associated with that position.

4. Thorndike, Edward, "The Constant Error in Psychological Ratings," 1920.

2. The Mediator Neutrality Checklist (presented later in this chapter).
3. Becoming mentally aware of a bias and counteracting it by acknowledging it to themself and not allowing it to influence or affect any statements made or actions taken.
4. Stepping out of the mediation to take breaks in order to maintain or regain their composure.
5. Allowing themself the space to accept terminating their role as mediator. It is never acceptable to sacrifice impartiality merely to stay on the job.

Racial or Gender Biases: Generally Defined by Social Construction

Racial bias is the preference, unequal, and unfair treatment (favoritism) of one race over another without any considerations other than race or perceived race, resulting in overall inequality. *Gender bias* is the preference, unequal, and unfair treatment (favoritism) of one gender over another without any considerations other than gender or perceived gender, resulting in overall inequality.

It is important to keep in mind that mediators and conflict professionals are human like everyone else, so it would be shortsighted to assume that simply because they act in a role as a neutral or impartial conflict interventionist that they do not carry with them certain biases. The majority of people do in one form or another. There are many factors that contribute to the creation of a bias, including lifelong experiences, isolated incidents, childhood upbringing, and cultural background. Racial and gender biases are two particular biases that are, unfortunately, part of the fabric of our society. They have long been overlooked in the construction and functioning of our daily lives. During a mediation, however, it is critical for a mediator not only to be aware of these possible biases, but to be in charge of them. Biases have a way of inserting themselves into statements and actions, often leaving an individual none the wiser until after the fact. It is never more important to be in control of any bias than when acting in the capacity of an impartial conflict interventionist brought in to assist with communication and possible resolution. The insertion of racial or gender bias from a neutral could have both immediate and deep, long-lasting impacts on the conflict and the disputants involved. The disputants' ability to shift into effective communication as well as their ability to function toward conflict resolution might be derailed as now there could be added to the conflict a new layer of mistrust toward any individual there to provide assistance.

To combat any real or perceived bias, mediators must ensure that their statements and actions are as equally balanced as possible toward all parties. This can become tricky, however, when CHMs and Communication Styles factored into the equation require a possible change in tone, behavior, or content from the mediator, thereby creating an instant disparity between the ways in which they interact with the disputants. Of paramount importance is that the mediator's change in behavior is reflective only of that need to interact with each disputant in the way dictated by their individual CHM and Communication Style and not relating to gender or racial identity. By the mediator remaining focused on what the conflict requires, the facts of the case, the various needs of the parties, and their wishes regarding resolution, there should be very little room for a racial or gender bias to present itself. If, however, a mediator begins to sense that they might be influenced by a bias, they should certainly take a moment to reflect on how to proceed, including referring to the Mediator's Neutrality Checklist at the very least, and removing themself as mediator at the utmost.

If a disputant identifies either a perceived or real racial or gender bias from a mediator, two scenarios could follow: The first is the possibility that the disputant could increase aggressivity toward an opposing disputant by misdirecting anger that should rightfully be pointed at the mediator, or become so upset, understandably, that they refuse to proceed with that mediator or with any mediation process at all. The second is that they will express their recognition of the bias to the mediator and choose to engage in an open dialogue about it. This scenario is preferable to the first in that it could allow the mediation to proceed. As biases can be either conscious (purposeful) or unconscious (implicit), a conversation between a disputant and a mediator about a bias could be productive and informative for all parties to the conversation. It could also build a layer of trust between the disputant and the mediator as they engage in what could be a difficult, vulnerable, emotional, and often highly polarizing topic. A conversation can provide the opportunity for a disputant to express their feelings, provide possible clarity, and furnish information to the mediator regarding their perception of and experience with race or gender relations. Boundaries can be created that the mediator will need to respect to continue with honest and productive conversation and a fruitful mediation. Indeed, many of these points sound difficult, to say the least, and scary to purposefully engage in, but the benefits of doing so can outweigh the discomfort along the way. Although not all mediations will require this level of depth in relationship-building between disputants and mediators, some will, making it an important skill that can result in a mediator's ability to manage that depth. The more skilled a mediator becomes at engaging in open dialogue with disputants, including their own real or perceived biases, the better they will become at controlling the timing and depth of necessary conversations, enabling parties to refocus on the conflict and to set a mediation back on track.

Note to the Reader

While the preceding discussion of gender and racial bias is directed through the lens of mediator neutrality and biases possibly affecting mediators, these important open dialogue steps are equally applicable when mediating discrimination cases. Concerns about how to mediate such disputes are warranted, as these can involve many layers of conflict and pain with seemingly unattainable solutions. Although this might hold true for some cases, as it could for any category of conflict, it does not have to. Building into mediations safe, controlled spaces for disputants to express their experiences, feelings, grief, and what they might need to move forward can be constructive and beneficial. Simultaneously, an opposing party will be listening, perhaps for the first time, to these expressions. There are often miscommunications, misunderstandings, a lack of sensitivity or empathy, and an inability to grasp the magnitude of impact that words and actions can have. A mediator should keep an eye toward creating a revised understanding and form of communication among disputants that has the potential to correct these circumstances, and this combination of expression and listening within the confines of the mediator's facilitation can enable that forward movement. Establishing ground rules early in the mediation, including prohibiting specific language and behaviors that are inappropriate, could contribute to the creation of the interaction style necessary to enable a new atmosphere among the parties. Having an ADR Advocate's Representative present could also be valuable when one (or more) party feels victimized or disadvantaged and might find comfort in additional support.

FLASH CHALLENGE

Where Do You Stand?

1. Familiarize yourself with the various Cognitive Biases (see Chapter 10 for a complete list) and discuss your position:
   a. Biases can be removed completely.
   b. Biases can never be removed completely and instead require proper management.
2. If you believe the answer lies somewhere between these two ends of the spectrum, explain and provide examples.

FLASH CHALLENGE

I Am Biased

1. Come up with a small fact pattern or scenario in which there is a conflict with at least two sides or opinions and room for discussion about the topic. Consider a conflict you have engaged in personally, one that you have witnessed, or a scenario that may have been reported on the news.
2. Select at least one of the cognitive biases discussed above and engage in a conversation as a mediator who demonstrates that bias in their response(s).
3. Before you begin each discussion, keep your chosen bias a secret from those who are listening. It will be up to them to guess which one is being demonstrated when the discussion has concluded.
4. Your audience can ask as many questions as they like in their quest to figure out your bias, and your answers should be representative of a mediator speaking through the lens of the bias.

MAINTAINING IMPARTIALITY

Let it not be said that remaining impartial, unbiased, and unaffected is not without its challenges. When in a mediation with a conflict that is familiar or resembles a past experience, or when there is a clear injustice unfolding before them, it can become extraordinarily difficult for a mediator to maintain the tenets of third-party impartiality and remain an even-handed neutral. What about mediations that are gut-wrenching, terribly sad, and difficult to listen to without becoming emotional? Mediators will likely face challenges that push them to struggle to maintain their neutrality. Being confronted with situations that shake one's resolve in this regard can be concerning and anxiety-inducing for mediators. Having a mental list of questions and statements to turn to when managing neutrality and feeling emotionally vulnerable and concerned about whether or not they can continue performing their role as an impartial mediator can be extremely beneficial.

MEDIATOR NEUTRALITY CHECKLIST

1. Am I able to see beyond the specific and bias-provoking issues in this conflict to assist and facilitate the communication process?
    a. Managing personal biases involves asking:
        i. Do I have adequate awareness of potential personal biases?
        ii. What am I basing my decisions on while acting as mediator or conflict interventionist?
        iii. How can I push back against my biases? If you sense that your decisions and actions are being affected by personal biases, question them and check in with yourself.
        iv. Consult your Mediator Neutrality Checklist.
2. Are the issues too personal or sensitive for me?
    a. It could be possible that the content of a conflict involves disputants discussing topics that are of an intensely personal or sensitive nature that could cause the mediator to become uncomfortable working with such information. It could also be that the topics revealed are too similar to issues the mediator might have in their personal life. Either could lead to a mediator becoming uncomfortable in their ability to proceed in a neutral fashion.
3. Can I separate myself, my feelings, and my experiences from this current conflict and these current disputants?
4. Am I involving myself in this conflict too much and taking it personally?
5. Are any of my words expressing my personal feelings about the issues that are being presented?
6. Am I relating too much to a particular disputant and therefore inadvertently favoring one side over another?
7. Can I provide impartial assistance, encouragement, and leadership as needed by the disputants?
8. Am I having any emotions that are becoming too strong to keep separated from my job performance?

9. Am I upset?
   a. Sad
   b. Mad
   c. Frustrated
   d. Hostile
   e. Agitated
10. Am I taking up a cause by engaging in this mediation?
11. Am I advocating for any particular position?
12. Am I attempting to sway any disputant positions for the benefit of a position I believe in?
13. Am I becoming invested in this mediation concluding one way or another?
14. Am I comfortable taking this mediation to settlement, should that be what the disputants desire?
15. Am I comfortable proceeding as mediator, or do I wish I were somewhere else?
16. Am I uncomfortable and questioning my abilities to proceed?
17. Can I empathize with this disputant even though and in spite of the fact that they . . . .

Answering *yes* to any one of these questions does not automatically necessitate removing oneself from the mediation. It would, however, require taking the time to think about which questions are met with a *yes* answer, whether or not those feelings have affected the mediation thus far, and whether they can be addressed in a way that sustains proper mediator decorum. Confronting issues that result in affirmative responses to the questions and statements above could help develop the skills that take power out of topics that can affect mediators, thereby fortifying the wall of impartiality between third-party neutral and disputant.

FLASH CHALLENGE

Are You Neutral?

1. Choose a topic you feel passionately about. It should be a well-known topic in which two sides are represented.
   a. Examples: Death penalty, abortion, climate change, vaccination mandates
2. Now ask two people to participate in a discussion about your chosen topic, each defending a side.
   a. They should know enough about the topic with developed opinions to engage in a full discussion.
3. You will mediate their discussion, reframing and facilitating to assist them to:
   a. Hear each other.
   b. Listen respectfully.
   c. Understand what the other is saying, including expressing the reason(s) for their position.

4. The mediation could include creative ideas about how to better communicate and discuss the issue between the two of them, as well as on a larger scale.
   a. Can you reach a point where mutual brainstorming can ensue?
5. When the mediation is complete, ask the participants:
   a. Did you, as mediator, maintain your neutrality?
   b. Did they interpret any part of your behavior as less than neutral?
      i. If so, ask them for specificity in describing your actions.
         1. Acting as a balanced mediator, do you agree that those specific actions were outside the lines of neutrality?
   c. Were there any times that they wished you had acted more:
      i. Aggressively
      ii. Compassionately
      iii. Controlling of the situation
      iv. Quietly
      v. Removed from the conflict so they could discuss something themselves without your input
6. Your concluding thoughts:
   a. Draft a description of the topic you chose specifically detailing your position and thoughts on the matter.
   b. Immediately follow with a description of how you were able to balance your personal position with your need to remain neutral.
   c. If you were not able to remain neutral, explain how and why you should correct your behavior next time.

A NEW VISION OF NEUTRALITY

What if disputants have a need or desire to remain in conflict? Should mediators and conflict interventionists be viewed as able to assist parties engaged in conflict when the goal of one or both disputants is not to conclude the mediation with a settlement or resolution in any traditionally recognized form? Are they capable of performing in that capacity? The answer must be *yes* to all of the above. In his 2004 book *Beyond Neutrality*, Bernard Mayer presented additions to the established concept of a conflict resolver, challenging the boundaries within which neutrals have regularly operated. This shift moves away from acting exclusively to resolve a mediation with a settlement agreement regardless of options that might be more favorable and preferred by the parties. Although not all mediators and conflict interventionists are comfortable with the prospect of expanding their role within the conflict intervention framework, the idea of intervention as opposed to resolver only inherently implies the concept of *more.* That more is a necessary consideration when determining the manner and extent of interaction with parties and conflicts. When a disputant's desired end goal is other than a mediated settlement agreement, a mediator should be prepared to work with that disputant on their terms and toward their chosen outcome. For example, in a case involving workplace racism, it would not be inappropriate for a mediator to reinforce the position that racism is never acceptable and racist behavior should always be addressed and remedied. This intervention from the mediator might permit the aggrieved party's true interest and mediation goal to be met, which could be contrary to their original demands that initiated the need for mediation. Their true goal may be only to receive the assistance of a neutral third party to engage in a very difficult conversation and to develop an improved way of communicating as they move forward. Prior to the mediator's intervention, this would have appeared to them to be unattainable. This verbalized position against racism represents an expansion of the traditional concept of mediator neutrality while remaining concomitant with elements of traditionally defined neutrality such as impartiality. Providing assistance to those in conflict comes in varying forms, and to address that reality, so, too, should the skills, creativity, strengths, and neutrality of mediators.

Expanding the Role

It has already been established that it is not appropriate for a mediator to enter into every mediation or conflict with a preexisting plan to settle the case no matter what, without consulting the parties about their positions on resolution. There are times and issues that require and are best served by other means of conflict management, inclusive of better communication and better conflict behaviors. How does this translate to a mediator or conflict interventionist? You will remember that a baseline skill for a mediator is the ability to manage and facilitate communication during times of conflict. During mediations, that description expands to include possibly bringing parties to a mutually agreeable settlement by using creative solution options. However, less widely discussed are the skills that enable a mediator to assist disputants in maintaining a conflict (not working toward resolution) and engaging in the communication process in a way that enables the parties to speak to each other more respectfully, efficiently, clearly, and productively. Participating in a conflict that is framed as an important topic of conversation rather than as a means to an end (settlement) is a much different form of mediation, but mediation nonetheless. This alternative form of mediation happens to be a potential bridge to accessing people of diverse backgrounds who might be less willing to engage in a traditional form of mediation that carries with it the specific goal of settlement. By increasing the ways in which mediators and conflict interventionists are able to assist parties in conflict, options begin to develop that encourage disputants to turn to those trained in conflict and communication management. Additionally and specifically, mediators must be prepared to engage in their mediations in varying ways, including by providing aid to parties who choose to remain in conflict but seek assistance in having more productive conversations, and possibly finding creative approaches to understanding each other and working together. Clarified and improved communication might surprise the disputants and cause them to begin to view their conflict, options, and true desires differently. What began as a form of mediation with no desire for settlement just might end up as a more traditional mediation with parties deciding to reach a settled agreement after all. Mediation requires disputant inclusivity in the process as well as in settled agreements, so it should also be practiced in a manner that is as inclusive as possible to as many people as possible who have varying concepts of conflict, intervention, and resolution. To accomplish this, mediators must be flexible in how they practice and conduct their mediations, in the processes and options they provide to parties, and in their mediation conclusion objectives. A mediator's hat is not only that of one who brings feuding parties to settlement. It is also that of one who engages with parties and conducts mediations with an amalgamated approach to conflict management and an accommodating and variable concept of the purpose of mediation and to the ends it can meet. With resolution being only one part and only one possible desired outcome of mediation or conflict intervention, when applicable, deeper conflict engagement should be the priority rather than an immediate and unwavering focus on resolution, unless that is determined to be the desired outcome.

By removing the limitations of closed-ended definitions, a new identity can be created for conflict resolvers and mediators that expresses our relevance in any and all conflict situations. *Conflict interventionist* is a wide-open, inclusive, and expressive description of the importance of conflict interaction from the facilitator, as opposed to *conflict resolver*, the cursory definition of which carries with it a narrow focus on resolution—not always the desired or most advantageous outcome. This broadened language reinforces the understanding and acknowledgment that conflict interventionists do not necessarily serve the isolated purpose of bringing conflicts to resolution in the traditional sense. To the contrary, it is their understanding, training, and skills applied to conflicts that are the significant characteristics. The fact that the conflict resolver or interventionist is neutral is folded into their very ability to perform their job properly, shifting the idea of neutrality to one aspect of the role instead of being its central identity. Not only does this change the concept of the profession, but it can also begin to address the many difficulties that a narrow concept of neutrality brings with it, including but certainly not limited to the fact that it is confusing and ambiguous for parties, the general public, and the professionals themselves. Neutrality is practiced differently from one conflict interventionist to the next, it is not necessarily a characteristic that all disputants seek, and it can be a deciding factor that turns many possible participants away from informal dispute resolution practices such as mediation. Shifting the focus and most pronounced aspect of this role away from framing the position of conflict interventionist in terms of neutrality and instead toward the unparalleled conflict understanding and intervention work that is possible at the hands of someone in this position could very well be the way forward for those in the field. The world of conflict engagement, intervention, and management is not one-size-fits-all for the various parties or facilitators involved, nor is it exclusionary to any categories of conflicts, so titles and descriptions of the practice should reflect that. We are indispensable in the landscape of conflict intervention and, in its many forms, resolution.

FLASH CHALLENGE

Get Involved in the Conversation!

1. How do you interpret Mayer's challenge to the boundaries of neutrality?
2. Compare and contrast the traditional role of neutrality with this new view:
   a. Conflict resolver only vs. conflict interventionist with expanded boundaries.
3. Should mediators and conflict interventionists expand into this new role beyond resolver?
4. How can the role of a traditional conflict resolver be expanded?
5. Might an expanded role affect a mediator's neutrality?
   a. Would this require a new definition and understanding of neutrality?
   b. Does neutrality as a heavily discussed tenet of mediation need to exist when the mediator is a stranger to the parties, with no previous relationship, and no vested interest in the outcome of the case?
6. How might the title Conflict Interventionist rather than Conflict Resolver shift the way disputants view the role of the mediator?
   a. Might disputants expect something different?
   b. If so, provide possible examples.

FLASH CHALLENGE

Mediate the Case!

Using the Mediation Example at the beginning of the chapter:

1. Mediate the case
2. Upon completion:
   a. Considering the facts of the case and the demeanor of the disputants, were you able to maintain your neutrality as you mediated the case?
      i. If you found maintaining your neutrality difficult at any point, how did you remedy this?
         1. What was required to maintain your neutrality?
         2. Discuss your thoughts and actions.
      ii. If not, what did you do?
         1. Did you express your struggle to the disputants?
         2. Did you decide to remove yourself as mediator?
            a) If so, at which point?

FLASH CHALLENGE QUESTIONS

On completion of the mediation, answer Flash Challenge Questions 1-3 a second time (repeated below). Discuss any differences between your answers before and after mediating the case.

Flash Challenge Question #1: Considering the facts of this case, how might a mediator's struggle to maintain neutrality affect the way they interact with the parties and mediate the case?

Flash Challenge Question #2: Are there any elements within this conflict that may cause the mediator to feel compelled to state or reinforce a position? (See "A New Vision of Neutrality" earlier in this chapter.)

1. Provide your answer(s) in dialogue form.
2. Explain your position and thought process.

Flash Challenge Question #3: Pick three of the enumerated Mediator Thoughts. For each:

1. Discuss and expand.
2. Are there any conclusions you are able to draw?

ADDITIONAL THINKING POINTS

1. Actions taken by mediators are based on value judgments that are formed over a lifetime of circumstances. This facet of the role of mediator continues to ignite conversations about neutrality because without the injection of impartiality into value judgments before the mediator takes action, the question of neutrality lingers. The dichotomy of thought connected to mediator intervention (should they, shouldn't they, and if they do, to what extent?) is that for many mediators, based on their understanding of their position, training, and experience, this is what they were hired to do. Anything short of bringing that experience and training to the table would be a dereliction of their duties. Refereeing, reframing, restructuring communication to be less harmful and more effective, reshaping the narrative into one that is less combative and more of a mutual puzzle that has yet to be solved, and creative settlement options and discussions are merely a sampling of what is taught under the umbrella of conflict intervention, resolution, and mediation training. What is the benefit of a third party if they are not there to inject impartiality and to assist in the process? The idea is that parties to

a conflict who have come to mediation are there because they have been unable to work through a conflict on their own. It would then only logically follow that adding another person into the room who contributes in no way other than as a referee would not necessarily be providing the assistance the disputants are seeking. Taking it one step further, if that is the environment they would be presented with, what would be the point in their participation in mediation at all? If the disputants know that settling outside of litigation is their best option, but have not been able to do so on their own, and are therefore asking for the assistance of a professional, a mediator, should they not receive it?

2. There is a logic game, wherein a doctor suddenly can no longer see patients on Sunday, and the task is to rearrange her Monday through Saturday schedule to accommodate the lack of Sunday appointments. When we find out that the answer is actually one appointment on each day, Monday through Friday, with all of the remaining appointments on Saturday, and against all logic of an evenly spread-out schedule, there pops the answer: 1, 1, 1, 1, 1, 5. As mediators, we are reminded that we must not bring our logic to the table if we are presented with facts to the contrary, or a situation devoid of our personal sense of logic or logic altogether. When you are in a room with disputants who have agreed that 1 + 1 = 11, then 1 + 1 = 11. No matter how much you know that 1 + 1 = 2, and no matter how much you want to tell them, you must not. To do so would be an act beyond a neutral position and would not respect party self-determination. "The difference between truth and fiction, is that fiction needs to make sense."[5] Even when a disputant's truth is perhaps bizarre and not based in our commonly understood and accepted reality, at least for that moment, it is their truth. You will mediate on their terms or you will remove yourself. There is a fine line that separates controlling one's biases and preconceived ideas, and not doing so. Train well in the distinction and management of the two, and it will serve your conflict intervention skills and mediation career well in the long run.

5. *The International*, 2009.

chapter 6

Listening

You Are Heard

When a mediator becomes a listener, essentially a captive audience of their disputants, they are also, in fact, a blank slate for those disputants. Whoever they are outside of the mediation, however they behave in their day-to-day lives, whatever they were doing even moments before entering the room and becoming the mediator, all is immediately suspended as far as the disputants are concerned. Barring any disputant behavioral readjustments and discussions about ground rules that could take place at the start of the mediation and necessitate the mediator proving to be capable of controlling the process, the first and most important role the mediator will play is that of listener. The listener does not yet have a personality, an opinion, or any behavior associated with them. They are like water, cushioning and enveloping, with the information they are receiving flowing in and out, devoid of the need to react to any of it. Consider water for a moment. It can be calm and healing or extremely dangerous, even deadly. There is a middle point that lies between those extremes, which is water that is perfectly still, quiet, and indecipherable. Without exposing any characteristic from either end of the spectrum, the stillness holds secrets and the ability to transform into anything it needs or wants to become at any time. That is also the characteristic of a listener who knows the benefit of stillness, and who is masterfully aligning the pieces on their mental chess board to plan for any situation that will require them to undergo a metamorphosis for the purpose of better suiting the disputants, their conflict, and the mediation. All of this lies within the information that the mediator has yet to receive, identify, sort through, and draw conclusions from. Just as water is one of the most powerful forces on earth, the limit of which knows no bounds, so, too, is the potential and reach of a practiced and skilled listener when there is information to be gathered, whether anyone – themself included – realizes it or not.

You are a detective, the likes of which we watch on television shows such as *Law and Order, Dateline, The First 48,* and other true crime shows. If you have ever seen detectives at work, you will notice that they are chameleons in their entirety: tone of voice, questions posed, and body language. Their job, like yours, is to extract as much information as possible to build a full picture of the exact nature of the conflict. The explanation for these chameleon-like interactions is that people are capable of storytelling, lying, and manipulation in any given situation to make themselves look better, cover up that which could cast blame onto them, and absolve themselves of guilt. That type of behavior does not comport with collecting the truth or the requirement of determining the facts to the goal of reaching creative settlement options. One might call these circumstances of possibly distorted truth less than desirable working conditions for mediators, but they are by no means unpredictable. Now the idea of playing the role of a detective enters the picture. Detectives must be flexible enough to mold themselves into the shape that best serves the information extraction process on a case-by-case basis. As the detective moves through tone of voice, types of questions to be asked, and body language, so, too, does the mediator. In addition, mediators will find it necessary to flow through Mediation Styles, Communication Styles, and Conflict Handling Modes (CHMs). The single thread that runs through the behavior and actions of a detective during an interview is that of listening, and it is equally so for a mediator during a mediation. Listening, and all that it encompasses, is a powerful tool that can change the landscape of any mediation: knowing how to listen, what to listen for, what the information means, the hidden information inside words and behaviors, what to do with that information, how to mindfully manage it, how to let it tell a story, how to dissect it, how to spread it out to find wiggle room, how to see through it to find creative settlement options, and on and on the list goes. "Good listening can increase your negotiation power by increasing the information you have about the other side's interests or about possible options. Once you understand the other side's feelings and concerns, you can begin to address them, to explore areas of agreement and disagreement, and to develop useful ways to proceed in the future."[1] How, though, does one decipher important and helpful information from information considered background noise? How do mediators ensure that they are not getting bogged down by this background noise, especially when there seems to be no shortage of it, and it is coming at them from all directions and in full force? What about when the disputants themselves fail to realize, or at the very least fail to admit, what the important information really is? What about when information pertinent to the resolution of the conflict dates back to an earlier time and is packed in emotional baggage that the mediator has not yet discovered? While listening to and mentally interacting with the information provided by disputants, the mediator will engage in a process. Subsequent movements and behavior during the mediation will directly reflect how efficiently they do the following:

1. Listen
    a. Purposeful Listening with the intent to gather information only.
    b. To identify CHMs.
    c. To select which Mediation Style to use.

---

1. Fisher, Roger, William Ury, and William Patton, *Getting to Yes: Negotiating Agreement Without Giving In* 2nd edition, 1991, p. 87.

   d. To find safe answers and wiggle room.
   e. For positions that overlap.
   f. For elements that necessitate reframing.
   g. For avenues that could lead to potential settlement opportunities.
2. Process
   a. As information is gathered, there must be internal sifting, categorizing, and decision-making.
   b. What is done with the information is equally if not more important than receiving it in the first place.
3. Churn
   a. After internal decisions are made for how to proceed with the gathered information, there should be mental checks and balances.
   b. Consider the potential outcomes of each possible move.
4. Chess
   a. Plan
      i. Settle on which moves to make, while considering how disputants may respond.
      ii. Consider the mediator's responses or moves back to them.
   b. Play
      i. Make your move.

SKILLS-SPECIFIC EXERCISES

Total Recall

1. For Listening
   a. Begin with 60 seconds of listening in total silence to someone speaking directly to you. It should be about something new to you.
   b. Recite back to them what they said at the end of the 60 seconds.
      i. How well can you do this?
   c. Build up from the 60 seconds in 15-second increments to two minutes.
2. For Asking Questions
   a. Repeat Part (a) of the Listening Exercise above.
      i. Write down open-ended questions as you listen. Your goal is to encourage lengthy answers – the longer the better, and to see how much new information you are be able to extract based on your questions.
      ii. Write down closed-ended questions (yes/no). Your goal is specific clarification.
   b. Now ask all of your questions to your speaker and write down their answers.
   c. Note the effectiveness of your open-ended and closed-ended questions.
      i. Were you successful in achieving your goal of obtaining new information based on your chosen question structure?
         1. If not, can you rewrite the question(s) to be more effective?

The type or types of listening the mediator employs at any given moment will depend entirely on the requirements of each specific mediation. Although the listening types vary, the remaining constant will be that the listening will be purposeful. It will have a goal for which that particular type of listening is the appropriate choice, and it will be the mediator's internal process that immediately precedes their actions. The listening descriptions that follow discuss the thought processes that shape how the mediator will proceed.

Listening is not only about hearing and understanding words. It is also about understanding the way the words are expressed. The International Listening Association defines listening as "the process of receiving, constructing meaning from, and responding to spoken and/or non-verbal messages." The frequently elusive recognition, let alone understanding, of a disputant's delivery (verbal and nonverbal) will enable the mediator to reach a better understanding of whether a disputant is happy, sad, frustrated, stressed, or hiding information, regardless of their actual words and delivery. The skill of listening reaches far beyond simply taking in the spoken word. It permeates the realm of body language to search for clues into a disputant's attitude and mental state, because just as a duck might appear calm traversing a body of water, we know better. We know that with a mere glance under the water's surface, one will see the feet of that same duck paddling fiercely. The deceptively calm appearance of the duck will not fool a seasoned mediator who knows all too well that looks are just that: deceiving.

Listening, or being on the receiving end of information, is one of the most multifaceted and multi-dimensional tools at a mediator's disposal, as the impact of information received and acted on can be limitless. Becoming situated into the position of receiver is not always quick or easy, but it is an absolute necessity. The crucial task of convincing parties to put themselves into potentially vulnerable positions with you, the mediator, in order to discuss their feelings is only one segment of the mediator's role.

TYPES OF LISTENING

Listening types are not so discrete that there is no overlap. They are used in a mélange, and at the mediator's discretion. For example, if a disputant were to say, "I went to the park," the mediator could employ Informational Listening to take in the stated information and then might immediately employ Discriminative Listening, followed by Critical Listening without a single additional word from the disputant.

Informational Listening

This is a passive form of listening used for the purpose of learning, whereby the listener is neither maneuvering nor manipulating the information they are receiving and only taking steps to clarify when necessary. The listener is not judging, criticizing, taking a position for or against, dissecting, critiquing, evaluating, or working through any of the information they are gathering. Some obvious forms of Informational Listening are asking for directions, attending orientation day at school, or becoming informed about a standard operating procedure at a new job. A frequent and interesting example of Informational Listening involves a devout student in biology class listening to the teacher's presentation on evolution. To effectively practice Informational Listening for the sake of learning, they must suspend their religious beliefs so as not to overlay them onto any of the information they are currently receiving and not use their religious beliefs to form or support arguments against the ideas that the teacher is presenting. In the alternative, it would no longer be considered Informational Listening. There is both a more and less appropriate time and place for everything, and Informational Listening is a crucial skill to practice as a mediator and a method that can be suggested to disputants. Listening to information and someone else's story without judgment, forming arguments against it, looking for gaps and illogical components, or comparing it to one's own experiences is a skill integral to communicating, cooperating, and frankly, coexisting with other people. It is also certainly one of the pathways out of conflict and toward settlement. If you are seeing validation between the lines here, you would be correct. Personally stepping back and validating information that someone else expresses without comparing it to one's own experiences and beliefs is a core tenet of Informational Listening, as well as the mediation process. Simply because it did not happen to you does not mean it did not happen at all; it also does not mean that someone else's experience is not valid. This is, in other words, enabling someone to feel and be heard through the use of listening, and thereby engaging them by way of validation. Listening to what someone is stating without funneling it through the lens of possibly contradictory personal experiences and beliefs automatically validates what they are saying. Engaging in the opposite, by in fact listening and interpreting the information through your lens of personal experiences and beliefs, has the reverse effect of instantly invalidating it.

Also integral to Informational Listening is the requirement of intense concentration. As this form of listening does not include actions beyond listening, clarifying, and storing information, it can be more difficult for the mediator to remain focused and easier to become disengaged. While the tactics below are intended for engagement purposes and specifically for clarification during Informational Listening, the nature of mediation is fluid. Using a tactic at this point could conceivably catapult the mediation to a more advanced point or even directly to a settlement conversation. Additionally, although there is repetition in the use of the same skills during the course of a mediation (e.g., reframing and showing empathy), the intended and desired outcome of using those skills varies according to what the mediator deems necessary at that moment and depending on what the mediation requires.

Helpful Mediator Engagement Tactics

1. Taking notes.
2. Questioning timeline, location, and people involved in the conflict.
3. Asking clarification questions:

a. "Am I hearing correctly that you mean . . . ."
b. "Would I be correct in stating that you . . . ."
c. "Would you say that upset you?"
d. "If they had not said that, would you still think it was wrong?"
e. "Please correct me if I am wrong . . . ."

4. Reframing statements
   a. "So in other words, you are upset because . . . ."
   b. (In response to the statement: "I hate him!") "Within the context of the conflict we have been discussing, what you have expressed is that you hate his actions. Would you agree with that?"
   c. "Let's see if we can rephrase that statement to be more specific about how it has affected you and your feelings, and less about what she has done."
5. Showing empathy in restating their statements
   a. "It sounds like that experience of . . . was extremely difficult for you."
   b. "I understand that your experience of . . . pained you greatly."
   c. "It is understandable that going through . . . has affected you in numerous ways."

If at this point you are questioning your ability to receive information purely as information without passing it through the lens of your personal experiences and knowledge in the course of receiving it, you would not be alone in such a concern. Remaining nonjudgmental can be a very difficult skill that requires practice to ensure that even if a mediator does have a judgmental reaction to disputants' statements, they are able to make sure that those judgments remain internal and do not interfere with the mediation process. There can be no element of judgment in comments or suggestions from the mediator. That would break the position of neutrality and jeopardize or end the mediation if not remedied immediately to prevent interference from mediator biases, opinions, judgments, or disputants' awareness thereof.

If the mediator is still experiencing difficulty listening properly and effectively during their mediations, having exhausted the above strategies, it is possible there are alternate issues to consider.

Potential Barriers to Effective Informational Listening

1. Lack of interest
2. Prejudice or bias
3. Preconceived ideas or positions
4. Being judgmental
5. Previous experiences
6. Closed-mindedness

Comprehensive Listening

Comprehensive Listening involves understanding the actual message or messages that are being communicated – the meaning of the words being used. An immediate concern should be evident: Is it really all that often that two or more people listening to the same comments, especially in a conflict situation, will understand them in the same way and to mean the same thing? For example:

Statement: It's not ready.

Disputant A's interpretation: It's not ready yet.
Disputant B's interpretation: It's never going to be ready.
Disputant C's interpretation: They aren't even working on it.
Disputant D's interpretation: They are slacking on their job and are probably slackers in other parts of their life as well.
Disputant E's interpretation: They never planned to do it in the first place and are stealing my money, which was clearly their plan all along.

Additionally, will the listener(s) understand statements as intended by the speaker? For example, the speaker who stated, "It's not ready," simply meant that they needed a little more time to complete the project. One message could have an unlimited number of misinterpretations, multiplied by the number of listeners present, the intensity of the conflict being discussed, and the probable heightened emotional state of parties to the mediation.

When Comprehensive Listening leads to confusion, go back to the basics. Ask for definitive clarification immediately, not only for the sake of everyone listening, but also for the speaker's sake, to make sure that their words do in fact support the messages they are attempting to express. For example:

1. "I am interpreting what you are saying as . . .
   Is that what you intend for us to understand?"
2. "I think I am a little bit confused about what you mean.
   Could you please explain it to me further?"
3. "It sounds like you're saying . . . .
   Is that correct?"
4. "I just want to make sure I am understanding you correctly.
   Would I be correct in saying . . .?"
5. "Okay, I think I understand what you mean.
   However, would you mind explaining it to me one more time so I can be absolutely sure?"

Encourage everyone to ask questions in their quest for clarity, as clarity is the only way to dispel miscommunication and misunderstanding. Asking questions to clarify confusing communication, word choice, language barriers, and employment-specific jargon provides answers that are effectively a form of reframing. Continuously pursuing truth and clarity through asking questions, checking in, and reframing significantly aids both mediator and disputants in removing any accidental misunderstandings and misinterpretations of both spoken and unspoken messages.

A natural progression from misinterpreting and misunderstanding the intent of a sentence or word choice is misinterpreting and misunderstanding the accompanying tone. For example:

Statement: What are you doing here?

Disputant A's interpretation: What are YOU doing here?
Disputant B's interpretation: What are you DOING here?
Disputant C's interpretation: What are you doing HERE?
Disputant D's interpretation: WHAT ARE YOU DOING HERE?

Employing Discriminative Listening together with Comprehensive Listening assists in building a fuller and deeper understanding of the conversation.

It is little wonder so many conflicts arise from electronic communication – text messages and emails – when the listener does not have the benefit of either seeing the speaker to gauge their body language or hearing the speaker's tone in their delivery.

Discriminative Listening

This is the most basic form of listening. In contrast to Comprehensive Listening, it does not involve understanding the meaning of the words being used; rather, it is the understanding of different manners of tone and expression used in the verbal delivery. For example, there is an ability to distinguish between happy and unhappy or stressed and anxious in contrast with calm and carefree, irrespective of particular word choices. Many of us have experienced asking a friend, family member, or significant other in the aftermath of a heated interaction, "Is everything okay?" only to be met with, "I'm fine." Although the word *fine* carries with it the implication that everything is indeed okay, one had best use Discriminative Listening to read through the lines of that verbiage to confirm its validity. When a mediator is able to separate tones from words, those tones provide clues to issues beneath the surface. The combination of the meaning of tone along with clear understanding of words aids in the overall comprehension of the message that a disputant is attempting to deliver – both consciously and subconsciously. Discriminative Listening is also applied to *listening* to body language, which is invaluable to understanding the speaker more fully. In the frequently used expression, "If looks could kill," where a message is delivered through merely a look on a person's face without any verbal accompaniment, a look speaks volumes and the meaning could not be clearer for those who know how to listen. Imagine the repercussions of not understanding a look that is intended to mean, "Stay away from me," "I am not ready to talk to you," or "This relationship is over." The question is how to apply the Discriminative Listening skill. The answer is to do so on a sliding scale of experience. When the concept of interpreting the nonverbal side of communication is new, the best course of action is to act under the assumption that your understanding of everything being said is wrong and therefore requires clarification, and that any and all disputant statements might or might not be truthful. This interaction could come in this form:

Disputant: That's fine with me. Go ahead and tell them I agree.

Mediator: I hear that you are saying it is okay with you and that you agree to the terms they are offering, but I want to make sure that I am understanding you correctly and that we move forward with what you genuinely want.

Disputant: Well, I guess I am not really okay with their offer, but I just feel desperate to get this mediation over with.

By simply requesting clarity in a nonthreatening and nonconfrontational manner, the mediator was able to draw out the disputant's true feelings, which happened to be in stark contradiction to their initial response.

Note of Caution

Remember that a conflict is a circumstance or disagreement that can escalate to an indeterminate level as a result of misaligned interpretations and disproportionate responses. Now consider a mediation in which at least one party resents being involved in the conflict and subsequent mediation. Add to that the possibly heightened and irrational emotional state of the disputants. It would behoove the mediator to absorb these realities into their approach when questioning the disputants. On any other day, a person might understand the exact intention of an innocent *why* question, but on a day when they are a disputant in a mediation fighting over a conflict with possible financial, emotional, and future consequences, they might not interpret that very same *why* in the correct and intended way. On such a day in mediation the mediator's *why* question could cause the disputant to feel accused of being a liar. Unless the mediator can call that train back to the station in a hurry, what follows next could be a cascading series of outcomes that include broken trust, outrage, fury, defensive behavior, and ultimately impasse. Asking carefully crafted questions that are completely devoid of accusation or presumption, as is the case in the example dialogue above, that invite the disputant to provide clarity and reassurance to a mediator who clearly has only their best interests and confirmed true intentions in mind, is the pathway through *why* questions. In the context of mediation, without applying this skill, at the very least you are looking at serious reframing, emotional handling, and a very displeased disputant. At the worst you have just walked into a potential impasse.

FLASH CHALLENGE

It's All in a Look

1. Find two people who speak a common language that is foreign to you.
   a. It is important that you do not understand anything they are saying.
2. Ask them to engage in a conversation while you listen.
3. Pay close attention to:
   a. Body language
   b. Tone of voice
   c. Gestures
   d. Facial expressions

- e. Verbal expressions that do not use words
  - i. Sighs
  - ii. Grunts
  - iii. Laughter
    - *1.* Is the laughter genuine, forced, or at the expense of the other person?

4. Take note of what you are witnessing and what you believe to be the possible meanings behind their behavior.
5. Begin to form a picture of what you believe to be going on.
6. When the conversation is over, explain your conclusions to the participants.
7. Were your conclusions close to the true nature of their discussion?
   - a. Close conclusions include understanding intentions and feelings, even if you were farther off in your guess of the content.
8. Were you completely off the mark? Discuss.
9. Were there areas of behavior that you thought meant one thing, but that you subsequently learned meant something different?
   - a. Can you take this new understanding and apply it to that same behavior the next time you see it? For example, during a mediation?
     - i. Could this aid in your overall work in understanding how to listen properly to behavior?
     - ii. How can that help a mediator during the mediation process? Discuss.
     - iii. Could a lack of proper interpretation of behavior be detrimental to a mediator during the mediation process? Discuss.

Therapeutic or Empathetic Listening

Arguably the most important listening style that the mediator will engage in, Therapeutic or Empathetic Listening employs listening to understand feelings and emotions, including putting oneself into the speaker's shoes. First, the mediator must be clear about the difference between sympathy and empathy. To differentiate, sympathy is having compassion and feeling sorry for someone while maintaining emotional distance and often includes statements of silver linings from those trying to help. Empathy is a realization and understanding of another person's point of view without minimizing it. When discussing the difference between sympathy and empathy, the story of a person who fell into a hole and is lying on the ground at the bottom is often presented. The person who walks to the edge of the hole above ground, looks in, and yells down to the fallen person about how sorry they are for their fall and any injuries that might have occurred is expressing sympathy. The person who finds a ladder, drops it into the hole, climbs down to meet the fallen person at the bottom to talk about what happened, and then shares in their feelings, is displaying empathy. The most important distinction between sympathy and empathy is that empathy expresses the understanding of another person's thoughts and feelings from their point of view within the situation, rather than with a point of view from the outside looking in. A basic tenet of empathetic listening is to "seek to understand before being understood and . . . to connect emotionally with another person while simultaneously attempting to connect cognitively."[2]

When a disputant is not necessarily making demands, but is nonetheless behaving in an uncooperative and nonproductive manner, a mediator might conclude that they are feeling unseen and unheard. Empathetic Listening could be a useful tool for both the mediator and an opposing party, as the presence of compassion and dedicated listening is a remedy to consider in such circumstances. Listening and truly hearing one another, often for the first time and in a situation that regularly impairs such desires and capabilities, could prove to be a useful tool for both the mediator and an opposing party that can silence the noise of tension, aggression, and conflict. It is an exercise in truly listening to another person, hearing their words and concerns, and thereby providing the validation that they have sought and perhaps not previously received. With this fulfilled need, the disputant might be able to shift their behavior and proceed through the conflict resolution process. Whether or not the disputants can use Empathetic Listening with one another will be dependent on the nature of the specific mediation and the atmosphere within the room. These variables could lead to a mediator's determination to move into caucus. Once there, the opportunity is available for the mediator to use Empathetic Listening with parties individually to address unmet needs, bringing about a less contentious, more agreeable atmosphere. This might enable the mediator to bring the parties back into joint session, where they might then be able to listen empathetically to one another.

Empathetic Listening can be key to deciphering explanations and true intentions of messages because they are often encased in irrational statements and behaviors that cannot be accessed without empathy.

Empathetic Listening *does not* require agreeing with the speaker. Disputants can be encouraged not to shy away from this tool simply because they do not see eye-to-eye on the facts of the case.

> If you're uncomfortable introjecting (summarizing while your partner is still talking), picture a butter knife inserted in a stream of water: if the blade is parallel to the flow (empathy), inserting it doesn't disturb the flow (your partner's focus and thought stream). Inserting your own needs, opinions, or thoughts is interrupting, which is like turning the knife blade sideways in the water flow. Doing this usually signals you're locally controlled by a false self and your awareness 'bubble' excludes your partner, so effective communication is unlikely.[3]

2. Huitt, W. "Empathetic Listening," Educational Psychology Interactive (Valdosta, GA: Valdosta State University, 2009) http://www.edpsycinteractive.org/topics/process/listen.html.

3. Gerlich, Peter K. MSW, NSRC Experts Council, "Empathic Listening."

Examples of Actions to Avoid When Attempting to Use Empathetic Listening

1. Comparing pain or experiences:
   "I know exactly how you feel. One time . . . ."
2. One-upping:
   "Oh, you think that's hard, this is what happened to me . . . ."
3. Judging:
   "Why would you do that?"
3. Sympathizing:
   "I feel bad for you."
4. Giving advice:
   "You should . . . ."
5. Invalidating feelings or experiences:
   "Don't be ridiculous."
6. Belittling:
   "That's not a big deal at all. Get over it."
7. Taking over the story:
   "Oh, that's like when I . . . ."

EMPATHETIC LISTENING EXERCISE

Whenever, Wherever . . .

1. Engage in a round of "tough questions" directed at any disputant who is exhibiting behavior that is particularly lacking compassion and is not attempting in the least to understand any perspective other than their own.
2. The questions should include but do not necessarily need to be limited to the following:
   a. How would you feel if your family member or friend were being spoken to and treated in this manner?
   b. Would you speak differently if it were a family member or friend sitting in front of you?
   c. If you were interacting with a friend or family member right now, how would your behavior be different?
3. Based on the answers above, the mediator can move on to the following role-play if necessary for additional empathetic reinforcement. Otherwise, the disputants can be encouraged to absorb this shifted perspective into their behavior as they move forward.

Empathetic Listening Role-Play

During a mediation that would benefit from empathy:

1. Ask the disputants to suspend the mediation in its current state.
2. Now encourage the disputants to reengage in the mediation in a manner as if they are interacting with a friend or family member.

> a. If the mediation is Transformative, the mediator can encourage the disputants to remember back to a time when they were not in conflict and to engage with each other the way they would have at that time.
> b. Even if it is not Transformative, with parties arriving as strangers and leaving the same way, a difficult mediation could be aided by the disputants interacting with each other as they would with family members or friends.
>   i. Strangers does not have to mean enemies, and it also does not have to mean that it is not worth the time or energy to extend kindness and courtesy to one another. It takes neither more time nor more energy to be just that, kind and courteous.

Critical Listening

The opposite of Informational Listening, Critical Listening is an active rather than passive form of listening that relies on analyzing, evaluating, scrutinizing, and dissecting the information being received. To what end?

1. Forming opinions
2. Analytical commentary
3. Problem-solving
4. Decision-making

With Critical Listening, the time to analyze the information is the moment it is received. A mediator has their mediator hat squarely and securely on their head at this point, having already processed the appropriate information in a strictly informative capacity. Suffice it to say, a mediator's nerve endings are tingling now, and the mental chess game has officially begun. With an end goal in mind, the mediator is now moving pieces around on the playing board in their head.

Mediator Engagement Tactics

1. Be inquisitive when contemplating information.
2. Question everything!
    a. Make sure those questions are guiding disputant(s) toward the purpose you have set out.
3. Begin drawing connections between the pieces of information that the disputants are providing.
4. Use questions to find answers that provide wiggle room for settlement options to present themselves.
5. Use questions to find answers that provide wiggle room for disputants to work collaboratively.
6. Use questions to find answers that require disputants to provide further and deeper explanation to open up isolated conversations rather than conflict discussion as a whole.

7. Do I detect a lie?
   a. Consider either direct or indirect inquiry.
8. Does the disputant's body language indicate feelings or behavior other than what they are expressing verbally?
9. Is the information helpful or harmful?
   a. To disputants
   b. To the mediation process
   c. To reaching settlement
10. Does the information provided present a hurdle to settlement that the disputants will require assistance to overcome?
11. What can I do with this information to transform it so it assists in accomplishing the goals for the mediation?
12. Is it possible to reframe this information to change the trajectory of the mediation?
13. How can I use the information to shift the narrative into one that better serves the disputants' mediation goals?

Remember that it is possible to be engaged in a mediation that requires only a financial negotiation process facilitated by a mediator. Although this might seem straightforward, the application of Critical Listening skills could benefit the way in which the negotiation is managed, as well as the way in which offers and counteroffers are presented. For example, if the mediator can detect an eagerness from Disputant A to see the mediation reach settlement, the mediator might be inclined to guide the process toward a smaller financial concession on the part of Disputant B, as the motivation to end the dispute might be greater than the motivation to save money. On the other hand, if the opposite should prove true, the mediator could encourage a look at creative nonmonetary options to supplement the financial offer. Critical Listening can provide insight into any situation that unfolds during a mediation, and the bottom line is that it is applicable to all mediations, including those that are based in financial negotiations. If possible, why not perform in a manner and at a level that even the disputants thought unnecessary or impossible? Just because a mediation could be resolved with a simple exchange and agreement about numbers does not preclude the possibility that critical and creative thinking could assist disputants in achieving better settlement options.

Thinking Critically Creatively: A Mediator's Considerations

1. Have I given the disputants their day in court?
2. Do they need:
   a. More time?
   b. More empathy?
   c. More support?

   d. An opportunity to acknowledge and express their emotions and work them through to move to a more rational and logical position?
3. What do I already know?
4. What does or does not make sense?
5. Does that piece of information fit into the presented timeline?
6. What can I determine to be fact or fiction?
   a. It does not necessarily matter, so the mediator will decide which way to mentally categorize the information to move toward settlement.
7. Where can I find wiggle room?
8. Should or could anyone apologize?
   a. Would that help this situation in any way?
9. What can I reframe to remove any potential misunderstanding?
10. Do I need to seek clarity anywhere?
11. Where can I ask questions to prompt and shift thinking?
    a. For example, prompting a thinking shift from argumentative and accusatory to receptive, respectful, and forward-thinking.
12. How can I bend and shape this situation?
13. How many conflicts am I actually working with?
14. What do I need to do to get the disputants to trust me?
    a. How can I neutrally align myself with the disputants?
15. How can I introduce brainstorming into the conversation so that it can begin immediately?
    a. Ideally it should come from the disputants, but how?
16. Can I find an opportunity to encourage one disputant to ask questions seeking clarity from another as a means of unobtrusively finding common ground and fostering and advancing collaborative effort?
    a. The discovery of this potential common ground and collaboration can further enable the mediator to encourage the disputants toward a willingness to work together for a settlement agreement.
17. Based on the information I have, how creative can I possibly be with settlement options?
18. How can I encourage the disputants to recognize that they can work on the conflict and toward resolution together instead of in opposition to each other?
19. Can I assist in creating "aha!" moments?
    a. An example of such a moment would be during discussions, when disputants realize that they are in agreement about something or some aspect of an offered solution.
    b. This would be extremely beneficial and could go a long way toward boosting confidence in the knowledge that it is in fact possible for them to both work together and achieve a settlement that is mutually acceptable.

FLASH CHALLENGE

From Informational to Critical

1. Find two people who are willing to allow you to listen to them discuss a conflict they are engaged in with each other.
2. You will not be mediating unless they ask you to, of course. Instead, your involvement will end after they each describe their perspective of the conflict to you, preferably one at a time.
   a. You can choose to engage with them jointly or separately based on your determination of what best serves the goal of receiving clear information.
3. Create an Informational Listening outline of the case.
   a. Use your Informational Listening skills to outline the entire case, detailing all facts presented.
   b. You might choose to create two separate outlines if each side's facts are vastly different, or you can merge all of the facts into one outline.
4. Now, using your Critical Listening skills, add notations in a different color to the Informational Listening outline you just created.
   a. Discuss your critical thinking process.
   b. Using Critical Listening skills, what are your first thoughts upon hearing the information?
   c. How does the information change as you flow from Informational Listening to Critical Listening?
   d. Which questions are you asking yourself?
      i. Refer to the list "Thinking Critically Creatively: A Mediator's Considerations" earlier in the chapter.
         1. Are any of those questions on your list? Discuss which and how they worked for you.
         2. Do you have any questions to add to the list? Discuss your added questions and how you used them.

Example Informational Listening Outline	Example Critical Listening Outline
1. A: The car accident happened on Tuesday afternoon right after lunch, and his children were in the car. *2.* The car accident happened Tuesday morning, and A was alone in the car. Also, Tuesday is a school day, so A's children would have been in school.	*1.* If it was a weekday the children should have been in school and would not have been in the car. *a.* Find out if there was a call to school to verify if the children were in class on Tuesday or not. *b.* Is there a police report? *c.* Insurance coverage? *2.* Timeline issues: Who (children or not) and When (Tuesday or Saturday)?

Example Informational Listening Outline	Example Critical Listening Outline
3. A: It was actually on Saturday, because his children were definitely in the car.	3. Was there an intentional lie to change the day from Tuesday to Saturday by A? a. If so, why?
4. B: It was definitely not on Saturday, because he was out of town—it was definitely on Tuesday.	4. Did the individuals know each other prior to the incident? a. If so, what is the nature of their relationship?

5. Based on the information, do you foresee any hurdles to resolution?
   a. If so, what are your plans to manage them?
6. Based on your information and the application of Critical Listening, which Mediation Style(s) would you use to mediate this case?
7. If possible, identify disputant Conflict Handling Modes, and in turn, which Conflict Handling Modes you would use to engage with them.
8. Develop mutually agreeable creative settlement options.
   a. Compile a list of possibilities.
   b. What are your plans for transforming the information to improve its usefulness toward settlement options?
   c. What are the steps you plan to take to get there?
      i. Are there any additional questions that might be important or necessary to ask?
      ii. Describe your thought process.
9. Do you get a sense that the conflict could end in impasse?

Rapport Listening

A fundamental task for the mediator is to build trust with the disputants. More specifically, the mediator needs to build a relationship in which the disputants trust the mediator enough to believe in the mediation process and to rely upon the mediator to guide them through the necessary steps to reach their desired end goal, settlement or otherwise. To develop that trust, however, it is necessary for the mediator to create a connection that is inclusive of understanding and effective communication. Listening with the intent to build rapport requires identifying specific details in the narrative and areas in which new narratives can be built.

Building Rapport:

1. When listening to a disputant's story, if there is an emotional aspect that they share, respond with empathy and compassion.

a. It would not be appropriate to use statements that could be interpreted as taking one side over another or seeing one side as more valid than the other. However, conveying sentiments that validate an experience a disputant is relating is appropriate and at the crux of building and establishing a relationship of understanding and trust.

THIS STATEMENT

It is understandable that your experience was difficult for you.

RATHER THAN THIS STATEMENT

Oh yes, yours is the more difficult position to be in.

2. Building rapport benefits both mediator-disputant and disputant-disputant relationships.

a. If possible, the mediator can seek out common ground among disputants to discuss and use as a technique to build rapport. What do a dog and a rosebush have in common? Not much, until a little more investigative work uncovers that the commonality lies in a parallel, lifelong devotion to each. This rapport can extend to and aid in settlement conversations. Where there is common ground once, there can be common ground twice. With settlement in mind, the mediator should work backward to see whether it is possible, even if there is not enough information yet to be sure. The mediator should:
   i. Ask for background and stories.
   ii. Ask for details, and the details in the details, and then more details on top of those.
   iii. Tease out as much information as possible, and even when it is not yet known if there is information being concealed, the mediator should always proceed as if there is more to be found.
   iv. Act as though every word heard and every fact learned is a drop in the bucket of information waiting to be discovered.
   v. See the crumbs for the clues they are.

MEDIATOR STRATEGY

To invite each disputant to discuss a personal interest that is meaningful to them with the goal of the disputants identifying parallel feelings, those of commitment to their respective interests.

1. Tell me about how you got started doing that.
2. What inspired you to continue?
3. Do you have any mentors?
4. Have you ever considered sharing your information by teaching it to others?

TO DISPUTANT A

It sounds like this is something you really care about and have put a lot of time into. Can you tell us about how you got started doing it?

TO DISPUTANT B

You mentioned that this is a time-consuming hobby of yours that you really enjoy. Can you tell us about it?

COMMON GROUND

The common ground being built with these statements is the opportunity for each disputant to share a personal interest that is meaningful to them. Eventually this can be used to develop a creative settlement option that intertwines their interests with a mutual understanding of the time, effort, and financial commitment each requires.

3. Building rapport can be as simple as a shared experience. The mediator could playfully overemphasize the annoyance about the amount of paperwork they require—whoever *they* is does not matter. The point is that everyone present in the mediation will address that same matter in the same way. For at least this brief moment, disputants are not treated nor do they see themselves as separate parties or even as if they are in conflict, and witty banter during the signing process has been known to happen. The resultant camaraderie among disputants from this shared experience of equal footing can carry over and extend throughout the mediation.
4. Be confident, calm, and relaxed in your demeanor and delivery. A mediator confident in their abilities and in what they are saying will have a better chance at building a relationship of trust with disputants. If the mediator trusts themself and it shows, the disputants will feel more comfortable following suit.
5. Make sure all parties are included in the conversation, whether in joint session or in caucus, so that a back-and-forth flow can be achieved. This reciprocal action between mediator and disputants can very quickly form a habit that feels comfortable and reliable, even expected and accepted. The benefit to settlement conversations could be the acceptance of creative, mutually considerate settlement suggestions from the mediator as potentially valid options.

Reflective or Mirror Listening

This form of listening uses verbal responses to express to speakers that they are being heard, understood, and validated when appropriate. Rather than simply listening to information and moving on to questions or statements based on that information, employing Reflective Listening requires additional steps to ensure that the speaker feels heard, understood, and validated.

In Reflective Listening, a listener reflects back to the speaker the thoughts, feelings, and opinions they are expressing, completely devoid of any personal input or interpretation. The listener is creating an exact reflection for the speaker.

1. In creating a reflection, the listener is enabling the speaker to confirm that they are being heard and understood correctly. The speaker is also being provided with the opportunity to make any necessary changes based on the reflection.
2. The reflection can also do what reflections tend to do, which is to point out certain things in oneself. In listening to their own words reflected back to them, they might realize that they do not actually like or agree with what they have been saying. Sometimes hearing a mirrored reflection reveals a necessary other perspective that has gone unrecognized but can alter the landscape of a conflict. They might even be willing to do something about it and to become cooperative to change.
   a. If during self-reflection a disputant can question some part of what they have said or done, why not encourage them to question other parts as well? The mediator should be prepared to expand upon any questioning a disputant does in self-reflection. Any discovery that indicates a less than helpful statement or position should be called into question and examined. A conversation about alternative behavioral options should follow.
   b. If the opportunity presents itself, the mediator should begin maneuvering the discussion toward collaborative resolution, regardless of whether or not they have addressed it yet. Evidence of a crack in aggressive or confrontational superficial posturing or other behavior that has thus far been hindering the settlement process or the realization by a disputant that they were wrong about what they thought they wanted or how they were approaching conflict communications should lead to the mediator's swift and immediate shift in strategy toward settlement.

If the mediation is in joint session, Reflective Listening can be a tool that the mediator uses to assist disputants to engage differently with each other.

1. For example, if disputants are having difficulty speaking to and hearing each other and are instead speaking at each other, the mediator can suggest that they engage in a Reflective Listening exercise to assist in the communication and listening process. With each disputant reflecting back what they hear and understand, all parties will receive the opportunity to clarify any misunderstandings and reframe their own statements to be better understood.
   a. A mirroring effect could take place in which on seeing what they look like, one or all of the disputants might decide to change and pivot their previous position, choosing to instead adopt a more collaborative, agreeable, and reasonable course of action.
2. Encouraging the disputants to use Reflective Listening can also be a tool for the mediator to keep them focused not only on what each is saying, but also the specific topic that is being discussed at any given moment.

a. When engaged in conflict, it is not uncommon for one disputant to appear to be listening, when in actuality they are furiously crafting responses to each point with which they take umbrage, keeping track only of their own planned replies to be unleashed when it is their turn to speak. Having disputants engage in Reflective Listening subsequent to the conclusion of each one's comments will force them to focus on the information being stated instead of their own planned rebuttals.
   i. Focusing on Reflective Listening might provide a disputant the added benefit of derailing any ensuing plans to respond with attacks that would have been carried out had they been given the option to respond immediately. (See "Take a Beat" exercises later in this chapter.)
   ii. While Reflective Listening is an excellent tool to shift the tenor of a conversation, it is important for the mediator to consistently keep control of the way in which disputants preface their statements. If the statements are not framed correctly, disputants on the receiving end might feel attacked, judged, and as if they are being told how they are feeling, what their intentions are, and what they did or did not do.

There should be no perspective or opinion offered while practicing Reflective Listening.

1. Judgmental statements to avoid:
   - "You should have done . . . ."
   - "If you had done . . . ."
   - "You messed up because . . . ."
   - "That was a mistake."
   - "You were wrong for doing that."
   - "Obviously you did that because . . . ."
   - "I can't believe you did that."
   - "If you don't . . . then . . . ."
   - "Have you done the research to . . . .?"
   - "Have you looked into other options?"
2. Solving statements to avoid:
   - "You should . . . ."
   - "If I did that I would . . . ."
   - "You need to . . . ."
   - "Go do . . . ."
   - "This is what you're going to do . . . ."
   - "Clearly you need help, so I'll tell you what to do."
3. Invalidating statements to avoid:
   - "It's not that big of a deal."
   - "Look at the bright side . . . ."
   - "It could be worse . . . ."
   - "It's not that bad . . . my friend dealt with something much worse."
   - "You should be grateful it was just that."

- "Oh yes, this one time I . . . ."
- "I know exactly how you feel. I had the same thing happen to me when . . . ."

A variation of Reflective Listening is to reflect back to the listener what it *seems* that they are expressing.

1. Unlike previously described Reflective or Mirror Listening, which involves no interpretation or opinion, this variation necessitates exactly that. It is the opportunity for the listener to reflect back to the speaker the message in their statement that goes beyond their exact words.
2. Generally speaking and specifically in conflict situations, it is very difficult to listen and hear without adding a layer of personal interpretation and opinion. The action of the listener reflecting back to a speaker how their message is being interpreted is crucial for both parties, as it provides the speaker insight into how their words are perceived, whether or not their message is clear, and if they are being understood correctly. The speaker then has the opportunity to clarify any number of miscommunications, misunderstandings, aggravations, and arguments by reframing statements to be less inflammatory and hurtful, as well as for them to rethink the way in which communication and conflict are being handled.
3. The listener can also reflect back to the speaker the effect that their words are having on them, so the speaker might have the choice to change the way they speak and apologize for any unintentional harm that has been caused. However, if that is exactly what the speaker intended, then that is good information for both the listening party and the mediator to have.
   a. A disputant who is intentionally mean and aggressive must be managed in a specific way aligned with their Communication Style and behavior for a mediation to progress toward settlement. At the very least this could involve caucusing with discussion about why they feel the need to behave in such a manner and whether that behavior can be shifted through reason and the comprehension of potentially detrimental impacts if the behavior is unchanged.

Reflective or Mirror Listening can be augmented into Reflective or Mirror responses from the mediator.

1. If it becomes apparent that a disputant is having a difficult time interacting with those who have different Communication Styles or different CHMs, it could become beneficial for the mediator to adopt an interaction style that reflects or mirrors that of the disputant as closely as possible. In other words, try to speak the same language to reach them. If the obstacle is one of communication, mirroring can go a long way.
   a. The caveat to mirroring a disputant's interactional behavior is that there are times when the exact opposite is required. For example, a disputant with a CHM might only be willing to back down and collaborate if they feel they have won something and overpowered someone. At this point, the mediator should move into caucus, where they would have

an opportunity to mirror back an opposite CHM by stepping in to offer themself as collateral damage, so to speak, playing the necessary role to mitigate the disputant's current Competitive mode. By absorbing the impact of the Competitive mode, the mediator can spare an opposing party this impact, and minimize the damage to the mediation as a whole. "What they can't hear can't hurt them," as they say, so shielding one party from another comes with the territory of handling angry disputants who sometimes lose track of the larger goal, and their BATNA within it. Additionally, this absorption by the mediator provides the competitive party with the opportunity to maintain an interaction style compatible with their preferred CHM. Satisfying this need to win will come at no cost to another party or to the mediation. After engaging with the mediator in this fashion, the competing party might be able to shift their thought processes toward settlement.

Whether the mediation is in joint session or in caucus, when settlement discussions have begun, the mediator should reflect back to all parties involved the exact details of any offered settlement option. It is imperative for all parties to know exactly what they are being offered, will be considering, and ultimately would be agreeing to.

1. Just before disputants sign any settlement agreement, the mediator should engage with them in a final reflection of the details of the agreement to ensure that all parties are on the same page and that they fully understand and agree to the settlement.

FLASH CHALLENGE

Reflective/Mirroring:
I'm Listening, and This Is What You Feel

1. Find two people to engage in Reflective Listening with each other.
2. Request that one tell a story that holds some emotional value for them.
   a. It should not be overly complicated, and mostly consist of the facts. Some emotional commentary is acceptable but not too much, as the listener should have the opportunity to figure that out on their own.
3. When the speaker has finished, ask the listener to detail back (reflect back) to the speaker the information they received, recounting the facts as they heard them.
   a. It is okay for the listener to take notes while the speaker is telling their story.
   b. The listener should practice reflecting back with statements that begin with:
      i. "It sounds like you...."
      ii. "I think I heard you say...."
      iii. "If I understand correctly...."
      iv. "I believe you said...."
      v. "From your point of view...."

4. The speaker can have an opportunity to correct any misunderstanding or miscommunication when the listener is finished.
5. Now ask the listener to describe their *interpretation* of the story including any additional details they may have inferred.
   a. Ask them to include the feelings they believe the speaker had pertaining to their story.
   b. This should be a presentation of the speaker's feelings that go above and beyond what they expressed during the telling of their story.
   c. The listener should practice reflecting back with statements that begin with:
      i. "Based on what I understand, you feel/you are feeling . . . ."
      ii. "It sounds like you feel . . . ."
      iii. "That type of situation can make a person feel . . . ."
      iv. "When you were telling me what happened, you looked . . . ."
      v. "Your feelings are coming across as . . . ."

LAYERED LISTENING: CHESS IN YOUR HEAD

Layered Listening is an application of all listening styles, layered on top of each other in an order conducive to reaching the desired and necessary mediation outcome. This involves listening to information and mentally structuring it to create a plan of action, to initiate a strategy through questions and statements to the disputants, and to reach an end goal.

Just as there is a process for most things—building a house, baking a cake, learning how to do a backflip—so, too, there is a process for listening, gathering, and using information, tailoring it for each specific mediation. During the course of conflict intervention, information does not exist in a vacuum with one piece not directly affecting another. There is cause, effect, purpose, placement, opinion, truth, fact, fiction, and more. The benefit of Layered Listening, gathering all the information and subsequently moving around the pieces, is that much clearer pictures tend to be revealed. Layering is also critically important, because the understanding of multiple parts of information woven together can be completely different than the picture a lone piece of information creates. Perhaps there was a stabbing, a violent act worthy of harsh penalty. However, if the causative event was that a gun-wielding invader broke into a home and was physically assaulting someone, the stabbing in self-defense might be considered a life-saving act of heroism. Imagine looking only at the violent response without taking into consideration the preceding incident. Without layering every element of a story, how reliable can that story really be? The movement of the pieces of information generally happens internally as the mediator is listening to the story, mentally shifting those understandings and ideas in the direction necessary to reach settlement. However, there is a time and a place for this discussion with one or all of the parties involved in the conflict that can shed light on possible miscommunications, misunderstandings, and less than factual comments and beliefs. Both options can reach the same goal of reshaping the narrative and planning moves toward settlement, but knowing and deciding when to use which will depend on the conflict, the disputants, and the mediator. Whereas verbal discourse leading to layering might not take place in every mediation, mentally layering information must—without exception—as the job of the mediator is to listen, understand, categorize, layer, plan, and execute.

DISCUSSION EXERCISE

Dive! Dive! Dive!

Disputant Statement

I don't want to be here anymore. I can't handle this.

Pause, think, and work. That's exactly what should immediately go through a mediator's mind when a disputant makes such a statement. On the face of it, the disputant is stating two facts: First, that they do not want to be in this mediation now and want to leave; and second, that they feel they cannot cope with it. This information is helpful to a mediator who is putting their listening skills to work to find the literal meaning of what is being said. Let us understand in no uncertain terms that the disputant has made a telling statement, the depths of which a mediator will need scuba gear to address.

Discussion

Questions and possibilities the mediator immediately begins considering upon hearing:

I don't want to be here anymore. I can't handle this.

1. Lean toward caucusing parties to privately encourage the disputants to give open and honest answers.
   a. This will also begin to lay the foundation for a trusting relationship between the mediator and disputant, which is crucial in this case as there could be many emotional layers to get through, and the disputant's emotional state is driving their words and actions.
2. Ask why they don't want to be here if being here could move them forward toward settlement and put this conflict behind them.
   a. Most people do not choose to be in conflict circumstances that require mediation and would rather spend a day doing something else, but this disputant still feels the need to make the statement. This is a telling signal for the mediator.
3. It seems to be a statement of anxiety, especially when combined with "I can't handle this."
   a. Do they regularly deal with anxiety issues?
      i. Was there childhood or adult trauma that has led to post-traumatic stress (PTS) or post-traumatic stress disorder (PTSD) and a limited or

stunted ability to interact with what they perceive as conflict, stressful, or confrontational situations?

b. Do they have behaviors or mechanisms for coping with anxiety?
   i. If not, will their anxiety worsen and potentially turn into more extreme anxious behavior as the mediation progresses?

c. Are they sensitive about having anxiety issues?
   i. They did not come out and say they struggle with anxiety, so perhaps they are unwilling or not prepared to reveal this.
   ii. How can I address this without directly saying the word *anxiety*, at least not before the disputant does?
   iii. There is a clear need to tread lightly while proceeding with the mediation process.

4. Exactly what is the *this* that they feel they can't handle?
5. How do they regularly address and manage conflict?
6. What do they need to feel more comfortable?
   a. How can I put the disputant at ease to be able to discuss the facts of this case?
   b. What can be done to separate the facts of the case from the disputant's emotional response to the conflict and to the mediation so that there is a chance of moving toward settlement?
7. How can I encourage the disputants to open up about what they are experiencing, the conflict in its entirety through their eyes, and the rest of their feelings on the issue(s) to move forward with a productive mediation?
   a. What do I need to do for them to see me as:
      i. An ally.
      ii. A safe person providing a safe space.
      iii. Someone with whom they feel comfortable speaking about personal issues.
      iv. Someone who does not judge them.
8. The time for settlement discussions will be later in this mediation. All of my focus, energy, compassion, empathizing, questions, and conversation will be focused now on their emotional state and what they need to discuss at this moment.
   a. I will guide the conversation toward a goal, not merely a discussion session about why they are upset.
   b. There are no questions I ask simply for the sake of asking questions. They are all guides to move through this and other emotional moments toward a position where we will try to find reason and logic to begin settlement discussions.
9. How can I unlock their brainstorming and problem-solving abilities and willingness to use them to work on settlement options?

FLASH CHALLENGE

Just Flow With It

Part 1

1. Respond to each of the questions and statements in the above discussion.
   a. Discuss and describe if they are similar or not to how you would approach the disputant's statement.

Part 2

1. Based on the above Discussion Exercise and discussion, create and fill in a flowchart with your responses to the disputant's statement below. You should create multiple responses to their statement.

I don't want to be here anymore.
I can't handle this.

2. Include disputant's responses as you imagine they would reply to each of your questions or statements.
   a. Empathize as much as you can with the disputant's position to imagine and include their responses.
      i. How would you respond if you were the disputant in this situation and the mediator were speaking to you?
3. Create as many conversation circles as you find necessary.
4. When appropriate, your questions and statements should illustrate your:
   a. Creativity.
   b. Search for pertinent information.
   c. Support.
   d. Strength.
   e. Direction.
   f. Additional thoughts.

Careful listening to find opportunity and to gather enough information to then ask nonthreatening questions is critical, especially when one word, one misunderstanding, or one miscommunicated thought could preclude a settled conflict. It is not hard to imagine the requisite mediator attention necessary to be placed on received information prior to their response. The mediator will now be engaged in the listening process in a fully active and purposeful way, categorizing, shaping, and positioning the information being presented. There is no conversation about listening without a discussion of what to do with the information being collected, inclusive of what must happen to that information before it becomes a response, a question, or a statement from the mediator.

Listening and speaking can have potentially deleterious consequences when performed improperly and used as weapons for disputants to hurt each other, so to assist them in avoiding further issues, the mediator might encourage implementing rules governing both the listening and speaking processes. This is a strategy that the mediator can discuss at the beginning of the mediation to set the tone for its entirety. Additionally, by discussing it at the beginning of the mediation with all parties at the same time, the mediator can avoid any disputant feeling singled out. As the mediation progresses, this will also help to prevent disputants from feeling that their behavior is being interpreted by the mediator as problematic and something for which they would be punished. Avoiding possible disputant misinterpretation of the mediator's actions as targeting them is wise, as that misunderstanding could cause a disputant to lash out. Planning for a variety of possibilities beforehand rather than seeming to mete out punishment after the fact is a course of action most beneficial when attempting to keep emotions and tensions in check.

EXAMPLES OF LISTENING AND SPEAKING RULES

1. The mediator will monitor that all rules are adhered to during the communication process, and if a rule is not being followed, the mediator and the mediator alone will be the one to step in to provide a reminder specifically identifying the rule that is not being observed. The rule must be adhered to before any communication continues.
2. If any rule is broken, either accidentally or intentionally, an apology should be made immediately.
    a. Even if the disputants are angry and aggressive toward each other and the thought of extending an apology is completely outside the realm of acceptability, the mediator can present (reframe) this necessary apology as one strictly for breaking a rule that disputants mutually agreed to.
        i. The apology rule will be included and presented at the beginning of the mediation along with any and all listening and speaking rules, to be mutually agreed to by the disputants.
        ii. This apology rule is isolated to the listening and speaking rules only.
        iii. An apology can and will come from any disputant who breaks an agreed-on rule.
        iv. As the rules will have been previously agreed to, any disputant apologizing for breaking a listening and speaking rule does not need to feel that they are being weak or giving up any leverage, power, or position in the overall conflict and mediation process.

Note to the Reader

Here is a little trick of the trade: An apology rule leading to the disputants getting into the habit of and becoming comfortable with apologizing for mistakes made and as a measure to de-escalate emotions can be strategy that you, as the mediator, can keep to yourself.

3. When a disputant is speaking, they will not be interrupted by any other disputant. They are allowed to finish speaking, and then the speaking turn will be passed to the next disputant.
4. If the listener chooses to ask questions when permitted and called on for their turn, they must be respectful and use no accusatory or blaming language.
5. All speakers should use "I" statements and should describe any effects of the conflict on them personally. They should not relate what they did, how they did it, or their reasons for it.
   a. Disputants should be directed to speak about personal experience and personal impact, rather than blaming another party for what happened. Fault can be dealt with (or not) at a later point.
6. There can be a designated time for rebuttals and responses by the listener to statements made by the speaker.
   a. The mediator can allow the disputants to present all of their information, including reflecting and asking any questions they might have. A separate time should pe provided for rebuttals and direct responses to a speaker's statements.
   b. Response statements should be devoid of opinions about the speaker's actions or personal beliefs about what should or should not have happened.
7. The mediator can also carve out time for disputants to seek help reframing their statements.
   a. The disputants might have become aware that their statements are being interpreted in unintended ways (e.g., aggressive and inflammatory). They might choose to seek the assistance of the mediator in reframing their statements to accurately reflect their intentions. This will most likely happen in brief caucuses between shifting roles from speaker to listener.
      i. If the mediation is in joint session, there is a possibility that the disputant will wish to remain there while their statements are reframed. The mediator can suggest the rationale based on the contents of the statements to make this decision either to stay in joint session or to move into caucus.
8. If it appears that listening disputants are not accepting or validating speaking disputants' statements, the mediator might ask each party to express

how they would feel if the shoe were on the other foot and their positions reversed.

a. This might be an activity that the mediator engages in with each disputant separately during caucus so that they feel more comfortable expressing understanding and validation for each other. They might feel if they do so in joint session that they will be giving up ground, admitting that they are wrong, or acquiescing to the strength of another position. The benefits of this move into caucus could be equally applicable to disputants developing a willingness to discuss settlement options that could be fair and mutually agreeable.

ASKING QUESTIONS AS STRATEGY

Although listening does not necessarily require asking questions, there is little doubt about whether questions will be part of the conflict intervention process. Desired mediation end goals necessitate the management of information, including asking questions in a purposeful and strategic manner. As a cyclical pattern of listening and asking questions develops, strategy, creativity, and potential settlement options emerge.

There are many reasons for asking questions, with an equal number of benefits, detriments, pros, and cons. There are also immediate decisions to be made regarding which types of questions to ask and consideration of a combination of types, all of which require forethought. Asking questions without at least a strong idea of what the answer could be is a scenario that should be avoided, unless, of course, the mediator is in a strictly information-gathering phase of the mediation, which can be at any point and continue for any duration.

1. Purposeful Listening
   a. As mentioned more than once throughout this book, listening is a foundational and fundamental part of conflict intervention in general and mediation specifically. It does, however, require training and practice to learn how to listen efficiently and to a desired end. Listening to be bathed in information for no good reason serves no purpose. The mediator is always listening with a purpose that changes and varies as disputants traverse the conflict resolution process. The skills of listening purposefully and asking questions intersect in potential opportunities and strategic planning. The mediator seeks out specific information that can provide a catalyst to drive the mediation ever closer to settlement. To identify that specific information, though, requires attention to and mental juggling of the many layers of the conflict, disputants' positions, their true underlying concerns, and taking advantage of moments that present wiggle room to the mediator in the form of openings for mutual collaboration, settlement options, or both. The questions that are formulated based on these considerations have the purpose of bettering some part

of the conflict, managing disputant emotional states, providing clarification, and guiding the mediation process toward resolution. The requisite emphasis placed on asking the right questions at the right time and for the right reasons is not exclusively for purposes of the mediation's forward progress. When the right questions are not asked at the right time and for the right reasons, the repercussions could be as serious and impactful as a mediation's complete derailment and impasse.

2. Identify the problem
   a. By focusing on a problem that needs to be addressed and dispelled, questions are turned into targeted approaches or attacks with a very specific and clear agenda.
      For example:
      i. The mediator will decide whether or not their agenda should be made evident to the disputants, and if so, a calculated choice will be made as to when and how to expose it. Perhaps it will be in the form of asking open-ended questions leading one disputant to "independently come to a new realization" that they believe is their own original idea. This, however, could produce a problem.
         1. Identified problem arising from the strategy
            a) An opposing disputant might feel an imbalance in contribution to the successful outcome of a mediation if they are not also contributing to the same degree.
         2. Mediator intervention
            a) The mediator might deliver additional questions based on this disputant's need to reinterpret their position of feeling imbalanced.
            b) The mediator can involve this disputant in brainstorming about the new realization. Even though they might not have come up with it, they can become part of developing it into a fully formed idea and bringing it to fruition.
3. Identify whether or not additional information is necessary
   a. Without adequate information including details, timelines, clarity, and nuance, a question is immediately risky—the value of the unknown cannot be underestimated. This danger emanates from the unknown nature of a disputant's responses to inquiries posed to them. For example, on commencement of the mediation, a disputant might be asked, "What do you need to settle this today?" Their unexpected response could be deemed completely inappropriate, disrespectful, and disagreeable by another party. In joint session, a dangerous answer from one disputant in front of another could derail an entire mediation by causing an impregnable impasse. In caucus, notwithstanding the mediator's efforts to repackage and reframe messages, an impasse might still occur if a disputant's answer to a question causes them emotional upheaval on such a level that it cannot be defused. In their effort to create pathways leading to safe answers, the mediator will use skillful, open-ended questions to

reconstruct the pieces of the entire narrative that shaped the conflict. In a layered fashion with levels of critical information, reframed inflammatory statements, and details clarifying previous unknowns, the mediator has created the opportunity for safe answers.

b. Questions that lead to safe answers can be repeated and expanded on to create an atmosphere that is cooperative and possibly empathetic where the same language can begin to be spoken by all disputants, leading to potential settlement. Safe answers can be the key to bringing parties together and onto the same side to work collaboratively within the conflict. An example of a safe answer is one that expresses hurt feelings rather than anger. The response to an angry communication compared to the response to an expression of hurt feelings can change mediation outcomes. The latter can culminate in a resolution of the conflict and the possible salvation of a relationship, whereas the former might contribute to bringing about impasse. Asking questions to gather additional information prior to "What do you need to settle this today?" will enable the mediator to make a better informed decision about whether:
   i. This particular question should be asked at all.
   ii. If it is asked, whether it should be in joint session or in caucus.
   iii. It requires reframing prior to being asked.
   iv. It will be interpreted as an attack that will be met with a response in kind.
   v. It will be interpreted as a power imbalance indicating that the one being asked has the power to make the decision about how the mediation can reach resolution.

Based on any additional information, if the mediator concludes that asking "What do you need to settle this today?" will increase the likelihood of a favorably received and better understood response, then they will feel that posing the question could be appropriate and beneficial. Asking questions to collect supplemental information is a generally advantageous approach when the mediator senses that one party is becoming increasingly agitated and angered by what they are hearing for reasons that are not readily clear. Without identifying the cause(s) of their responses, the mediation could find itself in jeopardy of not reaching settlement. Information is one of the deciding factors that can tip the scales in one direction or the other.

A mediator listens not only for information to assist in the negotiation process or to create a timeline, for example, but also as a true observer whose job it is to seek out opportunity, possibility, and creativity where there is seemingly none. These answers provide space for new understandings, new conversations, and new relationships between disputants, as well as with the conflict. The resultant safe answers may also encourage disputants to ask each other questions which express interest and show validation of thoughts, feelings, and ideas. This new interaction allows disputants to reposition so that when they are speaking, they are answering questions and providing information to an interested party who cares about what they have to say.

c. If a mediator has a suspicion or determines that information presented by the parties is not factual, this is an indication that seeking out additional information might be necessary. However, seeking truthful information could be a sensitive course of action for the mediator once the disputants have already presented their stories that include mediator-identified untruths. The mediator should avoid any implication that a disputant is lying, simultaneously encouraging additional discussion. Through the use of open-ended questions, purposeful listening, and inviting as much detail as the disputant has to offer, the mediator should be able to differentiate factual from not factual information without directly accusing the parties of lying.
   i. Note that there are occasions when seeking out additional information to determine fact from fiction is not the best course of action. Doing so during discussions involving facts determining fault is irrelevant and actually destructive to moving forward toward settlement. That determination need not have a seat at a resolution discussion table when the mediator focuses the parties on moving past the conflict positions they are currently in to reach settlement, regardless of what brought them to mediation.
   ii. Asking questions in various ways, all revolving around the same subject, is a method by which the mediator can separate and cross-reference answers. If the mediation is in joint session, there will be commentary from the disputants contradicting statements each believes to be untrue. The mediator might propose that the disputants speak one at a time, retelling their tale of the conflict, making statements, or answering questions, alternating with one another and repeating this process as many times as necessary to separate fact from fiction. If the mediation is in caucus, the mediator could pose the same questions to each disputant and weigh the answers against each other. Even if they are mostly different, there might be common elements that the mediator can determine to be truthful or not.

FLASH CHALLENGE

Three Lies and a Truth

1. Find a partner and ask them to tell you three lies and one truth, on any topics. Make sure they do not disclose to you which is which. You will be discussing them all, so instruct your partner to be prepared with a full story for each and to give answers to your questions.
2. Engage with them about each statement and take notes for yourself.
   a. Ask questions.
   b. Ask for details.

c. Ask cross-referencing questions.
d. Ask for context.
3. When you feel ready, make your guess as to which are truths, and which is the lie.
4. If you guessed all correctly, great! Find another partner and practice again.
5. If you did not guess all correctly, also great! This is a perfect opportunity to take a second look at their answers to your questions, including the specific way they delivered the information to you.
   a. Was there anything you missed that you can identify on closer inspection of your notes and additional review of the conversation that can lead you to different conclusions?
6. Consider discussing with your partner where you could have asked additional questions or asked them differently to reach answers that would have led you to the correct conclusion.
7. Repeat this challenge with at least three people and keep a log of all conversations and outcomes.

4. Identify what must be avoided
   a. During a mediation, the mediator might conclude that certain topics are inflammatory and triggering, having evoked highly emotional responses. In deciding that these topics are not integral for the disputants to reach settlement, it is the mediator's responsibility to guide the parties away from those topics and onto an alternate track. It might be the first instinct of the parties to engage with each other on issues that have been and continue to be inflammatory. The mediator, however, can create a dialogue that does not provide further opportunity for interaction about anything other than what is productive for settlement by pivoting and choosing a different line of questioning. Through the use of carefully and specifically chosen questions, the mediator may be able to avoid those triggering topics.
   b. If, however, those triggering topics happen to be components of the conflict that must be addressed and discussed, the mediator should focus on restructuring the way the topics are presented. The triggers and points that must be avoided could, in fact, be in the packaging of the message rather than the message itself. That is a manageable task for the mediator.
   i. For example, hearing a claim such as, "It was an accident; I didn't mean to," might be triggering for a disputant who associates that phrasing with denial of responsibility and an unwillingness to repair any harm or damage that was caused to them. Repackaging that phrase into "It was my mistake, I apologize, and I would like to make it right," would likely sidestep any triggers and move the mediation forward.

5. Goal
   a. A broad goal is more closely associated with information gathering for the purposes of crafting strategy, approach, and possible settlement options. Questions should be wide and open, designed to extract from the disputants as much information as possible about everything imaginable. When there is no clearly defined path to settlement identified or formulated, when everything and nothing is on the table, and when the mediator is wading through the muddy waters of "What the heck is going on here, and why?" the wisest choice would be to ask broad questions and to collect all of the information that they can. Yes, that does include the sister-in-law's best friend's neighbor's hair color, because that detail could eventually prove useful when intense creativity is the only option a mediator has to navigate toward a settlement. One never knows.
   b. With a narrow goal in mind, possibly to get to the bottom of a specific point in contention or that has caused confusion, questions that pertain only to the pertinent topic are most appropriate. Questions should focus the disputants' attention exclusively on the relevant point, remaining there either until resolution of the point is reached or it is clear that it would be more beneficial to set it aside and shift to other equally specific points, or to the broader goal of settlement. It is not always necessary to address every point along the way to reach a mutually agreeable settlement, especially if the mediation is not Transformative. Strangers do not need to agree about or understand everything about each other if a solution option is deemed acceptable by all parties. The collective goal of putting the conflict and the mediation behind them can be enough, and fortunately, mediators travel with extra-large rugs capable of covering quite a bit that is swept underneath them.
6. Be crafty
   a. Open-ended questions are usually asked for the purpose of encouraging disputants to open up and discuss the conflict in their own words. A commonly used tool during interrogations and conveniently also applicable during mediations, open-ended questions are designed to bring forth conversation on any topic in an attempt to reach a flow that might lead to additional information spilling out. This could include certain unintended disclosures on the part of a disputant (or person being interrogated), and information that they had not planned on disclosing to the mediator. It is important to keep the questions as open-ended as possible so that disputants will have plenty to discuss, with a lot of story to reveal.
   b. Closed-ended questions—those with yes or no answers—are a topic of far less discussion, but they do serve a valuable purpose. When a conflict has become convoluted, with complicated conversations and frustrations abounding, a direct yes or no answer can provide organization and clarity. When the mediator asks a question that a disputant is inclined to answer with a long-winded, circular, possibly nonsensical, and potentially

antagonizing response, a concise yes or no can close doors on unimportant points that have been belabored to no avail due to the argumentative nature of conflict. The goal is to move the mediation out of its current position and into a new one. It can aid in nipping superficial posturing in the bud and can also cut through to concerns beneath the surface. Requesting a direct and succinct answer in the form of a yes or no eliminates the opportunity for extraneous commentary, which is the desired outcome in these circumstances.

FLASH CHALLENGE

Yes, No, Maybe So, and Can You Tell Me More About That, Please?

1. Using the Ms. Shi v. Ms. Vito fact pattern, come up with open-ended and closed-ended questions that apply to the various components of the conflict and that might be beneficial in working toward resolution.
2. You should have one list of open-ended questions and one list of closed-ended questions for each disputant.
   a. Discuss your reasons for choosing each question.
   b. Which part of the fact pattern led you to make each of your questioning decisions?
3. Include what you imagine would be potential responses to each of your questions.
4. Extra Credit: Provide your replies to each of their potential responses.

7. Desired responses
   a. Unless the mediator is a glutton for punishment, enjoys living life on the edge, or happens to be gathering information, there is no reason to ask a question without an end goal in mind. Lacking any information about the conflict or the case, that end goal could be to reach effective communication among the disputants or to bring the mediation to a settled agreement. However, with the addition of new information and new answers to questions, that goal will likely begin to include more elements, such as a repaired relationship or a new understanding.
8. Potential responses
   a. A mediator should always plan for the unexpected as well as the expected. Many people have first aid, earthquake, or survival kits at home as part of being prepared. Consider this strategy to be the mediator's first aid, earthquake, and survival kit rolled into one. By being mentally prepared for all types of answers that come their way, including those that might be less than desirable because they present a cognitive bias or require an immediate reframe, the mediator will be ready with follow-up questions and responses. Applying one of the strategies presented above such as

refraining from asking questions (for purposes other than information-gathering) without at least an idea of the answer is another valuable item packed in the mediator's kit. In other words, never be caught off guard, and always be at least two moves ahead.

Even when disputants are able to communicate in some measure effectively, the mediator must continue purposeful lines of questioning to actively guide the conversation and ensure that it stays on a correct track. Regardless of how much mediator facilitation is required, an across-the-board recommendation to anyone who asks for help dealing with any sort of conflict large or small is to *take a beat.* Between the thought forming in one's head and the words exiting one's mouth, pause or take a beat to make sure that what is about to be said will reflect correct intentions, whether making an initial statement or responding thereto, and that less harm than good results. In fact, this is always good practice before speaking. If a disputant expresses uncertainty about how to structure a thought or is concerned that it will be interpreted in a manner other than how it is intended, that means they are exhibiting self-awareness, concern for others, and a desire for cooperation. An ensuing conversation will likely transpire in caucus for the disputant to discuss privately with the mediator the best way to structure their thoughts, based on their intentions. The mediator should direct the disputant to stop, breathe, take a beat, and self-reflect about the intent behind their messages. They should also be encouraged to ask the mediator as many questions as necessary until that best structure is reached and expresses complete clarity of their intentions, as well as their desired outcome. Exploratory questions from the mediator asked at different times during the disputant's self-reflection and considerations could provide necessary guided direction. Understanding each other properly and knowing exactly what is transpiring before any form of a response is made is imperative to participants in mediation, both disputants and mediator alike. It is of the utmost importance to take a beat to ensure that perceptions are correct and that there are no responses made in kind to messages that might have been misunderstood or misperceived as inflammatory, aggressive, or disrespectful. This *take a beat* plan of action should be implemented before every answer or response among disputants.

TAKE A BEAT

If/Then Statement #1: Try this Instead

If disputants are unable to exert self-control while speaking, then advise them to shift their approach and repackage their message by saying:

> *It sounds as though you are saying you don't care about my feelings, and that you are blaming me for something. I would not think that you would feel that way, or say something like that to me, so please help me figure out what you mean.*
> *("Please" should help soften a message and create a collaborative instead of combative environment.)*

Without this act of taking a beat, there could be incorrect conclusions drawn that carry with them unintended consequences. Those conclusions might include:

1. If I explain myself in a way that makes sense to me, it will make sense to them as well.
2. I am speaking perfectly clearly and rationally, so they must understand what I am saying and see that I am correct.
3. I understand what they are saying.
4. I know I am right so they must see that I am right as well.
5. I am using specific words for specific reasons (for their definitions) and they understand them in exactly the way I intend them to be understood.
6. If I explain what happened and how big of a deal it really is, they will see it as a big deal as well.

The unfortunate and unwelcomed ramifications of incorrect conclusions can stretch farther than the eye can see and deeper than the mind can comprehend. Imagine someone running toward a foreign embassy, yelling and waving their arms while being chased by gun-wielding soldiers who are also yelling. The embassy has orders to shoot anyone who tries to storm their grounds and does not heed their commands to stop. The runner is not slowing down in spite of the shouted command of "Stop or we will shoot!", and is about to cross the embassy threshold. In a last-minute, split-second decision, the commander of the embassy guards directs his troops, "Hold fire!" The runner launches over the gate and lands at their feet, while the soldiers giving chase stop just outside the perimeter. The runner is a citizen of the country represented by the embassy and was about to be captured and punished for protecting an innocent child from being beaten by the soldiers. Had the embassy commander not taken a beat, which led to the decision not to fire, the guards could have wounded or killed one of their own countrymen instead of providing needed and deserved protection. There is no reason to take a chance, so take a beat.

Ms. Shi v. Ms. Vito

Inaccurate Perceptions and the Unnecessary and Avoidable Damage They Cause

The perceptions of Ms. Shi and Ms. Vito are that each is attempting to take away or deny something that the other wants or needs, and that each is disregarding the other's interests and feelings. Ms. Shi believes that Ms. Vito wants to kill the fig tree that she loves so much, which has deep emotional significance, is the vehicle by which she engages in her bird-watching, and is one of the main reminders of their fig business that helped her to buy her home in the first place. She has become anchored to her position of distrust and aggression toward Ms. Vito.

Ms. Shi perceives that the life she has built is being threatened. She is negatively biased against Ms. Vito, as evidenced by her attitude of denying responsibility for Ms. Vito's daughter's injury and for the maintenance of the portion of the tree that hangs onto Ms. Vito's property. By acknowledging that the dropped figs, and the tree by extension, are responsible for the injuries and general harm, Ms. Shi feels that she is providing Ms. Vito with additional ammunition and evidence for the tree's removal to be appropriate and warranted. Additionally, as a result of the deterioration of the relationship and complete breakdown in their communication, Ms. Shi has thus far been unwilling to partake in any civil communications with Ms. Vito about:

1. General responsibility.
2. Appropriately acknowledging the daughter's injury and taking financial responsibility.
3. Addressing previous property damage due to dropped fruit and rodents.
4. Working collaboratively on options to clean up after the tree to avoid any additional damages.

Without a willingness to provide and receive proper or clarified information, shifting away from their perceptions of each other's actions and behaviors will be almost impossible. Had Ms. Shi been willing to ask (and accept the answer), she would have learned that Ms. Vito had gone out of her way to seek out potential options for the management of the tree, including cutting and harmless removal of the roots that are doing serious damage to her house and pool. This information might have been enough to shift Ms. Shi's attitude and perspective sufficiently to change the dynamic of the conflict and their interactions because it is likely that at least part of her unwillingness to accept any responsibility, or least her attitude about it, is based on her inaccurate perceptions. Based on these misperceptions, Ms. Shi is now using her assumption that Ms. Vito wants to kill the tree as a tool to justify her position and behavior. She is in pure fight, protection, and defense modes. Ms. Shi refuses to engage in any form of effective or productive communication, and because of that Ms. Vito perceives Ms. Shi to be:

1. Mean.
2. Heartless.
3. Stubborn.
4. Unwilling to listen to information and facts.
5. Unwilling to hear that she, Ms. Vito, has been traumatized by her daughter's injury and subsequent medical treatment and care.
6. Unwilling to hear that Ms. Vito is facing major foundational issues with her house—her personal residence to which she, too, has a strong emotional connection.

Their perceptions have created a scenario in which:

1. According to Ms. Vito, Ms. Shi is uncaring, cold-hearted, stubborn, narcissistic, unreasonable, unwilling to listen, completely irrational and illogical, and incoherent in her false accusations.
2. According to Ms. Shi, Ms. Vito is cruel for wanting to destroy the tree that she loves, deliberately lying and creating a false bad image of her in stating that she does not care about the injury, and threatening her livelihood by demanding so much money from her in general, and in such an aggressive and accusatory manner specifically. She believes that there is no way the medical and property damage bills could come close to equaling $175,000, so clearly Ms. Vito is trying to steal her hard-earned money: "How could a few little figs and some roots cause property damage, anyway?"

The disputants have no communication at all, and each perceives the other to be unable and unwilling to listen. Each woman believes the other is "out to get her" and that they are at war, on opposites sides of an issue, when in actuality, they could and should be partnering together to determine solution options that respect and address as many as possible interests, needs, and desires of both sides. As a Transformative mediation between family members, there are more considerations than simply negotiating who pays how much to whom.

TAKE A BEAT:

If/Then Statement #2: What If . . .

If everything a disputant says is defensive and combative, then ask:

> *Is it possible that while the opposing party is actively speaking and stating their positions, emotions, and experience, that you are crafting rebuttals and mounting defenses in your head, instead of listening and truly hearing what they are saying to clarify and deepen your understanding of how they are approaching this mutual conflict? Consider that while doing so, you are missing crucial information that could entirely change the face of the conflict and this mediation. You are also potentially missing areas where you agree, as well as areas of previously unrecognized and unrealized misunderstanding. Can you see that a more beneficial plan is to listen, learn, and repeat for clarity before proceeding with a response?*

The guiding principle is for disputants to be led to understand that their goal is one and the same—to be rid of the dispute. The sooner the narrative can be shifted, the better. "How can we solve this together?" and "What do we each need to be willing to reach settlement?" can replace "No, I want that instead of this and you need to do it my way!"

FLASH CHALLENGE

Seeing the Forest, Not the Trees

During the next Mediation Exercise that elicits aggressive attitudes from the disputants that the mediator identifies as possible unnecessary overreactions, try stopping and asking the disputants to answer the following questions about each other:

1. Can you restate in your own words what they have been expressing?
2. What do you believe are their true intentions?
3. What do you believe to be the elements that are most important to them?
4. Can you identify any areas of commonality?

TAKE A BEAT

If/Then Statement #3: Better Together

If the parties are not working together toward settlement, then direct them to:

> *Brainstorm together. You are here together, so why not try a different approach and actually make an effort to work together? In other situations, when doing something one way doesn't work, we stop, pivot, and try it a different way—or try something else. Why not do that here and now, together? Suspend reality for a moment and forget that you are in conflict and pretend you are seeking each other's counsel to solve this problem. Why not? No one likes to be in conflict. No one would choose to be engaged in a dispute. By working together, you're adding another in-common element. No one wants to continue being upset by the dispute, constantly thinking and worrying about it, possibly being kept up at night, and causing rollover conflict with those around them. Let's put an end to all of that today.*

Note that If/Then Statement #3 is applicable barring those specific mediations in which one or all of the disputants determines that remaining in conflict is their preferred course of action. (See Chapter 5, "Maintaining Neutrality.")

TAKE A BEAT

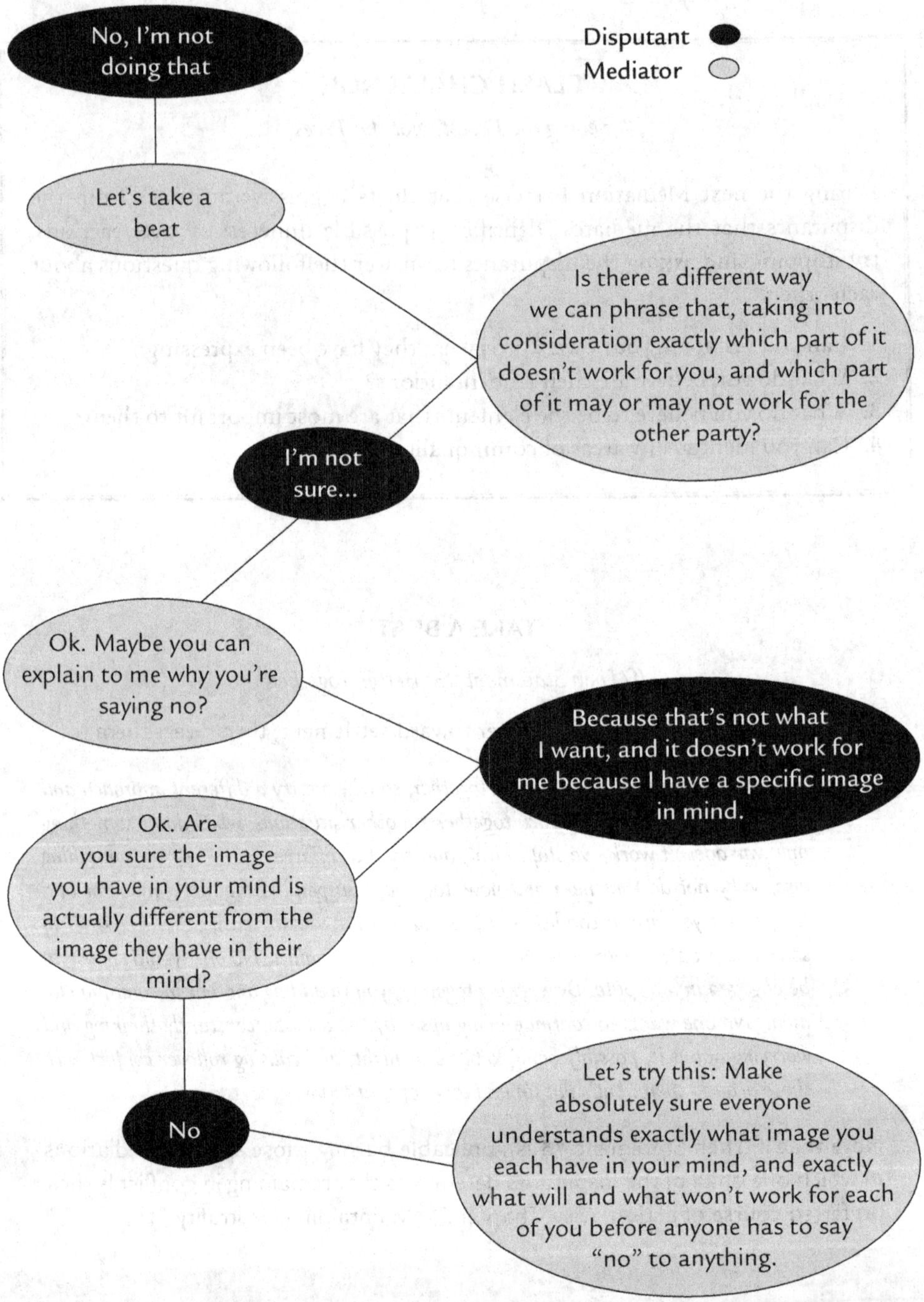
No, I'm not doing that
Disputant
Mediator
Let's take a beat
Is there a different way we can phrase that, taking into consideration exactly which part of it doesn't work for you, and which part of it may or may not work for the other party?
I'm not sure...
Ok. Maybe you can explain to me why you're saying no?
Because that's not what I want, and it doesn't work for me because I have a specific image in mind.
Ok. Are you sure the image you have in your mind is actually different from the image they have in their mind?
No
Let's try this: Make absolutely sure everyone understands exactly what image you each have in your mind, and exactly what will and what won't work for each of you before anyone has to say "no" to anything.

FLASH CHALLENGE

Mediate the Case!

Quick, somebody close the window: Reason and logic are loose in the building and trying to get out!

The Facts

1. Mr. and Mrs. Balloon are a married couple heading toward divorce. They have sought you out to mediate a current dispute over scheduling their divided time for the use of their summer home.
2. It is five minutes into the mediation. You have just finished your opening statement, and the couple has agreed that it is acceptable for Mrs. Balloon to speak first. You have asked Mrs. Balloon to explain, in her own words, why you are all there today, to which she responds, "Because my husband is a narcissistic, egomaniacal, self-centered, selfish . . . ."
3. They are now screaming at each other. Cheating and "bad spouse" accusations are flying left and right, and you can't duck fast enough to miss the insults they are hurling at each other. All semblance of reason and logic is lost.
4. You know with certainty that this level of aggression is not about the summer home, even though it is currently presenting that way.
5. Neither Mr. Balloon nor Mrs. Balloon has cheated on the other, but both are convinced to the contrary.
6. They have two children, twin 12-year-old girls, whose custody they plan to share.
7. The twins have been acting out very badly, which has caused an additional strain on the marriage.
   a. The twins are furious at their parents and heartbroken at the prospect of divorce. The family has gone to two counseling sessions together so far, which has been very traumatic for all involved, adding stress and tension to the situation.

Instructions: Review Appendix, "Mediation Exercise Instructions"

1. Find two people to portray the disputants, Mr. and Mrs. Balloon. Inform them each of the facts, including providing secret information to the appropriate party—make sure that the other party cannot hear this.
2. Inform your disputants that they are each grappling with issues below the surface of what they are openly presenting, as outlined in the Secret Information section below. They should keep this information from you, the mediator, until they choose to reveal it.
3. There is no time limit on this mediation.
4. Because you already know that this is a contentious situation, decide right away if you would like to meet with the parties in caucus after your mediation opening statement or if the parties are able and willing to remain in the same room as each other to proceed in joint session.

Assignment

1. Address disputant needs that are not being met and create a safe and responsive environment for them. Take them to the BAR . . . or to buy a BRA!
   a. **B**eat: Have them take a beat before they speak and before and after they answer.
   b. **A**sk: Ask them questions to get to their needs below the surface.
   c. **R**eframe: Reframe their inflammatory and aggressive statements into being respectful and solution-oriented.

   and/or
   a. **B**eat
   b. **R**eframe
   c. **A**sk
2. Are you able to settle the mediation?
3. If so, how?
   a. When the mediation is over, ask your disputants what changed once their needs were met and how it helped move them toward settlement.
   b. What is the mutually agreed-upon settlement agreement?
4. If not, explain why.
   a. Ask your disputants why it did not work, in which ways their needs were still not being met, and what they felt could have been done differently.

Secret Information for Mrs. Balloon

1. Stay-at-home mom Mrs. Balloon has felt neglected by her husband. He does not express interest in a date night, never compliments her, and on the rare occasion that they are alone, they have nothing to talk about anymore, other than their children.
2. Mrs. Balloon is convinced that separating is the best course of action.
3. Mrs. Balloon is immediately presenting as only interested in a divided use settlement because she is considering getting back into the dating scene.

Secret Information for Mr. Balloon

1. The extra responsibilities Mr. Balloon has taken on at work over the past nine years have enabled them to buy the summer home, but Mr. Balloon feels that his hard work has gone unnoticed and unappreciated by his wife and family. He is resentful that his long, hard-working hours have led to his wife wanting to divorce, as he only agreed to do it in the first place to buy her the home that she wanted! The time spent apart has taken a toll on the couple.
2. Mr. Balloon is not so sure because he thinks they might be able to save their marriage. He will discuss this with the mediator in private, but not in front of Mrs. Balloon.
3. Mr. Balloon is secretly open to settlement options other than divided use of the home.

chapter 7

The Art of the Reframe

The Tilted Kilt

MEDIATION EXAMPLE

Your Pillow or Mine? A Mediation Pajama Party Sleepover

THE INVITATION

This mediation had all the elements of one written for the big screen; feuding students, a teacher in the middle, verbal threats, shouting matches, crying outbursts, sides being taken . . . and that was all before the mediation even started! I was approached to mediate for two horribly feuding students of the same drama teacher, who simply could not be in the same place at the same time with each other without explosive outcomes. I agreed. One of them suggested, "I think it will be a good idea for us to have a sleepover. We will all be in our pajamas, sitting on the floor with pillows everywhere, and really talk. With *you* there as our mediator." I won't lie. Somewhere between sleepover, floor, and pillows, I began checking in with myself to make sure I wasn't completely hallucinating. "Sure, no problem," I heard myself say, with my painted smile, controlled nod, and fully packed toolbelt at the ready. "Definitely, absolutely. I think that's a great idea. Very innovative." There was no doubt that they both felt unheard, would need apologies, and would need to be validated, so a little immediate validation from me would only help nudge us in the right direction. It's never too early to begin laying the groundwork as a mediator.

Emotions were already incredibly high for the parties, and it was clear that they were only going to increase. This mediation is included in this chapter on reframing because that was the skill most relied on and continually engaged during the mediation. In addition to hurt feelings, a complete breakdown of communication, and aggression coming from both disputants, there were more misunderstandings and misinterpretations than is usually the case. When we refer to people speaking *different languages*, this scenario is representative to an extreme of the implications of the expression: different backgrounds, different upbringings, different family dynamics, different educational experiences, different employment histories, different experiences with conflict and trauma, different Conflict

Handling Modes (CHMs), and different Communication Styles. As presented by the parties, these differences could not be confused with the sort of differences that constructively and cohesively "make the world go 'round." Rather, the presented differences were interpreted by the parties in a manner that resulted in distorted, negatively shaped perspectives of each other.

The interesting thing about the origin of this mediation is that I was approached by one of the parties completely of his own volition, so at the least there was a willingness from one party to move into a different relationship with the other, who, as it turns out, was not quite as willing. Because this was not a standard mediation, we will consider it to be conflict intervention in an informal mediation process, with the application of the same mediation skills. It began with a pre-mediation call to the less amenable party.

THE PRE-MEDIATION PHONE CALL

Not knowing anything about this disputant, Disputant B, other than that he was not the one who approached me in the first place, the call I made would really be considered a cold call. His hostility toward the opposing party, Disputant A, immediately overflowed and was consequently projected toward me and any considerations I had of meeting together to resolve their issues. I immediately began reframing this conflict resolution proposition into how it could benefit him, highlighting how being embroiled in this conflict could be negatively affecting him, his work, and those around him. I detailed at great length my role as a facilitator of communication, and an impartial third party to make sure boundaries are not crossed and that respect for everyone is at the forefront of any question, statement, or action. This call also took us to some of his concerns below the surface beyond his interactions with Disputant A, which included the impact the situation had on his personal life and the rage he harbored about it. Among his concerns was questioning his ability to remain controlled enough during a mediation to express himself in a clear and organized manner. In response to this concern, I offered a number of suggestions available to both sides:

1. Caucus, which would allow time to process everything being discussed before responding.
2. My continuous and immediate intervention if either disputant were to conduct themselves in an unacceptable manner.
3. My perpetual preparedness to provide reframes if either party should need assistance getting their points across.
4. Offering the option to write down responses as opposed to verbally communicating them if they should feel so inclined.

By the end of the call, he felt comfortable with my abilities and my intentions. He thought it would be best for everyone involved, especially himself, if they were able to move past the conflict and into a different way of communicating and interacting with each other.

THE CONFLICT INTERVENTION: AN INFORMAL MEDIATION

Part 1: Moving into Caucus

Although initially I viewed the idea of a pajama party mediation to be completely wild, I found my perspective of it shifting in a different direction once the parties arrived. It was readily apparent that the pajama party scenario afforded a more relaxed and comfortable space for the parties, and considering just how emotionally charged the entire situation was, that became something that smoothed the edges. I expressed my shifted perspective to the parties who agreed, providing us all a moment to discuss something in common and a respite from the anger that the conflict elicited. Sensing tension in the room, and some immediate aggressive comments, I decided to move the parties into caucus right away to let off some steam with me privately as they detailed their accounts of how they ended up in their current position. I was able to work on reframing messages (questions, answers, statements) separately with each of them, discussing and identifying with every potential reframe:

1. How their initial message could be perceived and misinterpreted.
2. How the reframe would uphold the intention of their message, using more respectful language.
3. How the reframe should come from a place of "I" instead of blaming.
4. How the reframe will allow space for true dialogue and an exchange of communication and validation.

Additionally, I discussed with each of them some of their histories, both of which included extensive trauma, fending for themselves, and being their own advocate after feeling taken advantage of in many situations over the years. We were able to discuss how this background could have colored their interpretations of some of the other party's messages and behaviors, as well as the ways in which they responded. I could not disclose the similarities in their histories because the discussions were in caucus and only shared with me after several trust-building exercises that included intense validation. I felt that I should work to see if I could encourage them to discuss some of their background openly with each other in joint session in light of the commonalities, which would provide necessary insights and could be an instant eye-opening moment for both. Although this process took quite some time and involved a great deal of shuttling between the rooms, the parties finally came to a point where they felt comfortable being in the same room together, curious about what the other had to say, and looking forward to working out a settlement plan that they would both agree to and maintain.

Example Statements and Reframes

Initial Statements

1. He is crazy!
2. He has acted so horribly to me in the past, and I have done nothing to deserve it.

3. This entire situation is his fault.
4. He does not know how to act or talk to people.
5. I did nothing to deserve any of the abuse I have endured from him.

Initial Statements Reframed

1. I do not understand any of his behavior. It is completely foreign to me and unlike anything I would do myself, and like nothing I have ever seen before. I do not know how to process it or how to interpret it any differently. I think clarification of intentions would really help me here, and I am willing to listen.
2. It has never been my intention to behave in any manner that would elicit such explosive and aggressive responses. My intentions have always been to try and get along, but based on his responses it is possible that my true intentions were somehow lost in translation in the beginning. As the conflict escalated, there was so much emotion and frustration that it became impossible to act with any semblance of civility toward one another. Neither one of us has been able to give each other the benefit of the doubt in a very long time. Maybe never.
3. I do not believe that I have been the one to initiate disagreements between the two of us. I have, however responded in kind and that has not helped the situation. It is also possible that he has misinterpreted and misunderstood my words and actions and has therefore taken them as insults or as aggressive behavior. I would like to go through any instances that stand out for each of us and discuss them to provide clarification to each other.
4. His position is that I have not understood or interpreted his statements correctly and that other people also have been incorrect. If that is the case, I am willing to listen to his explanation of his intentions. Maybe we can discuss alternate ways of communicating that will allow us each to express our thoughts so that they will be received in the manner that we intended.
5. Since I know my true intentions, I know that they are not deserving of being met with hostility, rudeness, or aggression. However, I believe I can make space for the fact that he has not understood me thus far, misinterpreting my words and actions at every turn. He has believed that I am attacking him, and that he needs to defend himself, so that is what he has done. I suppose the same can be said for me. Maybe if we can explain ourselves to each other we will be able to see that nobody actually meant any harm, but that everything just spiraled out of control with emotions and hurt feelings being added into the mix.

Part 2: Joint Session

Once each party was able to see that it was at least possible that there were misunderstandings at a fundamental level and that there could be additional factors accounting for some of the aggressive behavior from both of them, they became willing to hear each other out. Heading into joint session, I recognized the similarities in their past experiences, and I knew that if they would be willing to open up and discuss them with each other (a very difficult activity to contemplate as there was absolutely no trust between them), they might possibly recognize some of the reasons behind their actions and responses toward one another. I decided to use myself as an example and provided some instances of my own responses in heated situations that had less to do with what was going on in the moment and more to do with my past experiences involving completely different people. I also discussed how I handled situations when my words and actions were taken incorrectly, including how each was addressed and eventually overcome. In spite of their anger and aggression toward each other, I was able to guide them away from accusatory "you" statements and positions to presenting those same messages from "I" perspectives. This led to the parties being willing to discuss the emotional impacts of the event being described, and when they became comfortable, also relating how they wished the situation would have transpired instead of how it really did. I was relying on the fact that at the end of the day, neither party really wanted to be in a conflict situation, much preferring to enjoy their lives, have happy experiences, and even to make friends whenever and as often as possible.

CONCLUSION

Little by little, with assistance in reframing and while exhibiting appropriate composure, both disputants gave and received the time and opportunity to discuss themselves, explain their intentions, and also detail how they would like their relationship to be. "You did this . . ." began to shift to "I felt that you were . . ." and "There is no way this can ever work . . ." became "Maybe if we both . . . ." Together they opened up the door for a new way of interacting and understood that by allowing space and taking a beat as necessary (see Chapter 6, "Listening") when they felt hurt or attacked by one another, they would be able to express themselves in a nonaggressive manner, could provide clarity, and thereafter would be able to avert misunderstandings and avoid future blow-ups. Although they still did not trust each other, a fact that made perfect sense based on their history, we discussed that trust did not actually need to be a part of the conversation just yet. It would be acceptable for them to take each other at their word, believing that when either party said that they really did not mean to say something hurtful or act in a hurtful way, that they meant it, and afterward that everyone should move on. They would prove their intentions through their words and actions. They did not have to like one another, but they could approach their situation in a way that would make their lives easier and better, and who knows, maybe even become pleasant down the line. With quite a few tears and a timid hug at the end of the night, a plan was in place for addressing future potentially upsetting situations, and the idea that a different relationship could be formed was planted.

Your tongue is your horse; if you look after it, it protects you;
if you ignore it, it insults you.
—*Jordanian proverb*

Billy's cousin and attorney Vinny is describing to him how facts and evidence are shaped and manipulated as needed to support a position, in this exchange, the DA's presentation of Billy's supposed guilt. By using a playing card to simulate the shape of a brick, Vinny explains the similarities between building a case and building a house, both requiring strong foundational support—bricks for a house and solid (like brick) facts and evidence for a case. Vinny demonstrates how looks can be and are purposefully deceiving through reframed information, as not all unadulterated facts connected to a case necessarily reinforce a desired position. Vinny tells Billy that the DA will show him ". . . bricks . . . (with) straight sides . . . the right shape . . . in a very special way so they appear to have everything a brick should have. There's one thing he's not going to show you. When you look at the right angle, they are as thin as this . . . card. His whole case is an illusion . . . because you're innocent." Vinny then flips over the playing card he has been using for his demonstration and it is different than the one he had been using all along to illustrate his point.
—*My Cousin Vinny* (1992)

What would it look like if the same idea were presented with different intentions, motivations, strategies, and desired outcomes? By taking the core of a message and devising different ways to package it, each variation could evoke a different response from a listener. What is the speaker's desired response? Work backward by focusing on getting to the desired outcome by removing all components of the statement that are extraneous and not helpful. Satisfying a need to lash out, punish, make a point, or inflict pain are not helpful components of a statement or conversation when there is a larger goal and a desired outcome that will be to the benefit of the speaker and, likely, to the listener as well. Reframing can be so fundamental to mediation that a mediator might be in the position of reframing the concept of the collaborative process as requisite to ensuring that parties will engage in the mediation at all. It is not uncommon for disputants to feel that collaboration, an elemental base of the mediation process by its very definition, requires giving up or losing something that might be of great importance to them. In addition, they will have to work with an opposing party who has brought them harm or represents something they are fighting. Working against this perspective, a mediator might reframe the very idea of mediation as a collaborative process in its totality, into one of being a potential means to an end that avoids litigation. Agreement to mediate as a result of this reframed perspective could lead them to giving up nothing, gaining an exit to the conflict, keeping them out of court, and arming them with an unlimited number of creative options to accomplish settlement or resolution as the disputants determine.

The immediate purpose of reframing is to alter messages (questions, answers, statements), often shifting them from aggressive and inflammatory to explanatory and enlightening. The ultimate purpose thereof is to achieve behavioral shifts, thereby making communication more effective and settlement, when appropriate, possible. (In addition to reframing, mediators can use Motivational Interviewing to assist in shifting disputants' behavior. See Appendix, "Motivational Interviewing.") Reframing is a tool that will become virtually synonymous with mediation. It is an alternative language that mediators must learn to speak and use for translating in order for them to be most effective. The reframing process might include:

1. A question-and-answer period in which the mediator will seek clarity to ascertain the speakers' true intentions.
2. Discussion of anecdotal background.
3. Discussion of potentially altered delivery for the statement to better express the disputant's feelings and intent.

The mediator listens, hears, rearranges, and then reframes original messages, maintaining true intentions but presented in a different manner, which lends itself to a more desirable outcome. When an original statement clearly breaches disputants' boundaries and a direct line can be imagined from statement to impasse, being inquisitive serves a mediator well, especially when a reframe does not immediately present itself. The framing, or presentation, and reframing of issues and messages is a critical part of the mediator's job, shifting perceptions of information from inflammatory to supportive and competitive to collaborative and clarifying that aggression might stem from pain. (Praying while smoking sounds acceptable; however, smoking while you pray? That sounds questionable.)[1] As the facilitator of communication and in their neutral capacity, the mediator often acts as a barrier through which certain messages must not pass.

TILT THE KILT

1. Shifting the narrative
   a. Whether a conflict story is presented one way or is supposed to be told another way, so what? If the conflict existing in its current form, being understood and interpreted in a particular way, is not conducive to resolution and settlement, tilt the kilt! Grab the information in your hands and rotate it, flip it around, and turn it inside out until you can find a shape and position that suddenly exposes space for cooperation and

1. Folberg, Jay, Dwight Golann, Thomas J. Stipanowich, and Lisa A. Kloppenberg, *Resolving Disputes Theory, Practice, and Law*, 3rd ed., 2016.

settlement options. Just as a kilt is meant to be worn one way and one way only, or else, so, too, is the traditional nature of conflicts: two opposing sides, one being right and one being wrong. Well, not so fast. Why does that have to be the case? Why not tilt the kilt? Why not tilt conflict? Why can't it be that conflict itself is the opposing party, and the disputants present are in it together on the same side working toward resolution so they can both be free of any further entanglement with the conflict? That would involve tilting the kilt and pushing back against an unnecessary systemic understanding and acceptance of conflict that has gone on far too long and has allowed for far too much damage. From the broadest tilting the kilt and reframing of the perception of conflict and of mediation to the targeted application onto specific messages and case-related details, shifted perspectives clear new pathways.

b. Think about the facts of a case in a three-dimensional box. Now slowly begin to turn, tilt, and shift that box. In each new direction, not only might there be opportunity for different perspectives on the existing case, but an entirely new case could be shaped.
   i. Imagine a kaleidoscope containing a collection of glass shards. With each turn there is a new view even though the original elements remain the same.
   ii. Rotating and tilting a box of facts generates new vantage points of the same conflict, creating a new landscape.
   iii. Every new angle presents a new perspective, opinion, vision of facts, and the opportunity for additional creativity, conversation, and options.
      1. *New* can provide calm to a tumultuous mediation, even a new perspective allowing disputants no longer to feel that they are losing ground (should that have been an issue they were previously facing). Actual or perceived loss of control can be an impenetrable wall in the conflict resolution process, so any opportunity to address and shift away from this position is a gift to the mediator and to the mediation.

Depending on the specific perspective that has been tilted and reframed, the resulting conversation could be so new and distinctly different that an entirely new concept and understanding of the original conflict has been formed.

2. Consider
   a. Consider what the outcome of the statement should be and take a moment to determine how a reframe could benefit the disputants and the mediation, rather than causing harm, as would be the case with the statement in its original form.
   b. If the mediator believes that it could be beneficial to involve the disputants in this process, the mediation should move into caucus. Once there, the mediator can create a diagram of possible deleterious outcomes should the particular statement be allowed to stand as is. Assuming none

of those outcomes were aligned with the disputant's true intentions, they might now be willing to discuss possible reframing variations until there is a proper reflection of their intentions.

i. This process can assist the disputant not only by enlightening them to the way their messages can be misinterpreted, but also to assist them in realizing and working through some of their feelings and concerns about the conflict itself. This might even lead to a discussion about settlement, and their desire for resolution weighed against continuing on with the conflict.

c. Depending on the atmosphere in the room, the open discussion of implications and intentions of messages could be practiced in joint session. This would provide disputants with an opportunity to meet face-to-face to express hurt feelings and unintended consequences of each other's misinterpreted messages.

i. For Transformative mediations, this could be beneficial to building habits for the future and to practice a communication style that involves taking a beat and giving each other the benefit of the doubt.

ii. If the mediation is not Transformative, and is tense in any way, it may not be necessary or beneficial to engage in this practice at all, particularly not in joint session. Any questions the mediator might have about intention can be directed to that disputant in caucus. At that point, the mediator can make one of two decisions: Either engage the disputant in reframing discussions simply for the benefit of making the conflict intervention process and their interaction style more manageable, or reframe on their own, without disputant engagement, based on clarified intentions and the removal of unnecessary and potentially damaging additions to the message.

3. Vacuum

a. Take in as much information as you can: The more information you have, the more options you have. Reframing sometimes requires a series of manipulated messages in an attempt to find the ones best suited to a conflict and disputants' needs. Having multiple variations of reframes at the ready can be crucial to maintaining control of a mediation and keeping it on track. It can be complicated to determine what will anger a disputant and send them into a rage or trigger an emotional outburst. Mediations do not always provide the time required to thoroughly excavate a disputant's emotional trauma and pent-up aggressions; some do, but not all. The solution has to be options—the options that mediators carve out for themselves built on the stack of garnered information. A discerning ear will separate helpful from unhelpful and detrimental information, and a keen focus on disputant goals will enable the mediator to align potential reframes.

4. Scoop

a. Mentally categorize collected information:

i. Like items.

ii. Items that could be linked together toward the end goal.
iii. Items that should be separated and kept far apart.
iv. Items that need to be clarified.
v. Items that have caused and continue to cause elevated emotions.
vi. Items that need to be reframed.
vii. Items that have been and continue to be misunderstood and misinterpreted, but, if clarified, could lead to behavioral and atmospheric shifts, thereby opening the mediation for resolution possibilities aligned with disputant goals.
viii. Items that could be used during settlement discussions.

5. Piece together
   a. Piece together those fragments of a statement or question with the original intention and sentiment, but in a new, reframed way that will no longer be interpreted as inflammatory or aggressive and that will not send the entire mediation into a tailspin, ending in impasse.
   b. Although a reframe might sound quite different from an original statement, it is crucial to ensure the presence of the intended message. The intended message, however, might be difficult in nature, so it is possible that the mediator will choose to deliver it in the form of multiple reframes and not in one, as originally expressed by the disputant. In some situations, slow and steady will win the race, so the mediator should not feel pressured to express information in the same manner as the parties simply to maintain the same pace. In fact, a reframe could also serve the purpose of slowing down the delivery of information by adding cushioning around difficult points, and not simply the restructuring of a statement.
6. Target
   a. If mediation is a target, meeting disputants' goals is the bull's-eye and messages are the arrows. Use reframes to keep the arrows pointed at the target with the bull's-eye in your crosshairs.
   b. It is common for intentions, needs, and fundamental concerns to be lost by virtue of the ways in which disputants communicate during conflicts. This could cause them to veer off track during the mediation, losing sight of resolution as their desired outcome, and instead fixating on fighting, proving points, blaming, and winning. Reframing can become a helpful and necessary tool for the mediator to realign disputants with their mediation goals. Reframing messages to become clearer, more direct, and more focused could allow parties to shift back, or for the first time, onto a path that could lead to meeting those goals.
      i. Whether this purposeful reframing takes place in caucus or joint session will depend entirely on each mediation. If disputants are exhibiting behavior that leads the mediator to believe they will have a hard time controlling themselves and de-escalating, then entering caucus might be a wise course of action. If the mediation is more civil and parties are communicating in a way that exhibits empathy

or a desire to understand each other, then the mediator could opt for joint session.

ii. Whether in caucus or joint session, reframing is extraordinarily helpful even if only to assist disputants to see themselves more clearly, regardless of the atmosphere that the conflict and the parties have created. In other words, reframes can be an excellent teaching device when it becomes important or necessary to assist a disputant to recognize the interpretation and impact of their messages more clearly. Additionally, of course, a skillful reframe can immediately remove aggression from a statement, taking it from being a weapon wielded by one disputant against another, and turning it into an expression of mutually accepted fact wrapped around an olive branch, swathed in vulnerability and invitation.

7. Cover and calm
    a. More often than not, the goal of a reframe is to deescalate and to keep a mediation moving forward. When disputants are angry and in the heat of a moment, their messages could become reactionary instead of purposefully crafted to bring resolution to their conflict. When this happens, parties can become so emotionally affected that they are not able to reframe their messages to benefit the mediation process on their own. In these circumstances, it becomes the job of the third-party neutral, who must not be emotionally affected by the conflict or any messages therein, to find the purpose in disputant messages, and as necessary, to restate them to benefit the mediation process.
    b. When the desired outcome of the reframe is in fact to deescalate, the reframe should land on the disputants as a blanket that extinguishes the heightened emotions and furious flames of the dispute, and in their place allows a new conflict landscape to be created.

Listening to the details of a conflict that precipitated mediation, if a mediator can parse out elements that might have inflamed the conflict and are identifiable as conflict exacerbators, the mediator could choose to address them right away to aid in the overall settlement goal or attempt to avoid them completely. Additionally, if a mediator can become hyperaware of potential conflict traps or triggers during the communication process between disputants, those could become messages that are immediately reframed, redirected, or avoided.

A STATEMENT MANIPULATED

"There's no way I'm going to do that."

1. Weaponized
    a. As a weaponized statement, "There's no way I'm going to do that" is a defiant, oppositional, possibly insubordinate statement from a person who is being told what to do. It might also be a rebuke to someone who is trying to offer helpful advice or a possible solution option.

i. A disputant might respond to a proposed settlement agreement with this statement. This response could be out of spite, frustration, or anger, regardless of the validity of the offer.
   1. If the conflict is contentious enough, the proposed offer could be taken as inflammatory and sufficient to cause an opposing party to respond in kind.
   2. In conflict, absolutely anything could be perceived as inflammatory and triggering.
   3. A mediator's course of action should be to immediately reframe and attempt to identify the intention of the statement—the feelings behind it that have been packaged in a less than desirable way.
   4. If the mediation is in joint session, the mediator will likely need to be prepared to engage in damage control, as there would not have been an opportunity to step in before the statement was heard by a listening party. If the mediator is able to encourage the listening party to continue to listen while there is an unwinding of the offending statement into an alternate form that expresses true intentions and feelings in a way that is no longer offensive or inflammatory, then the mediation may be salvageable. An apology with an acknowledgment that the original statement carried with it an unintended message, together with a reframe devoid of aggression, could have a beneficial impact.
   5. If the mediation is in caucus, the mediator might have a similar conversation with the speaking party, but with the benefit of privacy and without also necessitating the management of the listening party being exposed to the statement in its weaponized form. Regardless of whether or not the mediator is successful in assisting the speaking party to see that their statement does substantially more harm than good and is possibly not truly indicative of their interests and subsurface feelings, it can be reframed or possibly dismissed entirely.

2. De-weaponized
   a. As a de-weaponized statement, "There's no way I'm going to do that" could be stated for a completely different reason.
      i. A disputant might respond to a proposed settlement offer with this statement. This response could come because they perceive the offered agreement to be unfair to the party proposing it. Perhaps the offering party has swung too far to the collaborating or compromising side of the negotiating spectrum, and although their offer would greatly benefit the receiving party, it is not accepted by them for exactly this reason.
      ii. It is possible that the mediation is Transformative, and although the nature of the relationship is currently conflicted and in turmoil, the party receiving the offer believes that sometime down the line the relationship will heal, but not with an agreement such as the one that has

been proposed. The offer indicates that the proposing party clearly wants the mediation to end at any cost, as the settlement is skewed in favor of the receiving party. Although it might seem to be in the best interest of the receiving party to accept the offer in its current form, being advantageously skewed in their direction, their concern is for the future relationship, which is not something they are willing to jeopardize.

1. In this manner, the statement is not only de-weaponized in and of itself, but it is also a de-weaponized statement that could have the power to de-weaponize subsequent messages from all of the parties involved in the mediation. Used in this fashion it could have the power to entirely shift the atmosphere of the mediation and change the interactions of the parties.

iii. A mediator might take this opportunity to encourage the receiving party to explain to the offering party exactly why they are declining the offer in its current state. This could be a healing moment for the disputants, or at least a chance to begin to lay the foundation for an improved relationship in the future. However, it is possible that the offering party will not be receptive to hearing this explanation. They might still be too angry or hurt, which is understandable considering the parties will have potentially traversed a road laden with difficult experiences that brought them to mediation. Whether or not the offering party is able to accept the explanation for the refusal, the action of the refusing party will remain and perhaps be accepted and appreciated eventually. In the meantime, the mediator should continue to work with the parties until an offer is found that is perceived by all parties to be fairer and better balanced.

3. How to use the statement, "There's no way I'm going to do that"

a. To defuse

i. If the statement is weaponized, it would require de-weaponizing, reframing, and shifting to use it to defuse. However, if the statement is de-weaponized, it could present an opportunity to illustrate deeper feelings below those presented in the current conflict. A disputant's action to decline an advantageous settlement offer (by using this statement) in favor of preserving the possibility of a recovered relationship is also one that can defuse a hostile environment, a hostile opposing party, or both. Such an act of putting an opposing party's needs above one's own could deescalate and shift an interaction.

ii. As a weaponized statement, it is identified by the mediator as an indicator of an area of the conflict or a perspective that needs to be addressed and defused. It is indicative of the party's emotional state, their inability to think and communicate rationally and logically, and exactly how far they are down the conflict rabbit hole and away from possible resolution. This understanding can be helpful to a mediator in defusing situations that arise as a result of the disputant's emotional state.

1. After hearing such a statement, a mediator might immediately engage in a conversation with the speaking party to examine the reason(s) for the statement because it is an indication of intense emotional involvement. The conversation will also involve peeling back any layers of emotion that are covering up the disputant's interests and needs to discover information that remains beneath the surface and has yet to be expressed.

b. To persuade and convince

i. As a weaponized statement, it could be used to convince a listening disputant that the speaking party does not have any concern about seeking a mutually beneficial agreement, that attempting collaboration is not a currently available option, and that the speaking party is in a heightened emotional and perhaps irrational state. This could be an indicator to the listening disputant to stop a useless negotiation during which they have already disclosed to the mediator a willingness to pay, and it has become apparent that the speaking party is negotiating for sport and in bad faith. The mediator might highlight this statement to illustrate to the listening disputant that settling with a party who makes such a statement and behaves in this manner is, unfortunately, the best option – right away, especially if an impasse leading to court might be unfavorable.

ii. As a de-weaponized statement, it is a look into the intentions of a speaking party and can be used as a tool to persuade and convince a listening party that the settlement terms being offered are last and final and there is no further opportunity for negotiation or wiggle room. In this case, it is an indication of a bottom line.

c. To answer

i. As an answer, "There's no way I'm going to do that" changes with extreme measure in concert with the tone of its delivery.

1. *Aggressive or combative tone*: As you would imagine, when said in an aggressive or combative way, this statement might be perceived as an attack that requires a defensive response from a listening party. It would present a defiant position that is immovable and unconcerned with anyone else's feelings, interests, or needs. It is fully self-centered and not open to input, discussion, or mutually agreeable negotiation.

2. *Submissive tone:* In a voice that gives power away, with the speaking party possibly feeling defeated, deflated, or exhausted, the listening party might disregard this statement altogether. It could easily be dismissed by a listening party who identifies that there is no position or power behind it, and the conversation progresses forward as if it were never made at all.

3. *Commentary tone:* The statement might mean nothing at all, and both the statement and reaction to it might be similar to a person standing on the edge of a cliff about to bungee jump, who, out of fear and a burst of adrenaline exclaims, "There's no way I'm going to do that!" As they have already made the decision to jump and are experiencing some well-placed fear and might be in need of encouragement and a good old-fashioned pep talk, those around them cheer them on, moving them toward the edge for the jump. The statement carries no weight other than an emotional outburst to be set to the side while plans progress.
4. *Collaborative tone:* This statement is a conversation opener and can be interpreted as a tone of questioning or hesitation. It indicates a lack of certainty that a decision might be correct, being open to discussion about it, and amenable to a final conclusion that it is right.

d. Scare

i. As a scare tactic, a speaking disputant is using this statement to send a clear message to a listening party that, at least at the present moment, they are not receptive to accepting an offer and settling. Their intentions might also be to scare the listening party into believing, whether true or not, that if they do not receive what they require, the speaker will gladly allow the mediation to conclude in impasse, resulting in a future court hearing.

ii. If a mediator believes that the listening party is not negotiating in good faith or does not have a proper understanding of their BATNA or WATNA, the mediator might then decide to use the speaking party's statement as a scare tactic aimed toward the listening party. It is an opportunity for the mediator to have a mediation vs. litigation conversation that is connected to a strong statement indicating that the speaking party is ready and willing to go to court, an outcome that would be undesirable for the listening party.

iii. The listening party could also use this statement as an opportunity to call their bluff, responding with words to the effect of *likewise.* If the speaking party is using it as a strategy rather than to reflect their true intentions, a response in kind might cause them to back down and reassess their willingness either to accept the terms they have been offered, or to begin negotiating in good faith.

1. If the speaking party does not reassess their position on their own, and it is clear to the mediator that they are only using this statement as strategy, a move to caucus to discuss their options and potential responses might be appropriate. The mediator may not wish to suggest directly that they reevaluate their strategy, but it might be possible to guide a conversation that allows the speaking party to come to that conclusion on their own.

2. If the listening party has not made the decision to respond in kind on their own and is exhibiting distress over how to manage the current negotiations, the mediator could move them into caucus to discuss their options. If the speaking party is interacting with a Competitive CHM and the listening party is operating with a Collaborative or Cooperative CHM, it might require encouragement and confidence-boosting discussions to enable the listening party to see options that they might not realize are available to them.

e. Settle
   i. The mediator could use the import of this statement to remind the parties that they are not forced to be in mediation, that they have the ability and power to decline any offer that they do not find acceptable, and that they can exit the mediation at any time and for any reason. The mediation process can be scary and intimidating, especially when the conflict could have serious consequences for the parties, so this statement can empower them to feel that they can engage more fully and freely in the process without panicking that they will become trapped or forced to accept an offer.
   ii. The statement can also be used by parties in response to various aspects of the conflict to reflect certain points that they will not yield on—no matter what. It is a form of mutually agreed-upon ground rules set in place to ensure that the focus remains on interests and needs without the nonnegotiable points being brought up and interfering.

FLASH CHALLENGE

So Many Arrows in the Quiver

Assignment

1. While engaging in the Mediation Exercise, choose five sentences (questions, answers, or statements) that were used by the disputants and discuss them.
   a. Identify if they were:
      i. Weaponized
      ii. De-weaponized
      iii. Used to defuse
      iv. Used to persuade and convince
      v. Used to answer
      vi. Used to scare
      vii. Used to settle
2. Discuss how you were able to identify in which manner the sentences were used.
3. Were the disputants' intentions successfully expressed in their messages?
4. Discuss the impact of the sentences on the listening party and if any mediator intervention transpired.

MEDIATOR CONSIDERATIONS WHEN CRAFTING A REFRAME

1. Once I begin reframing, will that process require changing the way I am conducting this mediation? Either a move into caucus from joint session, or vice versa?
2. What needs to be accomplished by the reframe?
3. Can I distill out the disputants' true intention(s)?
4. Are their true intentions beneficial or detrimental to the mediation?
5. What should I remove from their statement to de-weaponize it?
6. What must be added to de-weaponize it?
7. How can the necessary elements be added?
8. Can I use this reframe to de-escalate a potential response to their original statement and instead elicit one that is neither aggressive nor inflammatory?
9. Can I use this reframe to de-escalate existing tensions and to reach feelings and issues below surface-level posturing?
10. Can I provide a reframe that will create a safe emotional space for the disputants?
11. Is the information I have gathered thus far sufficient to reframe necessary messages to achieve disputants' mediation goals?
12. Is additional or different information required to provide the necessary options to craft reframes?
13. Will the reframe be one of presenting different information or one of a different approach with the same information?
14. Do I need to weave additional skills such as empathy or asking questions into my reframe to achieve receptiveness from the listening disputant?
15. If I were on the receiving end of a statement, how would I need it to be reframed to actually hear it and be receptive to its message?
16. Can I draw on my personal experience with various Conflict Handling Modes to help with my reframe decisions?
17. Can I draw on my personal experience with various Communication Styles to help with my reframe decisions?
18. Should the reframe be presented as coming from the speaking disputant, or should I take the information and weave it into a conversation between the listening disputant and myself?
19. Based on my limited experience with the listening disputant, do I understand what they need and how to get through to them?
20. If I discuss reframing the statement with the speaking disputant, will they be receptive to it and could it possibly shift and improve their communication dynamic with the listening disputant?
21. Could I use this reframe to begin to highlight to the disputants and subsequently dismantle their mutual misunderstandings, misinterpretations, and miscommunications?
22. Can I use this reframe to draw attention to the damage that can be and has been caused by ineffective communication as a result of unclear intentions in original messages?

23. Can I use this reframe to alter and change the narrative to one that can lead to reaching disputant mediation end goals, including settlement?
24. If this is a Transformative mediation, can I also use the reframe to shift and change the parties' dynamic as they move forward in their relationship?

EXAMPLE

1. ORIGINAL STATEMENT

I want you to wear that dress, otherwise what's the point of even going. You don't even need me there, go without me.

Potential Issues and Misinterpretations

a. Exerting power over someone else.
b. Making decisions for someone else regardless of how they feel about it.
c. The speaker's feelings and wishes are more important than those of the listening party.
d. "Who put you in charge?"
e. "Don't tell me what to do."
f. Guilt.
g. Manipulation.
h. Attempting to force someone to do something they don't want to do just because you want it that way.

Reframed Statement

After inspection, the mediator discovered the information necessary to craft the following reframed statement:

I love that dress. I bought it for you to express how much I love you, and when you put it on for the first time your eyes lit up and you had so much confidence in yourself. It made you so happy, and it made me feel like you believed I could make you happy. But, of course, I don't want you to be uncomfortable in any way, and if you are, maybe we can go buy a new dress together. I have been feeling like you don't need me at all lately, and like you have moved on in your life without me.

a. Although the details included in the reframe are not readily clear from the original statement, what is clear is that there seems to be something missing between the two sentences of the statement in its original form.

2. ORIGINAL STATEMENT

I can't believe you did that! Only a liar would do something like that.

Potential Issues and Misinterpretations

a. Has an aggressive tone.
b. Includes name-calling.
c. Virtually demands a defensive statement from the listening party.

d. Implies that the speaker knows all the facts and is speaking factually.
e. Does not leave room for clarity from a response.
f. Is accusatory.
g. Impugns the listening party's character and integrity.

Reframed Statement

Your actions in this situation surprised me and hurt my feelings. I feel betrayed because that was in confidence, and I trusted you with that deal and that information. I do not understand why you did what you did, and I am confused how we even got here today. I am angry at you because I thought we were so close, and now I feel like a fool. I feel like you should want to clarify why you did what you did and said what you said, and I am willing to hear what you have to say.

3. ORIGINAL STATEMENT

I told you not to do that.

Potential Issues and Misinterpretations

a. Being told what to do.
b. Being corrected.
c. Acting as though they have the authority to dictate someone else's behavior when they don't.
d. Hierarchies.
e. Questioning competency.
f. Asserting power.
g. Abusing power.
h. Causing immediate defensive position.

Reframed Statement

We are working together on this project, each in charge of our own departments. You are marketing and I am engineering. I advised you that making that particular change was impossible, and that the tests I ran prove it cannot be done. Why would you turn around and tell our boss that it is not only possible but will be profitable and beneficial to the company? Now I am on the hook for something that is impossible, as I told you from the beginning, and I look incompetent and as though I am not doing everything I can to help the company be more successful.

4. ORIGINAL STATEMENT

How should I have known?

Potential Issues and Misinterpretations

a. Easily interpreted as rude.
b. Easily interpreted as though the speaker does not care.
c. Implies that the responsibility is on the other person to have informed them.
d. Implies that the other person neglected an action or did something wrong.
e. Implies a lack of interest in figuring out an answer.

Reframed Statement

I had no idea that there was additional information I did not know. I genuinely thought that when we last spoke, I asked all of the necessary questions and received all of the necessary answers, including any and all information there was to know. No one said anything to me after that conversation. If I had known to ask for anything additional, I absolutely would have. The last thing I want is to have a conflict over a misunderstanding and simple missed exchange of information. I respect you, and I believe I show that every time I come to you to seek answers and consult with you before we engage in our projects. My intention is for us to always be on the same page as each other.

FLASH CHALLENGE

You Take It from Here

1. Consider the following statements:
   a. "I am not interested."
   b. "You don't understand."
   c. "I know exactly what you mean, the same thing happened to me but even worse."
2. As you read each statement, create a short story in which the statement fits.
   a. What are the potential issues and misinterpretations?
3. Provide one reframe per statement.
   a. What is your end goal for each reframed statement?
   b. Discuss how each reframe addresses the potential issues and misinterpretations presented by the statements in their original forms.

Ms. Shi v. Ms. Vito

Reframed

There are a number of issues in this dispute that could benefit from reframing, one of them being the future of the fig tree that is currently presenting as central to the conflict even though there is clearly more beneath the surface. In addition to providing privacy and bird-watching opportunities for Ms. Shi, the tree also signifies the past the sisters-in-law share, which is an issue that will need to be addressed if this case is to find resolution. The foundation of the reframes pertaining to the tree might center around this statement: "We all want the tree to be seen and loved for what it provides and represents, and not to be thought of as a source of destruction, frustration, or outrage."

To frame the issues differently, a mediator could encourage each disputant to discuss and explain a passion: bird-watching for Ms. Shi, for example, and Ms. Vito can share a passion of her own. Through a deeper understanding of what each disputant loves, there can be a humanizing aspect, a commonality found in passions, and more space to build creative solutions incorporating the protection for those passions through strategies that can include brainstorming together.

"What solutions can we devise together that help us all reach our goals?" The issue is framed as one that affects both parties together, rather than pitting them against each other with opposing interests, needs, and desires. The mediator might say, "What can we come up with that will help you as neighbors and family members to move forward in your relationship with each other, with common respect for this beautiful tree that represents a time in your history together, which you both (eventually) can agree you want to keep?" Not only should the mediator be framing the issue as a mutual interest, but it should be framed in a way that allows the disputants to find themselves as partners working together against the conflict. All reframes should reflect messages that are devoid of blame, presenting an "I" perspective instead that is then expanded into a "We" perspective to reflect the immediate importance of aligning the disputants on the same side. Neither would actually want the tree to cause harm to the other, nor would they want the harm to be caused to their own property or family. By switching roles to encourage empathy and understanding, reframes should reflect this commonality.

With guided assistance from the mediator, the disputants can begin to brainstorm and come up with creative solutions that address their mutual and personal interests, needs, and desires. There will be no judgments permitted during this brainstorming, and if a statement or idea should come out that way, the mediator will immediately act to reframe it so that it can be shifted and rotated from a weapon of harm to a tool of solution. The mediator might treat addressing and reframing the issue of and conversation about the tree as a gateway into conversations about other elements of the disputants' relationship that need to be identified and addressed or that are unresolved. This discussion will likely present as a key factor in subsequently having a rational and logical conversation about the injury, property damage, and tree location without it being eclipsed by emotional turmoil.

Discussing the elements that are contributing to the conflict and the disputants' behaviors within it will also require reframing. As this will likely be a sensitive and difficult conversation, necessitating vulnerability and honesty that the disputants are unaccustomed to, the mediator will likely be reframing their own questions, as well, to avoid triggers and automatic defensive responses that present as slammed doors. In a sample reframe of the issues for mediation, a mediator would include no mention of the monetary demands that have been presented, as they are possibly inflated due to disputant misperceptions and overreactions. Monetary demands can be (temporarily) set aside when issues below posturing positions are reached. Reframing can also breach culture, upbringing, and individual experiential gaps, all of which are issues that could be involved here as well.

The following reframes have been extrapolated from conversations that might have transpired during the mediation of Ms. Shi and Ms. Vito. They are not separated by disputant and are in no particular order.

Reframes

1. "I did not know how to respond to you."
2. "I did not know how to express myself."
3. "I would like to explain what I meant when I said . . . ."
4. "I understand that my actions came across that way, but what I actually meant was . . . ."
5. "The tree means so much to me because . . . ."
6. "I feel like you hate the tree, want to remove it, and do not care about my feelings about it. But I realize that I have never given you the opportunity to fully explain your feelings and to correct me if I have misunderstood, so would you please explain to me how you feel about the tree?"
7. "I feel like you are accusing me of being a bad person and that makes me feel very hurt."
8. "I am confused about the way you feel about our business relationship because I am beginning to realize that you and I feel differently about it."
9. "I do not understand why you are upset with me, but please know that it was never my intent to hurt you in any way. Would you please explain your feelings to me?"
10. "I realize that I lash out when I feel hurt or that I am being attacked, even if that is not the case, and that I do not allow the other person to explain themself to me. I know I have done that to you and I am sorry. Would it be okay with you if I explain myself and my actions to you and you can do the same for me?"
11. "I feel that you do not care about or respect everything I did for our business; however, I realize that maybe you do not really know everything I was doing when I was away from the office. I never explained it to you. I would like to explain that to you now. Would that be okay?"
12. "Do you feel hurt by me?"
13. "When I was growing up . . . and it is not an excuse, but it shaped the way I communicate and I struggle with it. Maybe you can help me by telling me right away when I have hurt your feelings so that I can address it."
14. "I feel that I have gone out of my way to try and talk to you about the issue of the tree for a long time now, and every time I did you ignored me, snapped at me, or laughed in my face. Am I misunderstanding that? Can you please explain to me what happened all of those times?"
15. "What was it in the way that I attempted to communicate with you that caused you to get angry with me or to feel that I was attacking you?"
16. "Is our conflict or even the tree itself more important to you than your nieces?"

17. "I feel like you do not want to work together, and that you just want to continue hurting me out of spite, but I realize that I have not asked you so that you can answer that yourself. Do you want to work together toward resolving this dispute?"
18. "I feel like you do not want to repair our relationship, and that you just want to continue hurting me out of spite, but I realize that I have not asked you so that you can answer for yourself. Do you want to repair our relationship?"
19. "I want to express how much I care about my nieces and our family, but I do not know how. However, it is the truth and I would like to talk about that for a moment."
20. "I think it would help if I wrote down some of what I would like to say and then gave it to my sister-in-law. I know my words are not coming out in the way I intend, which is very frustrating for me and I can see that it is adding to the problem."

The following are original messages that have been extrapolated from conversations that might have transpired during the mediation of Ms. Shi and Ms. Vito. They are not separated by disputant and are in no particular order.

Original Messages: Questions, Answers, or Statements

1. "You . . . ."
2. "I can't believe that you actually . . . ."
3. "If you think for one second that I am going to pay for that . . . ."
4. "The tree is on your property and it is yours. It is your responsibility, period."
5. "You are going to pay one way or another."
6. "You don't care about your own niece, and that is disgusting."
7. "I want nothing to do with you."
8. "You have shown through your words and actions exactly what type of person you are, and I want nothing to do with you anymore."
9. "Clearly you're not smart enough to understand what's really going on here."
10. "Why should I try to cooperate with you now, when all along I have tried and you have done nothing but be rude to me, to my daughters, and have slammed the door in my face every time I tried to talk to you about this issue."
11. "All I have done is speak nicely to you and to ask you to clean up after YOUR OWN TREE, and this is what I get. Ridiculous and pathetic."
12. "You make no sense."
13. "Clearly you can't handle anything if you can't even behave properly when your own family member brings up an issue being caused by something that YOU OWN."
14. "Not checking in on your own niece after she was injured is a crystal-clear message and can only mean one thing . . . ."
15. "No one on the planet would behave the way you do. It is YOUR TREE! How can you even argue with that?"
16. "How can you possibly imagine that I am going to pay for damage that YOUR TREE caused?"

17. "If I acted the way you're acting, I never would have gotten to where I am today."
18. "Obviously you only care about yourself and what is best for you. Even when people get hurt you still act this way. Shameful."
19. "I shouldn't be surprised by your behavior, though, considering how you acted when we were in business together—all about you and always putting yourself first."
20. "You care about money, a tree, shade, and birds, right? Who cares that your own niece broke her wrist and was in the hospital! That's exactly the person you are!"
21. "Now I see why everyone calls you mean and a bully with no heart!"
22. "You're such a drama queen!"

FLASH CHALLENGE

You Can't Hang a Picture Without a Frame . . . or at Least You Shouldn't

1. Using the reframes above, create a new original message for each.
2. Using the original messages above, create a new reframe for each.
3. For original messages 1 and 2:
   a. Come up with three full sentences that might have come from Ms. Shi.
   b. Come up with three full sentences that might have come from Ms. Vito.
   c. Come up with one reframe for each of the original messages you created.
4. Can you devise other potential reframes focusing on the tree and its impacts?
5. Based on the *Ms. Shi v. Ms. Vito* fact pattern in its entirety (see "Prefatory Information"), can you devise other potential reframes focusing on additional issues central to the conflict?
   a. For example, the injury Ms. Vito's daughter sustained and Ms. Shi's related behavior.
6. How can reframing help Ms. Shi discuss her past with Ms. Vito?
   a. Provide some examples of possible reframes the mediator might suggest.
7. Can reframing help Ms. Shi explain the reasons for her behavior and attitude toward Ms. Vito?
   a. If so, how?
   b. If not, why not?
   c. Provide some examples of possible reframes the mediator might suggest.
8. Is reframing beneficial for Ms. Shi and Ms. Vito?
   a. Why or why not? Discuss.
9. Include a brief discussion of the general purpose of reframing and when and how it can be beneficial.

FLASH CHALLENGE

Telephone

1. Break into groups of five to seven students, seated in a circle.
2. One student will come up with a statement and whisper it into the ear of the student sitting next to them.
   a. Each member of the group should have the opportunity to come up with a statement and be the first speaker.
3. The student receiving this original statement will listen, consider the message, and then reframe the statement as they pass it to the next student. The game will conclude when the final reframe is delivered to the original speaker.
   a. Both the heard and spoken message should be written down and kept hidden until the end of the exercise.
4. Once the original statement has made its way around the circle and has been reframed by all members of the group, each student will present the reframe they received as well as the reframe they subsequently created. The final reframe along with the original statement will be shared by the student who initiated the game.
5. Each student will explain how they interpreted the statement they listened to and how they came to their decisions for their reframe.
   a. The discussion of the decision-making process should include intended consequences of their reframe.
6. Compare the original statement to the last reframed statement.
   a. How are they similar?
   b. How are they different?
7. After hearing the original statement, is everyone still confident in their reframe?
   a. Why?
   b. Why not?
8. As a group, discuss the possible impact of the original statement when compared to the possible impact of each reframe.
   a. What are the different ways the original statement and each reframe can be interpreted, thereby creating different effects on the disputants who hear them?
9. As a group, discuss whether the intent of the original statement can still be identified in the final reframe.
   a. If not, begin with the final reframe and continue in reverse order to locate where the original intent was lost.
      i. Identify how it was lost and recreate a new reframe in its place that incorporates the original intent.

FLASH CHALLENGE

Teamwork Makes the Dream Work!

Instructions

1. Divide into small groups of at least three people.
2. Using the *Ms. Shi v. Ms. Vito* fact pattern, create a dialogue that will become a mediation. This dialogue will be between the disputants with a series of problematic original messages (a combination of questions, answers, and statements) that should be reframed to benefit disputants' participation in and overall success of the mediation. You should have at least eight original messages.
3. The students will act out the mediation. It should be no longer than 10 or 15 minutes.
   a. Student #1 will play the role of the disputant presenting the original messages, Student #2 will play the role of the disputant who is receiving the original messages, and Student #3 will play the role of mediator.
   b. These roles should change after each mediation is complete with each set of original and reframed messages acted out.

Assignment

1. As a group, create reframes for each original message.
   a. Each reframe should address the issues presented by the original messages.
   b. Discuss the process of coming up with each reframe.
   c. What are the issues each reframe addresses?
      i. How does each reframe address those initial concerns?
2. Once each mediation is complete, each student should discuss:
   a. How the original messages made them feel.
   b. The differences between reactions to original messages and to reframes.
   c. Whether or not the reframes had a beneficial impact on the mediation.

CREATIVITY AND REFRAMING

Reframing is a particularly exciting area of conflict intervention for mediators to express their creativity, problem-solving, and solution-oriented skills. One of the most iconic scenes from the 1989 film *When Harry Met Sally* illustrates how one friend, Harry, attempts to calm down his weeping friend, Sally, by reframing (in one way or another) everything she says:

Sally: What's [wrong] with me?

Harry: Nothing.

Sally: I'm difficult.

Harry: You're challenging.

Sally: . . . too structured . . .

Harry: . . . in a good way.

Sally: I'm going to be 40!

Harry: When?

Sally: Someday.

Harry: In eight years.

Sally: . . . it's there . . . it's not the same for men. Charlie Chaplin had babies when he was 73.

Harry: . . . but he was too old to pick them up!

The scene concludes with her feeling better, demonstrating one example of the power of a reframe.

As long as conflicts persist, there will be no shortage of situations and disputants alike who will undeniably benefit from a reframed question, answer, or statement that has been either hurled at them or that they have spewed, both with landings that carry ramifications that often neither the speaker nor the listener can imagine. In those situations, and in so many others, reframing—the more creative the better—is an integral part of the conflict intervention and resolution processes.

chapter 8

Empathy

The rock in the water doesn't know the pain of the rock in the sun.
—*Haitian proverb*

MEDIATION EXAMPLE

Being Heard and Validated

In this example, an Americans with Disabilities Act (ADA) case required mediation, and the introduction process began with pre-mediation briefs. However, it is what remained hidden beneath the surface that proved to be the driving force behind the conflict.

BACKGROUND

Petitioning Party

1. Due to the necessary use of a wheelchair, Petitioning Party was unable to access a portion of the property owned by the Responding Party (Property Owner).
2. Because the establishment is designated for use by the general public, Petitioning Party claims that the Responding Party is in breach of the ADA as a result of the inaccessibility.
3. Asking for compensation in the high six figures—above ADA established fines.

Responding Party (Property Owner)

1. Argued that, because the property was "natural" and not man-made, she should not be responsible for accessibility issues.
2. Listed others who also would not have access to the area in question in defense of why this case should (and would) be thrown out.
3. Claimed that there were plenty of other areas on the property that were easily accessible for wheelchairs.

Part 1: The Mediation in Joint Session

This mediation began with all parties and their attorneys gathered in one room to hear the mediator's opening statement and to sign paperwork. Immediately following the completion of both, the parties dispersed into separate rooms for the mediation to proceed in caucus. Because both parties were represented by their own attorney, the mediator requested a joint session with only attorneys in attendance to allow each case to be presented in a more factual and less emotional manner without the disputing parties present. Based on attorney recountings, a disparity was immediately apparent in the representation of the facts and what each side believed to be the crux of the matter. Although there seemed to be agreement on many details, there was an undeniable misalignment weaving its way through the center of the case that was presenting a communication and comprehension incompatibility and would require clarification from the disputants.

Part 2: Moving into Caucus

It is interesting to be in the presence of a singular and mostly agreed-upon set of facts with two such dramatically distinct perspectives, interpretations, and understandings of the problem. On the one hand, the owner of an establishment was engaged with the mediator in a heated debate about exactly what was "fair and reasonable" to demand that they fix or change at their place of business to make it fully accessible. The conversation ranged from using drawings and rulers to demonstrate what change was and was not possible due to the outdoor, natural setting, to discussions about those who could not access the property, and those who were not expected to be able to do so, including children, the elderly, and anyone with a physical impairment due to the location's difficult, dangerous terrain. The property owner delivered considerable argument about precisely what was covered by the ADA, including the definition of "fair and reasonable" turned upside down, inside out, and back around again.

On the other hand, the Petitioning Party claimed the establishment to be inaccessible specifically to those who use a wheelchair. Much like the Responding Party, the Petitioning Party began with a description of the events, the landscape, and a detailed explanation of exactly how and why the area was inaccessible, also stating that there should be no area in a place designated for "public use" that is inaccessible to any person. The conversation very quickly shifted to a focus on the emotional impact of being denied access to a place of "public use," and that is where it remained. The impact was tremendous, described by the disputant as embarrassing, disrespectful, dehumanizing, belittling, and terribly upsetting. Certain reactions and responses, including settlement demands, were a direct result of these deeply felt emotions. It was clear, however, that this point was lost on the Property Owner whose lack of understanding would need to be addressed. As long as parties remained in caucus, that responsibility would belong to the mediator. When financial demands are high, disputants have a tendency to focus only on the payouts they might be facing, but it seemed possible that the non-monetary factors involved in this case would outweigh even a potentially large financial outcome for the Petitioning Party.

After the mediator returned to speak with the Property Owner and began explaining the emotional components involved in the case, the Property Owner's confusion became apparent. The Property Owner perceived the settlement demand (their primary focus) to make no sense, being exorbitant and well above an amount that would balance any harm caused by "simply an inability to enter that portion of the property the one time the Petitioning Party visited the location." The conversation could not stop there, though, because forward movement and effective communication depended on an ability to understand the opposing party's position. Whether or not the Property Owner expressed empathy in regular, nonconflict life, it was not a skill they were using at that moment. Shifting position to a softened stance, broadening their perspective, and extending compassion to create empathy for someone they presently believed was trying to take an unjustifiable advantage would be critical to reaching a mutually agreed-upon settlement agreement.

THE EXPLANATION PROCESS

Imagining oneself in a position completely foreign to one's reality can be very difficult for some disputants, especially when their thought process is being shaped and taxed by a conflict, as was the case for the Property Owner. An explanation process could not begin until after the Property Owner provided their interpretation of the Petitioning Party's intent behind their exorbitant settlement demands and expressed anger and frustration about the high dollar amount. The mediator then engaged the Property Owner in a discussion that introduced the idea of the dollar amount reflecting a measurement of the emotional impact, rather than as an opportunity to collect as much money as possible. The mediator was also able to guide the Property Owner to consider challenges a person using a wheelchair might face, which of those were presented during the visit to the property, and how those challenges and their consequences could be affecting the Petitioning Party. The Property Owner was then asked what emotions they envisioned these challenges and their consequences could elicit, and many of the words used to respond to the question were aligned with the words used in the description of the event by the Petitioning Party. At that point, it was clear that the Property Owner was beginning to understand that there was more to the case than a dollar-and-cents negotiation in which the Petitioning Party was trying to take advantage of them. With this shift in perspective, the Property Owner gave the mediator permission to disclose to the Petitioning Party what transpired during their caucused conversation. The mediator conveyed the Property Owner's thoughts and then asked the Petitioning Party if they might feel comfortable explaining directly to the Property Owner the emotional impact of the event. The options to share these feelings included verbally in joint session or by writing them down to be read aloud while the parties remained in caucus. The Petitioning Party made the choice to write down their feelings.

Reframing to Develop Empathy

Initial Positions

Responding Party (Property Owner)

1. Angry
2. Defensive
3. Feeling that Petitioning Party was trying to take advantage
4. Financially focused
5. Lacking understanding of Petitioning Party and true nature of the conflict
6. Reactive

Petitioning Party

1. Angry
2. Defensive
3. Feeling dismissed by Property Owner
4. Using the large financial demand to reflect emotional state
5. Had not expressed emotions or explained personal position to the Property Owner
6. Reactive

The reframing that took place began with shifting the Property Owner's understanding of the possible reason behind both the settlement demand and some of the less-than-collaborative behavior that the Petitioning Party exhibited thus far. Reframing to attain that shift involved a substantial amount of conversation about the different ways emotions are expressed based on individual interpretations of situations and actions, life experiences, ability to communicate feelings and needs, and what is viewed as potential solution options. The conversation also included many reminders that all people are different, their intentions do not necessarily match their delivery, and one disputant's understanding or interpretation of the definition or reason behind an action or statement could very likely be different from another's. Additionally, individuals do not necessarily process information or express themselves in the same way, so taking a beat and seeking clarity before responding is a good philosophy in general. As this is a beneficial conflict-avoidance and de-escalation strategy to apply with friends and family members we have known our entire lives, just imagine the potential benefits with a total stranger whose behavior is completely foreign to you!

Reframing can be done at any point on a sliding scale, in large or small ways, from reframing the entire understanding of a conflict, down to reframing specific words and sentences. The most impactful reframing to develop empathy took place by shifting the Property Owner's understanding of the true emotional nature of the conflict and the Petitioning Party's understanding of the Property Owner's reactive and uninformed position.

1. The Property Owner's statements and actions were reactive, born out of fear and lack of information, and without true understanding.
2. The Petitioning Party did not understand that the Property Owner's reactive statements and actions presented as angry and aggressive as a result of fear and lack of information.

Understanding and accepting that the Property Owner was indeed coming from a place of fear, defensiveness, and a lack of understanding of the Petitioning Party's position and the true nature of the conflict helped defuse some of the Petitioning Party's aggression. Encouraging the Petitioning Party to express emotions and then teaching the Property Owner about both the emotional and logistical sides of accessibility shifted and reframed the mediation from one of contention and combat to one of collaboration and creative, solution-oriented thinking.

New Positions That Reflect Reframes and Empathy

Responding Party (Property Owner)

1. Curious and interested in deepening their understanding of the Petitioning Party and the true nature of the conflict
2. Informed
3. Empathetic
4. Compassionate
5. Apologetic
6. Interested in a collaborative approach to settlement
7. Creative in solution-oriented approaches to settlement options

Petitioning Party

1. Provided with the opportunity to express emotions
2. Heard and validated
3. Receptive to the Property Owner's interest, compassion, empathy, and apology
4. Viewed the shifted position as an opportunity to educate the Property Owner and to work together to ensure that the experience would never be repeated
5. Willingly and actively participated in creative settlement discussions
6. Acknowledged the benefit of nonmonetary solution options in this situation

CONCLUSION

The Petitioning Party's letter expressing emotions was so powerful, and understood so clearly by the Property Owner, that the case took on a completely new life. Following his lead, the Property Owner wrote a letter back expressing:

1. A newfound comprehension of the impact of the experience.
2. A deep apology for unwittingly causing such emotional pain.

3. A commitment to taking the necessary steps to ensure that no one would ever again be excluded as a result of inaccessibility on the property.

The letter concluded with an invitation to collaborate on ideas to transform the property into a space welcoming and inclusive to all. At that point, the case essentially started over. The parties agreed to recommence the mediation process in joint session, re-introduced themselves to each other, and began brainstorming solution ideas. The Property Owner was able to explain what was financially and environmentally possible, and the Petitioning Party was able to educate them about what was necessary and appropriate. With shifted perspectives that included new understandings and developed empathy for one another, the parties were able to mutually agree upon a collaborative settlement that was of a substantially different nature than originally anticipated.

Empathize in a way that is disciplined, rigorous . . . deliberate, and effective.[1]

An empathetic approach can change interactions during conflict intervention in a way that results in greater clarity in matters of perception, intention, interpretation, and consequences, as well as offering improved insight to connect pieces of information contributing to one disputant's understanding of another. When empathy is used properly, it can transcend language, cultural misperceptions, positional misunderstandings, and resolution barriers. An empathetic approach targets thoughts, feelings, emotions, opinions, outlooks, and experiences, which are present for everyone. Therefore, it would be a reasonable assumption that empathy has the capacity to work with and for all during times of conflict. However, it is one thing for a mediator to be able to express empathy and manage it properly during a mediation and quite another for disputants to be empathetic with one another. Among parties, empathy can create and encourage an ability to imagine that cooperation can be attained and that settlement can be reached. In the heat of a hostile conflict situation, we might all be able to recall a time when we looked directly into the face of a person with whom we were very well acquainted, but it was the face of an alien from Mars who looked back at us. Conflict has a way of causing disputants to suddenly become convinced that an opposing party must be from another planet based on interpretation of behavior and sentiments. For disputants in conflict, developing empathy can help humanize each other and can remind disputants that, contrary to their current Martian belief, all parties to the conflict are, in fact, human beings. It is altogether possible that commonalities can be found in experiences and corresponding emotions that might be more similar

1. Waldman, Matt, Center for Empathy in International Affairs, "Changing Minds," *Briefing on Empathy in Mediation*, April 2006.

than different. In a situation where empathy is the remedy, as is so often the case, a question comes to mind: If behavior is shaped by emotion, especially in conflict and trauma situations, why would and should there ever be a mediation approach that intentionally excludes empathy from the conversation? Would we use a butter knife to eat soup? There are far too many mediators and mediating styles that argue that rational decision-making through rational management and evaluation, a jewel in the mediator's crown, is in point of fact devoid of empathy. On a global scale of international relations, the following are examples from mediators participating in the Center for Empathy in International Affairs/European Institute of Peace Consultation discussing empathy or lack thereof:

1. *Vietnam.* Robert McNamara, the former U.S. Secretary of Defense, had said of the Vietnam War that the Americans and Vietnamese were fighting two different wars. He attributed this, above all, to a lack of empathy.
2. *Liberia.* In one area of rural Liberia, in 2004–2005, there was conflict between Muslim and Christian groups, partly due to resentment among Christians that Muslims didn't send their children to local schools. Empathy helped break the deadlock. In a critical meeting, Christian leaders came to understand the Muslim elders couldn't send their children to local schools because they had been founded as missionary schools. According to one participant who was present at the discussions, the former had been able to take and understand the latter's point of view.[2]

The more different and distant the subject, the harder it becomes to relate to them, and the less likely we are to empathize.[3]

Fortunately for both mediators and disputants alike, empathy is a skill that can be learned and practiced. Empathy and the various ways it is expressed might differ on an individual basis, but what does not differ are the effects and benefits that lead to newfound understandings and willingness to discuss settlement options. During certain times, certain situations, and with certain people, virtually everyone either has or will find the capacity to express empathy in their own way. In other situations, however, generally those that are related to conflict and with people who are strangers or disliked, empathy has not been a frequently used conflict resolution strategy. The important distinction is that expressing empathy in both realities is a choice. Bearing that in mind, the results of improving the understanding of the uses and benefits of empathy as a conflict intervention skill specifically, and as an improved personal characteristic in general, might come as a pleasant surprise. However, a person's aptitude for and later ability to empathize is directly affected by their understandings, interpretations, and experiences, so how quickly and efficiently empathy can be expressed falls on an individual timeline.

2. Id., p. 3.
3. Id., p. 4.

Disputants can be reluctant to express empathy and imagine themselves in the shoes of an adversary. A mediator could, of course, provide assistance to a disputant in moving toward empathy as a working skill in a quicker and more efficient manner. At some point, empathy became regarded as a weakness, a *less-than* characteristic or skill with no place at the rational and logical adult table. In countless circumstances, that could not be farther from the truth. It would be a fool's errand to enter a mediation or conflict-intervention arena without any and all skills and tools at the ready. Knowledge is power, as the old adage reminds us, and when the best possible outcome is the result of being as informed as possible to be able to make the most appropriate and beneficial decisions (which could have life-changing consequences), why even for one moment would a conflict interventionist intentionally exclude and not embrace a skill that can lay a pathway directly into the inner workings of adversarial or opposing parties? Within the context of mediation, the understanding and expression of empathy are essential for the development of an empathetic relationship between the mediator and disputants and disputants with one another.

Developing empathy is not always an easy endeavor, often made harder by the speed with which some mediations must be conducted—in the hallways outside of a courtroom, for example—as well as by the idea of strong versus weak labels placed on certain behaviors during conflict. These built-in structural and psychological barriers to empathizing are hurdles that the mediator might decide to devote energy to overcoming should they deem that a mediation might benefit from the presence of empathy and the development of an empathetic relationship. After commencement of a mediation, a mediator could strategically exude empathy by purposefully and continuously projecting it toward all disputants with the intent for them to follow suit and adopt empathy toward one another, either intentionally or incidentally. This might happen in a way similar to an accent that manifests when we travel to other countries—it is not intentional, but after being inundated and surrounded by voices speaking a foreign language, it happens even without our realizing or controlling it. A little impromptu empathizing never hurt anybody—quite the contrary, in fact.

MEDIATOR STRATEGY: DEVELOPING EMPATHY AMONG DISPUTANTS

> Often we deal in static or conventional notions of knowledge, when conflict is in fact dynamic, complex and nuanced—which empathy can help illuminate. In that sense, empathy can add more layers to our understanding.[4]

4. Id., p. 1.

1. Ask one disputant to describe how they feel from a place of "I" to the opposing disputant:
   a. More specifically, how the conflict has caused them to feel.
   b. Their feelings about the various components of the conflict.
   c. There should be absolutely no blaming of the opposing disputant in presenting their feelings.
   d. Encourage them to address their desire to reach settlement, including why it is important to them.
2. Ask the listening disputant to respond with any clarity-seeking questions they might have.
3. Next, ask the speaking disputant to respond to the listening disputant's questions.
4. Ask the listening disputant to explain what they understand the speaking disputant to be expressing.
5. The speaking disputant should be invited to correct any misinterpretations or misunderstandings the listening disputant might have.
6. Ask the listening disputant if they can imagine that they are a friend or family member of the speaker and that they are attempting to resolve this conflict, instead of someone who is involved in a conflict with a stranger or in a conflict that does not involve a measure of caring.
   a. Consider providing a moment for the disputant to shift out of conflict mode.
7. Ask the listening disputant to respond to what they have heard the speaker express, using their new perspective of a personal relationship.
   a. Encourage the disputants to engage in reciprocal dialogue from this different perspective.
   b. The disputants should continue interacting with the speaker coming from a place of "I," and the listener responding only to what the speaker is saying without introducing any additional and possibly contradictory commentary.
8. Once the exercise has been completed, ask the disputants to switch roles and begin the exercise again.
9. When the disputants have all participated in both positions, check to see if the atmosphere of the mediation can be maintained with this new sense of empathy and understanding. Inquire how each feels with their new insights, any new information presented, and with the knowledge that everyone is there to improve their lives by moving past the conflict.
10. Highlight the similarities and commonalities in sentiments expressed by the disputants.
11. Discuss a new approach to addressing their differences.
    a. Find a common thread, even if it is the act of attending mediation in the first place or their common desire to resolve the conflict, notwithstanding differing settlement demands.

STRATEGIES TO DEVELOP EMPATHY AND EMPATHY AS STRATEGY TO DEVELOP RAPPORT THROUGH ADDITIONAL CRITICAL MEDIATION SKILLS

Purposeful Listening

Purposeful Listening with the distinct goal of developing empathy is designed to understand and interpret someone in the exact way that they desire and intend, and not through the lens of the listener's personal experience, understandings, and interpretations. It can be equally important for a mediator to develop and display an empathetic relationship with each disputant as it is for the disputants to develop and display one among themselves. Depending on the nature of the relationship among the disputants, which could have begun with the conflict and might end the moment it is resolved, the need for the empathetic relationship during the mediation will not be beneficial or required on its conclusion when they return to their original relationship as strangers. However, if the mediation is Transformative and the disputants are in a position to have a continuing relationship outside of the conflict and after it is resolved, then building an empathetic relationship that extends beyond the conclusion of the mediation could be critical. Without it, the disputants could find themselves in mediation every time a conflict arises. Without an empathetic relationship between the mediator and the disputants, a barrier preventing the mediator from using the rest of their skills to the greatest extent possible might develop. Such a constraint could occur if the disputants do not sense empathy from the mediator, because with empathy comes trust, openness, willingness, creativity, and eventually the possibility of settlement. The chain of listening through empathetic ears to create empathetic responses in order to build an atmosphere of empathy leading to an empathetic relationship is a strong strategy to overlay onto any mediation process, interweaving additional skills as needs and opportunities arise and are presented.

Comfort

Empathy provides a comfort to disputants that can be critical in reaching settlement. It is through an empathetic relationship and a level of comfort that disputants might become willing to be more communicative about the true nature of their feelings and concerns, as well as openly and honestly discussing what is beneath the surface that they are presenting. In many cases, only once that information is uncovered can the mediation be brought to settlement discussions. Imagine opening up about issues that cause feelings of vulnerability to a perfect stranger within moments of meeting—not necessarily an easy, comfortable, or desirable task. Before a disputant sees the merit in that and is willing to do so, there must be action such as the construction of an empathetic relationship. That will produce an atmosphere of comfort conducive to the benefits that empathy brings, created by using methods including the following:

1. Empathizing.
2. Allowing disputants to express themselves as much and for as long as they might need.
3. Showing interest: using active listening, asking questions, reframing, and reflecting back what the disputant is saying.
4. Finding topics in common, whether related to the conflict or not.
5. Sharing stories from the mediator's experience, real or fabricated.
6. Listening silently while using nonverbal actions to express understanding and support. (See Chapter 6, "Listening.")
7. Making suggestions that take into consideration the best interests of the disputants based on what they have expressed.

Trust

Building empathy builds trust. When disputants express empathy toward one another, including feelings and positions in the conflict, they are building a level of understanding leading to the belief that they are being heard and understood. This, in turn, leads to trust in the fact that they are being validated and possibly moving onto the same side together in opposition to the conflict itself. This could enable the disputants to engage more collaboratively in the mediation process and to reach settlement options that would not be available to them without empathy building a layer of trust into their relationship.

Even in a situation where disputants are unable to express empathy toward one another, negating the ability to form trust, the mediator might still be able to develop a relationship of trust with each disputant individually by using expressions of empathy. Without earning the trust of the disputants, a mediator could find it increasingly difficult to mediate. In the absence of trust there is mistrust, which makes performing in the role of mediator an almost impossible task.

1. To develop trust with parties, the mediator should:
   a. Express empathy.
   b. Demonstrate understanding.
   c. Ensure that the parties feel heard and validated.
   d. Engage in the conversation.
   e. Ask questions, make statements, and provide suggestions that demonstrate that the best interest of each disputant is the mediator's only concern.
   f. Develop a relationship of mutual respect.
   g. Ensure that party interests and needs are reflected in questions, statements, and suggestions.
   h. Work equally for all parties involved in the mediation.
   i. Maintain impartiality in a manner that precludes any disputant from feeling that the mediator has taken one side over another.
   j. Be fair and make sure that the mediator's work always reflects fairness.

k. If in caucus, always maintain confidentiality unless and until specifically provided with permission to do otherwise.
l. Be honest with the disputants when discussing the case, their positions, their BATNA and WATNA, and their possible settlement options.

Mirroring

Mirroring is an industry favorite strategy in developing empathy because, as has been scientifically proven time and time again, people are most comfortable and relate most readily and freely with those they interpret to most resemble themselves. If a mediator mirrors back to a disputant similar personality characteristics—vocabulary, belief systems, and even mannerisms—it would not be uncommon for a disputant to find comfort and to identify an ally by that shared behavior. The kinship developed through mirroring can result in a disputant feeling that the mediator empathizes with them because they understand them. This concept shifts the mediator from the position of stranger and one with possibly questionable intentions to that of community member (think family, friends, and support system), which would afford them a substantially easier position from which to operate.

The purpose of a mediator engaging in mirroring is to encourage the parties to reach the necessary level of trust and comfort to disclose honest information to the mediator, if not to each other. If this can be accomplished, the mediator will be able to effectively guide disputants to negotiate in good faith, with effective communication leading to the possibility of being receptive to and accepting settlement options from the mediator. If parties do not believe that the mediator is operating on their behalf and with their best interests in mind, assisting them in accepting settlement options as wise decisions can be extremely difficult.

Openness

The use of empathy to build the foundation and framework for the existence and development of comfort and trust promotes disputant openness. This, in turn, engenders a more conducive work environment for both the mediator and the conflict intervention and resolution process. If ever a mediator has felt that they are treading water or running on a hamster wheel during their attempts to engage with parties during a mediation, a likely culprit is a lack of disputant openness.

A mediator can assume that their relationship lacks empathy or trust when disputants:

1. Do not detect or believe that the mediator understands them, their position, or their explanations.
2. Do not feel heard or validated.
3. Do not perceive the mediator to be an ally.

If this is the case, the mediator might decide to take strategic action and move away from discussing various details of the case or settlement options. The mediator can then pivot toward focusing on ways to engage differently with the disputant to develop empathy with the goal of fostering a relationship that can shift the current difficult dynamic. To accomplish this, a mediator might:

1. Focus on validation.
2. Only mention settlement options if brought up first by a disputant.
   a. Allow parties to guide the conversation to ensure that they have their day in court and do not feel rushed or pressured to get over it and on to settlement discussions.
3. Refrain from evaluating the case.
   a. Evaluating could be misinterpreted by disputants as pressure and a shifting of sides or ganging up against them if they have not emotionally processed and expressed their positions to a level of fulfillment enabling them to progress to a more rational and logical position.
4. Focus on their feelings, interests, and needs only.
5. Be supportive.
6. Engage in the conversation using tactics such as active listening, asking pertinent questions, and displaying interest in what the parties are disclosing.
7. Consistently maintain the goal of empathy development so all questions, statements, and responses have empathy woven through them and are reflective of an empathetic bent. For example:
   a. Asking a question that encourages a disputant to delve deeper into their story so that the mediator can "better understand where they are coming from."
   b. Making a statement that expresses support of their experience in a manner that indicates that their feelings are appropriate and matter and that "given those circumstances, feeling that way makes perfect sense."
   c. Circling back around to discuss whether certain proposed settlement options would in fact meet a disputant's interests and needs.
      i. Whether the proposed options do meet their interests and needs might matter less to a disputant when weighed against the possibility of resolving the conflict without escalating it into a courtroom. However, this decision might not be attainable without the disputant feeling that the mediator empathizes with them and cares about their position within the outcome of the case.

Information

Engage with information in an empathetic way. If disputants disclose information of a sensitive and personal nature, the mediator must lead with empathy and compassion in response. Sometimes information is provided by disputants in a cautious manner specifically as a test to see how a mediator will respond. This is a pivotal moment and an opportunity to demonstrate to disputants that their information is safe and that there can be a foundation of trust and empathy between the parties individually and the mediator.

1. When a mediator receives a piece of personal or sensitive information, or a disputant discloses hesitantly and possibly after struggling to feel comfortable enough doing so, it is critical to act in a manner that accurately and appropriately supports the nature of the information. Before the mediator begins to manage the information in any way, including reframing, asking

additional questions to identify truthfulness of the statement, or guiding it toward possible settlement options, their immediate response must reflect:

a. Validation.
b. Comprehension of the message.
c. Understanding of and compassion for the effort it took the party to provide it.
d. Recognition of the trust the disputant has placed in them by revealing it.

A mediator should remember to lead by example in managing and interacting with information provided to them. If parties are not interpreting and responding to information in a manner respectful to each other or beneficial to the mediation, the mediator should demonstrate a suggested improvement for their interactions by applying empathy. Lacking the empathy that certain topics and conflicts require can easily shift a mediation, taking it instead on an aggressive, confrontational, and competitive course, rather than one of understanding, cooperation, and collaboration that seeks a mutually beneficial and solution-oriented resolution. (See Chapter 7, "The Art of the Reframe.")

Settlement Options

The presence of empathy can contribute in large part to a mediation achieving effective communication and subsequent settlement. Both the expression and acceptance of empathy are critical parts of turning the tide. Empathy is a powerful tool that alters the way parties perceive and are perceived by each other, and resulting settlement options are generally more finely attuned to the participating disputants than those produced in a setting devoid of an empathetic lens. To shift to an empathetic perspective, the mediator might propose that the disputants reimagine the settlement offer they are extending as from the viewpoint of an opposing party and not exclusively from their own.

Settlement options that demonstrate and incorporate empathy stand a greater chance of:

1. Being reasonable.
2. Being respectful.
3. Being mutually agreeable and acceptable.
4. Remaining intact.
5. When appropriate, healing relationships that have been harmed by the conflict.

These options are produced from the work of mutual contribution by disputants who operate, at least in part, from a position of inclusivity of opposing disputant interests. If and when parties struggle to get to this position of their own volition, a mediator can direct their focus to a discussion of empathy, which will include the power of its potential impact on their conflict resolution—beneficially with its inclusion and detrimentally (potentially in spades) by its exclusion. Empathetic settlements can prevent a revolving door of mediating the same issues.

FLASH CHALLENGE

Testing Your Limits

Empathizing can sometimes prove to be a difficult exercise in managing and interacting with parties whose beliefs and actions are interpreted by the mediator to be disturbing. This can, however, be a consistent aspect of mediation or conflict intervention, so engaging in practices to develop the skills to reach empathy with even those who fit this category is a necessity. Becoming successful at empathizing with those parties also deepens a mediator's ability to maintain impartiality even when faced with challenging circumstances and to understand some of the more testing, additional requirements of mediation and conflict intervention.

1. Select an individual to empathize with whose actions you detest or whose views and positions you find deplorable or absurd.
   a. This can be an individual known to you that you have engaged with in the past.
   b. This could be an interaction you engage in for the purpose of this Flash Challenge.
   c. This could be an individual not known to you, but whose position and perspective you are familiar with enough to answer the following questions.
2. Discuss how you were able to put yourself in their shoes.
   a. What did you learn from doing so?
3. Would you be able to use empathy to accept:
   a. The reasons that brought them to where they are?
   b. The reasons that they believe what they do?
   c. The reasons that caused them to do what they did?
4. Do you see their side or position differently now?
   a. If so, describe your new lens.
   b. If not, explain why.

RISKS OF EMPATHY

1. If a mediator is not practiced in managing their empathetic feelings, they could become overwhelmed by them and lose their ability to maintain emotional control and impartiality.
2. If a mediator is not practiced in managing the expression of their empathy, they could be mistakenly perceived by the disputants as not being impartial.
3. Crossing the line from empathy to internalizing the details and emotions of a disputant's story can cause a mediator to favor one side over another.
   a. The mediator might begin to advocate for one side, feeling that they, too, have been harmed by the opposing party.

b. The mediator might also begin to develop disdain for a disputant if they become aligned with a chosen side, thereafter causing communication and settlement discussions to become more difficult or even impossible.
c. The mediator showing favor could embolden one side to refuse to be cooperative or collaborative and cease their willingness to continue any form of dialogue, instead choosing to proceed to court where they are sure they will prevail.
d. The mediator's credibility could be called into question if they are not able to remain neutral.

FLASH CHALLENGE

What Do You Think?

1. Discuss the relationship between empathy and professionalism in the field of mediation and in conflict intervention, including:
   a. Opposing positions.
   b. Potential psychology behind positions.
   c. Comparing and contrasting empathy as a weakness to empathy as a strength.
   d. Your perspectives about empathy in the landscape of mediation and conflict intervention:
      i. Yes, no, why, why not, when, where, how.
2. Discuss how a conversation about a shifting perspective of empathy might transpire and unfold.
   a. If you do not believe this conversation needs to happen, discuss your position.

chapter 9

Finding Interests and Needs Below the Surface

The Signal in the Noise

Quite frequently the strong emotional background of an issue and the personalities involved may be more significant than the facts.

— *William Simkin, Mediation and the Dynamics of Collective Bargaining (1971)*

On a fundamental level, all people need to feel accepted, respected, validated, and heard, which often requires reaching needs below the surface. Mediators can begin to address deeper and more authentic problems and issues, and for the types of mediations where this action is appropriate and necessary, this could be a channel to resolution and settlement. Without these needs being addressed, there could be wild mediations in store, frequently grounded nowhere near reality. The consequences of any of these needs not being met, let alone more than one at a time and during the heightened emotional state that conflict creates, can be heated discussions about fictitious grievances with the intention of diverting attention from conversation that might lead to addressing actual needs below the surface, resulting in impasse and the mediation ending without settlement.

A prime example of the external manifestation of a fundamental need not being met would be when two individuals are engaged in a conversation about what to have for dinner. All of a sudden, one explodes about how the other did not take out the trash three Tuesdays ago, never puts them first, does not care about their feelings, and is also pretty sure that they are being cheated on, because, "Now you're tying your shoes to the left instead of to the right!" More attention should be paid immediately and consistently during mediations to asking questions such as these:

1. "How are you feeling?"
2. "Do you need anything?"
3. "Do you understand what is happening?"
4. "Do you have anything to add?"

This would go a long way toward keeping disputants on topic with minimal emotional outbursts at a time when parties are substantially more prone to such expressions. Disputant answers will likely include expressing feelings such as these:

1. They are not being heard.
2. They are not understood.
3. They are ignored.
4. They have been disrespected.
5. Their feelings and opinions are being disregarded.
6. They have been and continue to be hurt.
7. Intentional harm has been inflicted on them.

It is the mediator's job to be responsive by guiding disputants to shift to new perspectives. Only then do disputants stand a chance at avoiding fighting about the oppressive and hideous color of the barn door and whose responsibility it is to paint it – obviously not either one of theirs – a point now being fought to the death, when the crux of the issue really is "Why wasn't that phone call returned yesterday?" The goal should be conversations that are unencumbered by a perceived or actual loss of fundamental needs. If fight-or-flight responses are firing because fundamental needs are not being met, how is it possible to expect disputants to cooperate and compromise, or even hear the logic or reasonable nature of the conversation? It is not. Do not waste time trying to negotiate settlement without addressing fundamental needs because leaving them ignored and unaddressed could result in impenetrable roadblocks. Instead, identify needs below the surface that are not met and address them before attempting to reach mediation end goals.

During the course of a mediation, more often than not, a cycle of issues arises in the areas of:

1. Trust and lack thereof.
2. Inadequate information caused by an inability to communicate fully and properly.
3. A breakdown of respect.

With these issues, parties will remain in positional bargaining with demanding and aggressive postures, unable and unwilling to hear each other. At this state of heightened conflict, disputants might as well be speaking different languages. With anger, frustration, distrust, and lack of or inadequate information added to the mix, the produced result is a recipe for a continuing dispute. The mediator has the power to interrupt this cycle and bring parties together. For example, a disputant in caucus may have provided additional information that can become a tool to be applied to disrupting the cycle. While still in caucus and after receiving potentially impactful new information, the mediator can begin to manage and reframe the information to bring down the walls of that disputant. The mediator might then find it worthwhile to ask the disputant for their permission to bring this information to the attention of an opposing party so that a move into joint session could result in parties interacting with the information together. With permission granted, this tool can be brought outside of caucus for disputants to use jointly, seeing and hearing each other speak about their needs and the true issues of the dispute. With all parties now aware of the newly shared relevant information, they can address and resolve certain aspects, if not the entire conflict.

On the other hand, if an issue or need below the surface remains unaddressed, it could interfere with the entire mediation causing impasse. No mediator wants to be in a position of being blindsided by a sudden demand after a settlement offer has been laboriously reached, or so they thought.

EXAMPLE

A mediator has spent hours guiding disputants through the mediation process and has finally reached a settlement that is mutually acceptable to all parties. This settlement was carefully crafted to encompass every single need and concern articulated throughout the day by both parties—a truly amazing feat. The agreement was signed by one disputant. The mediator turned to the other party and presented the paperwork for them to sign, when, out of nowhere, that disputant decided that although the settlement took into consideration all of their expressed needs and wants, suddenly there was more to address and the settlement did not, in fact, reflect the entirety of their concerns.

Take a moment to consider how a mediator would be feeling in that moment, how you would be feeling in that moment, and what thoughts would immediately come to mind. A list would most likely look something like this:

1. How could this have happened?
2. Did I allow this to happen?
3. How did I allow this to happen?
4. How could this new concern not have come up sooner?
5. Why did they not express this to me earlier while we were crafting the settlement?
6. Why did I not dig deeper beneath the surface to make sure that there was nothing else going on?
7. How can I now recover this mediation?
8. Is this settlement process now going to have to start over from scratch?
9. How is the other party going to react to this new piece of information—that there is actually more to the story which is now preventing settlement?
    a. Will they be receptive to it?
    b. Will it make them angry?
    c. Will they interpret it as a power tactic?
    d. Will they be offended by it and act out in some way?
    e. Will it draw out new issues and additional roadblocks to settlement?
    f. Was there a reason this information was purposefully withheld?

Without developing a relationship of rapport that includes delving beneath superficial posturing, the scenario just presented will be repeatedly replayed. Identifying needs and concerns below the surface must happen if only to avoid surprises at the eleventh hour of a mediation. For a mediator, having access to every possible piece of information is as important to their ability to perform as a conflict interventionist as it is for a construction worker to have hammer and nails, a pianist their sheet music, and a scientist their microscope. These tools are fundamental and foundational to the efficacy of job performance. It is not a choice; it is a requirement. The types of information potentially hiding beneath the surface during a mediation could include emotions as well as facts pertinent to the conflict and to subsequent settlement discussions. These emotions will be important for the mediator to bear in mind because they could easily affect the decisions disputants make. If a disputant is presenting as emotionally unaffected by the conflict, but on deeper inspection the mediator ascertains that this is not actually the case, it will be necessary to be addressed as settlement discussions evolve. The disputant might have a much harder time contemplating offers in a rational manner and could require more from an opposing party to even be able to entertain settlement. This need can manifest itself at any time and from any direction, so it is best to anticipate and offset the possibility. In contrast, if a disputant is truly emotionally disengaged or unaffected by the conflict, then it will be reflected by their ability to be rational in their consideration and acceptance of appropriate settlement offers. Even so, with this latter type of disputant, there is still the possibility of a problematic subsurface issue. The golden rule is to make sure, one way or the other!

WHAT MIGHT BE LURKING BEHIND ANGER AND BELOW SUPERFICIAL POSTURING

- Fear
- Loneliness
- Rejection
- Depression
- Embarrassment
- Anxiety
- Frustration
- Confusion
- Hurt feelings
- Sadness
- Isolation
- Guilt
- Shame
- Jealousy
- Outrage at perceived or real injustice
- Helplessness
- Overwhelming stress
- Humiliation

Although presented differently, all of these feelings are expressions of vulnerability—an emotion that most people in conflict go to great lengths to conceal with anger and superficial posturing as their exposed protective layer. All too often, vulnerability has been associated with weakness, making it a hurdle in a mediation setting. By recognizing and understanding that superficial posturing is to be expected as a form of armor against the exposure of true, possibly vulnerable feelings below the surface and by being fully aware of and prepared to address this issue, the mediator will be positioned to move through and eventually beyond to reach a point where potential cooperative settlement options can be discussed.

PURPOSEFUL LISTENING

For a mediation to move forward properly, those feelings that quite possibly and perhaps very likely stand in direct contradiction to the feelings and positions presented thus far must be accessed. Dismantling surface-level posturing to access those lower levels of information can be the backbone of a mediation. It is a task that requires Purposeful Listening to lay a foundation of trust and an emotionally safe environment for the cautious introduction of the mediator's guidance toward what must be accomplished to reach settlement.

When a mediator has determined that there could be information or emotions below the surface, the effort must be put forth beyond that of listening without action. Listening and hearing information for the sake of listening only is not enough. In the quest to ascertain subsurface elements, Empathetic Listening is one form of Purposeful Listening that employs support and encouragement rather than advice or criticism while building a relationship conducive to the search. Using Empathetic Listening and listening for inconsistencies such as an emotional response that seems overly dramatic or far too extreme within the conflict can reveal an indication of something additional or different transpiring below the surface. After hearing an inconsistency, a mediator could offer an expression of empathy to encourage a disputant to disclose additional subsurface information. Empathetic Listening targets opportunities where empathy might be required and could be beneficial.

EXAMPLES OF EMPATHETIC STATEMENTS

- "I appreciate that you trust me with this information."
- "I believe that I understand what you are saying."
- "Thank you for sharing this with me."
- "I can see why that is bothering you."
- "I am sure that must be challenging for you."
- "How did that experience make you feel?"

A note of caution is in order. Asking a disputant how an experience made them feel displays interest in what the speaker is saying, as well as a desire to learn more about their experience and to explore how that experience affected them – but there is a caveat. The mediator must be ready to reframe and pivot the answers toward possible settlement and solution options in a manner that can prevent those feelings from resurfacing and detrimentally affecting the mediation's forward progress. Asking for more emotion in an answer can be a slippery slope if the mediator is not prepared to drag a disputant out of an emotional bog and back onto solid ground fairly quickly.

FLASH CHALLENGE

Turn It Empathetic

Part 1

Engage in a conversation with someone you know about an experience they are involved in. It does not have to be based on an argument or disagreement but should have an emotional component. Here are some examples.

- A discussion about an obstacle being faced at work or a conflict they are involved in with fellow employees.
- A difficult breakup, either of a marriage or a relationship in some form, including possible child custody issues, or just the consideration of a breakup.
- Feeling overwhelmed with stress or anxiety—a discussion of those feelings as well as their possible causes.
- Siblings who are not inheriting equally and one (or more) is upset by it.
- A situation that involved a betrayal of confidence by an entrusted person that might have led to embarrassment or some sort of repercussions.

1. Insert as many of the above empathetic statements when appropriate and as make sense without stating that you are doing so. Do not call attention to or label them as such.
   a. Are you crafting and inserting any of your own empathetic statements that are not on the list?
      i. If so, what are they?
2. Discuss some of the opportunities that were presented through your partner's statements that opened the door for you to insert your empathetic statements.
3. What happened after you delivered your empathetic statement?
   a. How did they respond?
   b. Did it change the dynamic of the conversation?
      i. If it did, how?
4. Did they acknowledge your empathetic statements?
   a. Did they mention gratitude in some way?
5. Do you feel that the conversation benefitted from using empathetic statements?
6. Do you feel that you were able to build rapport or trust through the use of the empathetic statements?
   a. This might be more applicable when speaking to a stranger, unless you are receiving new information or have encouraged your partner to disclose something very personal.

7. Were you able to encourage them to disclose new, additional, or deeper information to you?
8. Did they disclose new, additional, or deeper information to you on their own following your empathetic statements?
9. If any new, additional, or deeper information was disclosed to you as a result of using the empathetic statements, did it alter any part of their original input into the conversation?
   a. Did it change their outlook and did they reflect about it to you in that changed way?
   b. Did they reinterpret the experience they are discussing with you in a different way following any of your empathetic statements?

Part 2

Engage in a similar conversation with a stranger.

1. Follow the instructions and answer all of the questions above.

Part 3

If the conversation in Part 1 or Part 2 was not about a conflict, engage now with someone else in a conversation and encourage them to discuss a conflict they are having in which you are not involved.

1. Follow the instructions and answer all of the questions above.

Extra Credit

Engage a person you are in conflict with to discuss the matter.

1. Insert as many of the above empathetic statements when appropriate and as make sense without stating that you are doing so. Do not call attention to or label them as such.
2. What happens to the tone of the conversation once you introduce the empathetic statements?
   a. Does their tone change along with yours?
      i. Do they attempt to employ any empathetic statements as well?
      ii. Conversely, does it anger them even more and do they interpret it as condescending, belittling, or as a "maneuver" on your part?
      iii. Can you identify a Conflict Handling Mode shift from them?
         1. If so, from what to what?
   b. Were you able to resolve your conflict?
      i. If so, discuss the settlement you reached and how.
         1. Do you believe your use of the empathetic statements assisted in resolving the conflict and reaching settlement? Discuss.
         2. Do you believe you would have reached resolution and settlement without the use of the empathetic statements? Discuss.
         3. Does the resolution and settlement reflect any of the new, additional, or deeper information you were able to receive? Discuss.

> *a)* If so, discuss how you realized it could be beneficial for resolution and settlement upon hearing it.
>
> ii. If not, why do you think that is?
>
> *1.* Do you believe you could reach settlement if you were to engage in a second and third conversation surrounding the conflict, each time using Empathetic Listening and applying empathetic statements?

RAPPORT

Developing a relationship of rapport, one that is comprised of understanding and empathy with the goal of leading to more efficient communication, is a predictable and straightforward strategy to access information below the surface. However, it is how we build that rapport that necessitates discussion. Managing disputants with the following traits is difficult:

1. Emotionally charged and embroiled in conflict.
2. Possibly attending the mediation only begrudgingly.
3. Completely suspicious of mediation, mediators, and intentions.

This is exacerbated by working within a time limit. If the mediator is able to develop a relationship of rapport, the difficulty level could be substantially decreased. The effort to encourage disputants to pivot initial positions to reveal what is hidden is a task that necessitates some level of rapport with the mediator.

Parties in conflict who enter mediation generally lack rapport with one another; otherwise they would likely have been able to communicate cooperatively and to effectively reach a settlement on their own. Logically, then, something must change to successfully move the disputants through conflict and into settlement. It is illogical to assume that this can be done with all factors remaining the same, particularly if there are unaddressed and unresolved needs or concerns below the surface. With improved communication creating an openness to cooperate, and in conjunction with the mediator's ability to reach previously undisclosed information and emotions, a shift can occur. This is accomplished through the process of building rapport between mediator and disputants. Whether this is done in joint session or in caucus is entirely dependent on the nature of the conflict, the emotional state of the disputant(s), their ability to control themselves, and their willingness to listen and work together. Remember, Rome was not built in a day, as the adage goes. Building rapport can be a daunting task that requires one step at a time. The process begins the moment a mediator invites disputants to describe the conflict that brought them to the mediation that day, effectively having their day in court, which will undoubtedly include at least some of their feelings about how they have been wronged by another party. Creating rapport cannot be rushed, and certain steps must be taken to get there.

Steps to Building Rapport

1. Give disputants their day in court.
   a. Allow and encourage disputants to get it all out for as long as they need to.
      i. The invitation to a disputant to discuss anything and everything they might need to express with the mediator's full attention is an invitation to build rapport. Taking that day in court is indicative of the disputant's acceptance and their willingness to engage in a relationship of rapport.
      ii. Once the disputant begins speaking, they are making the most of the opportunity to disclose information and feelings that they had not before, as well as to offer new hints and clues of potential wiggle room that the mediator can apply when settlement discussions begin.
2. Listen.
   a. Use the various listening types as the needs of the disputants and the mediation process present themselves.
   b. Knowing which listening type to use when, where, and how can assist the mediator in drawing out a disputant, at the same time providing appropriate responses to their various needs in any given moment as they are steered toward revealing additional details. A disputant might be relieved and comforted to know that a mediator who is a skilled listener makes for the perfect secret keeper.
3. Show interest.
   a. Even if a mediator must feign interest, do so. Showing interest demonstrates caring, which is integral to the rapport-building process, which is in turn integral to reaching subsurface information.
      i. Interest can be expressed verbally and nonverbally through:
         1. Statements of affirmation and understanding
         2. Eye contact
         3. Body language
            a) Leaning in toward the speaking disputant
            b) Sitting up straight
            c) Head nodding
4. Be empathetic.
   a. Be certain that there is absolutely no judgment in any responses or further questions.
      i. A judgmental mediator is not conducive to a disputant becoming willing to change their position or disclosing information that had been purposefully kept secret.
         1. During the initial discussion with disputants concerning the reason(s) for mediation, it is crucial to avoid pushing back against anything said including lies, misinformation, or misguided statements.
   b. Be an interested, supportive, understanding, and trustworthy mediator to whom disputants can tell their stories. Allow that trust to flow over

onto the disputants so that they realize that they can and should speak more deeply and truthfully.

5. Mirror.
   a. Consider matching the disputant's manner while attempting to demonstrate understanding of what they are saying and validate, for example, that the experience, "sounds like it must have been very difficult for you to endure."
      i. Matching the disputant's manner allows the mediator to provide the comfort of familiarity. With that comfort, a bridge can be built, leading the disputant to feel parallel comfort and become willing to disclose new potentially sensitive and personal information.
      ii. There is a difference between validating a disputant's emotions and agreeing with their portrayal of the circumstances of an event, and validation does not require agreement. Supporting their feelings and how an event affected them is necessary to show an understanding of what they are saying and how they are feeling. Agreement is not. In that understanding, the mediator might find the opening to become a confidant for the disputant.
6. Probe: Ask questions, and then ask follow-up questions.
   a. Probing leads to two distinct avenues of value. The first is gaining access to potentially critical information and the second is assisting in building an informed relationship, both of which are mainstays of a successful mediation process.
   b. Inquiries demonstrate interest, understanding as well as misunderstanding, and appreciation of information being expressed.
      i. The nature of asking and answering questions inherently leads to the potential for uncovering new information. The manner of asking those questions will vary in the context of circumstances. Inquiry styles may include:
         1. To the point
         2. Vague
         3. Pushy
         4. Gentle touch
         5. Leading
         6. Hidden meaning
         7. Ambiguous
      ii. Asking a probing question could be exactly what a disputant needs to open up about what is happening beneath the surface of what they have been presenting.
         1. It is possible that to date, no one has shown any interest in what they are feeling, what they are going through, and whether or not there is any more to their story. The simple opportunity extended by a mediator of an inquisitive mind with an interested ear might be enough to open the door to subsurface material.

7. Find common ground.
   a. People automatically feel closer to those who have had similar experiences.
   b. Be wary not to upstage what the disputant is saying. Expressing an element of a shared experience that might have led to a successful creative solution in that particular situation could be helpful to the disputant in finding a settlement to their own conflict as well. One-upping a disputant's experience will not be met with the same outcome.
   c. If the mediator senses that they could benefit from additional information being withheld by a disputant, they might attempt to share an experience of their own that is similar to what that disputant is presenting, but one that also incorporates elements that differ and might appear to be deeper, more emotional, or more complicated. The disputant will listen to a story that they find parallel to their own, combined with additional aspects that do not quite resemble what they shared, but might bear similarities to parts of their story that they have not disclosed. This could encourage the disputant to follow suit and reveal to the mediator what they have been hiding.
      i. If the mediator chooses to describe a factual story, but it lacks the different or deeper elements necessary to demonstrate further layers, the mediator could consider presenting additional information in the form of a question or reflective statement.
      ii. Here are some examples.
         1. "If someone had asked me if I was content with the way we resolved our conflict, I would have said no, even though I acted as though I was. But nobody asked me, so I didn't have a chance to tell anyone. Nobody cared."
         2. "I wish I had someone in my corner at that time who was there for me, who I could talk to and really open up to. It was hard for me to keep some things a secret at that time even though I felt that I had to."
         3. "Keeping my feelings and some parts of that story a secret for so long really affected me physically and emotionally. I wish someone had told me to just be honest no matter what, and that it would have been okay."
         4. "If we had someone to help us communicate better during that difficult time, I think I could have been comfortable talking about some of the things that I felt I needed to keep hidden."
         5. "Hearing that story out loud makes me realize how very important it is to be able to open up and talk to someone about what really happened."
         6. "I didn't think I was upset at the time, but now when I reflect back, I wonder if I actually was upset and whether it caused the conflict that followed."
         7. "When my friend became upset at me, I was surprised by the intensity of her response because it did not appear to match the event

that caused it. Do you think it is possible that sometimes responses require explanations?"

8. We are in this together.
   a. Express to the disputants that you are in this with them, by reframing "I" statements to "we" statements.
      i. For example, "I don't know what to do" is turned into, "We will work through solution options together until we find one that works for everyone."
         1. This statement is also transformed from one of despair to one of collaborative action with support, which can instill a sense of confidence and newfound possibility.
   b. There is strength in numbers and providing a disputant with a teammate could give them the strength and support they need to feel ready and able to discuss the entirety of what they are experiencing.
      i. If a disputant feels less alone, they might become more willing to share additional aspects of their story that they have been reluctant to thus far.
   c. The mediator is on everyone's team, so it is acceptable to show support to each disputant by encouraging them to tell their story, to stand up for themselves, and to be open to working collaboratively together against the conflict to move past it and carry on with their lives.
9. Open the floodgates.
   a. Encourage conversation and the expression of emotions or details that disputants might need to get off their chest or that the mediator perceives to be a necessary step for a productive mediation.
      i. The more information a mediator has, the easier it is to identify various issues involved in a case.
      ii. The more information a mediator has, the easier it is to develop creative settlement options that address diverse and possibly contradictory interests and needs simultaneously.
      iii. Parties have the opportunity to work through emotions that might be inhibiting them from engaging in the mediation in a rational, logical, and productive manner.
      iv. Aspects of the conflict that are confusing or being misinterpreted could be clarified.
      v. Parties have the opportunity to explain intentions that might not be reflected in their statements or actions.
   b. The opening of the floodgates might take place as a result of a developed empathetic relationship of trust, comfort, and support. This is a layered technique that applies skills to create a position (an empathetic relationship) to cause an effect (opened floodgates) for a desired outcome (effective communication and subsequent settlement).
      i. Layering will become a common practice for mediators, as not many skills in general, and in mediation specifically, stand on their own to

command change. Additionally, even if it were possible to use only one skill to shift parties, the outcome of a single-skill approach might not be as advantageous as the outcome of a multi-skill approach, and the process of getting there would likely be more difficult without the support of various skills working in tandem.

10. Momentum.
    a. Successful mediations are often built on the back of momentum and flow of conversation. This momentum can be created from:
        i. Parties reaching their communication stride with each other.
        ii. The successes of favorable responses to multiple negotiated offers during the course of a larger settlement discussion.
        iii. Beneficial atmospheres, including empathy, openness, and good faith engagement.
        iv. Excitement about developing creative settlement options that go beyond the confines of monetary offers.
    b. The creation of momentum, however, can be a tedious task, as it is bred out of a mediator's persistent, repetitive, unrelenting behavior through the application of any number of mediation skills, the scope and order of which will vary and shift with each conflict and disputant.
    c. Momentum, however, can swing both ways. As effective as it is at providing a pathway to a desired outcome, momentum in the wrong direction and developed out of the wrong behaviors can have the opposite impact on the same desired outcome. In these circumstances, where parties either enter the mediation with established detrimental and ineffective momentum or it is a pattern that parties develop immediately, the mediator will have to dismantle it. By taking apart what is not helpful and rebuilding with what is, a mediator can shift and realign the characteristics of the momentum so that it becomes a force that carries the mediation toward the desired settlement end rather than a force that stands in the way.
    d. Another approach to momentum is to think about it as habit development for a designated purpose. Habit development (think healthy eating) requires:
        i. A plan with a desired outcome.
        ii. Dedication to the plan.
        iii. The creation of new actions and behaviors that better serve the process of reaching the desired outcome.
        iv. Repetition.
        v. Refocusing and realigning when bad habits emerge to derail the current plan.
        vi. Help and support from outside sources (not always, but often).
        vii. Sacrifices (no longer eating cake, or not interacting exclusively with a Competitive CHM).
        viii. Removing obstacles.

ix. Determination at all costs when the desired outcome is important enough.

11. Balance.
    a. Balance is a key element that must be factored into the equation when applying mediation skills, styles, strategy, or approach, and especially during sensitive conversations to skillfully draw out additional or deeper information from disputants.

    To apply a mediation skill in a manner or with a strength (or weakness) that exceeds necessity could lead to an unintended result, transforming that skill from one meant to assist and be useful into one that potentially wreaks havoc on the process and the parties. Too much (or too little) of anything is not a good thing, so it is said, and generally speaking, on that point there need not be much argument. However, that is not where the discussion of balance ends when working with conflicts and disputants.
    b. As has become abundantly clear, all conflicts are different and correspondingly, disputants are different as well. With that in mind, a mediator should not necessarily presume that a specific type of balance is what a situation requires. For example, a mediation itself might require balance in the form of a mediator evaluating with a heavy hand and extending that behavior all the way through to the signing of a settlement agreement. This could be an instance of unequally balanced CHMs that become balanced by the mediator's application of a heavy-handed, direct Evaluative mediation style. Of course, there would likely be layers of balancing acts that the mediator performs, including the application of any number of mediation skills, in combinations and quantities determined by the specific lack of balance. Providing balance has many levels, layers, and applications, all of which depend on the requirements of the conflict and parties. Balance should not be thought of only as an even distribution, as it is often through the unequal distribution of a skill, style, strategy, or approach that balance is found or restored.
    c. The mediator also has the capacity to act as a conduit of balance by communicating and engaging in a manner that the mediation or disputants lack. Instead of attempting to shift or balance disputant Communication Styles or CHMs to create effective communication, for example, the mediator could decide to provide the necessary balance by funneling all communication through their own Communication Style or CHM—the one or ones required to reach the

desired atmosphere. Acting as the conduit, the mediator would apply strategies such as reframing before releasing the information back to the parties, to reflect the necessary balance in a disputant's message. (See Chapter 7, "The Art of the Reframe.") Another form of balance might present as the mediator providing the missing confidence and support a disputant lacks in conjunction with, and adding negatively to, an overly activated Compromising or Accommodating CHM. In this instance, the mediator would likely be attempting to shift the disputant's mode.

FLASH CHALLENGE QUESTIONS

Flash Challenge Question #1

1. What are possible reasons for Ms. Shi's overall behavior that escalated the situation to the level of conflict, including her seemingly uncommon manner in connection with her niece's injury?
2. What are possible reasons for Ms. Vito's overall behavior?

Flash Challenge Question #2: Using the Ms. Shi v. Ms. Vito fact pattern, what might be a creative strategy to approach any undisclosed or hidden information, considering the fact that both disputants are:

1. In attack mode.
2. Interpreting communication from each other as attacks.
3. Responding in kind.

In their book *Beyond Reason Using Emotions as You Negotiate,* Roger Fisher and Daniel Shapiro identify Five Core Concerns: Appreciation, Affiliation, Autonomy, Status, and Role. These basic human needs must be met to progress through a conflict-based conversation and into settlement without it being subjected to difficult emotional hurdles. The labels of core concerns might change, but the concepts remain the same. There is no version of a mediation or resolved conflict story that does not necessitate understanding, recognition, addressing needs, and subsequently meeting them. When considering the aftermath of concerns that have been disregarded when compared with those that have been addressed, it is not difficult to imagine the conversations that could follow.

WHEN CONCERNS ARE *DISREGARDED*…
…THE RESULTS ARE

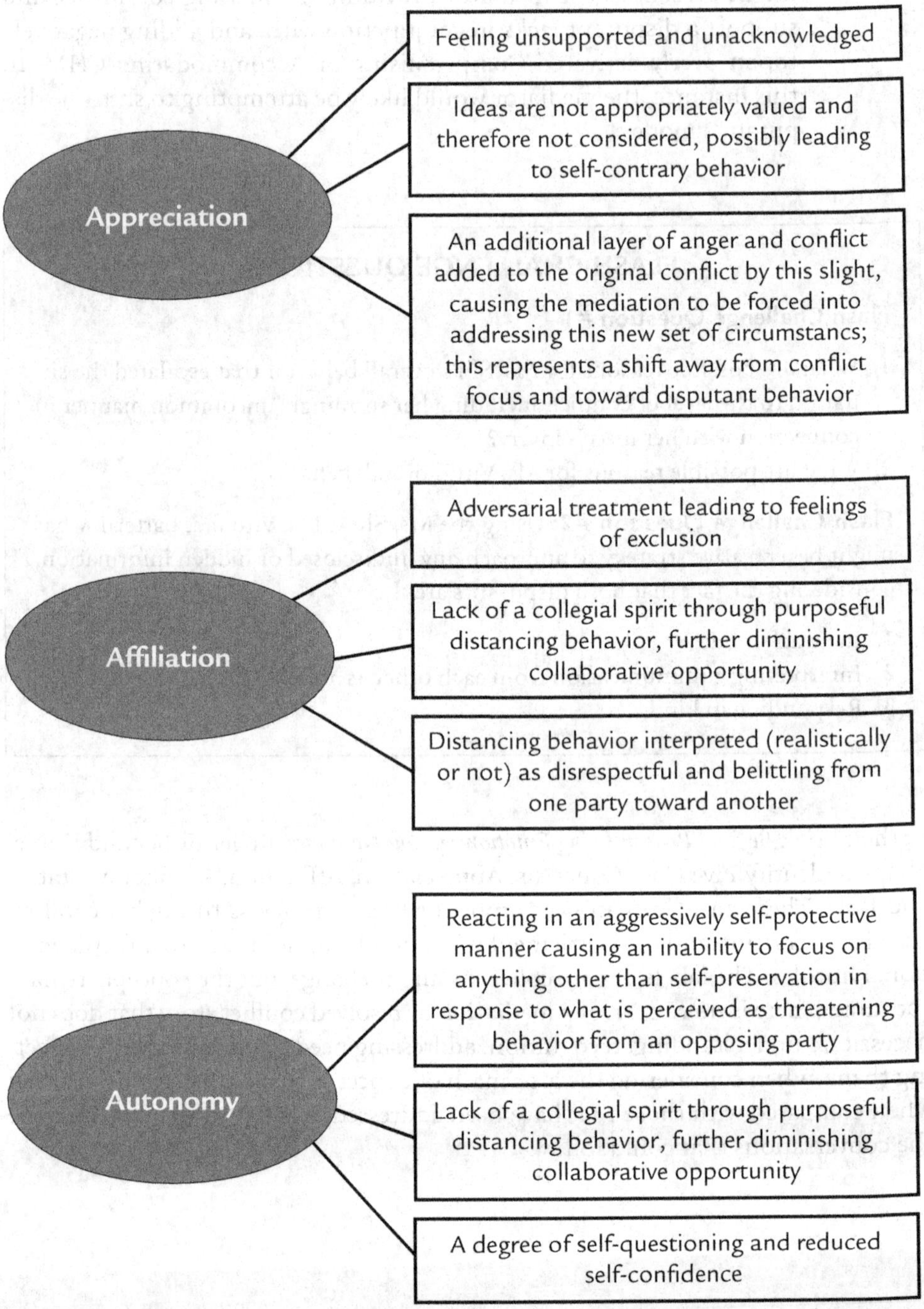

WHEN CONCERNS ARE *DISREGARDED*... ...THE RESULTS ARE

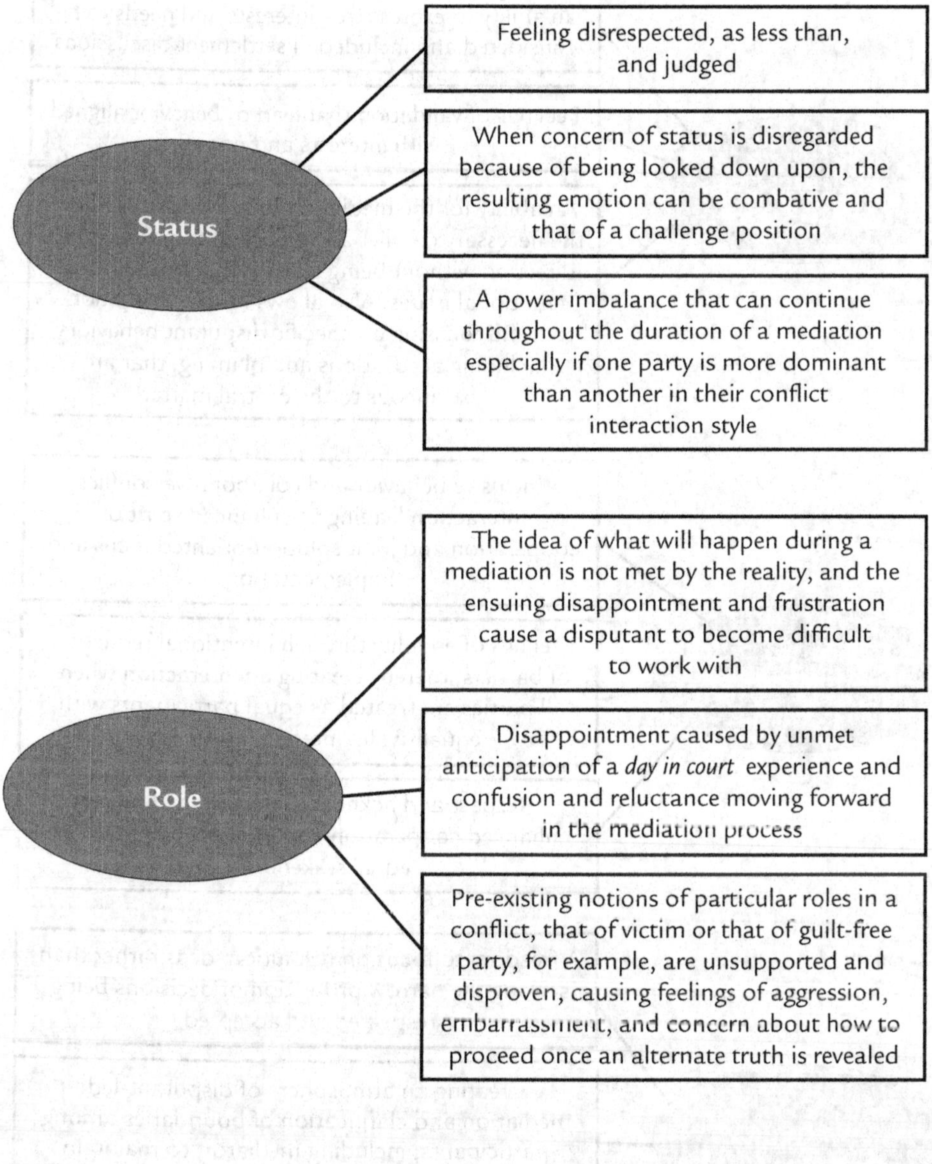

WHEN CONCERNS ARE *ADDRESSED*...
...THE RESULTS ARE

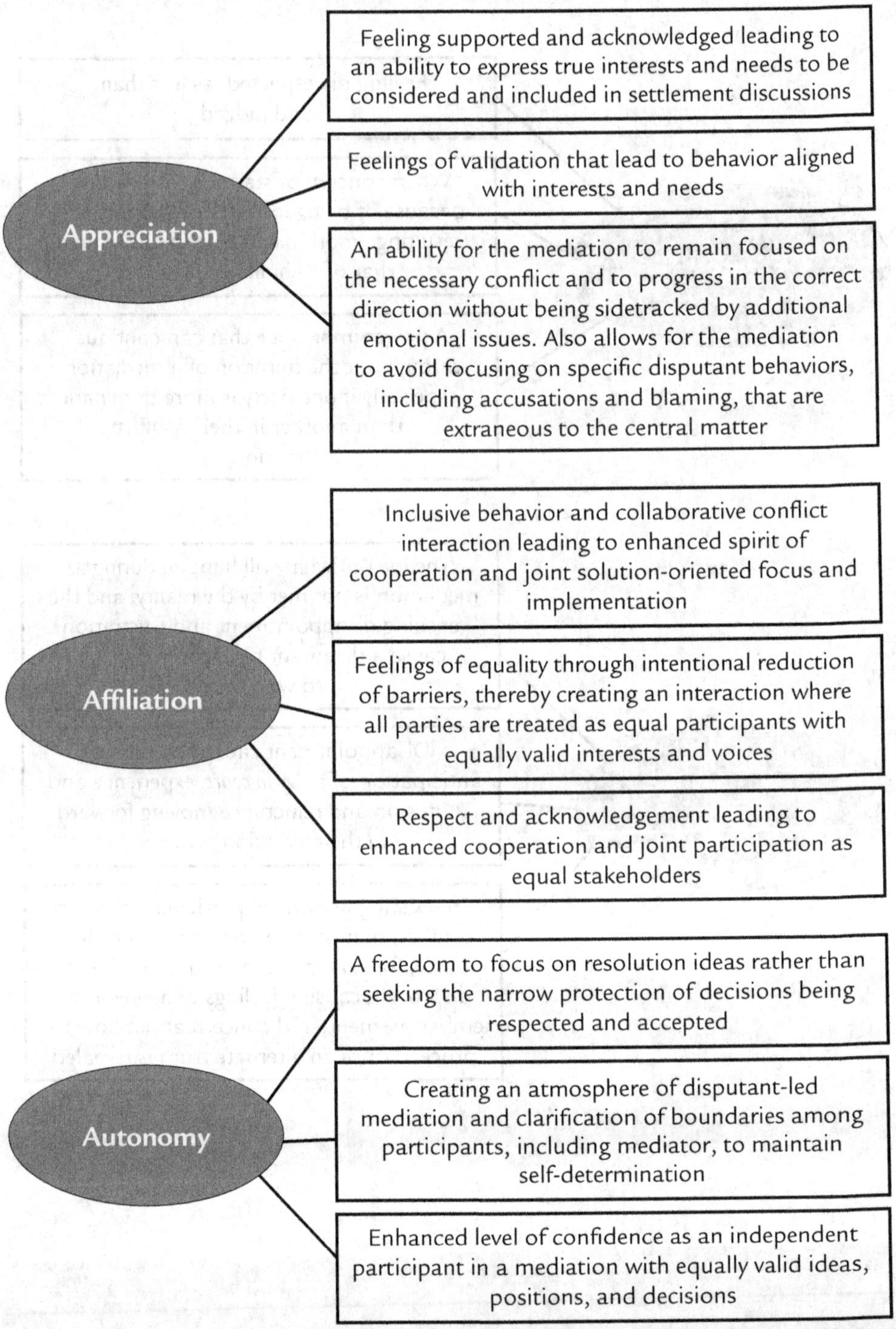

WHEN CONCERNS ARE *ADDRESSED*...

...THE RESULTS ARE

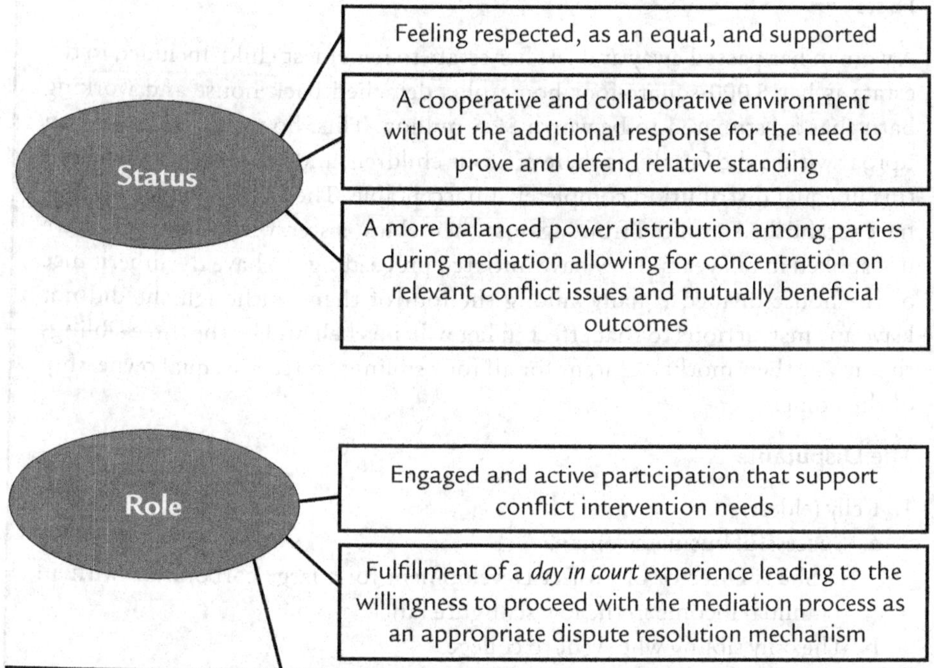

If a mediator determines that a disputant's pre-existing construct of their role within a conflict is inaccurate:

Option #1: If the collective realization could be damaging to the mediation, a move into Caucus should happen. There the mediator can enable that construct to remain intact while shifting focus to settlement discussions exclusively rather than discussions with the goal of determining details of the conflict. In doing so, the disputant can remain validated and secure in their chosen role while still proceeding with forward momentum toward conflict resolution

Option #2: The mediator may begin to guide the disputant toward re-envisioning their role within the conflict with the absorption of factual, and possibly new, information. Whether in Caucus or Joint Session will be determined based on the atmosphere of the mediation, the relationship between the parties, and the mental and emotional state of the disputant in question. The result is the disputant's role remaining within their control and the parameters of this new role being comfortable to them as it would be a result of their own design

In both scenarios, the disputant can proceed productively through the mediation process without aggression or embarrassment with a chosen role intact

FLASH CHALLENGE

Meeting Disputants' Needs vs. Not: Mediate the Case!

Facts

A woman has passed away and left her estate to her eldest child. Included in the estate is her 5,000-square-foot home plus detached back house and working barn that is estimated to be worth $2.5 million. This, however, has caused an uproar within the family, as there are four children, and the younger three find this unequal distribution completely unacceptable. The three younger siblings have established a united front against their eldest sister, with whom they have not spoken in ten years. They have initiated proceedings to have the inheritance of the house divided equally among the four of them. Although she did not leave any instructions to that effect in her will, it is believed by the three siblings that it was their mother's intent for all four siblings to receive equal ownership of the home.

The Disputants

1. Kelly (eldest)
   a. Successful businesswoman.
      i. She is Director of Project Development for a large corporation with an annual income in the low six-figure range.
   b. The only sibling who went to college.
      i. Her parents paid for her education, and five years after graduating, she paid them back in full.
   c. No interest in spending money on litigation and believes her siblings have absolutely no case, so is frustrated at being put into a position to deal with this.
   d. Has no relationship with her siblings and presents as not at all interested in what they have to say.
   e. Believes that their widowed mother left her the property because she is responsible and successful and is the only sibling who will make smart decisions with it.
   f. Believes that if the estate is divided up among the four of them, her siblings will vote to sell instead of keeping the property in the family, which her mother specifically told her she wanted (although these instructions were not left in writing).
   g. Cannot stand the idea of even one additional cent going to her brother Gabriel and has actually considered contacting the police to report him for elder abuse against their mother now that she has passed away; while alive, her mother begged Kelly not to take any such action as she viewed Gabriel as a victim of his addiction, and Kelly respected her mother's wishes.
   h. Also is disgusted by her sister Shannon receiving anything else from their mother, considering that their parents have supported her for her entire life, and she has refused to ever get a job even when she could not afford

to feed her children, choosing instead to "guilt" their parents into giving her money.

2. John (second eldest)
   a. Feels that although their sister is older, he should be in charge because he is the eldest son.
   b. Has a family of his own with four children and wants to sell the property immediately.
   c. Believes that the property is worth $4 million, although there is no proof of this higher value, and is negotiating for his share of this inflated amount.
   d. Would be willing to be paid off by Kelly for his share (of $4 million) if she wishes to avoid litigation, as he is convinced that the three siblings would prevail in court and that Kelly would be forced to pay all legal expenses.
   e. Believes that Kelly views herself as better than the rest of the siblings because of her "fancy education and big job" and freely says so.
3. Gabriel (third eldest)
   a. Has lived in the disputed residence for much of his life, being either homeless or sleeping on family members' couches on the numerous occasions that his parents asked him to leave due to his drug use.
   b. Has been employed to take care of their mother in the residence for the last seven years as a full-time job, being paid accordingly.
   c. Has a history of drug abuse and is still currently under the influence of various illegal substances.
   d. Has stolen from his mother in the past to support his addictions.
   e. Because of Gabriel's neglectful behavior, their mother was forced to hire additional help to get the assistance she needed.
      i. During his time taking care of their mother, Gabriel's drug use did not stop. He continued to steal from her, including taking her credit cards to buy whatever he wanted. He frequently stayed out of the home for days on end, leaving their mother to fend for herself or call her neighbors or the other siblings for help.
4. Shannon (youngest)
   a. Did not go to college, married young and had two children before the age of 23.
   b. Has never had a job.
   c. Received continuous financial assistance from their parents for years, including paying for both of her weddings and monthly assistance for rent and food.
   d. Three years ago, their mother stopped supporting her financially and Shannon did not speak to her after that.
   e. Has been through two divorces and is currently living with their brother John and his family.
   f. Feels that their sister Kelly is bossy, is a spoiled brat, has been given more by their parents throughout her entire life, and should not be allowed to have the house.

g. Does not believe that Kelly ever paid back their parents for college.
h. Believes that their parents also paid for Kelly's wedding and for the down payment on her home.
    i. There is no evidence that their parents paid for Kelly's wedding or gave her money for the house down payment, and Kelly refutes both points.
i. Believes Kelly has always stolen the spotlight.

Current State of Affairs

1. After multiple ferocious arguments among the four siblings, the younger three obtained the services of a lawyer, who filed to contest the will. They are now in mediation.
2. Gabriel is refusing to leave the property and is systematically taking items out of the house to sell.
3. Upon commencement of the mediation, they immediately entered into caucus with Kelly in one room and John, Gabriel, and Shannon in another. All parties are represented, with the three younger siblings sharing one attorney.

Assignment

Consider the graphics above. You will be conducting two mediations with the same fact pattern, but two different sets of participants in the roles of disputants. Remember to review the Appendix, "Mediation Exercise Instructions," with participants prior to engaging in the mediation.

1. The first time you mediate this case, you will do everything in your power to make sure that all parties' concerns are being met by either you, the opposing party, or both – try for both.
2. The second time you mediate this case, you will not spend any time or energy meeting needs or encouraging parties to meet each other's needs. You will immediately and exclusively engage in settlement negotiations, and the only mediation style you will use throughout will be Evaluative.

(Not all of the following questions apply to both conducted mediations)

3. What were some of the differences in the flow of conversation or the flow of the mediation? Discuss.
4. How did you ensure that needs were being met? Discuss.
5. How were you able to reach their real issues and needs below the surface if they were not forthcoming about revealing them? Discuss.
6. Was there any superficial posturing from the disputants?
    a. If so, how did you penetrate that superficial posturing? Discuss.
7. Were you able to settle the case either or both times? Discuss.
8. Was there emphasis on issues other than those directly pertaining to the case? In other words, did addressing needs, or not, have an impact on what the parties focused on and wanted to talk about? Discuss.

9. Did not addressing disputants' needs present any obstacles for you in attempting to move the mediation forward to eventually reach settlement? Discuss.
10. Did you uncover any hidden information in the course of addressing disputant needs? Discuss.

FLASH CHALLENGE QUESTION

Flash Challenge Question #3

1. How might the five core concerns be incorporated into an approach to mediating the Ms. Shi v. Ms. Vito case?
2. What purpose might they serve?

chapter 10

Managing Impasse

The task is . . . not so much to see what no one has yet seen; but to think what nobody has yet thought, about that which everybody sees.

— *Erwin Schrodinger*

ENCOURAGEMENT

A mediation has reached impasse and the parties have given up. They are packing up their papers and putting on their coats. The mediator is watching with disappointment that she could not assist these parties in reaching settlement, when a last-ditch idea enters her mind. Somewhere between guilt, validation, and encouragement, the mediator begins speaking:

> I just want to thank you for your willingness to participate in this mediation today. It was a difficult and vulnerable decision to make to come here and try to work out your conflict together to reach a better place in each of your lives that is beyond this dispute. This conflict has clearly been extremely challenging for both of you, and I want to express my appreciation that you were brave enough to discuss it with me and with each other here today. You worked hard and tirelessly to try and reach a settlement, and although it might not have happened, you both still put in the work and that cannot be taken away from you. I am impressed with the efforts that you have made and your dedication to trying as hard as you can. In my experience as a mediator, it takes an incredible amount of strength to sit down with someone with whom you are in conflict and work to change that position. It is unfortunate that you are leaving today without reaching a settlement because you deserve to be out of this conflict zone, which you have proven through your efforts during this mediation. However, I think you have a much better understanding of what you are each dealing with and experiencing from your different perspectives, and you have shown respect to each other throughout this process. There is no doubt that you have taken all of the necessary steps that can lead to resolution—you have just not gotten there quite yet. You did not give up on yourselves, and I will not give up on you. I am here for you to take your next steps as well.

A statement like this can be enough to encourage disputants to sit back down to work just a little bit harder and just a little bit longer toward settlement. This strategy of encouragement sparks the cognitive bias that causes people to believe that if they get a little, they can get a little more. For example, if they negotiate for a particular sum of money, and the opposing party agrees to it, they might think that where there is some there is more, and immediately change their demand to a higher dollar amount. The parties could be encouraged to consider that if they were able to do as much as they did so far, perhaps they could do more, especially if they were encouraged and praised for performing so well up to that point.

It would be uncommon for a mediation, regardless of how straightforward the conflict is, and how agreeable the parties are, to be without at least some twists and turns, including the possibility of impasse. So why not enter each mediation with an eye toward the possibility that impasse, in some form, will occur at some point, and be alert to it? Why not begin carving out and creating potential points of agreement, movability, and wiggle room for later settlement options after the very first disputant statement of the mediation? If you sense that impasse could be on the horizon, begin preparing for it immediately, especially while there is still a sense of collegiality in the room and among the disputants. Sometimes a mediation hits the ground running with extremely negative, heightened emotions and impasse looming right out of the gate. Other times, impasse does not come until reciprocal communication is no longer effective and all efforts cease. Somewhere in between the two extremes lies the circumstance when a mediator senses the possibility of impasse based on their experience with similar conflicts, certain statements the disputants have made that could become problematic later, or mood shifts beginning to occur. In any case, be prepared for impasse strategizing. The mediator is a creative being, purely liquid, and there to provide what is needed in any given moment by changing approach, strategy, and skill set from one minute to the next. Stay calm in the chaos and show the parties why they can trust you.

GETTING TO NO

No is an intensely sought-after word in the world of negotiations and conflict intervention, along with *yes* and *settled*, of course. Why should that be the case? The answer is that the word *no* is a definitive limit, or so disputant(s) think—but we will get to that momentarily. *No* is a baseline from which a mediator can work. In fact, it is the moment when true, concrete work can begin, because it is in that moment that a mediator learns the boundaries disputants believe they have. Using these boundaries, or walls, the mediator can begin to explore creative settlement ideas, discussion points, comfort level, and connection checks, and slowly but surely work up from this (possibly momentary and quite likely movable) bottom line. *No* is a challenge point and an opportunity to see just how sharp one's mediation skills truly are. A disputant's *no* is a thrust, and a mediator's expertly crafted reframe, immediately pivoted Mediation Style, sharp open-ended question, or calculated dismantling of a bias, is the parry.

It is likely that no one and nothing is immovable. It could, however, be movement that never presents itself during a mediation, thereby causing an ending in impasse. That is fine. It must be, because sometimes that is just the way it is going to be, and mediators must accept that. We enter into mediations with the knowledge that for various reasons, certain conflicts should not and will not be settled within the confidentially protected walls of a mediation. This would be an example of an immovable or unreachable settlement. Beyond that, the movement through impasse and into settlement might need to come at a later date and during a subsequent mediation, after certain actions have taken place, including the disputant's absorption of the previous mediator's hard work. The mediator does not always know those details, but should always remember that almost nothing is set in stone. Michelangelo said, "Every block of stone has a statue inside it, and it is the task of the sculptor to discover it." A Chinese proverb tells us, "He who moves mountains begins by carrying away small stones first." An American saying indicates, "The only difference between stumbling blocks and stepping stones is the way you use them." From Greece we learn, "It is drops of water that make a hole in the rock." There is no shortage of encouragement to remind us that little by little, step by step, we can accomplish even the seemingly most difficult of tasks. Never give up. Keep pushing with your eye on the prize, using laser focus, hard work, and dedication.

When looking at impasse, potential impasse, and what moving the immovable entails, consideration should be given to exactly what that immovable element is. It could be a disputant who has dug in their heels to a particular position that is barring the way to settlement, or it could be an issue for which the disputants cannot seem to find resolution. It is important to keep in mind that an immovable aspect of a mediation could be a person or a part or parts of the conflict so that nothing is inadvertently overlooked.

DISPUTANT PERCEPTIONS

Disputant A: So is the whole fight about a jacket?

Disputant B: It's not about the jacket. I cannot even remember anything about the jacket. Sue and I were in the exact same conversation at the exact same moment but in completely different realities. Now I think she's oversensitive, and she thinks I'm clueless.

It is said that there are two sides to every story, and then there's the truth. That generally implies that the sides are versions of the story that frame the speaker in a better light than the other party, who is sticking to their own side. That is true, but there is an additional meaning. The two sides are not intentionally manufactured stories for a particular reason, but instead exactly the truth as each party believes it to be. This is not a stretch to imagine, considering the widely differing backgrounds and experiences people have, inclusive of upbringings, cultures, religious beliefs, and political leanings. So different are the makeups of human beings that it is a wonder anyone can comprehend and reach a level of understanding and acceptance with anyone else at all. It is through our own personal lenses that everything we have contact with is viewed, so it only makes sense that a single event would be interpreted differently by many. In light of that, and during mediations, the question becomes this: How does the mediator manage that reality? What if we add the additional layer of the mediator's own lens into the mix? If there are two disputants and one mediator, are there now three sides to the story in addition to the truth?

Is there even really a truth at all? The reality is that all conflict is shaped by those involved, usually with vastly different interpretations and perspectives of events that transpired, so often the truth makes no palpable difference whatsoever. (And by the way, who decided what the truth is anyway?) What about a simple, innocent positional difference? Or depth and scope of previous knowledge? If all you have ever done for your entire life is walk up and down a very flat street that has no twists or turns, in a very small village that has not progressed with the times, imagine someone coming along trying to convince you that not only are there streets with all kinds of twists and turns, but also streets that can take you straight up the side of a mountain! Not only would this contradict your concept and limits of reality, but it would also contradict your understanding of the very definition of a street. Now you are speaking different languages, and this other definition of a street is crazy, unsafe, and wild. (Note that the nature of being presented with information so distant from an individual's reality can be interpreted as a personal attack and could trigger and result in trauma or an aggressive and defensive response.) This is a rather superficial example, but consider the same idea applied to a much more foundational belief—something that sits at the very core of a person's being. One of the problems with disputants' perceptions is that they have to be managed. In other words, now there are additional elements that must be addressed and reconciled. A disputant's perception that they were harmed to a degree far worse than any form of evidence portrays, for example, does not necessarily align itself with the strength of their case should it wind up in court being judged by our legal system, which presents yet another truth—that which is socially agreed-upon. Between the two is where mediation and the work of a skilled mediator rest.

PERCEPTION VS. REALITY

What if a disputant is interpreting a settlement offer or a scenario as an impasse, but you, the mediator, do not see it that way? What if the disputant is interpreting a settlement offer as one that does not meet their demands and will not satisfy their perception of fairness, when that actually might not be the case? This can be tricky because in some instances, a disputant's perception of impasse is as powerful as an actual impasse, and the results are the same. For disputants with this mindset, there is no amount of discussion, explanation, appealing to reason, creative strategy changes, or fancy moves that will result in a change of mind. A number of these disputants will have entered mediation with the decision already made that they will refuse any semblance of collaboration, will never settle, and will gladly shuffle off to litigation. Others will truly believe that there is an impasse and their emotional state, warranted or not, will not allow them to see or hear anything to the contrary. In other instances, however, it is possible for a mediator to communicate effectively enough to assist disputants in moving through a real or perceived impasse. Using any number of the conflict intervention, communication, and mediation skills covered in this book, mediators can work with disputants to dissect why they are perceiving a situation as that of impasse, exactly which of their interests they feel are not being addressed, and what they would need to move back into settlement discussions. Sometimes through the use of tactics such as clarification, empathy, validation, and reframing, an impasse can be just another moment of miscommunication and misinterpretation indicative of the reason the disputants landed in mediation in the first place. If that should not be the case, as is wont to happen, and a settlement offer that is understood correctly does actually lead to impasse, a mediator might consider going back to the drawing board and discussing with the parties what they need to see in a settlement to feel that they can agree. The mediator can then attempt to extrapolate from the current settlement offer those items that meet the disputants' requirements and reframe the language therein to match and mirror the way disputants presented their needs originally. (Recall that cooperation often rests hand in hand with comfort derived from familiarity.) Even if the proposed settlement does not entirely address their need(s), getting close enough could allow expansion of the edges of the settlement offer to include whatever it is that they need to feel satisfied. The mediator could also consider concluding the mediation with a partial settlement that:

1. Does not allow the inability to resolve certain elements of the conflict to affect the ability to resolve others.
2. Provides the opportunity for the disputants to work out the remaining unresolved elements on their own.
3. Allows a designated amount of time to pass to see if the other elements of the conflict work themselves out before returning for another scheduled mediation.
4. Allows the disputants to return for another scheduled mediation to work on remaining unsettled elements that are fewer, thereby enabling a less complicated negotiation.

A partial settlement could be enough to show the disputants that they can agree on something after all, that an agreement can work between them, and that they share a desire to end the conflict. It is possible that the partial settlement will form a habit of agreement that naturally carries over to the rest of the conflict that remains. If that should fail, the mediator can always diagram a comparison between mediation and litigation to ground the disputants back into the reality of what not settling in mediation really looks like (see the Appendix, "Mediation vs. Litigation"). BATNA and WATNA coupled with the reminder that loss of control, extended wait times, and potentially huge financial expenses are considerably less appealing in the cold, hard, light of day that is not infused with the emotional charges the disputants might be feeling at that exact moment. "I'll see you in court" is a lot less attractive when one considers exactly what that means for both the winner and the loser.

FLASH CHALLENGE

Making a List and Checking It More than Twice

Using the chart from the Appendix, "Mediation vs. Litigation," as a reference, create an accompanying chart that compares common misperceptions with the realities of the various aspects of each of the two dispute resolution approaches.

1. For example:
   a. Emotional components and their ramifications.
   b. Impact on relationships.
      i. While certain detrimental impacts might share some commonalities, be sure to include beneficial impacts as well and specifically where appropriate.
2. Reframe and expand on specific aspects of these two dispute resolution approaches that you feel are:
   a. Often or stereotypically misunderstood by disputants.
   b. Manipulated by disputants during the mediation process.
   c. Used as weapons during the mediation process.
   d. Used to create impasse during the mediation process.
3. Present possible impasse situations that could occur as a result of the misperceptions.
4. Include possible approaches to defusing the impasse situations.
   a. There could be multiple approaches to each impasse. The more approaches you can come up with, the better, as even if two separate mediations present with similar conflict characteristics, leading a mediator to use similar approaches to conflict intervention and impasse defusing, the presence of different disputants completely changes the landscape of any conflict intervention process. Be prepared with multiple approaches regardless of the similarities in the nature of the conflicts themselves.
   b. In responding to your listed misperceptions, provide examples of how you would use:
      i. Clarification
      ii. Empathy
      iii. Validation
      iv. Reframing
   c. Be creative!

IMPASSE VS. THE FEELING OF IMPASSE

The feeling of impasse occurs when disputants are overrun by emotional responses to their position in a dispute. Their ability to accurately interpret the mediation is blocked by their emotional state, often shaped by their feelings toward and about an opposing party, which results in their perception of impasse. In such a situation, a mediator should consider encouraging parties to separate the people from the problem[1] to de-escalate emotions and tease out underlying issues by

1. Fisher, Roger, William Ury, and William Patton, *Getting to Yes: Negotiating Agreement Without Giving In*, 2nd ed., 1991.

shifting the focus of the mediation away from "who did what, and how" conversations (blaming) and to, or back to, the issue(s) central to the conflict and disputant interests that need to be met. A move into caucus might be necessary to literally separate the people from the problem (the parties become the problem themselves when they can do nothing but blame and attack each other) so that appropriate conversation focused on the conflict and working toward settlement can occur.

Dismantling impasse often comes in the form of shifting from initial superficial posturing, with disputants who are defensive or aggressive and use accusatory language, insults, and demands, and moving their mindset and behavior into cooperative, creative, solution-oriented thinking and approaches. That process lies in the identification of the issues that have resulted in the current impasse and the subsequent application of the correct skill in the correct manner. It is imprudent to be stuck in one approach or to apply strategies without flexibility, as appropriately, creatively, and dynamically managing disputants' emotions is integral to handling impasse. Even if the impasse is simply two sides being so far apart in their financial demands that they believe there is no possibility of cooperation nor any solution in sight, it is through the application of mediation skills, including creativity, brainstorming, shifting mediation styles, undoing biases, and perhaps bringing disputants onto the same side as each other in cooperation toward a solution to their shared issue(s), that impasse can be dissolved.

COGNITIVE BIASES

> Most of our so-called reasoning consists in finding arguments for going on believing as we already do. . . . Greatness, in the last analysis, is largely bravery—courage in escaping from old ideas and old standards . . . .
>
> —*James Harvey Robinson, American historian*

In addressing impasse, no discussion would be complete without a look into the cognitive biases that could affect disputants' thought processes and the decisions they make. These potential hurdles are all too common in conflict intervention efforts, so becoming familiar with them will be to the advantage of a mediator or conflict interventionist. Cognitive biases are distortions and errors in rational thinking and therefore decision-making that are enabled by the failure to engage Systems 2 Thinking, which would have included the thorough analysis of complex situations in a slower and more comprehensive manner. With complexity mattering less to disputants as the nature of conflict overtakes nuance, the involvement of heightened emotions and impulsive reactions can immediately awaken cognitive biases, putting them to work as the first apparatus of response. This behavior of responding in a quicker and shortened manner, facilitated by operating through the lens of cognitive biases, is most recognizable as visceral or knee-jerk Systems 1 Thinking. As disputants receive information from one another and consider their relative positions, they begin to personalize and develop individual subjective realities for themselves as opposed to objective realities based purely on the facts of the case. These realities are specifically based on:

1. Perceptions.
2. Past experiences.
3. Best interests.
4. Personal biases and prejudices.
5. Possibly conflicting, irrational, and incorrect understandings of concepts and events.

When combined, a systemic error in disputant thought processes results. The presence of cognitive biases often culminates in baseless and problematic decisions and answers with, for example, a disputant jumping to a claim of fire when the facts only support smoke. Past events, prejudices, or a more direct inability to understand the facts of the case properly shape such an unsupported conclusion and can severely complicate the mediation process. Added to that is the reliance on assumptions emanating from biases rather than rational examination and the utilization of scant information combined with rapid reasoning to arrive at decisions. Cognitive biases inhabit the space between the intention of a speaker and a proper understanding and interpretation of:

1. The statement.
2. Motivations behind the statement and its components.
3. The character and trustworthiness of the speaker.
4. A personal position in relation to the statement—objective vs. subjective reality.

Because the potential impact cognitive biases could have on any mediation might be substantial enough to cause an impasse, becoming versed in their identification and management to minimize their adverse impact, and shifting and realigning perspectives to an advantageous outcome could be vital to the success of reaching a settlement agreement. Mediated cases often hinge on the ability to work with, around, and through cognitive biases.

The following cognitive biases are divided into two categories highlighting their more salient characteristics relating most closely to each category. Although there are areas of overlap, this division was created as an organizational tool.

What you see is not what others see. We inhabit parallel worlds of perception, bounded by our interests and experiences. What is obvious to some is invisible to others.

—*George Monbiot*

Conflict and Position-Focused Biases That Prevent a Disputant's Accurate Assessment of Information

1. Selective Perception and Selective Memory
   a. Selective Perception and Selective Memory bias occurs when a disputant only understands and remembers that which serves them and their position best. There are times when a piece of information, a statement, or an idea is so far outside the realm of a disputant's own experiences, belief structure, background, ideas, and position that they truly cannot receive or understand it as reality, let alone as a legitimate addition to their story. They might have an extremely difficult time factoring it into any equation they currently have constructed. Conversely, a piece of information or a statement could be so crucial to a disputant's structured reality that a story or understanding without it is impossible. It is most likely that a disputant with this bias will remain situated in defense of their position. (Selective Perception and Selective Memory serve to bolster a Confirmation bias.)
   b. With an incorrect perception or memory of an event, connections that should be made do not happen. Discussions about settlements that are reasonable comparative to the conflict could be drastically affected by such lack of connections. The resulting understandings of a case's strengths, weaknesses, and possible outcomes in court if not settled in mediation also are not accurate.
   c. Mediator intervention
      i. It can be extremely difficult for a mediator to introduce information to a disputant during a settlement conversation if that disputant is unable or unwilling to receive it. The disputant might begin to view the mediator as a liar and an enemy, aligned against them, and failing to behave in an impartial manner by attacking them while supporting an opposing party.
      ii. The mediator could choose to encourage the disputant to describe the conflict, including as many details as possible. As the description unfolds, the mediator can begin to ask questions that require the disputant to provide clearer, more specific, and more reliable answers. This practice might produce responses more aligned with the truth, as the sometimes alternate facts of selective perception and Selective Memory can be trickier to create with the quicker pace of interactive conversation and questioning and when additional details are required.
      iii. The mediator might also attempt to have a theoretical discussion about the strength of the case, as well as what disputants might be facing should they decide to conclude the mediation without settlement and instead proceed to court. The disputants might be more willing and able to understand and accept what is presented to them as true if the information is more detached, as it will no longer be

personal to them. As an outsider looking into someone else's situation, the disputant might be able to bring new objectivity to a revised assessment of the information, and as the mediator reintroduces the coincidental parallel to their own, it is possible that this shifted perspective could transfer.

2. Optimistic Overconfidence
   a. Optimistic Overconfidence is a relatively common bias for a mediator to expect from a disputant. Whether it is genuine, a strategy, or a defense mechanism, this bias causes disputants to have more confidence in themselves, their abilities, and their case than circumstances support. The decision-making errors that follow a rationale impeded by overconfidence are often the culprits that bring a mediation to the screeching halt of impasse.
   b. Overconfidence can cause disputants to have recollections that inaccurately represent details and events to their benefit, even though they cannot be substantiated.
   c. This bias can extend to disputants' evaluation of their expected performance and success in court, concluding that they will be more believable and convincing to a judge or jury, and that they will be afforded certain exceptions and benefits of the doubt based on their presentation of the case.
   d. Mediator intervention
      i. It is in the context of overconfidence that mediators bring out the big guns of a BATNA and WATNA conversation, guiding parties to see the realities of their situation, including the true value of their case as well as that of the opposing party, and what could easily happen if they proceed to court rather than settle in mediation.
      ii. Discuss specific facts of the case. The reality of where the case stands based on exactly the facts that are involved, factoring out any degree of overconfidence, could cause parties to reconsider their situation and possibly begin to question the strength of their case.
      iii. The mediator will want to steer clear of causing disputants to feel that they must continue to prove themselves, their personal abilities, or their case to anybody. Instead, the mediator should attempt to shift the parties to working exclusively toward creative settlement options. Any additional discussions focusing on fault and proving their case could prolong impasse, so removing those needs and behaviors entirely from the mediation might enable the parties to shift their focus to resolution only. That would be a great place to prove themselves and their abilities by engaging in activity that requires them to design settlement options and to be as creative as possible in doing so. This mediator strategy provides a new avenue for excelling at and being in control of something productive to demonstrate skills, simultaneously shifting the focus away from their overconfident, ineffective, and impasse-causing repetitive pattern. (Who can come up with the most creative option for settlement

that addresses all party's needs and concerns in a thoughtful and collaborative manner? If you can come up with it by working together that would be exhibiting the skills of a master.)

3. Reactive Devaluation
   a. Reactive Devaluation occurs when a disputant immediately and automatically disbelieves and disregards an opposing party's provided information, statements, and positions simply because of the nature of their relationship—at different ends of a conflict spectrum. Conflict elicits a number of emotions, as we have seen, one of them being distrust. When there is an air of fundamental skepticism and distrust, any form of compromise and collaboration can be difficult. Attempting to find common ground or agreement on certain facts or timelines can be complicated enough, but working on a settlement that necessitates mutual agreement among the parties and trust that each will follow through with an offer can be next to impossible. If you interpreted that last sentence as a challenge extended, you would be correct.

FLASH CHALLENGE

Seeing Eye to Eye

1. The next time you either witness a dispute or find out about one, offer to help resolve the conflict.
   a. It could be a dispute about an event, or a misunderstanding in a conversation—any interaction that resulted in a conflict with parties on opposite sides of the incident.
   b. Keep a written account of the details of the conflict and of the specifics of each side.
      i. Make sure to be clear on the differences between the sides.
      ii. Include notes about the similarities between the sides.
2. Your goal will be to see if you can assist the parties to shift and become open to accepting the possibility of the very different understanding of events and resulting position that they are hearing from the person on the other side of their conflict.
3. Were you successful?
   a. If so:
      i. How did you accomplish the shift?
      ii. Which mediation tools did you use?
      iii. Describe each party's process in shifting.
      iv. Were you able to build enough trust between the parties to form a settlement of some sort? Or did they end by agreeing to disagree?
   b. If not:
      i. Why do you think you were not able to assist them in shifting?
      ii. Would you do anything differently next time?

b. Mediator intervention
   i. When it comes to conflict, reactive devaluation is either confined to the conflict itself, remains attached to the parties, or is a combination of both. It may:
      1. Permeate newly presented information that was intended to shift a disputant's perspective of the conflict from intentional to unintentional acts.
      2. Prohibit the development of empathy.
      3. Block conversations from engendering new perspectives.
   ii. A mediator could choose to devote most of their time and energy to separating the conflict from the disputants themselves by depersonalizing the issues and helping them toward a more dispassionate view of the conflict and the manner in which it is being discussed. By eliminating any specific mention of party participation details of the conflict, which would almost certainly be in caucus to remove any reminder of an opposing party, the mediator might be able to keep the disputants focused on the issues, the conflict, what is best for them, BATNA and WATNA, and the various settlement options that could meet their needs regardless of who is on the other side of the settlement offer. This strategy can be implemented throughout the entirety of the mediation and not only during settlement conversations, as the mediator attempts to assist the disputants in shifting their positions to becoming open to receiving information that each is presenting, even though it contradicts their personal positions. The presentation of settlement suggestions should be funneled through the mediator and delivered as mediator suggestions.
   iii. Reactive Devaluation can be a central bias in highly charged situations. In-caucus strategies include reframing a proposed settlement offer as coming from the mediator instead of the opposing disputant. This shift might prompt the disputant to consider it because it is not a proposition from an opposing party that is lost to the effects of reactive devaluation.
   iv. Working within provided parameters might be helpful. For example, these monetary figures were provided by each disputant in caucus:

      Side A: We will pay $16,000.
      Side B: We will accept no less than $14,000.

      The mediator can create a new figure or set of figures that is positioned within those provided by each party. In this example, instead of automatically offering $16,000 to Side B, which is as high as Side A will go, the mediator will offer an amount in between the two positions — $15,000 — to each disputant, so that they both have the chance to leave the mediation feeling that they received a good deal in light of the circumstances.

1. The mediator's process: To Side A: "If I were to get Side B to X amount, could you live with that? You might not be thrilled about it, but could you live with it to get this settled and over with today?" Then to Side B, the mediator would have the equal and opposite conversation, but with different values, going back and forth until the disputants reach an agreement. Opportunities may lie within the common practices of a mediation process—shuttle mediation and standard negotiating in this scenario—but it is often at the discretion of the mediator to be creative and perceptive enough to find them.
2. This is a tactic that could be employed in the same manner regardless of whether the offers are close in margin or extremely far apart. Paying less and receiving more are always preferential outcomes.

4. Anchoring
   a. An Anchoring bias presents itself when parties are attached to a specific dollar amount or item(s) and requirements that must be in a settlement offer for it to be considered. Because mediated settlements often include nonmonetary components, these must also be recognized in a mediator's awareness of the bias. This then becomes the bar against which all subsequent numbers and items are measured. A disputant's anchoring item might be false and inaccurate, yet upon learning that, the disputant might pay no heed and continue to be anchored and fighting for it, whatever *it* is, nonetheless.
      i. The immediate problem is how to manage a party who is anchored to something that is completely erroneous, irrational, and impossible to attain.
   b. Anchoring can be extremely inflammatory and triggering for parties on an opposing side because it gives the impression that there is absolutely no room for conversation, negotiation, new understanding, or collaboration. This can be very unsettling to parties and to the mediation process.
      i. Imagine a disputant is trying as hard as possible to explain to an opposing party about the impact an event had on them and how it created painful feelings, but that they would like to have open dialogue about it. Now, imagine that this open and vulnerable position is expressed only to be met by a complete unwillingness to compromise from a disputant on the other end of the conflict who cares about no conversation other than one that involves attaining their anchor.
   c. A disputant might also employ Anchoring to have plenty of room to negotiate, and to make concessions to appear particularly agreeable and generous even though they are not. However, this would be considered participating in the mediation process in bad faith.

i. This purposeful negotiation tactic could become frustrating to a disputant on the other side of the table, as it can be a futile and time-consuming process based on intentional strategic action that is resistant to the actual mediation process and opposed to the genuine movement of working through a bias.
ii. Parties might become insulted by certain numbers or requests that they believe are inappropriate and fail to take into consideration the gravity of the situation and their feelings. (Remember that feelings can sway a mediation toward or away from settlement in the blink of an eye. Do not write off the impact that disputants' feelings have as unnecessary in the negotiation and mediation processes.)

d. Mediator intervention
i. Stay the course! Managing a party exhibiting an Anchoring bias might be difficult, but a mediator should remain consistent in their presentation of the facts and what the party could be facing if they refuse to settle, combined with a steady and firm continuous return back to reasonable settlement offers.
1. The mediator can use a bracket approach (high and low numbers that a settlement must be between) if all parties agree, to return the mediation to a sensible and appropriate negotiation range that can produce an agreed-upon settlement through continued negotiations to bring the numbers within the bracket closer together. Encouraging parties to move their goalposts to reset or bracket the negotiation into an appropriate framework can remove an anchor in favor of the opportunity to reach a settlement that is still within a range interpreted as appropriate.
ii. Ask questions! The mediator can ask the parties to explain their positions, to indicate how they came to their conclusions, to show evidence for extremely high or low numbers, and to explain why they believe their position is reasonable.
1. As the mediator unravels the answers, they might consider comparing the explanations and expectations to potential outcomes should the case end in impasse.
2. During the time it takes for disputants to explain themselves to the mediator and for them to respond to what the mediator has to say, they might begin to shift their position on their own as they realize some inconsistencies in their reasoning. The thrill of making wild demands and sticking to their guns (anchored position) might also begin to fade during the explanation process, especially when the position does not make sense and is often indefensible.

5. Confirmation
a. Confirmation bias is the tendency to understand, interpret, and use information and evidence as validation of preexisting beliefs and positions, even when, in fact, there is no confirmation and often it points in an entirely

contrary direction. It could also cause disputants to ignore facts that are inconsistent with preconceived ideas and beliefs. Any information that does not readily fit into a chosen narrative is either ignored completely, deemed a lie, or reshaped and reinterpreted to do so. In other words, supportive information and evidence are pursued, and contradictory or questioning information or evidence are devalued and dismissed.

i. Example: If Disputant A only speaks triangle, and the information they are receiving from Disputant B is in square, Disputant A's confirmation bias will immediately fashion that square information into triangle, and Disputant A will not think twice about it, nor will they give a second thought to the information that is disregarded in the translation process.

ii. Confirmation bias affects individuals in various other circumstances. This is important to recognize because when a bias exists in other areas of a disputant's life, it can be more difficult to manage when it is ingrained in and part of who they are. It is not strictly connected to their behavior during conflict, which is difficult enough to manage in and of itself.

1. An example is physicians who undervalue and disregard evidence that does not support their diagnosis of a patient and instead choose to focus solely on the evidence that does support their theory. Discounting as subpar and inaccurate the information and evidence not in line with their own position could place a patient's life in danger as a result of ignoring alternative and possibly more accurate theories.

iii. Example: In an academic study, randomly selected students were given identifying markers showing them to be gifted and talented. Subsequently, their teachers were provided with this information. What the teachers did not know was that those markers were intentionally created with baseless information simply for the purpose of the experiment, which was to see how this information would affect how the teachers behaved with these specific students in relation to the rest of the class.

1. In this scenario, the teachers' confirmation bias created a self-fulfilling prophecy. Even though based on a lie, it became true as a result of their actions toward the "gifted and talented students," who then excelled by virtue of additional attention and support in spite of not necessarily being any more gifted or talented than any other children in the class.

b. A disputant could easily overlook possible opportunities for settlement options as they:

i. Dispose of information that does not fit their preexisting beliefs in general and specifically pertaining to the conflict.

ii. Base their decisions on their perception of the invalidity of an opposing party's position and the validity of their own.

When disputants refuse to truly listen and receive what is being said, options for compromise, collaboration, wiggle room, and creativity are lost before they even have a chance to be discussed. The opportunity for hearing, learning, and empathizing fades, increasing the difficulty for the mediator and the disputants.

c. An unwillingness or inability to receive new and pertinent information also inhibits the process of clarification and correcting any misinterpretations or misunderstandings. This can immediately add to a disputant's inaccurate perception of the strength of their own case, and the weakness of an opposing party's case. A Confirmation bias could easily lead to impasse if a disputant does not recognize information that necessarily affects their case, often resulting in missing that information pointing directly to a settled agreement being their absolute best option.
   i. It is a slippery slope of confirmation bias overcoming rationality and logic while the validity of truthful and necessary information and facts is questioned, deemed inaccurate, and disregarded in favor of shifting out of an erroneous position.

d. Disputants' refusing to be moved despite credible and rational information being presented to them is, unfortunately, a rather common response when a disputant is faced with information that challenges their position. Bombarding them with contradictory information often has a tendency to root them even deeper into their position.

e. Mediator intervention
   i. In this situation, a mediator could attempt to dissect and discuss each point to see if a conversation can be had that naturally leads to other ideas and positions developing and coexisting. It could be possible to unravel just enough of a belief or position for a potential settlement option to present itself—one that does not appear to or have the feeling of destroying one position in favor of another. The mediator will have to look for opportunities for both positions to exist, but in different ways so that one does not present as right with the other presenting as wrong. When a disputant needs to continue believing that their position is the right one, find creative opportunities to discuss settlement options that move around positions, that do not need to question facts, and that focus on moving them forward in their lives. Shift the focus of the settlement away from the conflict and onto the physical and emotional benefits that settlement can bring to them, their family members, their friends, their livelihood, and possibly even their professional lives as well.
   ii. Face-saving options such as information posed in a brand-new manner that parties can agree to without feeling that they are compromising their image and position could be helpful strategies in this situation.

6. Sunk-Cost
   a. The Sunk-Cost bias manifests itself in mediation when parties make settlement decisions based on the financial investment they have already made throughout the duration of the conflict. In other words, they might be averse to a settlement, even if it is reasonable or skewed in their favor, that has a financial component requiring them to pay an opposing party if they have already spent money on any part of the conflict thus far, including attorney fees. As a result of this bias, parties often feel the need to justify any funds spent along the way by fighting it out in court. In their minds, that will be a winning day for them. A settlement in mediation that is perceived to be balanced and fair to all, involving give and take from each disputant, might not satisfy their need to feel that money previously spent was well spent and a smart decision on their part. Even though a mediation concluding in impasse and proceeding to court would, in fact, require the parties to spend additional money, and perhaps much more, that would still be the option chosen under the veil of the Sunk-Cost bias. The continued investment in the case is an acceptable loss to the parties because of what it has already cost them.
   b. This continued behavior, based on previous investment behavior and financial losses, does not take into consideration the fact that past money spent is just that—spent. No matter what, that money will remain spent, so a decision to reject the opportunity of a strong settlement offer that both minimizes future financial losses and puts an immediate end to the conflict is shortsighted and bias-driven.
   c. This bias creates an environment of being penny-wise and pound foolish, a thought process that the mediator must battle.
   d. Mediator intervention
      i. The mediator should remove any discussion of money previously spent from the conversation relating to anything other than ramifications of the mediation potentially ending in impasse. Discussions should focus on the benefits of nonmonetary and future-seeking settlement options.
      ii. At this point you might be thinking about potentially recoverable attorney fees, and you would be right to consider that. Attorney fees are often part of negotiations during mediation, so the traditional method of negotiating back and forth until parties can agree on a number would most likely be the chosen remedy when demands for these fees arise. However, if this is a sticking point that is contributing to or causing impasse, refer to the strategy of a partial settlement—dividing a conflict into portions that can be settled and portions that cannot. Settle as much as possible, possibly even the entirety of the conflict, and allow the attorney fee negotiation to stand on its own, separate and apart. The parties might immediately ride the wave of cooperative resolution all the way to and through

the settlement of attorney fees, or it could be something they circle back to at a later date. Either way, when possible and appropriate, settle what you can and see what effect that has on the parties, and the parts of the mediation that have not yet been settled.

7. Functional Fixedness
   a. The Functional Fixedness bias causes an inability to realize or accept that a position or attitude can be used or represented in a way other than previous personal experience or historical interaction dictates. To be succinct, disputants need to learn how to repurpose old conflict management tools in new, different, and creative ways.
      i. How did people even exist before figuring out that:
         1. A carrot or potato can be used to unscrew the remainder of a light bulb that has broken in the socket.
         2. A key can be used to push an elevator button so one does not have to touch it with their finger.
         3. It is possible to use a coin in place of a screwdriver.
         4. Pantyhose can be used as a strainer when there is no sieve.
         5. Peanut butter can remove bubble gum from hair.
   b. Effect on a disputant
      i. If parties either cannot or will not entertain the possibility that their counterpart(s) are capable of changing to new positions, moving toward cooperative and collaborative settlement could be difficult. Forward momentum with an altered understanding is virtually impossible without the acceptance of new information. This includes not accepting the presentation of a new, changed position or approach, by which a disputant is effectively stating that they do not believe the new statements or actions to be real or true, and are therefore a lie. In general, calling someone a liar often leads to a conflict situation. However, disbelieving them as they attempt to shift into a position that reflects the acceptance and understanding of newly disclosed information, deeper explanations of feelings and experiences, and the acceptance of possible cooperative and collaborative settlement discussions is an even deeper affront, requiring additional management. That can be hard to move on from, as it is a form of impasse that is the consequence of what is perceived to be a personal attack when one is in a potentially vulnerable position.
      ii. It is equally as detrimental to refuse to change a personal understanding or position as it is to refuse to believe that others can change their understanding and position. Each side of this coin can present a roadblock, or moment of impasse, during a mediation.
   c. Mediator intervention
      i. If parties exhibit difficulty as a result of a Functional Fixedness bias, a mediator could discuss with them how they would process the changed information and demonstrate examples of different conclusions and potential settlement options they might suggest based on

their own thought processes. As a professional creative thinker and problem solver, and having a reasonable and unbiased approach to any information they hear, the mediator could lead by example for disputing parties who are unable to do this themselves. The mediator might make settlement suggestions that help the parties avoid imposing any previous history or personal experience onto the presented information or subsequent settlement options.

ii. Seeing information and examples though the eyes of the mediator could assist the parties in becoming untethered from their own bias long enough to consider alternate realities that might benefit them during the course of the conflict and in the long run. If only approached from the confines of this bias, reaching a settlement that necessitates a shifted perspective of an opposing party would pose nearly impossible.

d. Effect on a mediator

i. The Functional Fixedness bias is problematic in its effect on disputants as well as its effect on conflict interventionists and mediators.

ii. Mediators who are unable to use strategies in differing and ever-changing ways or to devise new applications of traditional problem-solving techniques could face great difficulty assisting disputants to work their way out of impasse and to guide the mediation toward settlement. If their approach or a solution is determined only ever to be effective in very specific ways, the mediator is potentially cutting off an entire range of creative thinking that could be of paramount importance during the conflict intervention and resolution process.

iii. Mediators who are entrenched in a particular way of approaching problem-solving and possible solution options simply because they have worked effectively in the past could land in a difficult situation when that option does not work to address new circumstances that arise. They may find it challenging to work creatively and to reach into areas of possible resolution strategies they had not felt necessary in the past. They might not even know how to be creative, as thus far they had been relying on a particular set of strategies and approaches and entertaining nothing else.

8. Fundamental Attribution Error

a. A Fundamental Attribution Error bias can be distilled to determining who the disputant blames for the conflict and why. Their answer is that in conflict situations, it is generally believed that another party acted wrongly, and did so because of their bad character. External factors and actual details of the conflict diminish in presence and importance, and fault lies with the bad actor alone. (Of course, if Disputant A had done it herself, the bad thing that happened would absolutely not be a result of her own bad character! Instead, the cause absolutely would be external situational factors—those pesky details and realities of situations.) If a disputant views the harm, or perceived harm, caused to them as having been within the control of an opposing party and having been caused in a purposeful manner rather than by accident, the ensuing anger of that (harmed) disputant will be substantially greater and more layered than if this were not the case. Anger about a conflict combined with anger at a person for causing it, rather than anger about a conflict only, is critically different.

i. Remember the last time someone cut you off in traffic, or cut in front of you in line. Was your initial instinct to respond with something along the lines of, "Hey, what do you think you're doing? That's so rude and inconsiderate." Did you take a moment to consider that there might be a logical, necessary, or even emergency explanation for their actions? Probably not. However, if you were the one cutting someone off in traffic or cutting in front of somebody in line, there would obviously be an appropriate reason for your actions that had nothing do with being a bad actor or having bad character, and that would be the extent of your thought process (perhaps, "My wife is in labor and about to give birth, so I need to get through this traffic in a hurry!").

b. Anger without the proper understanding and acceptance of details, circumstances, and responsibility that led to a particular point or event—who did what, how, and why—can create instability for a mediation that is attempting to reach settlement. When situations arise due to a Fundamental Attribution Error bias, disputants are ceasing to consider the true nature of the conflict event, instead choosing to focus on shifting and assigning blame entirely to an opposing party, warranted or not.

c. Mediator intervention

i. Disputants who blame others while absolving themselves of any responsibility can pose a daunting obstacle to a mediator who is attempting to begin settlement discussions. There is no limit to what can happen when levels of anger and hurt are extreme enough, and that is inclusive of making bad decisions that can inflict self-harm if there is a perception that those decisions will inflict harm on an opposing party as well. There could be wishes for retaliation and at the very least, an extreme unwillingness to empathize at all, let alone factor anyone else's needs and concerns into the picture. Short of a disputant taking full blame, full responsibility, and agreeing to everything that is being demanded from them, the mediator should attempt to rotate the perspective of the conflict to encourage the parties to put themselves in each other's shoes by drawing on empathy. The mediator could attempt to expand any newly evoked empathy by suggesting the theoretical placement of friends and loved ones into the conflict in place of the current disputants. The imagery of a parent or child being wrongly blamed and suffering the consequences of defending themselves to no avail can be highly impactful.

ii. Ultimately, by having the disputant put themselves and their own well-being first and looking at the negative impact the conflict has had and continues to have on their lives, a mediator can motivate that disputant to more actively consider settlement. The bottom line is that most parties are likely to respond to "what will benefit me the most" more than any other strategy.

Disputant-Focused Biases That Affect the Way Disputants Process Information

1. Risk Aversion and Loss Aversion
   a. Risk Aversion causes disputants to be much more unwilling to participate in activity that would end in what they view as a sure loss, and to favor instead an activity that could result in a possible gain. For example, a party might view it this way: An agreement in mediation would involve a sure financial loss in the form of a settlement payment, whereas proceeding to court could result in a possible outcome that does not involve a financial payout. This perceived reduced risk is therefore preferable.
   b. Mediator intervention
      i. Mediators can reframe this understanding into exactly the opposite. The gain in mediation is that factors and outcomes are fully transparent, and participants are in charge of what happens and what they deem acceptable. Settlements in mediation can be uniquely creative, include a wide array of components that are nonfinancial, and act without the confines of the legal system. In a courtroom, the losses disputants might face could stand well outside their comprehension and extend to far beyond themselves and that day in court. The concept of losing what they already have and committing to a financial payout could be incredibly overwhelming for a disputant, so it is the mediator's job to put that into the perspective of how much more could be lost in a courtroom, which is an environment of unknowns affected by external factors over which the disputant would have no control. The mediator could also remind them of the physical and emotional cost of the conflict so far, and how much more might be added if the case did not settle in mediation but instead dragged on for an unknown amount of time waiting for the opportunity to be heard in court, with the added pressures and stresses of that process and its unknown outcome.
      ii. Additionally, the negotiation process that takes place during mediations, both before and during actual settlement discussions, should be discussed and viewed in terms of gains — what is gained collectively as understanding and clarification are reached and as the mediation moves toward settlement. The mediator may remind disputants that gains reached during the negotiation process should not be lost to impasse.

2. Tangible vs. Abstract
   a. A Tangible vs. Abstract bias can make it difficult for parties to fully grasp reasoning presented to them, such as the hypothetical and distant nature of a conversation discussing BATNA, WATNA, and what would be involved if they declined to settle in mediation and instead chose to proceed to court, when contrasted with what is in their observable present. These disputants are more influenced by what they can see, hear, and touch rather than what might or might not be, regardless of how severe those possibilities are. The magnitude of the detrimental outcomes they could be facing outside of a mediated settlement would be less important because they are only possible realities and not the current reality of the immediate moment.
   b. An example would be a company sending products to market when they have incomplete data on their efficacy, but doing so regardless because the products have immediate profitability and their retail presence ensures that the company will retain a competitive position. These tangible markers are the driving force behind what might be considered short-sighted decisions in light of known-to-the-company, long-term (abstract) product degradation. The relationship between now and later for those making the decisions in the immediate present is heavily skewed in favor of the tangible rather than the abstract.
   c. Following the logic of this bias, it would not be uncommon for a disputant to refuse to settle in mediation for what they feel to be a settlement that requires too much from them, in spite of the removed and abstract heavy price that the qualities of a case going to court carries with it.
      i. A disputant's refusal to settle in the moment because of a bruised ego might suit them just fine. However, their child, who could lose their entire college fund down the line after a ruling from a judge and exorbitant legal fees require their parents to use all of the money that was earmarked for the future, might feel very differently about it.
   d. There is an argument that this bias provides the ability to overlook negative consequences in the distance, and it does, but I would argue that a more accurate representation of the Tangible vs. Abstract bias would be to say that it provides the vehicle by which a party is given the opportunity to turn a blind eye to what is yet to come by highlighting what is in the present that does not suit them. Because they are abstract and farther removed, potential future events (including court proceedings) are not even recognized and included as necessary considerations, also diminishing their fear factor.
   e. Mediator intervention
      i. A mediator can employ a strategy of discussing in greater and more specific detail everything that could be included in a scenario with no mediated settlement. This could include, but might not necessarily be limited to:
         1. Present impact of the conflict on the disputant and those around them.

2. What an extension of this very difficult time could mean for and do to them.
3. Personal, familial, emotional, and financial impacts of taking a case to court.
4. Effort and time it could take to prepare for and go to court.
5. How the future might be a future now, but at some point it will be in the present and then an unknown outcome will continue well into the future beyond that.

Such a discussion highlights impactful and tangible details, including turning the abstract into tangible, and incorporates the effects of the conflict on those around them. A mediated settlement with no surprises, constructed by the disputants themselves, addressing their own needs and interests, and structured in a way that is as manageable and reasonable as possible for them, could become quite enticing in the face of the alternative.

3. Self-Serving
   a. Purely self-centered and self-driven, the Self-Serving bias causes disputants to put only their interests at the forefront of their comprehension and interpretation of a conflict, as the filter through which discussions transpire and move toward possible settlement options. This might sound familiar, as most parties fight for their side and what they believe they deserve; the difference is that with this bias, there is no acknowledgment that there is another side to the story, nor is there any effort to include others who have been affected and who might or might not have a valid perspective. The objective of a disputant with a Self-Serving bias is to better a personal position or outcome, leveraging information at their disposal to do so, even if it is to the detriment of those around them, and certainly to those on the other side of a conflict.
   b. The Self-Serving bias also includes taking credit for the good and turning to external forces to assign blame for the bad, even when both are at the hands of the same person in the exact same set of circumstances. This could easily distort a disputant's explanation of events, their unwillingness to accept responsibility for any harm that was caused, and their blanket ownership of being right.
   c. The self-serving at all costs nature of this bias is contradictory to the premise that mediation is a balanced process that requires conversation and negotiation in the attempt to reach a mutually agreeable settlement that is as fair as possible in the eyes of all parties. If one disputant, or more, is operating within the structure of a Self-Serving bias, reaching a settlement that reflects fairness and consideration to all sides is virtually impossible. The only way it would be possible is if the interests of both the Self-Serving biased disputant, as well as an opposing party, happened to be aligned: Enter the mediator and their toolbelt.
   d. Mediator intervention
      i. The mediator might attempt to bring the parties together against the conflict rather than continuing in opposition to each other, perhaps

by identifying and aligning commonalities such as the personal and possible professional impact of the conflict, certain feelings associated with events that have transpired, and a mutual desire to move past the conflict and on with their lives. In doing so, the Self-serving bias can be shifted from being directed by one disputant against another, and instead shifted to being collectively directed against the conflict. Blaming external factors instead of each other might also help in reaching settlement conversations. Biases are less likely to be expressed against those who are viewed as being on the inside, so forming an alliance between the parties to work together to solve a problem they are equally harnessed by could alleviate the impact of the bias on progressive discussions and possible settlement options.

4. Rationalizations
   a. Rationalizations are explanations devised to explain or justify behavior or positions, even if the explanations are neither appropriate nor logical. Disputants might use rationalizations to hide or manipulate their true intentions, details of the case, their actions, and the ramifications of those actions.
   b. Possible uses of rationalizations
      i. Honestly believing their explanation of events even though there is an obvious tilt in their favor.
         1. This is a potentially difficult situation for a mediator, as a disputant could fully believe their own rationalization, become unwilling to listen to reason or any other perspective, and remain steadfast in their beliefs and representation of their story. This could make for a steep uphill battle toward any form of cooperative settlement if an opposing party does not share their perspective and does not buy into their rationalization.
      ii. To make themselves look better in spite of the reality of their participation in the conflict.
      iii. Intentionally deceiving an opposing party.
      iv. Manipulating the reality of the situation to fare better in settlement discussions, offers, and outcomes.
      v. Removing guilt or shame for their participation in the actions that led to the conflict.
      vi. Fearing what might happen if the entirety of a truth were revealed.
      vii. Being fearful of the consequences of their true actions reflected in the outcome of the mediation.
      viii. Feeling embarrassment that they could have behaved in such a manner.
   c. Disputants use rationalizations in an effort to explain away wrongdoing, thereby concluding that they are absolved of responsibility. They might even reshape events to paint themselves as the actual victim, worthy of their own irrational requests in settlement demands. Without the ability to impress upon a disputant an understanding of their participation and

responsibility in a conflict, it could become challenging to reach a mutually agreed-upon settlement that considers the needs of all parties involved.

d. Mediator intervention
   i. To address rationalizations head-on or not to address rationalizations head-on, that is the question. In considering how to manage disputant rationalizations that are causing or maintaining impasse, a mediator must determine if it is best to address, correct, and dispel rationalizations directly or to reframe them in such a way that they support the truth rather than creating a new and distorted one.
      1. Direct Approach: To directly approach rationalizations, a mediator might request that a disputant explain and defend their statement or rationalization. As they begin to discuss it, the mediator can interject with additional questions, point out inconsistencies and inaccuracies, and acknowledge false statements. In a controlled and purposeful but respectful manner, a mediator can begin to shift the party away from their rationalizations and toward acceptance of certain realities such as their own wrongdoing and any harm they might have caused.
      2. Indirect Approach (Reframing Rationalizations): When a disputant is overly committed to a rationalization, a mediator could attempt to control the narrative using that rationalization. The mediator might maintain the broad idea of a disputant's created rationalization, but realign it to represent the information in a different fashion or to support a slightly different position. A disputant might not detect this marginally reframed rationalization as being reframed or changed at all, but instead as simply a discussion about their unchanged position, which could then translate into an expanded (as opposed to changed) position, possibly shifting their view of their participation in the conflict. With a rationalization appearing to be left intact in the reframe, a disputant might feel respected by the mediator and become more willing to listen and engage in conversation about the rationalization instead of a conversation questioning and challenging it, thereby allowing for possible malleability and an overall shift.

COGNITIVE BIASES: GENERALIZED MANAGEMENT STRATEGIES

The general strategy to manage cognitive biases leans toward working to slow down disputant thinking and decision-making to offset reactive heuristic responses (mental shortcuts) that are taking over. When the decision-making process is shortened to exclude in-depth problem-solving, consideration of consequences, and repercussions of decisions and includes the dismissal of future impacts, then disputants make decisions that do not necessarily best serve them. Mediators might attempt to debias parties by using tactics such as:

1. Asking open-ended questions that include explanations and support of their demands, decisions, and positions.
2. Seeking out issues and interests that lie beneath surface-level posturing.
3. Speaking in ways that do not require parties to defend themselves or their biases, the defense of which typically tends to strengthen positions.
4. Providing guidance toward slower and more thorough conversations.

Mediators could also do the following:

1. Reframe information or settlement suggestions to appear new or different to remove any connection a disputant might have to previous feelings or positions so that their biases do not reactivate. Reframing provides the opportunity to approach the information or settlement suggestions with clean slates, to be considered through unbiased eyes while saving face at the same time. This shifted perspective can afford disputants the ability to agree to settlement offers that are inclusive of components that were previously untenable due to their biases. Additionally, when the information comes from the mediator instead of an opposing party, a disputant might react to it in a more objective and less emotionally heightened or biased manner.
2. Assist parties to step outside of their own vantage points within the conflict to look at positions and options from other perspectives. Providing an example of a dispute with similar facts that removes the specific disputants from the conflict and inserts others into their places could shift the way they are relating to their situation, altering the conflict enough to find options for collaborative settlement discussions.
3. Work to remove blame from the mediation process, as engagement on that one point can be somewhat of a pattern leading directly to impasse, unless the parties happen to agree on that front; and you should be so lucky! Agreeing to disagree could work to set aside the blame game and to resolve the conflict, since it might not necessarily matter who is at fault. If the parties can agree to that, they might recognize that resolution is what matters, and it can be achieved without labeling or assigning specific blame. There is no need to compete to see who can win the war of pinning the blame on an opposing party when there is plenty of settlement problem-solving work to be done and, with opportunity, all parties can be helpful contributors.
4. Remember that in their back pocket they have their handy BATNA and WATNA and mediation vs. litigation comparison with factual information and perspective therein. Together with an outline of the detrimental emotional and physical impacts of conflict and trauma, they are prepared for a conversation they can have with parties and to bring them back to reality.
5. Remind parties about agreed-upon points, such as attending the mediation.
6. Shift the thought that any agreement is a loss into it being a gain.
   a. A disputant whose strict goal is to ensure that an opposing party does not gain is likely presenting a position and plan that is outside of their actual

needs and concerns. Discussing emotions, the cost/benefit of holding on to them, and what is possible to accomplish in mediation could undercut this biased position, thereby removing it from settlement discussions and eliminating a potential impasse.

7. Establish that differentiating between and conversing separately about positions and interests can be critical not only to reaching settlement, but also in the disputants' fundamental ability to achieve functional and productive communication.
    a. It is in that difference and separation between positions and interests where information is found, and where a solution could lie.
8. Stress that being in the confirmed majority of disputants who fared worse in court is undesirable, and that rejecting a settlement in mediation to seek one in court could require a sweeping financial win to position them advantageously coming out of the conflict. Anything short of that, inclusive of an equal (or marginally better) result to the one that they rejected in mediation, would likely not translate to a position that is proportionally equivalent to their win due to the encumbrances associated with trial. When there seems to be immutable unwillingness to compromise, the mediator might move the disputants into caucus to employ a more aggressive style, making an effort toward debiasing the parties by undercutting their convoluted interpretations that are at best, truth adjacent. A discussion should follow with a crisp focus on potential losses and punitive outcome in a courtroom setting, which is outside of their control and in stark contrast to the possible lesser loss options of mediation that are within their mutual control. This might have more effective results than a conversation focused on potential gains found in mediated settlements or even through a litigated outcome. With both losses and gains being of great import, however, and the shifting distribution of that import a result of the specifics of each case and the individual disputants, mediators should be prepared to discuss potential losses as well as gains, separately or in conjunction with each other, and in no specific order.

Although there are many methods of moving through impasse, it is conceptually important for the mediator to remember and remind disputants that regardless of severity or duration, the presence of impasse does not signify a permanent ending. Achieving the shift out of impasse is not limited.

FLASH CHALLENGE QUESTION

Flash Challenge Question #1

1. Familiarize yourself with the various cognitive biases above and discuss your position as to whether biases can be removed completely or remain in some fashion and must be managed.
2. If you believe the answer lies somewhere between the two ends of the spectrum, explain and provide examples.

FLASH CHALLENGE

Hide and Seek

1. Divide into small groups and develop a short fact pattern or scenario in which there is a conflict with at least two sides or opinions and room for discussion about the topic.
   a. A fact pattern might not be necessary if a topic is chosen that disputant participants have some knowledge about.
2. Select at least three of the Cognitive Biases discussed above and instruct the disputants to engage in a conversation in which they demonstrate their chosen bias in their response(s).
3. Before you begin each discussion, instruct the disputants to keep their chosen bias a secret from those who are listening. It will be up to you to ascertain which one has been demonstrated when the discussion has concluded.
4. You can ask as many questions as you like in your quest to figure out the bias, and participants' answers should be representative of disputants speaking through the lens of that bias.

MOVING THE IMMOVABLE IN TIMES OF IMPASSE

Partisanship is our great curse. We too readily assume that everything has two sides and that it is our duty to be on one or the other.
—*James Harvey Robinson, American historian*

Get Liquid

Begin to Flow Through Mediation Styles

When impasse presents, or the mediator can sense it coming, it is time to get liquid; in other words, become flexible and willing to change Mediation Styles with the changing atmosphere of the mediation. If the case presented as an Evaluative mediation in the beginning, it does not mean that when an impasse hits, a Transformative or Facilitative style would not or could not be helpful. For example, perhaps the facts of the case call for an Evaluative approach, and perhaps that worked up to a point; in actuality, though, the personality of at least one disputant necessitates a Transformative approach, along with action from the mediator to reach below their surface. Simply because the facts support the definition of one style of mediating over another does not necessarily have bearing on what the disputants themselves need. The mediator must assess the entirety of an impasse or problematic situation to identify what can assist movement through impasse and through the immovable. It would be shortsighted to forget that disputants are human beings who come to mediations with past experiences and potentially traumatic memories of conflict situations. Being currently engaged in a new conflict with a stranger with whom they have no history could have little impact on how much of their personal history influences the way they behave during the mediation and the mediation proceedings overall.

Use Other Conflict Handling Modes to Knock Them Off or Back Onto Balance

Familiarity and experience working with various CHMs is critical for a mediator as that is the way disputants communicate during times of conflict. The mediator will quite possibly be communicating with disputants whose CHMs differ, each requiring a different way of communicating with them. If a CHM is getting in the way of a disputant's willingness or ability to collaborate and settle—for example, if a disputant is acting in a highly competitive manner for reasons that do not necessarily pertain to the conflict, their opposing disputant, or the mediation—then the mediator might need to strategically interject. One strategy can be for the mediator to approach a competing disputant with an equally competitive style, especially if an opposing party is not communicating with the same Competitive CHM. Another strategy could be for the mediator to take an opposite approach with a CHM at the other end of the spectrum. It is possible that a cooperative, softer touch that involves more explanation, compassion, and a humanizing element could shake them out of their Competitive mode. Either way, communicating through shifting CHMs can be a beneficial method to create movement.

BATNA and WATNA

If parties are under the impression that they might need to take only a mediator's word for it, perhaps they would feel better hearing directly from Supreme Court Chief Justice Warren Burger with an opinion of disputants who bring cases to court that should have been settled in mediation:

> The anomaly is that there are "better ways of doing it"—of resolving private disputes—and in the public interest we must move toward taking a large volume of private conflicts out of the courts and into the channels of arbitration, mediation and conciliation.

BATNA: The Best Alternative to a Negotiated Agreement

What can happen if the case is not settled here today? Will the disputants be better or worse off? This is a topic of discussion that the mediator can use when deemed necessary as a realistic reference tool or one that can be addressed immediately to set the tone of the mediation. There are two schools of thought, but both lead to the same conclusion, which is generally that settling in mediation is the best alternative for myriad reasons, including but not limited to the following:

1. Mutual control of the outcome.
    a. No parties other than the disputants are making settlement decisions that impact their future.

2. Confidentiality.
3. Opportunity for creative settlement options.
   a. With both monetary and nonmonetary alternatives.
4. Possibility of a more advantageous settlement.
5. Disputants are able to engage in back-and-forth discussion with one another, providing the opportunity to ask questions, seek clarity, and clarify misinterpretations and misunderstanding.
6. Possible avoidance of the total destruction of a relationship.
7. Potentially repairing a relationship.

WATNA: The Worst Alternative to a Negotiated Agreement

This alternative focuses on the worst outcome a disputant could be facing if they do not settle their conflict in mediation. Whereas the answer to "What is a disputant's BATNA?" could be and generally is settling in mediation, the answer to "What is a disputant's WATNA?" sheds light on everything but settling in mediation.

The overlap between BATNA and WATNA is present because very often a disputant's BATNA is in fact their WATNA as well, making a negotiated agreement (settled in mediation) their best choice. To be clear, BATNA outlines other options to a mediated agreement and identifies them as best alternatives to a negotiated agreement. This should not be confused with best options for a disputant.

Decisions on whether to settle or to conclude a mediation in impasse benefit from a full understanding of exactly what those options might look like in the form of a possible mediated settlement rather than a litigated outcome. By presenting BATNA and WATNA, the mediator could provide the impetus to move through impasse. In caucus, the mediator will discuss facts and merits—or lack thereof—as well as BATNA and WATNA, to address possible biases. The mediator might ask an attorney present to explain how they would approach aspects of the case and, conversely, what they predict an opposing party's position might be. With this in mind, a mediator might then present potential courtroom biases and the elimination of control that disputants currently have in the mediation, as well as discussing the value of resolving their conflict that day and not continuing it. Incorporating an examination of BATNA and WATNA gives the value of reaching settlement today the potential to transcend the myth of the unknown's potential. The validity of a BATNA/WATNA conversation will remain a point of agreement among most mediators as long as there are disputants in conflict who do not recognize the value of mediation when compared to litigation, case permitting.

Empathy

If disputants can find it in themselves to empathize with one another, aided by the mediator, there is a possibility that the understanding they might find can move the mediation through actual impasse or moments of perceived impasse. Empathy can respond to, remove, provide clarity for, and reframe:

- Misunderstandings.
- Misinterpretations.

- Assumptions.
- Messages taken out of context.
- Ideas and statements that seem far-fetched.
- Biases.
- Stereotypes.
- Mystery.
- Unanswered questions.
- Unvalidated feelings and positions.
- Feeling attacked.
- Feeling alone.

Empathy can bridge the gap between parties even if it is just to remind them that, at the end of the day, they are all individuals with emotions, experiences, and needs, all of whom might inadvertently make mistakes at any given moment and for which they might have regrets and may be forgiven.

Almost everyone can relate to making a mistake, so empathizing can remind each disputant that the shoe could have been on the other foot just as easily. Focusing on settlement through this lens could drastically affect the nature and magnitude of potential settlement options and demands.

FLASH CHALLENGE

Okay, Prove It!

Use the Appendix, "Mediation vs. Litigation," and the chart you created for the Flash Challenge, "Making a List and Checking It More than Twice" earlier in this chapter.

1. The next time a disputant states that they believe they would be better served litigating their case rather than reaching settlement during their mediation, challenge them. Ask them, "How?"
   a. This can be during your Mediation Exercise or during real-life conflict intervention.
2. Encourage the disputant to outline to you exactly how their outcome in litigation would be more favorable for them than the outcome of a settlement in mediation.
3. Compare and contrast possible options from trial and from a mediated settlement.
   a. Include in your discussion the creative settlement options that are available to them in a mediated settlement only.

Getting the Disputants onto the Same Side

When resolution of any kind seems like a lost cause, impasse looms, and the mediator begins to feel the walls closing in, consider reconstructing disputant collaboration to mean working together against a common opponent—the conflict—rather than against one another, to ascertain what the conflict requires to reach resolution. The realigned dynamic is a collaboration with the goal of finding resolution in a new way, rather than continuing the unsuccessful efforts of addressing individual disputant interests and needs that are perpetuating an oppositional dynamic. Resolution in its many forms, including settlement, can be about a mutual interest such as ending the conflict, and not about agreeing on the facts, who is right or wrong, or convincing anyone of guilt or innocence. At this point, intentions need not mean anything, and impasse should be seen for what it is—an obstacle to ending the conflict—and for what it is not—an outcome by which needs and interests are generally met.

SKILLS-SPECIFIC EXERCISE

Let's Get Together, What Do You Say?

Using the Mediation Exercise, come up with a list of creative ways the parties can work together through the various elements of the conflict and toward resolution.

When interacting with the disputants, consider a suggestion such as the following:

> Try not to think of each other as monsters. Don't distance yourselves from each other, but instead try to relate to each other. Imagining yourselves as sharing absolutely nothing in common will make each other, and subsequent solutions, harder to see. You might not be able to solve this problem on your own individually, so share your ideas with each other and with the mediator. Seek help when you need it. Trusting is hard and makes us feel vulnerable, but your ability to allow yourself to be vulnerable here could prove to become your greatest advantage and strength over the conflict.

Cooperative Parties

- Parties have worked through disagreements and have reached agreement on certain aspects of the conflict. They will likely be able to consider each other's interests as well as their own when discussing resolution and settlement options.

Contentious Parties

- Parties are unable to reach agreement on any aspect of the conflict, refuse to accept each other's positions, and cannot find any common ground for settlement possibilities.
  - The mediator might consider reminding the parties that agreement on conflict points, understanding, and acceptance are not necessarily requisite to resolution. Their commonality is found in their involvement in a conflict, their presence in mediation, and in the eventual conclusion of the conflict—one way or another.

Assignment

1. Discuss potential impasse management strategies for the Ms. Shi v. Ms. Vito dispute.

a. If the mediator is interacting with the parties:
   i. Individually in caucus.
   ii. Collectively in joint session.
b. How could the strategies benefit the conflict in its current state?
   i. Which hidden issues might they help uncover?
      1. How?
   ii. Which specific element(s) of the conflict might they benefit:
      1. The most? Discuss.
      2. The least? Discuss.
c. How could the strategies benefit the subsequent mediation?
d. Provide an example dialogue for one strategy with consideration of how the mediator would manage the strategy, potential disputant responses, and the impact on the conflict as well as on the mediation.
   i. For example, if apologizing is one of the mediator's strategies of choice, provide an example interaction between the mediator and the parties illustrating this interaction with dialogue:
      1. How the mediator would broach the topic of an apology with each disputant.
      2. If a disputant is not immediately receptive to the idea.
      3. If a disputant is immediately receptive to the idea.
      4. If the disputant receiving the apology does not accept it.
      5. If the disputant receiving the apology does accept it.

Scare and Soothe

Reality checks such as BATNA and WATNA and mediation vs. litigation comparisons can impact a mediation stalled in impasse (see Appendix, "Mediation vs. Litigation"). By emphasizing potential outcome differences between creative settlement options in mediation and financially driven rulings in court, coupled with soothing parties by presenting facts about the benefits of reaching a mediated agreement, a conflict can be moved from the present and into the past. Sometimes a reality check on both or either end of the mediation spectrum, to scare as well as to soothe, can help disputants realize that impasse might not be their most favorable outcome and that certain facts outside of their conflict are actually more important than the conflict itself. When a mediation reaches an impasse, it is more often than not a consequence of either an aspect of the conflict or a result of a perspective or opinion the parties have of each other. That being the case, disputants will decide that there is something they just absolutely cannot get past, they become unwilling to listen and communicate any longer, or they will refuse to continue any attempt to reach a mutually agreeable settlement. At that point, a mediator might find it advantageous to leave the conflict and disputant opinions of each other behind and shift focus by highlighting the realities of the toll conflict can take on the parties, their friends, their family members, and their financial and professional lives.

With mediation concluding in impasse, disputants are willfully and knowingly forfeiting the wide array of benefits afforded by the mediation process in favor of a blind roll of the dice in a much stricter and less creative atmosphere, devoid of any semblance of their control over the process or their outcome. This can become an extremely lengthy legal process with a financial price tag that only increases as the court system delays hearing their case.

Once a disputant is thoroughly inundated by these scare tactics and has been scared straight, the mediator can pivot to a conversation extolling the many virtues of mediation, focusing on the wide breadth of benefits the parties could be reaping if they work together toward settlement. (This is, of course, based on the assumption that the parties have disclosed to the mediator that their wishes are to reach resolution, in whichever form that might take.) After the mediator has created discontent in a disputant's decision to conclude a mediation in impasse and to proceed to court, that is the time to swoop in with the soothing solutions and better options that mediation provides, offering the disputants an immediate answer to the newly created uncertainty in their decision for impasse.

Cross-Cultural Component

Mediators should remind disputants to recognize that differences exist, and that expecting all parties to be aware of and adhere to one another's cultural norms could be unrealistic. The mediator should try to understand each disputant's cultural norms by asking questions and perhaps stating, "There may be some things that I am not saying right, and it is not out of disrespect to you or your culture, it is because I am not knowledgeable, so please help me" (Mr. Smith, professional mediator interview, 2018).

Cross-cultural differences can have far-reaching consequences within the context of a mediation, both as a cause and an exacerbator of impasse. However, if there is an understanding that particular behaviors might be culturally based, and that intentions behind words and actions might mean something completely different from one culture to the next, it is possible that a bridge can be built between parties that clarifies some of the all-important intention questions. Information being the currency of negotiation, without knowing about the culture of the person with whom one is negotiating, it is extremely difficult to speak the same language, so to speak. Even the kindest gesture to one could be inflammatory to another with misunderstood fundamental interpretations of actions and behaviors that differ among cultures. Without understanding or remembering to listen and interpret words and behaviors of others within the context of their culture, as opposed to through the lens of understanding of one's own, there could be no end to misinterpretations and incorrect assumptions. Disputants with different cultural backgrounds who respond to one another as they would to someone with their shared background are often inaccurately recognizing messages and behaviors that would be found abrasive, dismissive, or intentional in their own culture. The cycle of perpetuated cross-cultural misunderstandings endures, leading to anger, confusion, hurt feelings, and possibly impasse. In this atmosphere of confusion, frustration, and fast-paced reactions lies the need for cultural understanding and sensitivity. It is not always easy or comfortable to allow for alternate and new meanings for words and behaviors that seem familiar. This will permit different constructs of interaction, coexistence of those constructs, and parties to become educated about them in order to move forward in concert rather than stalling due to a breakdown of the communication process.

Inadequate explanations and understandings can cause an immediate lack of trust, regardless of the conflict itself, as a direct result of the parties' misperceptions of one another. For example, a disputant might feel that an opposing party is behaving in an underhanded and deceitful manner. They could then make the decision to confront them based on their own cultural perspective, rather than being aware of a differing one that would appropriately explain the behavior. The other party, taken aback, might in turn note minor issues, and become confused about why they are suddenly being spoken to in an aggressive and clearly angry manner, denoting sudden mistrust. Adding to their confusion could be the fact that their demeanor, from their perspective, remained light and easy even as the opposing party became offended and furious, a clear example of differences and resultant misunderstandings in negotiations between two cultures. There was no trust exhibited by the one disputant who relied on misperceptions of the opposing party's behavior based on their own cultural understanding, even though the opposing party was in fact simply behaving in a manner aligned with their own cultural norms of pleasant and appropriate behavior.

Parties can be made aware of presented cultural differences that could affect the mediation and the way they interact with one another—their negotiating styles. For example, if a more aggressive style of communicating is explained to be the typical and respectful negotiation style associated with one culture or another, then the parties could wisely and appropriately conduct themselves with that knowledge, possibly bypassing any impasse that would have been a product of confusion and misconstrued messages or behavior. This explanation can be presented either in caucus or in joint session, likely at the prompting of the mediator and generally after an issue of misunderstanding arises. Impasse can sometimes be avoided with the clarification and acceptance of these differences.

Note to the Reader

Regardless of disputants' cultural backgrounds and whether or not that dictates their conflict interaction, communication, or negotiation behaviors, they remain individuals who have styles, modes, and preferred methods of communication of their own. A mediator's lack of experience in identifying and managing cultural differences does not produce an inability to properly interact with and manage a mediation with disputants who differ minimally or even greatly from one another. To be even more succinct, the manner in which cross-cultural issues are managed need not necessarily be separated from the general approach to managing mediations and participating parties, with the application of appropriate mediator skills addressed herein.

IMPASSE: CAUSES AND IMPACT

Impasse and Information

Although impasse can result from a lack of information, it has the potential to be transformed into temporary impasse with the addition of supplemental or clarified information. Disputants should feel comfortable and confident that they are making informed settlement decisions rather than decisions with any element of guessing or filling in the blanks on their own, or worse yet, feeling uninformed and therefore incapable of making any decisions at all. This could easily lead to a disputant feeling unable to settle as a direct consequence. Should that be the case, the mediator could divide the settlement into its various parts and encourage the disputants to go through them point by point, asking as many questions as necessary to become confident in making a decision. The questions can be directed either to the mediator or any other party and this activity could take place in caucus or joint session, based on their comfort level. The mediator should not treat this as an impasse, but rather as a continuation of information gathering and detail clarification. The mediation is not over just yet.

With the addition of either new material information, or preexisting information that has been repackaged and reframed by the mediator to give the appearance of being new, a disputant is provided with the chance to revise their current position that resulted in impasse and to move forward with the mediation by using a face-saving strategy. For a disputant, this can be the difference between changing their mind – an action that could be perceived as weakness of an easily manipulated party – and making an independent decision – an action that could be perceived as strength through the logic of a sound mind receiving new, and in their opinion, case-altering information. The realization that their position arguing the iron-clad strength of their case might not be as solid as they previously believed it to be, and that the benefit of settling in mediation might in fact outweigh the gamble of moving on to trial, is now a shifted position that they can act on with the new face-saving strategy. In the hands of a mediator, information can be positioned, repositioned, and used to enlighten, create opportunity, and provide impasse-avoiding strategies to disputants.

Impasse and Unsettled Issues

In the world of mediation, unsettled issues are essentially fouls on the play, because where unsettled issues persist, settlement will assuredly remain out of reach. If settlement has been reached, somehow, an unsettled issue hiding beneath the surface has the potential to destroy that settlement at any point. Fortunately, an unsettled issue is only unsettled until it is settled; however, how to do that is the $64,000 question. The answer relies on the nature of the conflict and the disputants themselves, so to map out exactly how to settle unsettled issues would be extraordinarily difficult. What can be done and the strategy that should be employed is an application of mediation skills beginning with listening to initiate the process of identifying the issues, leading to the correct and necessary ways to approach, manage, and possibly settle them. Only afterward can appropriately matched settlement discussions ensue and lead to possible success. The one constant a mediator can maintain even without having any knowledge of the conflict or the specific issues, is that if a settlement offer is already on the table when an unsettled issue or two present themselves, it could be a wise decision to remove the offer from any part of the subsequent conversation focusing on those issues. The reason for this is to engage in a separation of church and state, as they say. Keep the settlement agreement out of the potentially tough conversation that might follow to keep it separated and free from being tainted and pulled into this particular portion of the mediation process. In doing so, the current settlement agreement could remain a viable option as is, or with minimal amendment, once certain issues are settled. Whether or not those issues are settled in that same mediation will not preclude the opportunity to move forward with the agreed-upon portions of the settlement and returning to the unsettled issues at a later date.

Unsettled issues could also inhibit a disputant from making personally beneficial settlement decisions if that settlement simultaneously benefited the opposing party. Fixation on causing harm and as much suffering as possible to an opposing party could cause a disputant to refuse settlement that would see them gain in whatever it is that they are seeking. The unfortunate reality is that issues left unattended fester, grow, and all too often overshadow good decision-making skills in times of conflict. A focused discussion of that disputant's life and the ramifications of refusing to settle, devoid of any mention of an opposing party whatsoever, could possibly jolt them into the realization that at the end of the day it is their own life affected by their decisions that they will continue living. The other party will go off and live their life as well, so making decisions that include specific considerations, namely how to cause them pain and suffering, is unwise in that it is not putting personal well-being at the forefront of the decision-making process.

Impasse and What Lies Beneath the Surface

If a disputant's feelings, needs, interests, and concerns that exist below the surface have not been accessed and discussed, but remain crucial to both the conflict and to a potential settlement, the mediator will not be privy to them, an opposing party will not know about them, and the disputant themself might not even be aware of them. For example, it is possible that everyone involved in the mediation acted in good faith, discussing the conflict, and then collaborating on a settlement; however, when it came time to sign on the dotted line, a disputant suddenly stopped, becoming filled with emotions including anger over the terms that they just negotiated! (You will remember the conversation we had about dinner and the trash on that fateful Tuesday; see Chapter 9, "Finding Interests and Needs Below the Surface.")

A mediator might decide to bring any settlement discussions to a halt and to shelve them temporarily while pivoting the mediation toward addressing what is occurring beneath the surface of what the disputant has been presenting. Without addressing their feelings and allowing them to discuss what they are experiencing, the mediation is unlikely to conclude in settlement. If the underlying issues include anger and resentment, or feelings of disrespect, invalidation, sadness, or longing, then attention can be given to providing appropriate validation, needs-specific discussion, pertinent reframing, contextual specificity, and a realistic perspective of what the impact to their benefit or detriment might be of prolonging the conflict. A mediator who is responsive to those needs below the surface and is able to temporarily separate the broader conflict conversation to address determined and unresolved disputant needs could set the mediation back on track to signing settlement documents.

Impasse and Emotion

Emotions are truly a force of nature. On a regular day, emotions can cause people to act in ways that surprise even themselves, eliciting shock that they could be capable of doing whatever it is that their emotions drove them to do or say and that they come to regret. Now take that same person and their emotions out of that regular day and drop them into the height of a conflict, the day of mediation, face to face with the person with whom they are in conflict, and bring them to an agreed-upon settlement together. All things considered, arriving at impasse really is not all that surprising. On the other hand, disputant emotions can be managed. For example, perhaps you are mediating a divorce case, rounding the bases toward settlement, offers practically on the table, when suddenly Disputant A is triggered by the way Disputant B sighs, and explodes in a fit of rage about an issue that was discussed and supposedly resolved several hours earlier. At the end of the rant, Disputant A tacks on, "And there is no way on earth I am going to sign any settlement that gives you one piece of anything AT ALL that makes you even remotely happy!" This is a less than desirable moment for everyone involved, but the damage incurred could very well be mitigated. A few different approaches spring to mind:

1. If the mediation is currently in joint session, immediately caucus to calm each disputant in the very different ways they will require. To Disputant B, offer a reminder: "There are raw emotions for everyone involved. Not everyone is always capable of handling, controlling, or expressing their emotions properly and in ways that are not hurtful. Being hurt can be difficult to deal with, and no matter what, it has been clearly expressed that settling today is the absolute best outcome for both parties, so staying that course should remain the objective. Giving each other space to process even if it means acting out might need to be part of this mediation reality." To Disputant A, the one who lashed out, provide the private space to express exactly what they are feeling, thinking about, experiencing, and grappling with. It appears that the outburst did not have anything to do with the settlement specifically, but rather their relationship at large and the ramifications of the conflict, so discussing what they are feeling separate and apart from the settlement could be beneficial to circling back around to a willingness to sign it at some point. The mediator can allow the disputant to:
   a. Feel heard.
   b. Vent in any manner they need.

c. Process what they are experiencing.
d. Remember that mediation can be traumatic and bring up feelings about the loss of a relationship, good times, and memories.
e. Have someone in front of them to be on their side, by their side, and rooting for them to find success in a life beyond their current conflict-related pain.
    i. The mediator is on everybody's side during a mediation, and provides impartial support directly relating to the expression of feelings.

By allowing Disputant A this time, the mediator might be able to express the same or similar sentiment that they expressed to Disputant B: "There are raw emotions for everyone involved. Not everyone is always capable of handling, controlling, or expressing their emotions properly and in ways that are not hurtful. Being hurt can be difficult to deal with, and no matter what, it has been clearly expressed that settling today is the absolute best outcome for both parties, so staying that course should remain the objective. Giving each other space to process even if it means acting out might need to be part of this mediation reality." Whether the mediator decides to bring the parties back together into joint session after caucus will be a judgment call based on how the disputants feel, how they are behaving, and what they are saying. If they decide again that they are both ready to settle, that could take place either in caucus or joint session, whichever is less likely to induce another outburst. However, if the decision to settle in spite of lingering unsettled feelings or raw emotions is fragile, there is every reason not to move the disputants (back) into joint session. In that situation, caucus would be best to protect both parties and their decision to settle.

2. If the disputants have been congenial and seem to have an understanding of each other, including any pain inflicted in both directions, then it could be possible to keep the mediation in joint session and encourage the disputants to speak openly to each other. Depending on the way Disputant B reacts to Disputant A's outburst, the mediator might even refrain from reframing to allow each disputant to be raw and vulnerable. Nobody knows the disputants and the conflict better than the disputants themselves, so the mediator remaining strictly a facilitator and referee, if necessary, might be exactly what they need for the mediation to again reach settlement, as well as for their ability to move on. This could elicit a more authentic conversation, producing authentic apologies, and we all know the power of an apology, especially coming from someone with whom there is a deep, emotional history.
3. Receiving individually required communication assistance from the mediator to maneuver through emotionally difficult elements while in joint session involves all disputants as either participants or witnesses. For example, Disputant C has an outburst that is immediately addressed by the mediator. A conversation between Disputant C and the mediator ensues in front of Disputant D that involves looking into the true intention of their statement, the emotion behind and underneath it, the hurtful and damaging

(and possibly inaccurate) way it could be received by a listener, and potential reframing options Disputant C could consider. Disputant C's honesty and participation in this difficult and vulnerable conversation could enlighten Disputant D with information they did not previously know, perhaps including deeply hurt feelings as the root cause of any aggressive and nasty statements and behaviors. Disputant D could become moved to engage in the conversation with Disputant C's messages that have not been shifted and reframed, resulting in realizations, understandings, and possible apologies that did not exist prior to the mediation when listening and communicating were not performed or managed properly.

Emotions and feelings of anger, or being hurt, wronged, or attacked, can be difficult for disputants to move past and relinquish. It is not uncommon for them to want to cling to these feelings and to continually discuss them at great length regardless of how the conversation has progressed. This can be frustrating for a mediator to manage and especially challenging with the presentation of new or corrected information clearly pointing to a disputant being incorrect in their perception, understanding, and claim of being wronged by an opposing party. Despite any such confirmation, parties could remain steadfast in their position and the emotions connected to it, refusing to accept any new information that would shift their self-concept within the conflict. This, of course, can be extremely maddening to the other parties, who find it outrageous that this new, clarifying information that should completely change the conflict and resolution process, as well as connected positions and conversations, is not having that effect by purposeful intention. The outcome could be a double-sided desire for impasse: one from the disputant who refuses to budge and the other from the opposing party out of anger at that refusal. Although it would be logical to assume that situation-changing information would in fact change the situation, that is simply not always the case when the complications of emotions are involved.

1. A mediator might attempt to maneuver within this volatile situation by drilling down on the new information, becoming extremely detail-oriented so that there is no space to ignore or disregard it.
2. The mediator could also ask the party to discuss at greater length why they are having a hard time accepting this information, moving beyond their anger and hurt, and allowing the corrected conflict to become the one to focus on. They might have been living with these feelings for a long time, and the trauma of the conflict so affecting that they cannot readily understand how to give them up. Shifting into a new relationship with a revised understanding of what happened to them will bring with it new feelings, rendering their current ones inappropriate and inaccurate. They might need to work through a grieving and acceptance process of sorts that includes processing this transition and space to think and feel their way through it. Rushing into settlement discussions based on the new information and the clarified conflict could result in more damage and an even more entrenched position of impasse.

   a. Parties in this position could also find shifting to be intimidating. They might not immediately trust themselves with decisions that they will need to make based on new feelings. A mediator can help rebuild this diminished self-confidence by providing the disputant an opportunity to have a voice and to be heard. Working through fears and doubts out loud and with support is a strong confidence-building strategy integral to moving past impasse.
3. Beyond looking at new and old aspects of the conflict, as well as personal feelings, it could be beneficial to encourage parties to dissect and discuss their old and new opinions and feelings about one another. The mediator engages in this exercise as a listener and supporter, slowly guiding disputants from their old feelings about an opposing party and toward the creation of new feelings resulting from the information that clarified and changed the details of the conflict and positions therein. The mediator has the option to directly challenge the views, opinions, and positions the parties express about one another. In doing so, the mediator can more aggressively shine a light on the possibly erroneous assessments of one another, encouraging feelings of discomfort and discontent with previously held views as the conversation progresses. It can be a much different experience to think a certain way internally, as opposed to discussing it out loud, justifying and defending it to someone who is listening and responding. That could turn the tide of a position and viewpoint.

When emotions are heightened and rational thinking is gone, how can a mediator deescalate? To temper expectations and manage emotions to proceed toward what can be achieved, one strategy is to permit emotions to be expressed, followed by questions such as these:

1. "Where do you think that is going to get you?"
2. "How has it been working so far?"
3. "Maybe we cannot solve that problem here today, but what we can do is end the dispute and perhaps that will take away some of the pain and emotion and you can put it behind you."

This strategy discusses with parties the benefit of working to allay some of their emotional trauma, when it is not possible to allay all of it, even if some remains. Ending the dispute through a mediated settlement might still be worth it to the disputants even if it does not leave them feeling fully emotionally resolved. Some relief may be better than none at all.

Impasse as Strategy

A mediator might surmise that a disputant is behaving in a contrived, false manner while presenting a particular point as having great import or as part of their bottom line. Their position is a strategic ploy to motivate an opposing party to believe that if they fail to meet the terms there will be impasse, they will go to court, and they will be worse off for it. The mediator might also have discerned that the disputant is disingenuously participating in the continuation of a negotiation over that point as strategy to garner something else or to force an action from an opposing party. The mediator could choose to caucus and encourage the disputant to discuss the point more fully with them privately, and possibly disclose a genuine bottom line. It is possible that by defending and justifying their position, such as the reasoning behind a particularly inflated financial request, the disputant will realize that this false positioning has not resulted in any progress, nor will it. They should also converse about the potential for their strategic impasse becoming an actual impasse, and the impact that could have on them. As it is feasible that the disputant considers real impasse an undesirable outcome, they might be willing to shift strategies in favor of a more cooperative position that is less of a direct line to impasse, or possibly a line that does not lead there at all. Continuing on with their false position would not be worth a mediation that ends in impasse.

Possible Disputant Uses of Impasse as Strategy

1. To get more out of a settlement.
   a. Their intention could be to push an opposing party to find their limit, only to turn around and agree or offer alternate terms.
   b. Finding a limit might be a strategy to weigh against what they presume they could win in court.
2. To maintain contact and a relationship with another party.
3. To use the conflict to fill a void in their life.
4. To prolong the process for a currently unknown reason, but possibly relating to an eventual trial.
5. To wear down an opposing disputant until they agree out of frustration, fear, or simply because they have given up.
6. To develop a character or persona in the eyes of an opposing party.
   a. Possibly the persona of one not to be messed with, who is perfectly willing and able to refuse to settle and instead take the case to trial.

The Mediator May Question (either internally or directly to a disputant)

1. Why is the impasse occurring at this particular time?
2. Is it a negotiation ploy?
3. Is it to gain some advantage?
4. How does this disputant expect that threatening impasse will achieve an advantage?

Impasse might be an unintentional strategy when there are parties for whom resolution is not a desired outcome for reasons other than monetary gain. It is possible that they view resolution as too unequal a balance for the impact or nature of the conflict. For them, the depth of the conflict might be unmatched by any possible mediated resolution, as it may signify acceptance, capitulation, moving on, or no longer believing in the cause that brought about the conflict. If agreement is interpreted as surrender and turning one's back on one's beliefs, then reaching a traditional mediated settlement could prove tricky. It might need to be reframed into terms that incorporate the fundamental beliefs and require an untraditional settlement structure that does not focus on mutual solutions or an alternate platform.

Impasse and Context

Impasse can occur when disputants have lost all sense of objectivity with regard to their case. This is not a surprising phenomenon when we take into consideration the all-encompassing characteristics of the nature of conflict, defending oneself, worrying about an outcome that must involve another party's interests and settlement requirements that possibly contradict their own, and the fear of the unknown. Added to this mix is a cognitive bias known as the Endowment Effect, which simply means that if it is mine it is worth more and if it is yours it is worth less. A common example of the Endowment Effect is a homeowner listing their house for sale at an overly inflated price. They have lost sight of the price that the market will bear for their house, and instead have tethered their concept of the monetary value of their home to the emotional value they have developed over time and experiences. In their eyes it is essentially priceless, but according to the market, strangers interested in buying homes, and the rest of the world, who do not share those very specific and personal experiences, the house only supports and commands what the housing market allows. Within the context of mediation, this same bias can form between a disputant and their case, their pain, their suffering, their story, and ultimately their settlement demands. Impasse can occur when disputants are out of touch with the true value of their case as determined by what they might or might not be able to win in court, separate and apart from their bias and their emotional involvement.

There are not too many cases that cross a mediator's desk that are completely and totally new and unique. It is almost always possible to have some form of an evaluative conversation about potential outcomes should the case proceed to litigation. At the very least, the mediator can discuss the pitfalls that could be faced when comparing the characteristics of mediation against the characteristics of a trial (see Appendix, "Mediation vs. Litigation"). Value only exists if someone is willing to pay that amount for a house, or a settlement, so no matter how much a disputant believes they have been wronged, that an opposing party is at fault, how horrible their pain is, or how brilliantly their case would perform in court, none of that matters if there is no market value for their claims. For Disputant A, who is informed about the strength of their case and has consulted case law and legal counsel to determine that they could and most likely would win in court, their willingness to avoid going to court by settling in mediation and paying a certain sum to Disputant B should be seen as a victory for Disputant B. However, if Disputant B is controlled by the Endowment Effect, they could be incapable of seeing this situation for what it is, thereby causing impasse. It is not an easy cognitive bias to overcome, but it is possible for the mediator and the disputant to have a hard and honest conversation about the actual value of their case in which the mediator provides a reminder of the context to ground Disputant B in the reality of their situation. Shifting them out of the haze of the emotional connection they are experiencing does not negate their feelings, their pain, or their experience. Conflicts can have a nasty way of taking up all of the space in a room, and even in someone's life. They can become the only thing a disputant sees when they look around each and every day, so the mediator can choose if and when to remind the parties of the larger picture, which is their lives outside of the conflict. It would not be uncommon for a disputant to have forgotten how they felt before the inception of a conflict, that it could come to an end through resolution, and that they could find themselves with a life after the conflict reminiscent of how they felt before it ever began. A reminder of this perspective could help shift disputants out of a conflict-oriented mode and into one that is focused on resolution.

Impasse and Acknowledgment

The very nature of conflict implies that there is some form of relationship between the feuding parties, as without a relationship or connection there could be no conflict that involves those same parties and their interactions. Even so, acknowledging that relationship or the sheer existence of another party can be extremely difficult and upsetting for some disputants, leading to impasse for no reason other than that they refuse to admit that there is a side or position other than their own. The mediation process requires that the mediator pay equal and impartial attention to all parties, which can be an aspect too great for certain disputants to accept. They might assess one another as unworthy of being provided with the equal platform that exists in mediation. The mere equal presence and negotiation aspects of mediation could feel like giving up too much of themselves, their beliefs, and their dedication to whatever they view their cause to be that resulted in the origination and remains the essence of the conflict. When acknowledging each other is equated with determining who is right and who is wrong and an equality of the importance of the interests of all sides, then impasse can present itself to disputants as a far more palatable alternative.

If it is the decision of one or all disputants to decline working toward and potentially reaching settlement, the mediator can begin to assess the ways in which they acknowledge and communicate with one another. This can be accomplished by focusing on the following:

1. How the parties listen.
2. The way that parties express themselves and their messages, with clarity or not.
3. Disputants' appropriate usage and application of:
    a. Reframes
    b. CHMs
    c. Communication Styles
    d. Acknowledgment
    e. Validation

4. Feelings and issues about one another underlying that which is being superficially presented by each party.
5. The presence of any triggers that are shaping perception and interpretation.
6. How the disputants identify themselves within the context of the conflict and one another.
7. Exploring definitions that might differ or pose confusion.

This is a prime example of when dissociating the parties from the conflict could prove beneficial. In a conversation to be had, likely in caucus, the mediator should direct each disputant to focus on the reality that they are in a conflict situation, regardless of who else is involved, and it is presumably in their best interest to end that conflict. By working privately in caucus with each disputant, the mediator has a better opportunity to isolate discussions to pertinent conflict- and resolution-(if appropriate) related points, ensuring that it remains devoid of impasse-causing opinions about one another.

Impasse and Vindication

Stemming from the issues surrounding acknowledgment are the consequences of the need for vindication. Disputants generally describe their idea of vindication as akin to jumping up and down in the middle of a courtroom as the tale is being told about their harrowing experience at the hands of an opposing party who is completely in the wrong. They are, of course, completely in the right, with the judge on the edge of her seat, jurors captivated by what they are hearing, and an audience spilling out over the sides of the courtroom pews, mouths agape. Needless to say, the scene concludes with the judge "throwing the book" at the other party, as vindication is delivered. This is not quite how things usually work, a point the mediator will endeavor to explain to parties as they describe the differences between mediation and litigation coupled with certain, obviously critical, clarifications of the legal process, and what level of vindication, if any, they might expect to achieve. How then can the process of mediation or a mediated outcome, or both, address a disputant's need to feel vindicated? By dissecting and realigning it.

Sometimes the need for vindication is less a result of the particular position a disputant has in a conflict, and more a result of the communication process and interaction history the parties have had with one another after the initial event and as their conflict progressed. In such situations, the mediator can impress upon the parties a reminder of this and the fact that moments after the conflict is resolved the parties will either go their separate ways, never being forced to interact with each other again, or at that point and with improved communication, a new dynamic between them could be formed. This would preclude feelings of any need for vindication. In these cases, vindication becomes a perceived need rather than starting out as a need innate to the conflict. In accepting this, mediation conversations can shift to discussing necessary attributes of a possible settlement that satisfy the parties' true needs and interests without the contamination of an artificially created demand such as vindication.

If this is not the case, however, and the vindication a disputant seeks actually was bred by the conflict and is at least one part of their underlying and subsurface needs, then the mediator should focus the conversation toward the root cause of that feeling by ascertaining:

1. What the disputant believes vindication will provide to them.
2. Whether or not it is more important than possibly reaching a resolution that satisfies other aspects of the conflict.
3. What they believe a courtroom setting would afford them.
4. In which forms that vindication could come.

A weighted comparison between concluding the mediation in impasse and continuing to search for vindication in court might be a fruitful strategy. It could become apparent that walking away from a potential mediated settlement does not serve their best interest when it

1. Has worked to take into consideration the underlying needs and interests of all parties.
2. Is creative and multidimensional with monetary as well as nonmonetary components.
3. Might include apologies and position shifts to ones that are more inclusive.
4. Sets into place structures to assist the parties in communicating with one another as they move forward and address any potential future incidents or conflicts that might arise.

That is quite a substantial package to walk away from simply for the opportunity to jump up and down in a courtroom. (This assumes that parties actually intend to settle and are not maintaining impasse for an alternate reason.)

FLASH CHALLENGE

Vindication Is Mine! Or Is It . . .

Based on the above information, your interpretation, and whether you agree or not, as well as any additional thoughts you might have, form your own opinions to answer the questions that follow. Let's see your creativity at work!

1. Is it possible for a collaborative process such as mediation to provide disputants with real or perceived vindication? Can a mediator assist a disputant to feel vindicated? Explain.
   a. Could a mediator impartially facilitate an interaction in which one party requires vindication and to be acknowledged as the winner before they are willing to engage in any additional discussions toward resolution?
   b. Would a mediator be sacrificing impartiality if they worked toward one disputant bearing the brunt of the guilt and admitting that they are the loser or the one in the wrong?

i. What if a disputant does not consider themself to be wrong? Is it acceptable for the mediator to reframe it in terms of, "doing whatever it takes to resolve the conflict and they are just words that do not need to mean anything after all have signed on the settlement dotted line"?

2. Can a mediator assist parties to see that vindication might not actually be the answer to their underlying and sub-surface needs? Explain.
3. Can validation come in different forms?
   a. Is it always only in the form of an acknowledged winner and loser?
   b. Can it be more along the lines of agreement to work together as a mediation progresses?
   c. Discuss and provide examples.
4. Can parties move past an original concept of or perceived need for vindication if doing so will see a conflict reach resolution?
   a. Is this a settlement that will hold?
      i. What could be some requirements that should be included in a settlement that is reached in place of or that incorporates a revised form of vindication?

FLASH CHALLENGE

Let's Parse It Out!

This exercise can be performed by parties at the suggestion of the mediator, or by the mediator themself (and for themself) with the same goal, which is that of dividing disputant interests, needs, and demands into three lists[2] reflecting accurate and truthful levels of importance. The outcome of creating and reviewing these lists will be to demonstrate where there might and might not be room for negotiation and wiggle room during settlement discussions. The lists can also be used to identify areas of overlap with each other, areas that might require extra communication and clarification, and ideas for settlement options. An early and comprehensive understanding of these lists, including the Must List below, could contribute a great deal to the way a mediation unfolds, including whether it settles or concludes in impasse and the path it takes to get there.

The Three Lists

1. Must List
   a. Issues closest to nonnegotiable.
   b. Issues that will require the majority of the focus and time of the mediation.

2. Simkin, William E., and Nicholas A. Fidandis, *Mediation and the Dynamics of Collective Bargaining*, p. 77.

c. Issues that might require the majority of the mediator's assistance and intervention.
2. Intermediate List
   a. Issues that are important but retain some room for flexibility and creativity.
3. Issues Easy to Resolve List
   a. Issues that will not require the majority of the time or focus of the mediation.
   b. Issues that could be used for a horse trade. (See Chapter 4, "Conflict Handling Modes.")
   c. Issues a disputant can be extremely flexible and seemingly generous with to earn favor and develop "credit" with an opposing party.

Assignment

1. Engage in a Mediation Exercise.
2. During the mediation, ask the parties to create their own lists outlining the importance of their interests, needs, and demands.
   a. The parties should not necessarily share these lists with one another as they are likely still engaged in the negotiation process.
   b. This exercise can be done in caucus with each disputant or by and for the mediator's eyes only.
3. The mediator should create their own list simultaneously for each disputant based on their perspective of the information that has been expressed.
   a. This should be kept private and away from the disputants.
4. At the end of the mediation, the mediator should compare the lists the disputants put together with their own list.
5. How many of the items are:
   a. The same?
   b. Different?
      i. What might be the reasons for the differences?
      ii. Could the disparity be attributed to lying or exaggeration?
6. Did it become apparent that the disputants did not fully understand their own interests, needs, and demands at the time that they created the lists?
7. Could the result of an inaccurate or incomplete list be attributed to the need for the mediator to improve their listening skills?
8. Could any other mediation skills have helped the lists be more similar or even the same?
9. Can you see the benefit of the disputants creating these lists?
   a. Did they:
      i. Demonstrate where there might or might not be room for negotiation and wiggle room during settlement discussions?
      ii. Identify areas of overlap with one another?
      iii. Demonstrate areas that could require extra communication and clarification?
      iv. Present ideas or opportunity for the development of ideas for settlement options?

IMPASSE: BE ASYMMETRICAL AND PLURALISTIC

Asymmetrical and Pluralistic Thinking

Conflicting ideas can each be worthy of attention and respect. It is possible for more than one perspective and more than one viewpoint to exist as accurate, reasonable, true, and necessary. By being open to multiple perspectives and positions as possible truths and answers to problems, those embroiled in conflict, whether disputant, mediator, or conflict interventionist, should view and analyze information from multiple points of view before deciding on a particular course of action.

In a mediation that allows for the existence of multiple experiences, parties have the opportunity to feel validated and heard, with each of their positions counted. This atmosphere of accepting all positions as valid (positional validity), notwithstanding their conflicting nature, shifts the conflict resolution process from one that:

1. Dissects each element of disputants' proffered statements and explanations.
2. Seeks and assigns areas of fault and responsibility.

It instead becomes an approach that encourages parties to discuss their options not limited by singular exclusive correctness (nonmutual exclusivity) of their own position, concomitant with an appropriately corresponding settlement outcome. Resulting options are broader and less intrinsically tied to the push for symmetry of balanced fault and responsibility (positional balance) to be reflected in settlement. A 1:1 ratio of crime to punishment and pain and suffering to remediation is not always a plausible outcome of mediation, or elsewhere, yet often remains a position that must be addressed and realigned. In positions of impasse when disputants are vying for that elusive positional balance, but their BATNA really is to settle in mediation, asymmetrical and pluralistic thinking could present as an open window when all doors have been closed.

In adhering to a pluralistic philosophy that there is not necessarily one definitive way of deciding the best course of action, it is possible to create a conversation with multiple options for perspective, empathy, understanding, and resolution. With confines not that of right and wrong, there is an immediate expanse of collaborative, creative, and possibly even harmonious space within which to work. If there is no one right answer, there could be no one wrong answer as well, only answers that have not achieved resolution quite yet.

Asymmetrical and Pluralistic Approaches

Encouraging empathy is a strong tool for reaching a pluralistic atmosphere. By assisting the parties to better understand one another's positions, experiences, and feelings, the mediator can aim toward creating a process that welcomes each disputant and works with their specific perspective(s).

With the established thought process that nothing is inherently right or wrong, all settlement ideas are worthy of consideration – everything is on the table with no exclusions. The mediator should take pains to ensure that their personal position and beliefs about the disputants and the case do not cast shadows on ideas put forth by any of the parties. Every idea holds space in a pluralistic approach.

When disputant perspectives and interpretations differ greatly, the mediator should search for areas of commonality, large or small. By reframing, seeking wiggle room and possible overlap, the mediator can initiate a conversation with this information that is designed to cause a ripple effect from which possible mutually agreeable resolutions can emerge.

THE POWER OF AN APOLOGY

Clarification

The mediator should remind the parties that they are the experts on their own true intentions and reasons for their decisions, so if their messages and actions have been misunderstood, they can do something about it. If it is the outcomes of their questions, answers, statements, or actions that have been questioned and misinterpreted by others, and consequently led them to the conflict and mediation, it could be the explanation of their true intentions that provides the pathway to settlement and resolution of the dispute. As much as those messages or actions might have been misinterpreted in a way not reflective of the intentions behind them, though, they still could have caused pain and hurt feelings, and exacerbated the conflict. Therefore, an explanation combined with an expression of regret and an apology for an unintended impact could go a very long way toward mutual resolution.

1. If a disputant feels that they should not be held responsible for the incorrect way their actions were perceived by others and therefore refuses to apologize, a mediator might remind them that it costs nothing for them to make an apology and in fact, words of apology, even simply "I am sorry," could be beneficial to them. Apologizing is not an admission or acceptance of guilt. It is not even a statement of agreement. It is merely an acknowledgment that words or actions have hurt or caused harm to another person. It can serve as validation that the other party's experience was real and affected them, that their misinterpretation might have been reasonable based on the situation, and that their position is heard.
2. If a disputant is still finding it difficult to make an apology, they should be asked if they would be willing to say "I am sorry" if that would save them time, money, and continuation of the conflict. Regardless of whether or not it is a certainty, if there is a possibility that it could save them any of the above, would it be worth it to utter those three words?
   a. Any apologetic language or conversation beyond "I am sorry" might happen naturally on its own, but if a disputant is stubborn and angry, work toward a simple "I am sorry" to begin with. Let the ice melt a little after that. (Consider combining "I am sorry" with "I did not mean for my actions or words to be interpreted in that way. What I meant was. . . ." That is an apology with an added explanation and clarification of intentions in a way that presents remorse for the outcome and no more.)

Make sure any apology is combined with a clear explanation of intentions by discussing with disputants the difference between intentions and interpretations, and how only one is within the control of the acting or speaking party, no matter how clear they believe they are. Misinterpretations happen frequently all around the world, and if we are unwilling to accept apologies and clarifications, as well as the truth of a corrected misinterpretation, it would be nearly impossible for people who were not of identical minds to interact and coexist. Declined opportunities to provide apologies with corrected misinterpretations, and conversely not accepting apologies and corrections, should be steered away from during mediation.

The process of reaching new understandings about how actions are interpreted by others and possibly identifying patterns could be important personal learning and growth experiences that have the effect of beneficially impacting personal, social, and professional lives outside of the mediation.

Take a Beat

Directing a disputant to take a beat to stop an immediate and reactionary response gives a mediator the time to engage in a conversation about their interpretation of the message they are about to respond to, with possible alternative reactions that could be more advantageous or even simply more accurate. The mediator should reframe either to clarify a misinterpreted message or to shift the message from its original form (or both) to tilt the kilt enough to remove the need to respond in the originally intended manner. This might alter the disputant's understanding enough so that they choose to modify their initial reactionary response to one of empathy, explanation, and apology.

One of the benefits of taking a beat is that it can give a disputant the opportunity to be shocked that their own words came across the way they did and then to react and respond by rephrasing what they said, and even apologizing for any unintended effects. This can happen when another disputant makes the effort to express the impact on them in a respectful manner and their message is one of hurt and not anger. A moment of kindness, understanding, cooperation, and being on the same side is invaluable to the mediation process. We discuss time and time again the importance of an apology and just how far that can go toward reaching resolution.

SKILLS-SPECIFIC EXERCISE

The Apology

Take a moment to remember a time when you received an apology that effectively shifted an entire situation.

Answer and Discuss

1. Did it take you out of and end a conflict you were involved in?
2. What led you to believe that you should receive an apology?
3. Can you remember the language of the apology?
   a. Did you feel it was appropriate or sufficient?

4. Did you accept the apology?
   a. If not, why not?

Take a moment to remember a time when you gave an apology that effectively shifted an entire situation.

Answer and Discuss

1. Did it take you out of and end a conflict you were involved in?
2. What led you to believe that you should receive an apology?
3. Can you remember the language of the apology?
   a. What led you to choose those words specifically?

Answer and Discuss

1. Can you remember a time when you should have apologized?
2. What about a time when you knew an apology would have ended a dispute, but you could not bring yourself to do it?
3. Why couldn't you apologize, even knowing that it would solve the problem?
4. Can you now look back at that missed opportunity to apologize and craft the apology you could have given had you decided to offer one?
5. What is the advice you would give yourself about why you should and how to apologize?

Answer and Discuss

1. Can you make the idea and act of apologizing less intimidating and more approachable for your disputants?
2. What are your thoughts of the impact on a disputant of either giving or receiving an apology?
3. What can an apology do within the mediation or conflict intervention process?

WHAT NEXT: MEDIATOR ACTIONS AFTER AN IMPASSE BRINGS A MEDIATION TO AN END

1. If the mediation concludes with a partial impasse, some components of a settlement were agreed to, and it was a Transformative mediation, the mediator might consider discussing a plan of action for maintaining the integrity of the partial settlement as the disputants move forward.
   a. For example, if the conflict is between employees and the portions of the settlement that were agreed to included more open and frequent communication, the mediator might suggest that the parties devise a plan not only for the processes of communication, but also to determine how any future conflicts relating to communication will be addressed. It would be natural

to assume that the road to a better relationship between the parties might include conflict, so setting resolution structures in place could be key to maintaining the settlement.

   b. With tools to maintain their partial settlement, parties are more likely to find that the benefits of resolution and moving forward beyond conflict far outweigh impasse and remaining within the conflict. This bodes well for the chance that a second mediation will take place wherein the additional unresolved points of the conflict find resolution.

2. The mediator could speak with the parties about scheduling a future mediation.
   a. This attempts to ensure that the parties will still be committed to resolving the conflict outside of court.
   b. Looking toward the future keeps the momentum of the conflict intervention process going. Even if impasse caused the present mediation to end, scheduling a next meeting can frame the impasse as a mediation that ended with a pause and a confirmed second session, instead of a mediation that ended in finality with the conflict then moving on to court.
3. If parties are unwilling to commit to another mediation, the mediator might suggest conducting individual follow-up phone calls.
   a. Just because it is a scheduled phone call and not a scheduled second mediation does not mean the call will not end with the arrangement for a second mediation. Head into the phone call with as much energy and drive as you would entering a mediation.
   b. During these phone calls, the mediator should check in to see how the parties wish to proceed with the conflict intervention process.
      i. The mediator might set a personal goal to work toward party agreement to set a second mediation session.
      ii. The mediator might take the opportunity to remind the disputants of the known and unknown consequences they face should they decide to decline a second mediation and instead take their case to court.
4. If scheduled phone calls feel overwhelming for the parties, plan on emails.
5. If the parties are unwilling to commit to anything at all at this time, that is not a problem. Unless there was a previous specific request, there is nothing stopping the mediator from contacting the disputants at a later date. If the parties still do not want to speak to the mediator at that time, they can ignore the attempt at contacting them. However, without at least making an effort, the mediator could be missing out on an opportunity to speak to calmed, more rational, and more willing disputants who might be ready to reengage in the mediation process.
   a. If the mediator does not at least ask, the answer will be a definitive no. Be like Wayne Gretzky and take the shot because "You miss 100 percent of the shots you don't take."
6. The mediator should make it abundantly clear to the parties that the opportunity is always available for them to call or email if they are ready for a second mediation.

a. The mediator can also choose to be available to the parties after the conclusion of the mediation to answer any questions they might have about the mediation process, mediation as compared to litigation, or anything else that might arise.

Regardless of which form of communication the parties agree to, either with each other and the mediator or with the mediator only, some form of continued communication should be the goal at the end of the mediation.

FLASH CHALLENGE QUESTIONS

Flash Challenge Question #2: Provide an example of dialogue between the mediator and Ms. Vito addressing the $75,000 she is requesting for her daughter's medical expenses. This is presenting as impasse because on superficial evaluation, it appears that Ms. Vito has no reason to be flexible with the amount of her demand, as the tree that dropped the fruit responsible for the injury is owned by and on the property of Ms. Shi, regardless of where the branches are hanging. Ms. Shi was also notified multiple times by Ms. Vito of the problematic tree and its fruit.

1. Can you identify any wiggle room?
2. Can you find any leverage to encourage compromise?
   a. For Ms. Vito to compromise.
   b. For Ms. Shi to compromise.

Flash Challenge Question #3

1. Is this an example of a case that could be best mediated to partial settlement, with the remainder of the conflict addressed in a courtroom setting?
2. Might the scenario presented in Flash Challenge Question #2 above be an "agree to disagree" element that can be shelved and addressed by a judge alone so that the disputants' relationship can begin to mend and move forward in the interim?

CREATIVITY AND IMPASSE

> If an activity or function is unsuccessful, this simply means that the road is probably closed, and it is necessary to try another. The more difficult stalemated disputes may be settled only after a long series of persistent and imaginative approaches have been tried by the parties and the mediator.[3]

3. Simkin, William E., and Nicholas A. Fidandis, *Mediation and the Dynamics of Collective Bargaining*, p. 100.

When all else fails, be creative! Throw caution to the wind, leave your rule book at home, call your family and friends to let them know that you will be unavailable until next week, and hunker down. Impasse frequently strikes because the disputants become caught in a web of tradition: "He wants this from me, but I refuse to give it to him because he did that and I am angry," or "This whole conflict will be settled if I just agree, but I refuse because that will make her happy and I do not want to do that." Those are traditional positions where disputants often find themselves during a conflict, so the efficacy of traditionally used approaches perhaps should be questioned and subsequently avoided. It is in new and previously unconsidered creative solutions without claiming a clear winner or loser specifically tied to the conflict that an agreed-upon settlement can likely be found. The disputants and their mediation need to be thrown off balance, reset, and introduced to a newly developed pattern of interaction. Their current behavior can be characterized as typical adversarial conflict positions, each side digging in their heels and puffing up their chests. One strong strategy for shifting the entirety of the situation, narrative and positions included, is to inject fresh air, strange ideas, and foreign concepts that do not result in built-in opportunities for disputants to take up positions on opposing ends. For example, one particularly favorite creative settlement agreement can be summed up by one sentence: "My sister-in-law's brother's wife's cousin's window framing company is hiring, so. . . ." If a disputant refuses to agree to a perfectly reasonable settlement (reasonableness based on the facts of the case and what they could potentially be required to pay in court), by deeper investigation the mediator might uncover and discover that the refusal to pay is based on the disputant's present inability to come up with that particular sum of money. The mediator might break the impasse by suggesting a payment plan, or even an altered settlement offer incorporating a nonfinancial component, such as trading employment services in a field of expertise to work off part of the payment obligation. Without knowledge of the true reason for the disputant's refusal to settle, there would be no option for creativity applied to moving through the impasse.

chapter 11

Settlement and Beyond—And Beyond

Settlement . . .

Without doing everything possible to ensure that, at the very least, all parties know the same details about the dispute and what each side wants and needs for resolution, the mediator could be facilitating a conversation about exactly the wrong thing. For example, if Disputant A is hiding X from Disputant B, and Disputant B thinks R is actually Q, then how can settlement options possibly be determined? The mediator must take the time to detangle the disputants' understandings and interpretations of the conflict before there can be any forward momentum toward settlement. At that point, the mediator can kick their solution-oriented creativity into high gear.

Ms. Shi v. Ms. Vito

When and How Creativity Can Present Itself

Commonalities and wiggle room should be sought to develop space for creative brainstorming leading to solutions. Preferable solution options should address interests, needs, desires, and concerns that do not actually conflict and therefore might turn the disputants into partners instead of adversaries so that they can rebuild the relationship.

Potential Settlement Options

1. Moving the tree further onto Ms. Shi's property, remaining on the same side of her house so that she maintains the shade, shield, and privacy.
    a. This would simultaneously continue to afford Ms. Shi the shade, privacy, and view to which she has grown accustomed. Her bird-watching activities could easily continue, and with the tree now being fully on her property, she would be responsible for the leaves, the messy bird seed, the rodents, and the tree roots that are causing the damage to Ms. Vito's property.

   b. Ms. Shi could still enjoy her beloved fig tree but in the alternate location where the deleterious effects of the birds to Ms. Vito's property would be removed and the dropped fruit would remain on Ms. Shi's property only.
   c. Being required to collect the dropped fruit might cause Ms. Shi to develop understanding and empathy for what Ms. Vito has experienced on her property. This alone could create a large enough change in Ms. Shi's perspective of the situation that it might translate into a determined shift in their relationship at Ms. Shi's instigation.
2. Building a higher or additional wall to provide the shade and privacy that the tree currently affords Ms. Shi.
   a. Perhaps Ms. Vito would enjoy a higher wall as well, which could be a joint activity to plan.
3. Leaving the tree where it is, but extracting the invasive root system and pruning the branches that are causing the damage to Ms. Vito's property. This would be done in a manner that does not cause any detrimental impact to the tree.
4. Hiring a gardener or arborist to tend to the tree on a regular basis to prevent any further problems, keeping the branches on Ms. Vito's side trimmed and possibly cleaning up the leaves, the dropped fruit, and the messy bird seed.
   a. If Ms. Shi and Ms. Vito can address at least some of the impact their professional relationship has had on their personal relationship and the subsequent interactions leading up to the mediation, with a likely emphasis on Ms. Vito's daughter, her medical injuries, and the way Ms. Shi has responded, it is possible that Ms. Vito would agree to and possibly even enjoy keeping the tree where it is. Short of that, it is unlikely that Ms. Vito would be willing even to consider any settlement options that do not meet her demands in their entirety.
5. If it is decided that the tree shall remain where it is, assigning its care could also be a negotiable issue. If Ms. Vito agrees to it remaining in its current position, then Ms. Shi would become responsible for any and all maintenance of the tree.
   a. If that determination of responsibility were to be agreed upon, it is possible that at some future time, Ms. Vito might be able to shift her perspective on the tree to one of appreciation of its beauty, history, and delicious fruit.
   b. Perhaps Ms. Shi and Ms. Vito could eventually come together to plant other fruit trees, thereby creating a fruit tree orchard.
6. Moving the bird feeders to branches on the other side of the tree or to a different tree altogether to help keep the rodents away from Ms. Vito's property.
7. Allowing Ms. Shi access to Ms. Vito's property on specified days for cleaning, to include picking up leaves, dropped fruit, and anything related to the birds and rodents.
8. If the tree is left in its current location, installing a seed-catching device such as a net below the branches but above the ground so that the birds can eat but less seed will drop and fewer rats and squirrels will be attracted to the area on Ms. Vito's property. Costs will be paid by Ms. Shi as it is her hobby (and tree) that is causing the damage.

9. Placing a safety enclosure around Ms. Vito's pool equipment, either netting or a shed of some sort to protect it from the rats and squirrels, with the majority (if not all) of the cost to be paid by Ms. Shi.
10. Allowing Ms. Shi to organize and charge for scheduled public bird-watching on her property, and the money earned can be put toward the maintenance of the tree, including dropped fruit, leaves, extra seed, cleanup after birds and rodents, and repair of any damages to Ms. Vito's property.
11. Visiting a local grower or bringing one to the property to discuss options that cause no damage to the tree. They should choose someone who is acceptable to both of them and who will speak with them together so that they will each get the information firsthand.
12. Organizing a weekly family dinner as part of any agreement.
    a. The rest of the family can help bring the feuding sisters-in-law back together at least for the sake of their children. Doing what is in the best interest of their children might be an easy point they agree on.

FLASH CHALLENGE

It's a Wrap!

1. Come up with a list of any additional creative settlement options, including potential options that address the components of the dispute not covered in the above list. Consider:
    a. Ms. Vito's $100,000 demand for property damages.
    b. Ms. Vito's $75,000 demand for her daughter's medical bills.
    c. Management of emotions and possible misunderstandings from their joint past.
    d. Repair of their relationship.

It is unlikely that any creative, out-of-the-box ideas would be possible without first addressing the personal history, the previous business relationship, and Ms. Shi's continuing dismissive attitude toward the injuries Ms. Vito's daughter suffered. It is not typical for family members who were once close to respond to each other's children being injured with callous remarks and annoyance. Ms. Shi's attitude should thus indicate to the mediator that there is cause other than what is being superficially presented, and that it should be identified and addressed. That identification should lead to subsequent interaction to bring about understanding and effective communication between Ms. Shi and Ms. Vito with the disclosure of honest interests, needs, and feelings (at least in caucus to the mediator). If that can be accomplished, there might be an opportunity to optimize creative, solution-oriented strategies for resolution.

FLASH CHALLENGE QUESTION

Is there anything that might be adding fuel to the Shi v. Vito conflict? Possibly stemming from the disputants' time as business partners?

. . . and Beyond

The willingness to speak an unpopular or inconvenient truth is essential to effective leadership. As enticing as it might be to ride the waves of eased tension, newly cooperative conversation, and only slightly tense smiles, the mediator should not allow this temptation to create a distraction from addressing those bothersome additional issues that have been temporarily swept under the rug. The mediator should not shy away from asking difficult questions (". . . and what about . . .") and talking about any uncomfortable topics pertinent to the conflict and to a potential lasting resolution. In the event that the mediation is Transformative, addressing those questions and topics might also be required to benefit the relationship in its entirety. At the moment, the best that the situation is going to get for the disputants is right there in the mediation with a neutral third party helping them maneuver through issues, so the mediator should absolutely roll up their sleeves, get into it, and talk about everything. If the central elements within a conflict cause personal anxiety to the mediator yet they decide to mediate the case regardless, addressing those elements must not be avoided. Unless those elements are properly managed, they could subsequently return to cause additional problems and conflicts for the disputants, who will be on their own postmediation.

Mediation is not always a straight line where parties mostly agree on the facts, where the process consists predominantly of working on settlement options, and where the mediator is simply assisting to negotiate numbers back and forth between disputants. Mediations are often exactly the opposite. Buzz words – the words that we use to gauge and manage a situation, including which outcome(s) to expect from it – such as *perception, intention, reason, logic, reasonable, unreasonable, realistic,* and *unrealistic* are tossed into a blender and whirled into confusion and madness with the two governing rules of confidentiality and impartiality. Once we have that disclosure out of the way, it is anyone's guess what the face of the mediation to follow will look like. However, the mediator must still facilitate communication with efforts to bring parties to their desired resolution. These are the times that the arsenal of honed and razor-sharp mediation skills must be filled to the brim. Make a game plan inclusive of ground rules, acceptable and unacceptable behavior, trigger words to avoid, and validating language to use so that the disputants will have the benefit of a strategy in place for how to deal with future conflicts when they arise – because they will.

WHAT IF MEDIATION IS NOT THE CORRECT DISPUTE RESOLUTION APPROACH?

There could be several reasons that turning to mediation as the dispute resolution method to address a conflict is not the right decision. For certain disputants, mediation does not provide a large enough or public enough platform for their voice to be heard, as mediation is confidential. If disputants believe that confidentiality will limit their ability to properly and fully represent their case, their beliefs, and their needs, then remaining in a mediation process to address their conflict, whether or not they would be able to reach settlement, might not be desirable for them. When a disputant is seeking the particular power, position, and voice that only public dispute resolution processes can provide, mediation will not be the solution to meet these requirements.

And Beyond.

CONFLICT AND CONFLICT INTERVENTION

When it comes to the interplay between conflict and conflict intervention, whether on a micro or macro level, there is still general confusion, resistance, dismissal, and reluctance to acknowledge the viability of alternative approaches such as mediation. Engaging trained mediators and conflict interventionists to facilitate mutually acceptable outcomes during conflict or even inviting their rudimentary involvement as expert consultants in conflict circumstances have both been slowly on the uptick.

FLASH CHALLENGE

The Involvement of Conflict Interventionists

1. Discuss your opinion about why conflict interventionists are left out of important and impactful conflicts facing society at large.
2. How can conflict interventionists play a larger role in major conflicts?
3. What are different strategies, skills, and approaches that conflict interventionists could bring to an already crowded table?
4. How might decisions about public policy be benefited, reshaped, or different if conflict interventionists facilitated communication processes and were included in decision-making? Examples of such public policy areas are health care, immigration, capital punishment, racial discrimination, and gender discrimination.
5. Would you advocate for a policy dictating that a conflict interventionist be present and on the team to address significant public conflict, policy structuring, or decision-making?
   a. If so, discuss.
   b. If not, why not, and which conflicts should exclude input from conflict interventionists?

If the scope of approach to conflict remains narrow in understanding its very nature, its impact on involved parties, and approaches to management and resolution, then the applicability of including conflict interventionists will also remain narrow. Therefore, why should conflict not fitting such a narrow mold be considered within the wheelhouse of conflict interventionists? Shifting the perspective on conflict, broadening the way in which conflict and conflict management are viewed, and expanding the concept of the role of the mediator, conflict interventionist, or facilitator within and outside of the conflict management community are all components that together could bring about a change in the relationship between conflicts, resolutions, disputants, and those who stand at the ready, but who are still waiting, to help.

part III

Appendices

appendix 1

Example Opening Statement

Important Opening Statement Points:
Process Confidentiality, Party Participation, Mediator Neutrality

I would like to take a moment to explain the mediation process, after which I will ask if anyone has any questions or is confused in any way. Mediation provides a neutral third party who assists two or more disputants in conflict to reach their chosen outcome. This differs from arbitration and litigation in that the parties involved in mediation will make their own decisions with regard to a resolution rather than having an adjudicator—such as an arbitrator, judge, or jury—make these decisions for them. With time, monetary obligations, and energy drastically decreased in mediation as opposed to litigation and even arbitration, the ability to resolve your conflict in its entirety today is at your discretion should you mutually agree. During mediation, disputants can expect to receive time to provide their account of conflict events and to present their position(s), followed by negotiations between parties with the guided assistance of the mediator and then settlement option discussions. Parties may produce evidence and may choose to be represented by counsel.

I am here as an impartial, neutral third party. I will not offer legal advice, nor will I tell anyone what they should or should not do, including passing judgment on their chosen actions. I will, however, provide communication guidance, strategic conflict intervention techniques, and creative settlement assistance. I do not work for anyone individually, nor am I on any side against another. I work to assist all parties equally. My place here is to help facilitate open and constructive conversation so that you can reach your own resolution, together; it is not to make decisions for you as judge or jury. You are the driving force behind the mediation, and it is your participation that dictates the outcome of the conflict, as well as the terms of any settlement agreement. There will be time provided in just a moment for everyone to explain their viewpoints and feelings on the issues at hand, equally and without interruption. As one person will need to go first, I will ask the party who requested mediation to begin. If this does not feel comfortable, we can flip a coin. Are there any questions about the information I just provided?

You can choose at any time to request to speak separately and confidentially with the mediator alone in a private meeting called caucus. If you are uncomfortable now or become so at any time while in joint session (together in the same room), please let me know, and we will move into caucus immediately. What is discussed in caucus is kept strictly between the disputant and mediator present, unless permission is given to act otherwise. I will only carry messages or convey information from one disputant to another during caucus if I am asked to. We will continue to work privately and separately in caucus or we will come together into joint session, whichever will best serve all parties and the goal of reaching an agreed-upon resolution.

Mediation is confidential. Any information provided and settlement offers extended during mediation are confidential. Should the mediation result in impasse rather than a settled agreement, that information and those offers will not be heard in court. They will remain protected by mediation confidentiality as they were for the sole purpose of mediation engagement and resolution. If all parties agree, mediation confidentiality can be waived among disputants.

INITIAL GROUND RULES

Please do not interrupt when someone else is speaking. You will have a chance to address every issue that is brought to the table when it is your turn. If you are worried about forgetting something, feel free to take notes.

I generally prefer to keep things casual, using first names, but if that is not acceptable to you, please advise me as to how you would like to be addressed.

When we are ready to begin, I will ask to hear from each of you as to how you view the issue that brought you to mediation and what you would like to accomplish here. Please refrain from negotiating, arguing, or bargaining during your opening statements, and instead give your own summary of the events and issues as you see them. I will ask that you not interrupt each other during this time. Once each party has finished, and before negotiations begin, there will be an opportunity for each of you to ask questions for the purpose of clarification only. If there is anything you heard that you do not understand, please ask about it at this time.

If you have no questions for me [pause and look to both parties for verbal or nonverbal confirmation], let's begin.

IF YOU MOVE TO CAUCUS

I would like to remind you that everything you say to me in this caucus will be held in confidence by me, and I will not reveal it to anyone else unless you ask me to and I agree to do so. My goal right now is to understand as best I can how you view this conflict and, in particular, to understand your interests and what you will most need to achieve a settlement agreement or some form of resolution. That being said, please begin whenever you are ready by telling me anything that you perhaps did not mention during the opening meeting and would like to say now, or anything said in the opening session that you would like to underline or flag for my attention.

appendix 2

Get the Lay of the Mediation Land

AN INTERVIEW WITH A MEDIATOR

I knew I was speaking to the right person . . .

Interviewee Background

Practice area is estate planning, probate, and trust law with an emphasis in litigation and dispute resolution. A practicing attorney for over 40 years, a mediator for 15 years, and in mediations as a party attorney for more than 20 years. Predominately an Evaluative mediator, but believes in fluidity of mediation styles.

Interviewee Opinion of the Most Important Aspects of Mediation

Listening, allowing for and managing emotions, and evaluating the cases.

Insights from a Successful, Experienced Mediator

Interviewer: If you had to identify your single most important personal trait enabling you to be a good mediator, what would it be?

Interviewee: Listening.

He elaborated on the need for active listening, because most cases have emotional content driving them. In his area of practice by assignment over 30 years ago, estate planning, probate, and trust law with an emphasis in litigation and dispute resolution, he has found it of the utmost importance to hear the emotional side from parties to find the interests behind the positions. After parties speak emotionally, they might be able to approach their dispute from a less charged perspective.

Interviewee: I will say: "I hear that. I hear you. It sounds like it was really difficult for you and like you feel that you got a raw deal."

Often parties finally feel heard and realize that someone, sometimes for the first time, is listening to them; this can result in reducing anger, aggression, and spite—the latter in particular, as contributing factors to Reactive Devaluation and impasse—"preventing the proposer from achieving his goal, not because the offer declines in the affirmative benefits it creates for the recipient once it is made."[1] There is great need to ask probing questions and actively listen to recognize the interests of the disputants, regardless of the way issues might appear on the surface. Delving deeply into the topic of emotions led to another question.

Interviewer: When emotions are high and rational thinking is gone, how does a mediator de-escalate such a situation?

Interviewee: Permitting the emotions to flow, following with, "Where do you think that is going to get you? How has it been working so far? We cannot solve that problem here today, but what we can do is end the dispute and maybe that will take away some of the pain and emotion and you can put it behind you."[2]

Managing disputant emotions is a requisite skill for the mediator. Sometimes giving time to own and process emotions is a helpful tactic.

FLASH CHALLENGE, PART 1

Interview #1

Get the Lowdown: Interview a Mediator

1. Why did you decide to become a mediator?
2. What is your professional background?
3. What training did you go through?
4. What is the hardest thing about being a mediator?
    a. What was your most difficult case?
        i. What makes a case difficult in general?
        ii. How did you navigate those waters?
        iii. Did it settle?
            1. If so, was the settlement collaborative?
            2. If not, why not?
5. What is the most important thing you do as a mediator?
6. Is there one skill that you would say is the most important?
    a. Top three most important skills?
    b. How did you learn these skills?
    b. Do you use all of your skills during every mediation?
        i. If not, how do you know which skills to use when?
7. Do you use your mediation and conflict resolution skills outside of mediations as well?
    a. Do they help you in other areas of your life?
    b. If so, how do you apply them?

1. Russell Korobkin, *Psychological Impediments to Mediation Success: Theory and Practice*, p. 317.
2. Mr. Smith, Mediator interview, 2018.

8. Do you have a particular mediation style you stick with?
    a. If not, do you flow between mediation styles depending on the mediation?
        i. How do you know which mediation style to use and when?
9. What is your position on the neutrality discussion inside the mediation community?
    a. How do you present neutrality when you mediate?
    b. Where do you draw the line?
    c. Can you give me an example of a time during a mediation that caused you to struggle with your neutrality?
    d. Have you ever crossed the line of neutrality?
        i. If so, what happened?
            1. How did you mitigate your breach of neutrality?
10. How do you manage disputant power imbalances?
11. What is the most interesting and creative settlement you have been involved in?
    a. How did it happen?

FLASH CHALLENGE, PART 2

Interview #2

Inquiring Minds: Interview with Disputants

- As a result of this interview, the interviewer should develop an empathetic perspective for disputants who have been through the mediation process.
- Extra Credit: If the interviewer has been a disputant in a mediation, they might choose to answer the questions based on their own experiences in addition to interviewing someone else.
- If the interviewer is comfortable, they can consider presenting their personal experience to the class followed by a conversation with a question-and-answer component.

1. What led you to mediation?
2. Describe the conflict and its circumstances—the whole background leading up to mediation.
3. How did you feel in the conflict before mediation was even discussed?
4. How did you feel about the idea of mediation?
    a. Did you know what mediation was?
        i. If so, how did you know?
        ii. If not, what did you think it was going to be?
5. Did you prepare for the mediation?
    a. If so, how?

6. Describe the mediation process:
    a. Did the mediator give an opening statement?
    b. Were you in joint session? Caucus? Both?
    c. Was it amicable or aggressive?
    d. What is your Conflict Handling Mode?
        i. If the interviewee is not familiar with the various Conflict Handling Modes, define and discuss all five together.
    e. What was the other disputant's Conflict Handling Mode?
7. Describe the mediator and their role:
    a. How did the mediator approach the mediation?
        i. Describe how they handled it.
        ii. Describe how they spoke to you.
            1. Individually while in caucus?
            2. Collectively while in joint session?
        iii. Describe how they spoke about the conflict.
        iv. Did the mediator make settlement suggestions?
8. Did the mediator have to break up any fights?
    a. Did they set out any behavioral ground rules?
    b. Did they have to request civility?
9. Did the mediator encourage more discussion?
    a. Did they look into feelings or deeper issues?
10. Did the mediator listen well?
    a. Did they ask questions?
    b. Did they help with disputants' emotions?
11. Did the conflict settle in mediation (with a signed settlement agreement)?
    a. If so:
        i. How did you reach settlement?
        ii. Which methods did you use?
        iii. Did disputants brainstorm together and come up with resolution ideas?
        iv. Did disputants brainstorm separately?
        v. Did the mediator make settlement suggestions?
            1. If so, were they:
                a) Helpful?
                b) Thoughtful?
                c) Creative?
                d) Frustrating?
                e) Out-of-touch?
        vi. What was the most creative settlement suggestion?
    b. If not, why not?
12. Is there anything else you would like to add?

FLASH CHALLENGE, PART 3

Interview #3

Get Some Perspective, and Then Give Some: Interview the Inexperienced

1. Find someone who has never been involved in a mediation.
2. Ask them:
   a. Have they ever heard of mediation?
   b. What do they know about mediation?
3. Compare and contrast any misunderstandings they might have about mediation with the correct facts that you know.
   a. Fill in any blanks with your understanding of the mediation process.
   b. If they do not know anything about it at all, explain it to them.
4. Answer any questions they might have.
5. Now that they understand the process, ask them if they would consider engaging in mediation if they found themself in the position to need it.
   a. If so, ask them to explain why.
   b. If not, ask them to explain why not.
      i. Can you engage with them about their reasons for not being interested in mediation as a dispute resolution process?
      ii. Can you encourage them to see the benefits of mediation over other forms of dispute resolution?
6. Discuss with them the benefits of mediation and conflict resolution skills outside of the traditional mediation process. For example, when dealing with conflict:
   a. In their personal relationships.
   b. With a significant other.
   c. Between family members.
   d. In business relationships.
   e. With strangers.
   f. With neighbors.
   g. With community issues.
7. Can they see the benefits that the process of mediation and the use of these skills could have on a larger scale?
   a. The political arena.
   b. Between cultures with differing viewpoints, wishes, and beliefs.
   c. Between religions with differing viewpoints, wishes, and beliefs.
   d. Between citizens, communities, and police departments.
   e. Between citizens, communities, and their government.

New to Mediation

The following interview is a completed example of Flash Challenge, Part 3.

1. **Find someone who has never been involved in a mediation.**
2. **Ask them:**
   a. **Have they ever heard of mediation?**
   Yes.
   b. **What do they know about mediation?**
   Mediation is something you do to avoid going to court.
   Getting between two conflicting parties and getting to a resolution as a third, neutral party.
3. **Compare and contrast any misunderstandings they might have about mediation.**
   In its application – when mediation can be applied. After learning more about mediation, that understanding of when and how it can be used has been broadened.
   a. **Fill in any blanks with your understanding of the mediation process.**
   b. **If they do not know anything about it at all, explain it to them.**
4. **Answer any questions they might have.** [The following are questions from the interviewee.]
   If I wanted to hire a mediator, how would I go about doing that?
   Are there mediation services?
   Are there limitations to using a mediator?
   Are there certain scenarios when mediation is not the correct solution?
   Are some issues too serious or not serious enough?
   Are there points that could come up in a mediation that the mediator cannot or will not become involved in?
   Are there any times during a mediation that a mediator will say to the disputants that they should discuss the specific issues strictly between them and the mediator will leave the room?
   And vice versa – certain points the mediator will tell the disputants that they should not be speaking directly about and that should only go through the mediator?
5. **Now that they understand the process, ask them if they would consider engaging in mediation if they found themself in the position to need it.**
   Yes.
   a. **If so, ask them to explain why.**
   Because it provides a broader set of options that I did not know about before, and the options include keeping the financial burden at a place less than it would be in court with lawyers and potential rulings, and also the intensity of the conflict is kept at a lesser level than if the case went to court.

The creativity and flexibility a mediated settlement could afford is appealing, and certainly more accommodating than a court ruling would be.

Mediation is a safer bet when you need to maintain a relationship with the other party. It avoids the intensity of emotions that courts add to the equation and a potential looming financial burden that can cause serious emotional upheavals.

b. **If not, ask them to explain why.**

   i. **Can you engage with them about their reasons for not leaning toward mediation?**

   I would not lean toward mediation when I do not have a personal or long-term attachment to the other party, and it is strictly either a business transaction or one that has no long-term component.

   I would also not turn to mediation if I just want to sue someone who wronged me and I do not care about any of the benefits mediation affords, and all I want to do is sue and I will bring the best lawyer I can find and afford.

   ii. **Can you encourage them to see the benefits of mediation over other forms of dispute resolution?**

   I do not want to give the other side a chance for any form of a balanced or successful outcome. It is purely about punishing an opposing side.

   I do not want to have a conversation, just pay me or fix it, or whatever I am suing you for. No discussion desired.

6. **Discuss with them the benefit of mediation and conflict resolution skills outside of the traditional mediation process. For example, when dealing with conflict:**

   a. **In their personal relationships.**

   Yes, absolutely it would be beneficial. Conflict resolution skills can provide tools to access underlying issues that would not have surfaced if not for the skills. To access what is really going on below the surface—understanding true needs of other people. There is value in understanding as it relates to maintaining a relationship over time. Every step you take to better understand and know the underlying issues is a step toward extending the relationship.

   b. **With a significant other.**

   Because the emotions run higher, there is a lot more invested, a lot more expectation, which can make normal tempers run hot. You feel like there is more to lose whether that is true or not. There is more on the line, such as kids and other family members involved in the relationship, so using conflict resolution skills to truly repair any potential damage could become critical to the health and stability of the relationship.

c. **Between family members.**

Tools can help you get closer and better understand your family. The tools can help address certain assumptions family members have made and have been making for possibly a long period of time and need help to address. Conversations can be tricky and uncomfortable between family, so specific conflict resolution and mediation skills can provide structured assistance to allow everyone to be heard.

d. **In business relationships.**

Specific tools and skills provide guidance and assistance to anyone who is attempting to defuse a situation, gain insight into a state of mind, learn more about what someone needs, and learn how to best create a harmonious environment.

i. **Employee relations.**

It can be difficult for business leaders who are at a distance or detached from daily activities to understand the dynamics between employees. Structured skills can help address any concerns and issues that may be exist. HR concerns can be avoided.

ii. **Contract negotiations.**

Business with subcontractor or supplier.

International business where cultures and needs may be different.

e. **With strangers.**

Avoiding unintentional conflict.

Present as a caring person.

De-escalation tactics when you know nothing about the person.

f. **With neighbors.**

Avoiding small claims court over branches in your yard!

The nonfinancial component of a mediated settlement can benefit neighbors who share space in common, either a wall, a tree, or some other area that could be addressed to the mutual benefit of all parties.

g. **With community issues.**

Dealing with the police.

Addressing social topics that cause certain communities to be harmed and feel unheard.

Providing a structured outlet for discussion about difficult issues where assistance is truly needed.

7. **Can they see the benefit the process of mediation and the use of these skills could have on a larger scale?**

a. **The political arena.**

Yes. We are in an age of political, racial, and socioeconomic extremes, and now more than ever we need mediation to help give a meaningful voice to all sides and to avoid situations where the one who yells loudest is the only one heard. Also, to avoid situations where action only follows more extreme action instead of action following a conversation where all are heard.

b. **Between cultures with differing viewpoints, wishes, and beliefs.**
Yes. Different cultures might have different needs and communicate differently. Conversation that is facilitated, giving consideration to cultural variances, could be key to developing respectful and effective communication that is not currently present. The benefit of this is improved discussions and outcomes.

All sides must feel and be heard for progress and resolution that leads to changed behavior and action, so mediation and conflict resolution skills would provide the means to accomplish that with structure and ground rules that all participants can rely on to protect and honor them.

c. **Between religions with differing viewpoints, wishes, and beliefs.**
Religious disputes can consist of issues that run generations deep, and as the way they have been addressed and managed thus far is possibly not having the desired effect of change and collaboration, using mediation and conflict resolution skills to structure and harness new conversations could prove fruitful to a generations-old conflict that spans the globe and permeates all levels of society.

d. **Between citizens, communities, and police departments.**
There is such a long history of distrust between many communities and their police departments, that unfacilitated and unmonitored conversation could be dangerous at this point. Emotions are too raw, and experiences are too fresh in memories to have discussions about such large and impactful topics without assistance. Additionally, that assistance will come in the form of skills designed to accomplish exactly what is needed for communication to be successful.

e. **Between citizens, communities, and their government.**
The fundamental fabric of a society can become threatened when citizens and governing bodies are incapable of communicating, have lost touch with each other's needs and concerns, have dismissed grievances, and have moved into a pattern of performing activities and making decisions regardless of the costs to those outside of their immediate space. With conflict resolution and mediation skills, there could be a possibility of conversation, clarification, airing of grievances, presentation of requests, and discussions about what has been lost or taken away.

Collaborative action and possible resolution options could be discussed with a structure in place to ensure that no offensive action is taken that could derail forward momentum.

In this situation, ensuring that all participants are heard would be critical to the chance for change, and specifically change that incorporates what was expressed during any facilitated conversations that were had.

appendix 3

Mediation vs. Litigation

The following chart compares salient elements of mediation and litigation. The information can be used by a mediator or conflict interventionist to assist disputants in understanding the differences between the two processes and how those differences could affect them. The discussion of this material with disputants can be beneficial when they are making decisions such as whether or not to settle, whether or not impasse should be considered a viable conclusion to a mediation, and the resultant future impact(s) of their decisions – decisions with consequences that result in either remaining in mediation or finding litigation as the dispute resolution option according to what might be necessary or preferrable.

Mediation	Litigation
Includes, by definition, disputant participation in all aspects of the process from beginning to end.	Parties leave their fate in the hands of the judge and/or jury.
A Disputant in family mediation: I think the best thing for our kids is for us to be able to come to some kind of agreement on our own because at the end of the day the judge doesn't know our kids, doesn't truly know our situation, and I think that we will like the custody situation more if we are the ones who are deciding, rather than putting it in a judge's hands to make the final ruling.	
Parties have the ability to choose mediators who specialize and have experience in pertinent fields.	Parties have no voice in selecting their judge. Consequently, the judge presiding over their case might not necessarily have any expertise or experience in case-related matters.

Mediation	Litigation
Disputants are assisted by the mediator to work in concert and in collaboration with each other.	There is no requisite fairness or compromise when there is a necessary and proper ruling according to the law that the judge is obligated to impose on one or more parties.
Disputants discuss potentially acceptable and agreeable settlement options customized to their specific interests and needs before coming to a mutually agreed-upon settlement decision.	If there is a potential agreement between parties to end litigation via settlement, the judge might request to see parties' terms. However, consent is not guaranteed.
Disputants retain the ability to be active participants in making important decisions with immediate and direct consequences throughout. Such decisions are made exclusively by disputants.	Decisions, very likely requiring court approval, to withdraw the case and cease proceedings involve additional participants, are far less immediate, and carry financial consequences.
If parties do not find a settlement offer acceptable, they can continue negotiating in the attempt to reach a different settlement or end the mediation process in impasse.	Rulings are not determined by whether or not parties would feel satisfied by and agree to terms.
Confidentiality is provided by the process—during and continuing after.	Confidentiality providing protection from public exposure is not elemental to the process.
Time efficient.	Litigated cases can drag on for years.
Cost efficient.	Litigation costs can become exorbitant.
Mediations can be less destructive to relationships, and often incorporate a focus on their repair and reconstruction.	Court battles can result in destroyed personal and professional relationships.
There is unlimited potential for creative settlement options and no remedy limitations.	The court is bound by the laws of the legal system.
All disputants retain individual control over whether or not they remain in mediation—they are free to decide at any moment that mediation no longer works for them and can terminate the process.	Options have limitations and could cease according to initiating party and legality. The decision to terminate is not equal among parties.

appendix 4

Transcribed Mediation Example #1: *Transformative Employee Dispute*

DISPUTANTS

- R. Haradadian
  - R. Haradadian is 63 years old, and has been with the firm for 20 years
  - Legal secretary to V. Safarli, partner in charge of the firm
  - Also serves as office manager; the office consists of 10 attorneys, 10 legal secretaries, 23 assistants, and 4 receptionists
  - Uncomfortable with technology
  - Did not go to college
  - Known to have a short temper, to be difficult to get along with, very stuck in their ways, insists on acting as overseer, refuses to abide by the dress code
- T. Gwan
  - T. Gwan is 27 years old, and has been with the firm for 1.5 years
  - Legal secretary to Y. Herrada, also a partner at the firm
  - Has changed systems and implemented new technology at the firm
  - Was hired because of a graduate degree, and specialized training in a new technology field that will help the firm progress with the times; has already changed the firm's name and website
  - Has fresh energy, enjoys getting to know people in the office, plans activities for everyone, always has a pleasant and welcoming demeanor

MEDIATOR'S PRE-MEDIATION CONFIDENTIAL INFORMATION

- R. Haradadian: Admits to having sometimes made the work environment less than friendly for T. Gwan as a result of R. Haradadian's uncontrolled angry outbursts.

  Dear Mediator,

  My concern is getting the work done in a way that is going to benefit the attorneys and the firm. There have been projects that have been handled in ways that have caused problems for both myself and for T. Gwan, and I feel that I am here as a resource, being here for many years and I know the company inside and out—how things are done, how the company is run, what can help, and T. Gwan has pretty much avoided coming to me for any questions or advice and doesn't acknowledge the fact that I have that experience. As a result, it has

> landed us in hot water more than once. I don't know what's going on, but it feels like there have been many deliberate moves from T. Gwan to embarrass me, which I don't understand, and I don't think it is very productive. I just want to know what's going on!

- T. Gwan: Admits to having gone over R. Haradadian's head directly to V. Safarli on more than one occasion, even though that does not respect the chain of command, it is not how T. Gwan should have provided the information, and it reflected poorly on R. Haradadian.

> Dear Mediator,
> Let me give a little background information. Both R. Haradadian and I work for different people, so I feel that we are peers, and I feel that I am not being treated as a peer, but instead as a subordinate even though I am not because we each are legal secretaries to two different people. I feel that R. Haradadian is monitoring my every move, and I also am upset about the fact that R. Haradadian went to the person for whom I work to ask that I be fired, and I don't feel that there was any reason for that to happen. I feel the working situation is very, very tense around R. Haradadian in a way that I am not used to working. That is the situation in a nutshell, but most importantly I want to reiterate that we are on the same working level.

- Additional information from employers V. Safarli and Y. Herrada:
  - Detailed to the mediator, that if their legal secretaries, R. Haradadian and T. Gwan, don't resolve their issues during the mediation, one or both will lose their jobs. The mediator is instructed, however, to withhold this information from them until it becomes absolutely necessary to disclose it to force either a resolution or an alternate ending to the mediation if it continues on for more than six hours, as the attorneys are unwilling to provide and pay for any mediation beyond that point.
  - The employers have expressed very strong feelings of disappointment that the two employees have been unable to work together, have taken their disagreements to this level, and have forced the firm's hand—ordering them to mediation. They are unsure about whether or not they plan to keep either employee at the firm based on their terrible behavior to each other, and they plan to base a decision about future employment with the firm on the outcome of the mediation.
  - The employers would prefer for the disputants to finally show that they are, in fact, capable of cooperating with each other and working through their differences together, which is why they have requested that the mediator withhold certain information regarding their future employment at the firm from them until and unless absolutely necessary. Forcing their hands with the threat of termination is something the employers do not want to have to do, although they will if they have to, and they are also keenly aware that doing so will not solve any of the current issues that have landed the disputants in mediation.

THE DISPUTE

- Employment dispute between two employees who cannot get along and have been ordered into mediation by their firm.
- Both R. Haradadian and T. Gwan are legal secretaries to partners at a law firm who work on cases together, necessitating that R. Haradadian and T. Gwan communicate with each other and work jointly on a regular basis.
- There has been a last, very significant episode between R. Haradadian and T. Gwan that resulted in a missed deadline, and an incomplete project from T. Gwan, and R. Haradadian speaking directly to Y. Herrada (the attorney for whom T. Gwan works), and expressing the opinion that T. Gwan should be fired from the firm.

POINTS OF CONTENTION

- There doesn't seem to be space for both of them at the firm as it is now.
- They both feel that there is a substantial lack of respect for each other.
- Communication, misunderstanding, and miscommunication.
  - Lack of communication coupled with constant and consistent miscommunication
    - Styles
    - Lack thereof
    - Tone of voice
    - Language used
    - Chain of command
- No safe space to communicate and express thoughts and needs.

POINTS OF AGREEMENT

- The working environment cannot continue as it is.
- Their tension is affecting those around them.
- They fear that they could both be in jeopardy of losing their jobs.
- They cannot sustain a professional relationship without working through their issues.
- Their communication as it stands now is not only detrimental to their job performance, but also to their mental and emotional well-being.
- Although forced into mediation by their employers, both have admitted to the mediator in caucus that they are dealing with hurt feelings caused by the other, actually do believe that each has something to offer to the firm and to one another, and would like to come to a resolution today.

POINTS TO NEGOTIATE

- Each disputant harbors hurt feelings.
- Both want and need to keep their job.
- Both can learn from each other as each has a different skill set that could be beneficial to the other. In other words, they do not have to compete, there is room for each to bring different and equally helpful information to the table.
- Plenty of wiggle room because there has been a tremendous amount of miscommunication, misunderstanding of intentions, jumping to conclusions without taking a beat to gain clarity, and reactive behavior based on a fundamental lack of true understanding. Opportunity to explain and clarify will probably solve a lot of problems that have arisen.

DESIRED MEDIATION OUTCOME

- R. Haradadian:

  I don't want this kind of thing to happen anymore. I want to be used as a resource. I want to be recognized that I have value to this firm because of my experience, and to work together as a team on projects and not be left high and dry even when I ask for coverage.

- T. Gwan:

  I would like to be able to feel comfortable in doing my job without feeling that I am being monitored by somebody who is not my manager or my boss, and I would like there to be a more relaxed feeling in the office without any tension.

DISCUSSIONS IN CAUCUS

- Because the disputants were extremely combative upon entering the room together, toward each other as well as the mediation process in general, the mediator made the decision to perform the mediation in caucus.

  Mediator: Can you tell me a little bit about the course of the relationship? How was it before versus how it is now?

  T. Gwan: It was normal and problem-free until little by little, it feels as though at this point, so it probably happened over time, as though I have been constantly watched and monitored, and it's not comfortable in the workplace in a way that I usually like to feel which is relaxed, so there's a lot of tension, and when I found out that R. Haradadian was asking my boss to fire me, of course my reaction was well I don't even want to have to deal with somebody who is trying to get rid of me and I can just do my job without having to deal with them because it is unpleasant. There's tension, and then they were trying to get me fired, so that's not a very nice way to work in an office. It is very tense, and R. Haradadian is a little bit scary. I don't want to talk for other people, but I know they feel that way, too. It feels like if anybody makes a move, they are being watched by R. Haradadian as opposed to them being able to just work at their job and just do the job. Everybody wants to do a good job, but it feels as though R. Haradadian is like the mother hen, a very strict mother hen, when actually in my case, they are just a peer.

Mediator: Based on what you're saying, and regarding the project that inevitably brought us here today, on both sides, correct me if I'm wrong please, that there was a misunderstanding of intention. Is that possible? You felt that they were trying to do something malicious to you, and vice versa?

- It came as no surprise that the aggressive, superficial-level posturing behaviors from both disputants had little to do with what was happening below the surface
  - The disputants could have been reading from the same script.
  - Each felt deeply hurt by the other.
    - Their positions were not being respected by the other.
    - The work it took to get to where they are today was not recognized and respected by the other.
  - They each specifically wanted the respect and appreciation from the other.
  - They recognized that they each had skills that the other lacked, and that they could learn from as well as teach each other.
    - They were stuck at this hurdle, though, because they felt that admitting it at this late stage would put them in a weak position and they would lose ground.
  - They were both deeply disappointed that they didn't get off on the right foot.
  - They both felt completely misunderstood by the other.
  - The generational gap posed tone issues.
    - Older generations, R. Haradadian explained to the mediator, spoke in a more matter-of-fact manner, and it was hard to remember that the younger generation interpreted that as rude, and preferred a softer tone.
    - T. Gwan echoed this sentiment, explaining that the younger generation took more time to explain things, and to make sure there were no hurt feelings at the end of a conversation.
- Fortunately, after each disputant discussed their position privately with the mediator, including plenty of venting and validation from the mediator, and probing questions to reach levels below the surface, both disputants agreed to meet together in the same room to continue the mediation. Here the mediation essentially started over again, with each disputant explaining, in their own words, why the mediation was taking place and what led up to it—a vocalization of the confidential letters that were provided to the mediator prior to the start of the mediation.
  - As this was a Transformative mediation (TM), it was important to get the disputants back in the same room together. If they are incapable of being in the same room together for a mediation with a mediator controlling the room, how will they possibly move into a functional, comfortable, and productive working relationship once they are on their own?

THE COMBAT ZONE

Although the disputants agreed to meet in the same room and to move forward with the mediation jointly, they still required the opportunity to air their grievances with each other, resulting in multiple aggressive statements and contentious moments that are referred to as "The Combat Zone."

R. Haradadian: You don't respect my position at this firm. I have been here for 20 years, worked my way from the ground up, gave up relationships, time with my children, family gatherings, and evenings home to be where I am today, and you come in here, brand new, with no experience, and wave your fancy college degree in my face acting like you're better than me, and I know you're plotting behind my back to get rid of me—I can tell!

Mediator: R. Haradadian, that's an awful way to feel and would make it hard for anyone to work with another person if they believed that was going on behind their back. I'm sure T. Gwan would agree. Is this the first time you are expressing those feelings to T. Gwan? Maybe you can provide T. Gwan with some specific instances that led you to feel that way?

T. Gwan: I never even talk about college or my degree unless someone specifically asks me! You look down on me because I am new here, and didn't work my way up, but I worked just as hard as you did, I just did it in college! I worked myself to the bone getting good grades, working a part-time job, and taking care of my younger brother and sister! I tried to get to know you when I first started and all you did was ignore me! You would walk right by me saying "hi" to everyone except me! How do you think that makes me feel? You are so rude! It's really surprising to me that you would think that I, on purpose, did something that might sabotage your position, and very interestingly, it felt to me that you purposely sabotaged me. It is interesting to hear that you feel that I am the underhanded one. You talk about respect, but respect has to be mutual. I have something that I bring to this firm and I think it deserves respect as well. I haven't been here from the beginning—you worked your way up, I went to school and studied computer science and the legal system, and that is why I was hired. I was hired for what I have to offer, and you are here for what you have to offer, and so there is a mutual respect that doesn't seem to be happening.

PIVOTAL MOMENTS

Mediator: R. Haradadian, it's very clear that you're upset and have strong feelings about this situation. This is absolutely your opportunity to express those feelings, and to explain why, in your opinion, we are all here today, but maybe some of those expressions can be stated in a way that T. Gwan might be more receptive to. What about only using statements that express how you've been feeling, how you feel T. Gwan's words and actions are coming across, and how you'd like to feel, instead of telling T. Gwan what they did or did not do, what they did wrong, and how they need to change. Maybe you can consider asking T. Gwan if the way their words and actions are coming across to you are really how they mean them to. Maybe there is a miscommunication here, and a great deal of misunderstanding?

R. Haradadian: Yes that is something I would like to do, but I guess I am not sure how....

T. Gwan: And if I could do it again, I would have handled it differently, so that's my part in this, and I wish I had done it differently, but it felt to me as though when R. Haradadian brought it to me, they were aware that I could mess up because of my schedule, which I did, but it felt a little bit as though that was their intention – for me to mess up.

Mediator: Do you think it's possible that there is a fundamental misunderstanding of those intentions on both parts, since you already said that you didn't mean for R. Haradadian to feel certain ways? And maybe that could rollover into some other behaviors as well?

T. Gwan: Yes. We often don't know what another person is going through, if they are having a hard time, or the way we all act, so absolutely there could be something.

Mediator: R. Haradadian, would you like to respond now based on some of the new information you've heard from T. Gwan?

R. Haradadian: I am about the bottom line – getting things done, so there was no ill intention on my part in giving you something in a way that you couldn't succeed. But, I don't know why, ever, you wouldn't ask for my advice, knowing how long I've been here. You just completely ignore and avoid that conversation with me, and this last incident wasn't the first time, but it was really big and we were both really hurt by it. I could have helped out. I could have guided you in a way that would have helped you to be successful. That's why it feels vindictive to me, and this isn't the first time it feels like you did something like that to embarrass me by completely making it as if I don't even exist, and was never with the firm at all. So that's the part that I don't understand would be happening to begin with. I admit that I went into the office and I could have handled it differently, but just so you know, even involving your hire, they asked for my opinion. They have asked for my opinion on many different things even though I am not your supervisor. Not just you, but regarding other things as well, so I felt like it was my duty to say something because it didn't feel like you were cooperative at all in working with me, in wanting to work with me, or even just seeking out advice for things that could have been handled in a more successful manner. So, yes, in retrospect I was really upset when this last incident transpired, and I probably shouldn't have gone to your boss about it.

Mediator: It sounds like you wish the situation had played out a little bit differently, and maybe if the communication had been easier and more open between the two of you, you would have wanted to have more involvement together to work on the project.

R. Haradadian: Absolutely, absolutely.

Mediator: It also sounds like at some point, at least in the beginning of the relationship, you wanted T. Gwan to be there. You voiced your opinion that the firm should hire T. Gwan. Would that be accurate?

R. Haradadian: Yes, yes!

Mediator: Okay. Is there anything else you would like to add?

R. Haradadian: Well, just, you know, so that you hear it—if I had any kind of animosity toward you, I wouldn't have recommended that you be hired to our bosses.

T. Gwan: Well, you may not be aware of certain things the way you come off, and that might be totally not planned on your part, but you seem very judgmental, and including judging of the fact that I have a college degree even. You seem to mention about how you know the history of the firm a lot, and it feels like a judgment that I haven't been with the firm from the beginning, and I just got in on a college degree. Maybe you're not intending that, but there feels to be a judgment there, and you seem unhappy if you're not consulted about every move that I make. You may not be intending that, but that's what it feels like—that you're very judgmental.

Mediator: Okay, let's take a look at those intentions. It doesn't sound like you, R. Haradadian, were intending for T. Gwan to feel in that way, but, nonetheless, it happened that way. So, maybe you can tell us a little bit about what you *would* want T. Gwan to know?

R. Haradadian: I know your college degree speaks for itself, so I'm not discounting that or devaluing that in any way, but my goal is to work as a team and to have projects succeed. So, maybe I'm just too invested or too serious sometimes or intense about the firm because I have been a part of it for such a long time. I really look out for the best interest of the firm, and maybe I do oversee a little bit too much that isn't exactly in my job description to do because of that, and I can hear how that has bothered you, and I don't mean to have done that. I guess I'm not used to somebody who doesn't even come to me. It feels like you don't want to work on projects so that they are successful collaborations, you'd rather do it on your own, and maybe not have it succeed, and that maybe you don't even need me there. Maybe T. Gwan really doesn't even need me there, I don't know.

T. Gwan: Well, I think there's a buildup of . . . it's just that after something keeps on happening, like you keep on hearing that "you haven't been here so long," one starts to feel—I start to feel, and especially when then I hear that maybe I'm not needed at the company or that I should be fired, it just sort of—my response to that is to not even try anymore to deal with you, because I feel that there is nothing I can do to get your respect. So, maybe my reaction was the wrong reaction to make that happen, but it was just sort of a reaction that I had over time.

Mediator: It sounds like a lot of the words being used are in common, right? We are talking about respect, misunderstanding of intentions, "I didn't mean for you to feel that way," "maybe we can do this differently"—would you agree? It seems like if we can help everybody to feel heard, respected, that their opinions matter, and that everybody has something to bring to the table, you could have an enjoyable working relationship.

R. Haradadian: I think you're right. I think we are both talking about respect, I am hearing that too.

RESOLUTION

- The bottom line
  - Jobs on the line
  - Respect
  - Finding a way to work together productively
- Parties agreed to meet in the same room after they expressed themselves through the mediator practicing shuttle mediation. Once in the room together, they each took the opportunity to express themselves from their personal perspectives, excluding blame, and instead focusing on how they felt at different times—coming from a place of "I."
- Weekly communication schedule
  - Both an email and an in-person meeting would happen once a week
    - R. Haradadian was more comfortable meeting in person
    - T. Gwan preferred to send emails
    - The agreement was to communicate both ways to demonstrate to each other respect for individual preferences and also to work on becoming more comfortable with different forms of communicating
- An agreement to come to each other immediately with anything that was upsetting to them, but to give each other the benefit of the doubt
  - Take a beat
  - Ask for clarity
  - Explain how something came across to them, knowing that the intention was not to be hurtful
- To work on projects together whenever possible
  - There are benefits to old and new styles, so they will work on bridging that gap
- Mediator's ideas for implementation
  - Develop a communication system
    - Daily, weekly, monthly—find a schedule that works for all parties
    - Create a safe space to be able to approach each other with concerns immediately before anything gets out of hand
      - Learn how to approach each other
        - Ask each other the best way to speak to them
        - Come from a place of "I" versus "you did this," "you are doing that wrong," and "how could you do that?"

- TAKE A BEAT!!!
  - Ask questions!
  - Ask for clarity immediately
  - Provide space for unintentional misunderstanding and unintended consequences (hurt feelings), and then for the air to be cleared, followed by forward movement based on new information, understanding, and acceptance
- Identify trigger words to avoid
- Build in a respectful sentence structure for every communication
- Make sure both disputants are completely clear about why they are upset
  - How have they interpreted words and actions from each other?
    - Provide an opportunity for the parties to clear the air by explaining that they either did or did not mean what they said, did, or expressed in the way it was interpreted, and to provide a correct explanation of intent
- Approach while in caucus
  - R. Haradadian felt as though hard-earned respect and status were being taken away and lost and that their long-term position was being disrespected. It was very important for the mediator to make sure that R. Haradadian felt fully involved in the discussion about possible resolution options, rather than being told what to do and made to feel that yet another person thought they knew more and better by conducting the interaction in that manner. It was necessary to consult R. Haradadian for an opinion of possible options that would provide the opportunity to express their knowledge and skills acquired over many years of hard work at the firm.
  - T. Gwan was receptive to being shown new and different strategies when approaching R. Haradadian. Ideas included setting boundaries in place with R. Haradadian including parameters of T. Gwan's role at the firm, acknowledgment of the benefits of college education, and a stop to minimizing language due to being newly hired at the firm and not having come up through the ranks.
- Approach while in joint mediation
  - Find areas of commonality between the disputants and encourage discussion focusing on those commonalities – how, why, details
    - Common hurt feelings, common desires to have handled situations differently, common wishes to communicate better, get along, mend their working relationship, benefit the firm
  - Encourage disputants to comment and respond based on new, corrected information provided to them (by each other when given the opportunity to clarify and explain intentions) during the course of the mediation
  - Look into areas for apology
  - Focus on forward momentum, and strategies to address future issues that arise
    - If past behaviors should reoccur, set a correction plan in place
  - Create structured gridwork for how to proceed with each other, together

Mediator: Okay, let's look a little bit at how you would feel respected in your daily interactions with each other, as well as in these specific, larger projects where you both have a lot at stake, together. R. Haradadian, perhaps you have some ideas about what would make you feel more heard and respected?

R. Haradadian: Well, to use me as a resource. You don't have to reinvent the wheel to get things working more efficiently and effectively.

Mediator: T. Gwan?

T. Gwan: Well, I could do that. I feel uncomfortable when I feel as though I am being monitored in my coming and going, and I think that if I felt that you were okay with the way that I was performing, then I would feel comfortable to come to you, and talk just normally. There's a feeling of fear in the atmosphere, as though don't make a wrong move or else, and that's something I'm uncomfortable working with, I'm not used to that. I want to do a good job, and I think everybody does. We are all working toward the same thing, and we should be able to work together and to feel comfortable.

Mediator: Do you have any suggestions? Can you meet and communicate on a consistent basis? Perhaps a blending of these two very different communication and work styles. Based on what you're saying, you both want the best for the firm and to have a functional working relationship, but coming from two very different styles. So, let's look at some options to blend the styles allowing room for both.

T. Gwan: Okay.

R. Haradadian: Okay.

Mediator: Okay, so why don't you tell us a little bit about your preferred style.

R. Haradadian: I am pretty to the point, get the job done, so maybe that comes off as not willing to socialize, or something like that, but that's not my intention. I do socialize, but anyhow that's my style. Like I don't do flowery emails . . . I mean I'm not saying you do, or that that's bad, I'm just pretty direct when I need to say something.

Mediator: Okay, and when we're talking about someone who has a very different style than you have, would you be open to incorporating maybe a little bit of their style into yours?

R. Haradadian: Sure.

Mediator: Okay. T. Gwan? Tell us about your style.

T. Gwan: I'm probably the opposite of that in socializing, except for flowery emails—I don't do that, but I'm relaxed as I work, and I'm able to do the work while I'm relaxed, so I can be socializing, but it's not like sitting around socializing, it's actually being comfortable. It's not the exact opposite of yours. I'm also working, but I just have a different personality, and so the way I deal with things is a little bit less serious, maybe.

Mediator: Okay, that's a really good way of thinking about it. And do you feel that you would maybe be willing to incorporate a little bit of R. Haradadian's style, to provide a more comfortable environment to bring your two styles a little closer together?

T. Gwan: Well, I don't know if I could change my personality to become like R. Haradadian's personality, but . . . .

Mediator: Of course not, but maybe structuring emails in a slightly different manner, or including a structure that incorporates R. Haradadian's communication style? Maybe a planned weekly conversation?

T. Gwan: Yes, sure.

Mediator: Okay. Any other ways, either one of you, you feel could be beneficial in moving this relationship forward? As far as communication and validation? More ways you want to be respected?

T. Gwan: Well, I think it's important that we both know that each of us has a certain amount of experience, different experience, that we bring to the table.

Mediator: That's a really great point. Room for everyone's experience to be valid and helpful to both of you, and maybe an opportunity to share it on a weekly basis?

R. Haradadian: My concern really is about the work. I don't want this to happen again . . . okay, so that even probably comes off as bossy, maybe, I don't know now that I'm kind of hearing it, but I'd like to be included like I said—use me as a resource, because it's not good when things don't go well when they easily could have—I mean, that's why we're here, right?

Mediator: Exactly, and that's a point you both agree on. Okay. Let's look at some strategies! Let's look at some strategies to make sure you don't end up in this situation again.

T. Gwan: Well probably if we work together—if we feel that we are working together, as opposed to against each other, then if something is not going to work, we can have each other's back.

Mediator: Okay, let's open up the floor for everybody to brainstorm a little bit, maybe in the form of a scheduled communication together about projects, just meeting of the minds, on a daily or weekly basis? Tell us a little bit about what would work best for the firm.

R. Haradadian: That sounds good to me. To get on a project, like a team almost—a project team.

T. Gwan: Checking in to see what your boss has asked you to do, and what mine has asked me to do, making sure that we both know what's expected, and just discussing the projects?

Mediator: And T. Gwan, would you be able to go see R. Haradadian now when you need any advice or if you have any questions?

T. Gwan: Sure, of course, I would.

Mediator: Okay, let's start writing all of this down together. So, we talked about daily or weekly team meetings . . . .

R. Haradadian: I could make a project timeline at the beginning of each new project since I am more structured.

T. Gwan: Okay, that's fine. I could add some bullet points that I want to talk about.

Mediator: Okay, and is this something you would want to do in person, or over email, and with the rest of your coworkers there?

T. Gwan: It can be a meeting of all concerned.

Mediator: Okay, great. And how would the dialogue work? Would people raise their hands, or would you just jump into free-flow conversation?

T. Gwan: Raising hands works for me, does that work for you, R. Haradadian?

R. Haradadian: Yes, that's good.

Mediator: That's some good structure there! [Laugh from both disputants.]

R. Haradadian: And I think if you get the project, you would take lead, and if I get the project, I would take lead, that way there wouldn't be any confusion or issues there.

Mediator: That makes sense. And you could refer to each other for tips, pointers, and any helpful advice? Would you feel comfortable doing that at this point?

T. Gwan: Sure.

NO GUTS, NO GLORY

Although the parties were communicating completely cooperatively, being downright friendly, and had achieved a resolution that included active brainstorming and plans for future interaction, something felt not quite right to the mediator. Even if leaving certain issues untouched and undiscussed could end the mediation with a neatly wrapped resolution, without addressing absolutely everything, something would most assuredly derail any resolution down the line.

Mediator: T. Gwan, you seem a little hesitant. Is there anything else you'd like to get off your chest?

T. Gwan: Well, it's just going from everything being one way, to okay, now let's just ignore that and move on, that might take a little bit of easing into.

Mediator: And I think that makes perfect sense and is very understandable. I'm sure R. Haradadian, you may feel a similar way, but maybe you both have the same goal of moving forward, so at least you're willing to put the work in in trying to get there.

T. Gwan: Yes, of course.

R. Haradadian: [Nodding.]

Mediator: Are there any other suggestions? What about when you see each other in the office on a daily basis? Can you say "Hello," or "How is your day going?"

R. Haradadian: Yes, I think that would be nice.

T. Gwan: Yes, I mean if we are moving ahead from this and if we're now going to move on in a positive way, then that would be my natural reaction upon seeing you – to say "Hello." So yes, of course.

Mediator: That's great, and it's a pretty far cry from where you were when you walked into this room earlier today, right? The way it has been, you have had no communication except when absolutely necessary, so these casual conversations we are talking about now will build your communication skills with each other. Look, what you have been doing isn't working, and we're here to try something new, right? Let's throw it all on the table and do everything we can to make your professional lives better. This is your work – your profession. It takes up a lot of your time, so let's see if we can really make it a lot better.

R. Haradadian: And just to clear the air, again, because I was involved in the hiring process with you, and you were one of my recommendations, it's not like I came out of the gate with any animosity toward you, and the only reason I went to your boss, even though in retrospect I should have handled that differently, is because of the magnitude of the last incident, and I was really upset that it could have been avoided if we had worked together on it, and there had been more coming to me to get some information or advice or something like that.

T. Gwan: I think that there is some healing that has to happen, and it will probably happen while we are going through with these new steps toward communicating, and trust – being able to trust each other. I think that that will happen as we continue on.

Mediator: It is really great to be able to look at things we wish hadn't happened, and maybe are regretful of, and R. Haradadian, you mentioned something very specific you're regretful of. T. Gwan, is there anything you'd like to reiterate? Anything you wish hadn't happened between the two of you?

T. Gwan: Oh, well in terms of the handling of the project, I wish I had handled that differently, and I feel that it wasn't completely my fault the way it happened, but I didn't handle it well, and I would like to make that better, so there's that, and I do just want to be clear on the fact that we are both peers. That's really important to me.

R. Haradadian: Agreed.

Mediator: Okay, so it sounds like you have a good place to move forward to. Now let's talk about what to do if an issue should arise between the two of you. How can you handle it together? What makes you comfortable? Speaking openly? Bringing in a neutral third party? Emailing? Let's have a plan of action.

T. Gwan: You mean if there's a problem that we feel that the other person is maybe repeating some behavior from before?

Mediator: Yes, or something new.

T. Gwan: I'm comfortable with coming to R. Haradadian and saying something.

R. Haradadian: I am comfortable with that also.

Mediator: Okay, perhaps we can have some ground rules for that interaction. For example, always coming from a place of "I" and talking about your own feelings versus accusations. Can you agree to something like that?

T. Gwan: Yes.

R. Haradadian: Yes.

Mediator: Since you are seeing each other every day at work, and especially because it seems to be something that comes up for both of you, it would be good to try to express understanding and respect for each other. Perhaps you could try to work together to show that you respect each other's opinions, to incorporate that respect into questions you ask each other, and to acknowledge each other's contributions.

T. Gwan: I think it's great that you've worked so many years and that you know this firm very well, so certainly there will be all kinds of things that if I need to know, I have my repository of firm-related information right here.

R. Haradadian: Absolutely, and you could share with me some new tactics that you've picked up in college, from the educational end.

Mediator: Having come to this resolution, do you feel better now compared to the way you felt when you walked in today?

R. Haradadian: Yes, absolutely. I feel like now we can move forward.

T. Gwan: Yes, I agree.

Mediator: Okay, great. Then it's a wrap. Thank you for being a part of this mediation, and I wish you well moving forward. [Disputants smile at each other and shake hands.]

appendix 5

Transcribed Mediation Example #2: *The Disappointed Holidaymakers*

Mediator: Hello everybody and welcome to mediation. Let me start by asking: Is everybody comfortable being in the same room, at least so far?

Disputants [collectively]: So far, okay.

Mediator: Why don't I explain a little bit about mediation, we can sign confidentiality paperwork, and I will answer any questions you have. When we are finished, you can let me know again what your decisions are about proceeding with the mediation in joint session. I know you are all familiar with the mediation, but let me just remind you that mediation is completely confidential. When we are in joint session, everything in this room is confidential. If we decide to separate and move into different rooms, which is called caucus, anything we discuss in each room will be confidential unless you tell me otherwise. Does anyone have any questions about the process or what will happen here today?

Michaela [hotel representative]: I'm forgetting, are we going to be talking through you or directly to each other?

Mediator: You may communicate through me, or directly to each other. The manner in which you communicate is completely at your discretion, but because this is a facilitated negotiation process, I will ensure that we stick to the ground rules you mutually decide on and I will help in any way I can. When necessary and appropriate, I will evaluate, assist, guide, and offer suggestions that may be beneficial. Are there any other questions?

Disputants [collectively]: No.

Mediator [to Michaela]: Let's step to the side for a moment. How do you feel about remaining in joint session for now?

Michaela: For now I'm okay.

Mediator [to Joe, disgruntled holidaymaker]: How do you feel about remaining in joint session for now? You don't have to be okay with it, it is absolutely no problem to move into caucus right now if that makes you more comfortable.

Joe: No, I'm good with it. I want her to hear what I have to say, and I want to say it to her face.

Mediator: So, we'll stay here in joint session as you have both agreed that you would prefer to proceed in this manner at this time. Let's discuss ground rules. Anything in particular come to mind?

[Neither disputant responded.]

Mediator: I have not heard each of you discuss the details of the case yet, and I have not personally witnessed any of your previous interactions, so let me just say this: Let's avoid any name-calling and disrespect. If you are having a hard time figuring out how to say something in a manner that will accurately reflect your intention without causing any additional conflict, please direct it to me, so I can help you, and we will come up with alternate options together. Are you both agreeable to that?

Disputants [collectively]: Yes.

Mediator: Is there anything else either of you would like to add?

Disputants [collectively]: No.

Mediator: Okay, usually I flip a coin to see who goes first in order to make that decision in the fairest and most impartial way possible. Is that acceptable to everybody?

Disputants [collectively]: Yes.

Mediator: Okay. [Mediator flips the coin and Michaela goes first.] Michaela, why don't you tell us why we're here today – in your opinion?

Michaela: Actually, is it okay if Joe starts? Can we start that way?

Mediator: Joe? How do you feel about starting us off?

Joe: I feel fine with it.

Mediator: Okay, whenever you're ready.

Joe: We're here today in mediation because my wife and I were cheated out of our vacation that we saved a long time for, looked forward to for a long time, and were promised a great time and luxury accommodations. However, we were delivered none of that and we spent a lot of money and I think that we deserve compensation and a refund for everything that we put out because it was really, in my mind, a breach of an implied contract. From what I understand with this kind of thing, they say they're going to provide something, we pay them for that something they say they're going to provide, and then they provide it. If they don't, we are entitled to our money back and so that's what we want and then some for this horrendous experience and the aftermath that we have had to deal with.

Mediator: Okay, Joe, can you please tell me how much you spent on the trip in total?

Joe: Well, it was $650 per night for the package, which included the breakfast and everything. All in all, it was $650 per night, and we gave a deposit and actually sent in the money for ten nights, which totaled $6,500 just for the accommodation.

Mediator: Okay, and did the package include anything else besides breakfast every morning?

Joe: Yes, it included the car to and from the airport.

Mediator: Okay, car and breakfast, which you have indicated that you received. Is there anything else?

Joe: Yes, we got the car and were given the breakfast. Full use of the facilities at the hotel was also promised to us in the package deal.

Mediator: And how many nights did you actually stay at the hotel, two?

Joe: Yes, we stayed for two nights.

Mediator: And were you able to use the facility that was mentioned in the package?

Joe: No, not to the degree that would have been acceptable.

Mediator: And have there been any negotiations between you and the hotel thus far? Any kind of settlement offers or ideas on the table that we should begin by discussing?

Joe: No real settlement offers. I mean, they offered to upgrade our room, which they did, but we were basically trapped in our room because anywhere else we went was miserable.

Mediator: Okay, and what are you looking to accomplish here today as far as a settlement goes?

Joe: I'm asking for a full refund of what we paid for the package, our airfare back to Los Angeles, plus an additional $25,000 for our distress because we put so much effort into saving all year for this. I think $25,000 in the form of an apology would be appropriate.

Mediator: Thank you, Joe. I do have additional questions, but if it's okay with all parties, right now I would just like to get the facts from each of you. After that I will ask my questions, and we can proceed from there. Is that okay?

Disputants [collectively]: Yes.

Mediator: Okay, Michaela, why don't you tell me why you believe we're here today?

Michaela: Well, of course we're very, very sorry for the disappointment that this couple has, but I would like to point out that the regular price of their hotel room before the upgrade we provided to them would have been $10,000 more than what they paid. So, they paid $6,500 and normally that room would have been about $17,000. So, in comparison, they paid very little of what they would normally have been charged and got an excellent deal. Additionally, we did accommodate them in any way that we could, which included upgrading them and trying to make their stay as pleasant and enjoyable as possible. We understand that they were very disappointed, but there was still the possibility of going outside and beyond the grounds of the hotel, as they were still in receipt of this much reduced price, and phenomenal package for a hotel of this nature with stunning surroundings. They could have stayed and used their days. Yes, there was construction from 7:00 a.m. to 2:00 p.m., but there are ways around that. I don't think it's that unreasonable even though ideally one wants to go somewhere where there is no construction, but to have the opportunity to go to a place like this and stay in a hotel such as ours far surpasses any minor inconvenience the construction may have caused. Joe stated himself that without the package deal they would never have been able to afford it. So, this was an opportunity to afford coming to a hotel at this level of luxury for a very small amount, especially because they were upgraded to an even better and more expensive room. I think they could have somehow still found a way to enjoy this vacation even with the limitations of the construction. They could have gone out during the day, gotten up earlier in the morning to be gone by the time the construction started, and then returned back to the hotel for the afternoon when the construction was finished to go swimming in our fabulous pool. There were definitely ways around it is my point.

Mediator: Okay, let me ask you a question for clarity, if I may. The room they were upgraded to – what is the daily cost for that room?

Michaela: Their upgraded accommodation was one of our highest end luxury suites and costs $3,000 per night. It is completely top-of-the-line, and we did that for them so that they could enjoy their stay in complete luxury.

Mediator: And was that upgraded suite extended to them for the entirety of their stay?

Michaela: Yes.

Mediator: Okay, and what is the settlement offer you've extended to them thus far, or would like to extend to them now?

Michaela: Well, in addition to the upgraded suite and our continued apologies for the noise and the construction, we are willing to refund back to them all of the money they spent on the package they purchased.

Mediator: And thus far, you have not refunded any of their money back to them, correct?

Michaela: No, we have not.

Mediator: Okay, so they're asking for their money back plus airfare plus $25,000. Is any of that new information to you right now?

Michaela: Yes, it is.

Mediator: Okay, because there seems to be some new information, and there is a demand and an offer on the table, would everyone like to take a moment to process the information? And let me preface that question by reminding us all that we're here in this mediation today to try to settle this case, a fact that been expressed to me, in order to try and avoid moving to litigation, which could potentially add a tremendous financial expense to all involved, as well as an indeterminate amount of time before your case is even heard, and the added public nature of trials.

Michaela: Yes, thank you, I would like a moment please. Can we go over exactly what Joe and Louise received so far, and what they are asking for?

Mediator: Sure. Joe and Louise stayed two nights in upgraded suites. Now they are asking for a full refund of the package they purchased, as well as reimbursement for their airfare.

Michaela: Would it be possible to move into caucus for a few moments?

Mediator: Yes, absolutely. No problem.

MEDIATING IN CAUCUS

Michaela: I wanted to discuss with you privately what I am thinking about offering Joe and Louise and to get your opinion about it. I am inclined to offer them some very good stuff at the hotel, but not in the form of cash. What do you think about that?

Mediator [in Michaela's room]: You can offer anything you want, of course, and I do think you should think creatively. I think you should consider a few things, including the reality of what you could be facing if you don't settle in mediation. As it stands now you've offered them the upgrade and reimbursement, but that seems to leave other options on the table.

Michaela: Okay, I understand what you are saying, and I have some ideas. What they paid was 75 percent off what they would have paid, so for our hotel that is not an extreme amount of money. Giving them back what they spent to accommodate them is fine. If it is okay with you, I am ready to head back into joint session.

Mediator: Okay, give me a moment to check in with Joe and then I will come back to you.

Mediator [in Joe's room]: Hi, Joe. Thanks for accommodating the caucus request. Michaela is ready to rejoin in joint session. Does that work for you, or is there anything you would like to discuss with me privately?

Joe: I am okay for now, thank you. Joint session is fine with me.

Michaela [back in joint session]: I think I can understand their disappointment, and I understand this was their vacation time and I would ask for them to understand that that this was not our intent and that I really don't know why it was not advertised, but we acknowledge that it wasn't. I would also like to point out that yes there was construction going on, but we did accommodate them in whatever way we could, and as I said before, they easily could have gone outside of the hotel or adjusted their schedule slightly around the hours of construction. However, understanding their disappointment, even though they did stay for two days in the upgraded suite (one of our finest), I would be happy to include those two days in the refund – it was $650 per day which would be $1,300 of their package spent for those two days – of their full ten-day package price which was $6,500. That just leaves us with $1,000 for our troubles, and I think that should be enough.

Mediator: Okay, just so I am clear, you are willing to reimburse them $6,500, which is their full package amount?

Michaela: Yes.

Mediator: Okay, let me ask you one question before we shift over to Joe. Can you please explain to me exactly which areas of the hotel were not accessible to them, and to all guests, due to the construction?

Michaela: Anybody at the hotel could do anything they liked, but there was construction going on outside, so there was some noise, and some dust from the construction during the hours of 7:00 a.m. to 2:00 p.m. After that there was no noise and no dust, but everything including the swimming pool—every area of the hotel—was still accessible.

Mediator: And is the pool in the dust zone? If someone was in the pool during that time would they be impacted by the dust?

Michaela: The pool is not exactly in the dust zone, but there was construction going on, so we understand that it's not ideal to be in the pool between 7:00 a.m. and 2:00 p.m. due to the construction being done nearby.

Mediator: Is there a projected end date to the construction?

Michaela: Yes.

Mediator: Okay, so now let's shift over to Joe. We have an offer on the table for $6,500.

Joe: It's a start. Okay, I have to say that that their regular rate is really not relevant. They advertised this package for the amount that we paid, the brochure was beautiful—it showed an incredible, pristine view, and the pool was immaculate in the brochure. Everything looked wonderful and we expected a delightful vacation. You couldn't use the pool. There was a layer of dust over everything including the chairs, even the pool was like swimming in mud, so the pool was unusable, at the restaurant we couldn't even enjoy the complimentary breakfast because of the noise, and as soon as you walk out of the restaurant you're in a cloud of, who knows, possibly toxic dust. When she says there was no dust after construction—that would be impossible and certainly untrue. There was dust everywhere, they couldn't clean up the place right away after construction stops, it's not possible. A hotel of this luxury? Well, it wasn't a hotel of this luxury when we were there. I don't think their regular rate is relevant. They made a promise of a certain quality and for a certain price and they broke their promise. I think that the days that we stayed there were unacceptable in that we weren't using the hotel as promised—as it was promised to be available. I think that we should be refunded our airfares as well. We would not have made this trip—we wouldn't have thought about this for a second had we known what was happening on site, including the view. I mean, we look out our window and half the hotel is gone.

Mediator: It sounds like you planned the trip to only stay in the hotel and not go anywhere else off site, because if the construction was only at the hotel, then theoretically you could have had a perfectly nice trip to other places, visiting, exploring, and whatever else. What was your intent for the content of your trip?

STOP READING

FLASH CHALLENGE

Strategizing

1. Why do you think the mediator asked Joe about his (and Louise's) intent for the trip?
2. Might there be a particular answer, or answers, the mediator has in mind to hear in response?
   a. What are some of Joe's possible responses?
3. Might the mediator be mentally developing:
   a. A negotiating strategy?
   b. An overall strategy focus?
   c. A possible settlement design?
      i. Potential settlement options that could be appealing to Joe and Louise?
4. Based on what you believe to be Joe's possible answers, develop:
   a. Possible settlement options for Joe and Louise.
   b. Strategy to present your settlement options to Joe in a way that would be effectively received.
5. Broaden your settlement suggestions to incorporate possible options for Michaela's portion of the agreement – what would they be?
   a. Discuss your strategy to present your settlement options to her in a way that would be effectively received.

CONTINUE READING

Joe: Our intent was to have a relaxing stay at a luxury resort, to have drinks by the pool, to enjoy the tropical sunsets, this is what we wanted.

Mediator: Okay, I understand. And is this the only time that you would be able to come to this hotel? For example, if they said, "Okay, look, we're going to give you a full credit to come when the construction is done and you'll have a beautiful stay," is that something that could work for you and Louise?

Joe: We can only have a vacation like this once a year. This year's vacation was ruined. It was emotionally so disturbing that my wife is having trouble thinking about going back to work! We look forward to this all year, we book a luxury vacation every year, and this one was ruined.

Mediator: It sounds like a total letdown, and shocking for you—you had no idea what was happening when you got to the hotel. My question, though, is about what is more important to you—having your money refunded, or the possibility of having the experience you were thinking to have in the first place at another time?

Joe: Well, okay, so there are two issues. Yes, we would love to have a luxury vacation—that's why we paid for this package and we intended to have a great vacation, but we didn't get it and our window for this year is closed. But talking about future years? Yes, it would be nice to have another vacation, but what are we going to do about this year's vacation that was ruined? Those are two different, two different points.

Mediator: Yes. I'm wondering if we can factor the as-yet-to-be-had luxury vacation experience into the equation as well?

Joe: We can try.

Mediator: Okay, so they've offered you $6,500. Would you like to consider their offer and discuss accepting it or presenting a counteroffer?

Joe: I want $7,500 which includes our airfare, and I want our $25,000 pain and distress money. I think that we're entitled to compensation for the distress that they caused, and our ruined vacation for this year.

Mediator: Okay. I think we can look into some wiggle room. The distress you're feeling makes sense, of course, based on what happened. However, I'm wondering—and please just sit with it for a minute—if the promise of what you did want and what you did sign up for could be had in the future, even potentially next year if the construction will be done by then. Maybe that can offset some of your pain and distress.

Joe: If we were to get refunded this entire vacation, which would be the $7,500, then let's leave the other stuff out of this for now. And if we were guaranteed the vacation that we were promised, let's say next year, free of charge, we would consider a reduction in the amount we are asking for pain and distress.

Mediator: Okay, so let's shift over and hear from Michaela while you consider a new number.

Joe: Okay.

Michaela: So I think that we're being very flexible about this, and yes we would be willing to refund them the entire $7,500—that's fine. I do see, though, whereas he was saying that the two issues aren't connected, I do see them as connected for us. There's one issue, and this construction will be done at a certain point, and we can offer them a trip next year, and we're very sorry about the distress of this time. For next year, we can offer them the ideal, wonderful experience that they were hoping for. We think that that actually would take care of the distress, and so we would be willing to do that. We'll give them their money back that they spent, plus the additional $1,000 they spent on airfare returning home early, with a promise that they could come back in another year.

Mediator: Okay, and what about their trip next year? Can you please give me the details of what you are offering? Are you offering exactly this same package?

Michaela: This package price was an unusual and special deal that we do not offer generally. This was a one-time-only deal. So, we offered this exceptional price of 25 percent of the full price, and even though this will not happen again and prices will go up once the construction is over, we would be willing to give them the same special benefit for another year, or even for two years if they want to do this in two years. Actually, whenever they would like to do this, they can have this special offer, and it is a very, very special offer in that it's not ever done and it's not going to be done again.

Mediator: Okay, so let me make sure I understand. You're offering to refund their money in the amount of $7,500, plus the same package amenities at the same price for them to come back as their schedule permits. And, for the sake of details, that package will include a ten-night stay at exactly the same price—no change to anything.

Michaela: Yes, because they did also have access to areas outside of the parameters of the hotel, we understand that to go looking and exploring around wasn't their intention. They wanted to sit by the pool, have drinks, and watch the sunset, which we hope was still nice, and by the way, every day after construction ended, we did clean the pool as much as was possible. We did everything that we could to make every day as good as we could, but we understand and we will refund the entire amount for their output and, like we said, we'll give them the same deal even though prices are going up, and even though this package does not exist because it was a one-time-only offer.

Mediator: I think everything that you're saying goes a long way; however, I don't think we're addressing the largest part of the problem, which is that they were told that they would receive something, and they paid to receive something that they did not receive, and consequently a lot of things were ruined for them. They wait all year, they have one opportunity a year to go on this trip, they chose your hotel because it's beautiful, they've now said many times how beautiful they think it is, and that they would love to be able to come back and do it the right way. I think there are some very hard feelings because it was a very upsetting situation for Joe and Louise. I think any one of us can imagine how we might feel in those circumstances.

Michaela: Yes, and that is why we're willing to go out of our way to give them, at their convenience and on their timeframe, the full package that we offered to them originally. This is a spectacular package at an amazing quarter of the regular price, especially considering that we're not going to be offering that ever again. We can also consider adding in additional amenities for them while they are there.

Mediator: Okay, let's talk about those amenities because we do still have this $25,000 number on the table. Maybe we can do some negotiating there. So, let's talk about the amenities a little bit.

Michaela: We can add in some amenities that are not initially in their package, like to arrange some tours for them to actually leave the hotel, and these would be tours that they would have to pay for under normal circumstances. We will be happy to arrange those tours for them.

Mediator: Okay, and I understand that breakfast comes in their package, but what about another meal?

Michaela: Yes, breakfast comes in their package, but we would be happy to add in another meal.

Mediator: Such as dinners for ten nights at the hotel?

Michaela: Yes. This is a package, by the way, that doesn't exist. It is being tailored today to express to Joe and Louise that we value them as customers and would like a second chance to give them the vacation of their dreams. We know we can do it.

Mediator: Okay, thank you for expressing that. Just to be clear, the package that you're presenting to Joe and Louise is not the upgraded version, but is the exact package they paid for with the addition of the new amenities we're discussing?

Michaela: Yes, that is correct. The package will be the package that they wanted: the ten-day stay with breakfast included, beautiful room with a view, access to everything the hotel has to offer, but now we're talking about adding to the package dinner as well as breakfast, and arranging for them to go on tours. This is what we're adding to the package, which does turn it into what would be included in a much pricier package.

Mediator: Okay, to you Joe. Because we are still in joint session, you're hearing what's being offered to you, so let's talk about what they have done since the previous offer. They have come up another $1,000 to fully reimburse you for your trip, they're offering to arrange tours for you to visit any area you would like outside of the hotel . . .

Michaela (interjecting): Or anything like a tour or sightseeing that is of any interest to you or Louise.

Mediator: Okay, thank you for that clarification, Michaela. It sounds like they will arrange a variety of activities for you, and dinner for ten nights at the hotel, which you mentioned was very important to you and Louise—to be able to enjoy the beauty of the hotel. So now they've added an inside the hotel aspect, as well as an outside the hotel aspect, complete refund of your money, you can use this offer next year or the following year, and even though the package no longer exists they are willing to re-create it, plus more, especially for you and Louise.

Joe: Okay, I think we're making progress, but I want to address the fact that this year's vacation no longer exists, so I don't want to talk about, and I don't think that it's relevant to talk about this year's vacation because it really never existed, but the disappointment still exists from this year's vacation. So I appreciate that they're offering the same package—it's basically them wanting to do a rerun or a reboot of our vacation, so okay. These extras are not that impressive, I don't think that they really go much of the way toward compensating us for this huge, huge disappointment that we look forward to once a year! We don't make that much money, we both work very hard for our money, we squirrel it away, and we want and need this break. We didn't get it this year because of this situation, and in addition to not getting a break, we had this horrible stress of dealing with this and dealing with a staff that was so unaccommodating and so unprofessional toward us—the fact that we bought a package specifically seemed to cause the girl at the front to be very disdainful toward us. I mean, we were not treated well even under these circumstances. I think that we can come down from our $25,000 request with a couple things. I think if they added in spa privileges throughout the next vacation, plus full airfare to and from the hotel, whatever the cost it would be.

Mediator: So right now the package includes $1,000 toward airfare, so if it's more you are requesting that they cover the cost. Okay.

Joe: Right. And in terms of this year, well, we had to do a staycation and it was not very satisfying at all, so I'm thinking some compensatory effort to be made to make the rest of our year a little bit more doable. For instance, some sort of stress-reducing services, like massage in town, or whatever they think they can offer. I know they have a lot of properties, so maybe a weekend stay at one of their local properties.

Mediator: Okay. I appreciate that suggestion, Joe, and I think it's a really good suggestion based on exactly what you experienced, and I think that would probably be received favorably based on the nods I'm seeing from Michaela. Let's look some more into creating your vacation experience, and some additional pleasant experiences. So I'm going to shift back to Michaela, and please remember you can also speak directly each other if you would like to and are both comfortable with that.

Michaela: I was actually going to offer a weekend stay at our hotel that is right near where Joe and Louise live. I know that their ten-day yearly vacation time period is over, but I thought maybe a weekend in one of our hotels would be possible with their schedule and might help to deal with the present feeling of disappointment that they obviously missed out on a vacation. Hopefully by them going to the hotel for a weekend they can have some relaxation and then knowing that they have a year or two to plan for the vacation that they wish they had had, and they'll be able to have, they will begin to feel better.

Mediator: Okay, let's talk about spa privileges.

Michaela: We would be happy to add spa privileges.

Mediator: Now would those spa privileges extend to the reimbursed package in addition to the new hotel weekend offer?

Michaela: Yes.

Mediator: Okay. Joe requested that their airfare be covered regardless of the cost, meaning that if it should exceed $1,000, which would mean that is more than is allocated for in the package currently as the cost for the room is $6,500 and the entirety of the package is $7,500, the hotel would be responsible for paying any additional flight costs. Are you agreeable to that, Michaela?

Michaela: Yes. The package includes airfare, so we will continue to take care of that on our end when they come back.

Mediator: Okay, so let me make sure that I have all of the components of the offer clear. $7,500 refunded to them to be used on exactly the same package at any point in the next two years, including spa privileges, including their airfare fully paid for by the hotel, and a weekend at a local hotel, which will also include spa privileges.

Michaela: Yes.

Mediator: You have also added in tours (and related activities) and dinners to their package trip. What about for the weekend hotel stay? Are there any meals included or would you like to add the inclusion of any meals?

Michaela: We will include breakfast and dinner. It will be basically the same offer as the package, but it's a little different with tours because the location is different, but they will have a lovely weekend relaxing at the spa with dinner and drinks by the pool.

Mediator: Is that for two nights?

Michaela: Yes, that is for two nights.

Mediator: And the type of hotel room will be comparable to the package?

Michaela: Yes. But it is a different hotel, mind you, so it's not exactly the same – it's not international.

Mediator: Okay. Is there anything you'd like to add before we shift over to Joe?

Michaela: Just that we're very sorry that this was such a disappointment, but we feel that this is a good workaround and that we know that they will be happy with this arrangement.

Mediator: Okay thank you, Michaela. Joe?

Joe: Well, it's sounding really good. Just a couple of additional things I might ask for: I want to be guaranteed that the next time we book this package, all construction will be done and the renovation complete. I also want to be guaranteed an ocean view room for both of the packages, and the rooms will need to be above the fifth floor. If they can agree to those additions, I think we might be there.

Mediator: Okay.

Michaela: Well, there's no ocean view available in the hotel for the weekend getaway because there is no ocean there, but they will have the best city view the hotel has to offer, and above the fifth floor in both locations is fine.

Joe: Okay, a city view is fine, but it has to be on the premium side of their hotels.

Mediator: Okay, let's consider the original package to be a premium package, and this weekend stay will be of comparable quality. Is that agreeable, Michaela?

Michaela: Yes.

Joe: Well, Louise is not here today, clearly, but I am speaking for both of us and I'm going to go ahead and say, okay. I believe that she'll be okay with it also.

Michaela: I hope so, too, because I think that in apologizing for this whole thing happening, we have gone over and above in every way that we can.

Mediator: Okay, so let's just cross all of our T's and dot all of our I's as everybody writes the agreed-upon settlement down for themselves. We have $7,500 refunded to be used toward the exact same package either next year or the following year (two years), a guarantee that the construction will be completed. If that should take longer than the two years, you will extend their package?

Michaela: Yes, absolutely.

Mediator: Okay, and you are also including tours over the ten days, dinners for the ten nights that Joe and Louise will be at the hotel, spa privileges that will include massages per Joe's request, correct?

Michaela: Yes.

Mediator: Okay, and fully covered airfare. You are also including a one-weekend staycation, which is two nights at a local hotel including breakfast, dinner, spa privileges, and a comparable room above the fifth floor.

Michaela: Yes.

Mediator: As well, the room included in the package that you are reimbursing Joe and Louise for is also above the fifth floor.

Michaela: Yes.

Mediator: Okay. Are we okay?

Joe: I think we're there.

Michaela: I agree.

Mediator: Okay. Sounds good to me, and thank you. Are there any questions, comments, or concerns?

Michaela: I think that's it.

Joe: Okay. I appreciate the apology.

Mediator: Michaela and Joe, thank you for coming to mediation. I appreciate your active and respectful participation, and Joe—I think you and Louise will have two very nice vacations.

Joe: I think so also. Thanks for your help.

Mediator: You're welcome, anytime.

appendix 6

An International Interaction: *Mediating Across Cultures*

An analysis of the relationship between China and the United States and its impact on a negotiation over Chinese dissident Chen Guangcheng

Before a negotiation begins, parties must take many factors into consideration, including but not limited to, potential ramifications of words spoken, perceived slights or threats, the ability or inability to save face, and past and future relationships. Negotiations are made more difficult when there is a preexisting, often contentious and nontrusting relationship, as in the case of China and the United States. "Each set of negotiators is likely to see the interaction with the counterparty, at least in part, through the prism of the history of the relationship between their respective countries. How significant a factor this will be in the negotiations will depend on context: the countries involved, the nature of the deal being negotiated, and even the personalities of the negotiators."[1] This negotiation was centered around Chinese dissident Chen Guangcheng, who requested shelter from the U.S. Embassy. It was the moment that then Secretary of State Hillary Clinton made the decision to accept Chen Guangcheng into the embassy building that prompted negotiations with China. The volatility and hair-trigger pressure during this negotiation were not lost on the U.S. negotiating team, as they went into the negotiations with China knowing that the entire process could potentially be derailed simply by an ill-considered statement.

The stakes are even higher in negotiations such as this one, when world politics, the balance of power, and human rights are contributing factors. When a negotiation opens with one side "ripping into" the other, and hurling accusations of violated diplomatic practices, all parties fasten their seatbelts. Negotiations can take any number of wild and gut-wrenching twists and turns, and this negotiation was no exception. The negotiation team on the U.S. side of the table was made up of six State Department officials, including Assistant Secretary Kurt Campbell, legal advisor Harold Koh, and the U.S. Ambassador to China, Gary Locke. On the Chinese side sat ten Chinese officials in total, including a representative of China's Ministry of State Security and two unidentified men (one from an unidentified

1. Bradlow, Daniel D., and Jay Gary Finkelstein, *Negotiating Business Transactions, An Extended Simulation Course*, 2nd ed, 2018, p. 137.

branch of China's intelligence apparatus), and a diplomat named Cui Tiankai, who had previously worked with Americans several times.

Negotiations began on April 29, 2012.

The attendance of the "two unidentified men" on the Chinese negotiating team, named as such since they were never introduced at the negotiation table and they never uttered a word, opened a window into the way China operates. When forced to deal with potential cultural and national embarrassment, engaging with a foreign nation—the United States, as well as U.S. negotiators—China closed ranks, and kept their cards close to the vest. With the majority of the Chinese negotiating team remaining silent for the entirety of the negotiation, the U.S. negotiating team faced an uphill battle. China's political structure has its own culture and traditions; there are also many additional societal cultural norms and expectations. Whether China's silence was a political or societal cultural tradition, or both, it was a tactic that needed to be understood and recognized as such by the U.S. team so they could select tactics suitable for both dealing with and neutralizing its impact on the overall negotiation. The U.S. team was unable to use many of the strategies we are taught during negotiation and mediation training—in particular building rapport, finding common ground, and creating a relationship including trust—without which a negotiation might not achieve its goals both presently and in any sustainable fashion. With nothing reciprocated from any but one member of the Chinese team, these potential tools became impossible to put into practice. With skepticism and mistrust abounding and no ability to work it through, the negotiation would have to stand on the merits of the offers and concessions made by both the U.S. and Chinese teams.

When negotiating on behalf of the principal, the negotiator, or negotiating team in this case, must be prepared for the party in dispute to act in unpredictable ways. Here, at the eleventh hour, Chen Guangcheng went behind the backs of both the Chinese and the Americans and addressed the world about what was taking place. His action resulted in a complete breakdown in the negotiation process, nearly causing the derailment of the entire negotiation, and practically fracturing the relationship between China and the United States. Additionally, China felt unparalleled embarrassment and rage at what they perceived to be a slap in the face after they fulfilled their side of the agreement and honored their promises. To begin with, the Chinese considered the idea of negotiating with Americans regarding their own citizen to be unacceptable, so to have come all the way to an agreement and for it to implode due to Chen's very public actions was a substantial setback. At this point, the United States not only had to redouble their efforts to get a deal with China back onto the table, but they also needed to take Chinese culture into consideration and carve out a way for them to save face. This would prove to be a core tenet in the ability for an agreement to be reached and the relationship saved.

Another element in this negotiation that would prove to be extremely difficult was Chen's long history of publicly reporting on what he called "Chinese official abuses," and his multiple detainments by Chinese authorities. How would China, even if they could, negotiate to release him without looking weak? Beyond the act of releasing him, now the United States—a longtime competitive nation with whom China has had a strained relationship—had become involved. It would be the job of all of the negotiators, on both the U.S. and Chinese teams, to find a solution to the human rights problem arising around Chen, while providing China a way to save face, and restoring Chinese-U.S. relations.

After Chen caused what was perceived in the moment to be irreparable harm to the negotiation that the teams had labored to put together, Secretary of State Clinton decided it would be in the best interest of reaching a settlement for her to meet in person with China's senior foreign policy official, Dai Bingguo. Heading into the meeting on the morning of April 4, Clinton needed a strategy to skillfully provide China with an option to give the United States what they were asking for, while still being able to save face. A misstep from Clinton at this point would surely have ended the negotiations, and a lack of cultural knowledge and sensitivity on her part (a critical awareness, with its inverse of uninformed and insensitive), being fatal to the negotiation, would have swiftly undermined her ability to reach settlement. Clinton made a wise move by beginning her meeting with Dai by praising both teams for their hard work during the negotiations. She then proceeded to reframe a new proposal in terms of the first offer to which the Chinese had originally agreed before Chen lashed out and derailed it. In creating this reframe, Clinton adjusted and adapted her tactics based on the evolving landscape and changing dynamics of the negotiation, adapting to what the situation required. In conjunction with focusing on terms that had already been agreed to, as well as the respect her title brought to her in-person negotiation, Clinton was able to find common ground. Although the original U.S. negotiating team was unable to build rapport with the Chinese team, the sheer success of reaching an agreement created its own common ground and set the groundwork for Clinton. The originally agreed-upon arrangement was for Chen to end up studying at a university in the United States in two years; so why not just move up that timeline? This diplomatic, nonaggressive solution would become a winning scenario for all.

The Chinese face-saving move came in the form of a news report released by China's official news agency, Xinhua, stating that based on his Chinese citizenship Chen would be permitted to apply to study abroad. As part of their negotiating and settlement demands, it was necessary that China not appear to be yielding to outside pressure, nor making any kind of concession, nor coming to any type of understanding with the United States. This negotiation faced an incredible amount of public scrutiny, intensified by the constant, targeted media rhetoric. Confidentiality during the process was crucial, as we saw when Chen breached it by making a number of telephone calls, thereby derailing the first agreement. With confidentiality directly tied to media exposure of the negotiation, any public breach of this confidentiality would result in China losing control of the reframe of their involvement with the United States and any terms reached. The necessity of confidentiality would continue to be a key factor, as later revealed by the U.S. decision to decline comment in response to inflammatory and untrue press releases from China. Instead, all parts of the deal would be made to appear as an arrangement of independently completed actions, separate but still in concert with each other.

The U.S. team did not need to involve their pride in this negotiation, nor did they have interest in or designs on publicly touting any kind of power over China. Their primary goal was to reach agreement on certain points regarding Chen, but also to repair the relationship with China and ensure that it would be ongoing. When pride is involved, so, too, might be an automatic disadvantage. With pride often becoming a weakness, a lack of total rationality or ability to control emotions could follow. In discussing this negotiation, it has been noted that the days of destroying a relationship over a single person are in the past; so although China backed themselves into a corner with their unwillingness to be flexible about Chen's future, and to see both short- and long-term advantages, the U.S. negotiating team remained cool and let their creative ideas guide the negotiation toward their intended solution. There is a heightened level of respect for and pressure on maintaining relationships as parties coming to international negotiating tables are well aware of the stakes if an agreement is not reached, or if a negotiated agreement falls apart. Relationships matter and are understood in ways they have not been in the past. Because the core needs and desires of both sides were never truly in contradiction, the U.S. team had no problem allowing China to take the lead on how they would publicly address the closed-door agreement between these powerful countries. China in turn took to the press, creating their desired appearance of power and winning, in spite of the reality of the negotiation being more collaborative in nature.

During her meeting with foreign party official Dai Bingguo, Clinton never specifically asked for anything. She did, however, clearly tell him that she would be speaking about Chen to the press. This statement, or veiled warning, in advance of Clinton's actions, from one power player to another, allowed the time for China to release their own statement ahead of her press conference. Clinton made it clear, in a nonaggressive but authoritative way, that there was a clock on when the world would hear from her, a member recognized as the leader of the U.S. negotiating team, about Chen and a Chinese–U.S. agreement. Clinton set a hard deadline and allowed it to be the final impetus compelling action toward agreement. She did, however, allow that action to come from China ahead of the United States, acknowledging what was necessary to honor China's cultural mandates.

The press release from China stated that Guangcheng could travel to study abroad like any other Chinese citizen. Publicizing this piece of information enabled China to save face in front of the Chinese people as well as the rest of the world. It also left no room for accusations of China making any kind of deal with the United States or giving in to any demands that the United States was making, both points that were of utmost importance to China. By using the media to convey a tailored message to the public, China was able to fully control how the world would view their discussions with the United States. China used the media as the tool to reframe the situation, and Clinton was the motivating source to get it done. China's appearance of control in the media, versus the actual control that was arguably squarely in the hands of the United States, was enough to solidify the deal.

Certain strategies were used during this negotiation that were crucial in resolving the dispute. One strategy, a very effective tool in most mediations and negotiations, is to offer creative solutions. In conjunction with such options, it helps tremendously to have the path to that creative solution not only planned out, but also ready to go with little or no additional work needed from the offeree but to accept. Creative solutions can also provide for room to maneuver around sticky situations, deadlocks, and seemingly immutable points. The idea for Chen to attend university in China for two years and then transfer sooner than originally planned to university in the United States was just such a solution. The plan did not require China to lose any ground politically or publicly; it gave a legitimate reason for Chen to be leaving China; and the plan was ready to go and only needed China's agreement. Collaborative creative thinking is a variation of this strategy that can bring both sides together looking at new options, thereby moving away from points of contention during negotiation.

Another strategy was for the U.S. team to let China express displeasure toward the United States about the way they felt this situation was being handled. The United States, not responding in kind, did not fan the flames, maintaining a quiet and respectful presence. Allowing parties to express their feelings makes way for cooler heads to prevail. Removing emotion, as much as possible, from a negotiation allows all parties to get to their true concerns and interests. External posturing can be a major hurdle, especially when hurt feelings and pride are involved, so one way to move beyond them is to get them out on the table, and allow people to feel heard, understood, and addressed. Sometimes it necessitates an apology, as China demanded at one point, and other times it requires more, which could be in the form of additions to the settlement, that one party does not mind agreeing to, and the other party feels satisfied receiving. This makes it easier for all other parts of the agreement to progress and be settled. There were six times during the Chen negotiations that the U.S. team endured these types of meetings with the Chinese team. The meetings included insults, anger, and accusations of disrespect to the Chinese people. There are two important points to note here: The first is that not one of these sessions resulted in any member of either team walking away from the negotiating table. The second is that the hostile behavior was one-sided from the Chinese toward the U.S. team. Such behavior generally indicates where the power lies and who truly holds the cards, and in this instance, the U.S. negotiating team had the power and held the cards, as China had much more to lose and all parties knew it. They "danced the dance" that negotiations require, still respecting the Chinese team and facilitating the opportunity for them to accomplish what was necessary to be able to settle. Even after the settlement, the United States never communicated in a way other than respectfully with China's leaders, nor was the agreement spoken about publicly by the United States as a "win" over China. As long as China negotiated and agreed behind closed doors, their continuation to "denounce American interference in their internal affairs"[2] would be met with no public response from the United States. This pointed to the pride and culture of China, which had to be respected for the relationship to continue and for future negotiations to remain as options for resolving conflicts and settlements to be reached.

2. Hillary Clinton, *Hard Choices*, 2014.

We have learned that the most crucial part of a negotiation is to be prepared. That usually involves heading in with a plan. My experience in negotiating has been that having multiple plans might be the better way to go. To be clear, that would be multiple options all leading to the desired end goal. If certain points in contention are inconsequential to one side, but of tantamount importance to the other, concede. If it does not affect the bigger picture or your bottom line, agree to those issues and move on. This builds favor with the other party and can encourage them to mirror your behavior by conceding on points less relevant to them. Create a framework for the plan, but involve your counterpart in filling in the details. Sharing some control and choice across the table brings the other party with you into an ownership position of the agreement, creating a win/win result instead of a win/lose zero-sum game scenario that would most likely result in continued arguing and no agreement. We have learned to play chess in our heads ahead of time with every possible offer and reply that could come our way from our counterparts and to have moves ready in response to all. Of course, plans and strategies are all well and good until something unexpected happens midnegotiation and leaves everyone on your team speechless and staring wide-eyed at each other. That then requires spontaneous and evolving negotiating skills.

In hindsight, there is no doubt that the U.S. negotiators continued to chastise themselves for not monitoring Chen more closely and for giving him unsupervised access to those cell phones. In that moment there was not necessarily a reason to think that Chen would do anything to sabotage the agreement; however, taking his activist history into consideration, one can see that emotions ran too deep to take any chances. When a deal is as fragile as this one was, constant vigilance and minimizing external influences are of the utmost importance. To have nearly caused the premature conclusion of the negotiations and potentially dismantled the fragile political relationship between China and the United States by failing to monitor an unstable element is indicative of the need to focus on every possible detail. This is a reminder of the extraordinary importance of risk mitigation, in this case not to have permitted Chen to be alone with an opportunity to speak publicly.

When mediations and negotiations teams are comprised of negotiators from around the world, negotiating styles and personalities are likely shaped by vastly differing cultures. It can be a sharp contrast for negotiators who are unaccustomed to negotiating with people from cultures outside of their own. The impact of cultural norms and practices on international negotiations can be equally and often more important than the issues in question. Learning about the culture of counterparts in advance of the negotiation is a critical component in the preparation process and an important part of being involved in international mediations and negotiations. It would not be out of the realm of possibility for a negotiation to stop before it has even begun due to a misplaced handshake or misspoken word, each inaccurately interpreted as disrespectful. Negotiators can be taken aback by what they perceive to be aggressiveness from their counterparts, not understanding right away that such behavior was simply their cultural norm. Negotiating itself can also be part of the problem: In some cultures, negotiating or haggling is absolutely mandatory, regardless of what is being negotiated, whereas in others it is a sign of disrespect to attempt to negotiate at all.

Any negotiation between China and the United States was and is fraught with possible cultural mismatches, potential for misunderstandings, and an extremely blurry line between what is respectful and what is not. In the Chen negotiation, team members with previous experience interacting with individuals from both countries, in addition to their experience as negotiators, greatly aided the process and smoothed out issues that could have caused it to crumble had they not been as experienced. Whether you are a believer in negotiation psychology, tactics, or plain old good moves – perhaps a combination of them all – there is no doubt that both the U.S. and Chinese teams played hard, ebbed and flowed with the rolling tide, and bobbed and weaved with the punches, finally landing on the ground – maybe not entirely solid ground, but together on the ground, nonetheless.

REFERENCES

"Chronology of Chen Guangcheng's Case: Chronology of the Case of Chen Guangcheng, a Blind Lawyer Persecuted for Exposing Official Abuses in China." *Human Rights Watch,* November 13, 2010, www.hrw.org.

Wan, William, et al. "National Security: Negotiations over Dissident Chen Guangcheng Offered Rare Glimpse into How China's Leadership Operates, U.S. Officials Say." *The Washington Post,* May 19, 2012.

appendix 7

Mediation Exercise Instructions

The purpose of Mediation Exercises is to participate in a mediation, as mediator or disputant, in an environment as close to reality as possible.

The mediator should apply different combinations and varying degrees of the approaches, strategies, and skills discussed in this book. Since these exercises are simulations, the mediator should make every effort to practice as many as possible of the wide-ranging conflict intervention strategies presented herein. Applying these skills to the various exercises will give the mediator sufficient opportunity to gain practical experience in preparation for actual cases.

When acting in the role of disputant, participants should endeavor to become that character in the conflict with as much conviction and realism as possible. The participant's interpretation of the disputant's character will require behavior to include Communication Styles and Conflict Handling Modes (CHMs), for example, aligned with the details of the conflict. It is totally acceptable to create a fuller character while staying true to and following the given information. Behaving realistically is a requirement to deepen the learning experience.

GENERAL INSTRUCTIONS TO PARTICIPANTS AS MEDIATOR, DISPUTANT

Read the material, consider all of the elements, and start planning a strategy to reach the desired mediation end goal. Take a few minutes to review – don't rush this part of the process. There is no predetermined conclusion to any of the Mediation Exercises. Whether the mediation concludes in a settled agreement, an impasse, or an alternate end goal lies in the hands of the disputants facilitated by the mediator. To the participant playing the role of mediator, offer the disputants the possible inclusion of an advocate (see "Prefatory Information: ADR Advocates") and make sure to have the Mediator Assignment in front of you as you proceed, as there are questions for before, during, and after the mediation.

appendix 8

Motivational Interviewing: Changing Behavior and the Transtheoretical Model of Change/Stages of Change Model

What we need more than new discoveries in the physical sciences are better interactions between human beings.
— *Carl Rogers*

Motivational Interviewing (MI) is identified as "a collaborative, goal-oriented style of communication with particular attention to the language of change. It is designed to strengthen personal motivation for and commitment to a specific goal by eliciting and exploring the person's own reasons for change within an atmosphere of acceptance and compassion."[1] For the purposes of mediation, conflict intervention, and conflict resolution, consider MI and its focus on change as the process of a disputant changing their current position from one of being in conflict to not being in conflict. This tool could assist the mediator in guiding disputants in their process of transforming from being obstacles prior to changing to becoming stakeholders in the beneficial conclusion of the process by making effective and advantageous choices (changes). MI positions disputants in the driver's seat during mediation (and other forms of conflict intervention processes), from whom all ideas, goals, and intentions are derived, with the mediator positioned to provide support and encouragement. MI keeps the disputants at the center of the activity and helps maintain mediator behaviors of facilitating and encouraging, instead of dictating and diagnosing, which could lead the mediation into trouble. MI enables the principle of disputant self-determination to direct the way the mediator engages and shapes the mediation process, and it can be used at any point during any mediation when determined to be most appropriate and beneficial.

The end goal of MI is to encourage disputants to see the value of changed behavior, and thereby increase their personal desire to change (a necessary behavioral shift in many mediations to reach settlement). Therefore, it is important for mediators to be versed in skills that can assist in such shifts. It should come as no surprise that assisting disputants to reach their goals is that much easier when they

1. Miller and Rollnick, *Motivational Interviewing: Helping People to Change,* 3rd ed., 2013, p. 29.

themselves are not standing in the way. If disputants can be assisted to realize that changes in their attitudes and behaviors could be the vehicle through which their goals are reached, then the process can happen that much quicker and with that much more ease for everyone involved. To that end, the mediator will have interacted with the disputants as a strong network of support and skilled guide at the most and, at the least, as a facilitative assistant.

Questions and probing statements are designed to assist disputants to address ambivalence about making decisions that might lead to a change in their situation, including committing to a settlement that would bring an end to their current conflict. They are additionally intended to promote:

1. Greater awareness of a problem.
2. Recognition of the advantages of change.
3. Increased intent to change.
4. Elaboration on a topic related to change.

Exploring elements to the benefit or detriment of a decision in question can be a deeply helpful and impactful approach. It is important for the mediator or conflict interventionist to discuss with the disputants specific and potentially various consequences as they evaluate and decide whether or not to make changes to their present situation. Comparing and contrasting their lives before, during, and potentially after the conflict could be a useful strategy. The mediator should take care to remind disputants that ambivalence or fear about the prospect of change and all that it entails is a normal and relatable aspect of life. There is a process to everything, so disputants can and should feel safe and comfortable working through their personal process to reach their decision(s). Encouraging parties to discuss their situation, possible decision options, and the potential outcomes of making a decision to change their behavior and current circumstances, as well as the consequences of not doing so, is integral to effective Motivational Interviewing.

Example Questions

1. How are the present circumstances impacting you?
   a. How important is that to you?
2. What can be gained by changing?
   a. How important is that to you?
3. What are the benefits to you of the present circumstances?
   a. How important is that to you?
4. What concerns do you have about making changes?
   a. How important is that to you?

Disputant responses to these and any additional questions could provide insight for the mediator into how the disputant intends to behave with regard to decision-making and their attitude toward change throughout the mediation.

Motivational Interviewing: Assisting Disputants in Examining Their Situation When:

1. Ambivalence is high and disputants have mixed feelings about change.
2. Confidence is low and disputants doubt their abilities to change.
3. Desire to change is low.
4. Importance is low and the benefits of change and disadvantages of the current situation are unclear.

MEDIATOR STRATEGY: EXPLORING DISPUTANT CHANGE PERSPECTIVE

MI serves a twofold purpose as a strategy to change behavior and also embodying a shifted perspective on the process of changing behavior. This process often involves many elements as it progresses through a series of stages until the actual change transpires. If, during this process, a disputant feels that they are being perceived as unwilling, taking too long, uncooperative, or a failure, the natural process of behavioral shift might be stunted and brought to a halt, resulting in possible mediation impasse. The shifted perspective encouraged by MI does not ignore the intricate and multilayered nature of behavioral change, but instead strives to support those changes that must be made to reach a desired end goal.

1. When a disputant struggles to see the importance of change, MI could help to explore their interests and goals by asking the following or similar questions leading to the exploration of the necessity of the change.
   a. What are some of the things in your life currently that you wish to move away from?
      i. Asked in this broad manner, this question speaks to the bird's-eye view of a disputant's overall position recognizing that they are in conflict. It can be appropriate when a party is struggling with their willingness to change or to see the value in changing for the purpose of ending the conflict. Presenting such an expansive and open-ended question will allow the mediator to encourage the disputant to join them in taking a large step away from the conflict conversation and then to work their way back in.
      ii. This question can also be presented in a manner to highlight specifically that the things in their life that they wish to move away from exist as a result of the conflict and can therefore be removed if the conflict were to be brought to a mediated conclusion.
   b. When you think about the future, what are some things you would like to have in it?
      i. The goal of this question is to draw a disputant's attention to the conflict as a potential barrier or obstacle to the things they would like

in their future, and more specifically, that those things might not be possible as long as they remain embroiled in conflict. Ergo, settlement could be their way toward achieving what they desire for their future.

c. When you were a child, what did you dream about doing with your life? Has that changed?
   i. Nostalgia can shift perspective and cause behavioral change. The ideas children have are generally rife with enthusiasm and optimism, holding no space for conflicts, their repercussions, and the bad behaviors that they elicit.

d. If we were to be successful in our work together, what would that look like?
   i. One answer to this question might be *to* resolve the conflict with a mediated settlement. Such an answer can provide a convenient impetus for a mediator to engage a disputant in discussing how to reach their desired outcome.
   ii. It is possible that a disputant will have a difficult time answering this question as a result of immediately responding by blaming another party for the circumstances and seeing that party as the obstacle to the disputant's success. If this is the case, the mediator should help the disputant reorganize these thoughts to focus exclusively on the conflict and the potential benefits of their own changed behavior.

2. When a disputant has little desire to change, exploring the discrepancy between their values and the current state can be an effective method to encourage discussing change.
   a. A clear distinction between a disputant's values and their current circumstances might assist them to recognize that something must take place for them to achieve or reinstate those values. That something will likely be in the form of a behavioral change.
3. Explore the disputant's current values by asking the following or similar questions:

Broad, Bird's-Eye Perspective	Narrow, Targeted Approach
What is most important in your life at this moment?	How has the conflict affected those things that are important to you?
What do you value and prioritize?	What are the things that you value and prioritize that have been affected as a result of your involvement in the conflict?
	How has your involvement in the conflict affected the things that you value and prioritize?
	How have you had to change the things that you value and prioritize as a result of your involvement in the conflict?

Broad, Bird's-Eye Perspective	Narrow, Targeted Approach
	Have you had to sacrifice something you value and prioritize as a result of your involvement in the conflict? If so, how?
How does your lifestyle reflect your values?	In which ways are you unable to live out your values as a result of your involvement in the conflict?
	Does your current behavior fit within your values?
How important to you is it to live your life according to your values?	Do you accept (will you continue to accept) that the position you are in has allowed someone to interfere with your ability to live according to your values?
How can your values help achieve resolution to this conflict?	What are some of your conflict-related behaviors that might need to be changed to align with your values?

4. Discuss what their future could be like if they put this conflict squarely in the past and move on.
    a. Place the disputant's behavior in the context of their desired future.
        i. Do you believe that your current behavior supports ending the conflict and achieving your desired future?
            1. If so, how?
            2. Can you do more now to help support ending your involvement in the conflict?
            3. If not, what can you do to change your current behavior?

PRINCIPLES OF MOTIVATIONAL INTERVIEWING

1. Empathy from the mediator: Must be expressed to develop a trusting relationship with disputants. Without it, why would or even should disputants feel supported and listen when considering behavioral shifts? (See Chapter 8, "Empathy.")
    a. Expresses understanding, respect, acceptance, sincerity, and support.
    b. Develops a nonjudgmental and collaborative relationship.
    c. Focuses on listening rather than speaking.
2. Realizing discrepancy: Discrepancy between a disputant's current position in conflict and their expressed, desired future postconflict must be excavated and revealed to provide the impetus showing the necessity for a behavioral change.

3. Managing resistance:
   a. During the course of a mediation that requires disputant behavioral shifts to progress to settlement, it should come as no surprise that momentum might not be consistently in a forward direction. Change can be an arduous process in and of itself, but within a conflict environment involving parties who are angry, emotional, and who do not like each other, it becomes that much more difficult. The mediator must be prepared for second-guessing, pushing back, and general resistance to change.
   b. The answer to resistance to behavioral change does not always mean having a solution for it. It also means being prepared to assist in guiding disputants through that resistance so they can come to their own conclusions. Change can be interpreted as losing power, so encouraging and supporting disputants to reach decisions about change on their own can allow them to feel that they are reclaiming an element of power, control, and decision-making even as they agree to shift their behavior.
   c. The mediator or conflict interventionist should avoid arguing with disputants despite any presented resistance. There should be no attempts at convincing, but rather a decision to employ reframing and shifting perspectives in acknowledgment of the reality that decisions belong to disputants whether they are ultimately beneficial or detrimental.
4. Self-efficacy: A mediator's support as a disputant makes decisions can provide unparalleled benefits. For a disputant who is unaccustomed to being heard, respected, having power, having anyone in their corner and on their side, or believing that they are capable of taking the necessary steps to realize their desired outcome, such support or lack thereof can propel or inhibit behavioral change. In moments of difficult decisions and self-doubt, support from the mediator or conflict interventionist can be immeasurable in building self-confidence and self-efficacy. From there forward, the disputant might feel more capable of behavioral changes that will result in making impactful choices, making difficult decisions, and reaching their desired mediation end goal and postconflict reality.

FLASH CHALLENGE

It's All About the Confidence

1. Choose a person with whom you interact and see multiple times throughout the day.
2. Identify two areas in which you could verbally compliment and support them.
   a. For example, if they are in school, acknowledge their hard work, that you have complete faith and belief in their abilities, how impressed you are with what they have accomplished, and so on.

b. If they have a job, consider statements to the same effect, but possibly include their impressive ability to lead a team, make decisions, create products, and so on.
c. If they attend school and have a job at the same time, comment on that combination as well.
d. If they are a parent, acknowledge this and the difficulties they might have faced and overcome thus far and continue to do every day—all evidenced by the amazing child they are raising.

3. After making these comments, see if there is any evident behavioral shift or mood change.
   a. Make sure to persist with the comments throughout the day.
   b. This process could take several days, or even a week, but keep track of any changes.
4. Is there an identifiable difference?
   a. If so, describe it.
   b. If not, attempt to shift to other areas for compliment and support.
      i. Maybe they need something else.
         1. Can you identify another avenue to traverse to build their confidence and develop increased self-efficacy?
5. Has there been any change or shift in the way you interact together?
   a. Have they been friendlier toward you?
   b. Are they more willing to disclose information to you by discussing:
      i. Their day.
      ii. Issues they are dealing with.
      iii. Issues that are upsetting them.
      iv. Personal difficulties they are having.
      v. Personal information in general.
6. Could you incorporate this strategy during a conflict that you are involved in? Would you?
   a. This would more likely be possible during a conflict with someone who is not a stranger, a Transformative interaction.

THE FUNDAMENTAL PROCESSES OF MOTIVATIONAL INTERVIEWING

The processes of MI describe the flow of a conversation, and moving back and forth between those processes is appropriate and to be expected.

1. Engaging: This is the foundation of MI. The goal is to establish a productive working relationship through careful listening to understand and accurately reflect a disputant's experience and perspective while affirming strengths and supporting autonomy and self-determination.

2. Focusing: With the guidance of the mediator or conflict interventionist, an agenda is decided on that incorporates a disputant's current position and desired mediation end goal. This agreed-upon purpose gives the disputant direction and support moving into a conversation about change.
3. Evoking:
   a. Emphasis is placed on disputants identifying and accepting in their own words why change should occur. Personal reflection on their current conflict situation when compared to what their reality without conflict could be might be a helpful strategy in determining the why.
   b. Disputant ambivalence about change is discussed without judgment and dismantled into component parts to build certainty into each fragmented element. Through this nonjudgmental discussion and the normalization of ambivalence, disputant relationships with and perspectives toward change could be shifted.
4. Planning: The creation and implementation of a plan developed out of the disputant's input. With the mediator or conflict interventionist's support, commitment to this plan and to change is strengthened.
5. Acceptance:
   a. A mediator or conflict interventionist utilizing MI will take a position of:
      i. Nonjudgment.
      ii. Expressing empathy.
      iii. Seeking to understand the disputant's perspectives and experiences.
      iv. Highlighting disputant strengths.
      v. Respecting the right to make informed choices about changing or not—disputant self-determination.
   b. The mediator does not attempt to influence the disputant, but instead encourages them to direct their own behavioral shift based on:
      i. Processing new or reframed information.
      ii. Gaining a better understanding of the present situation and what could be removed from it should their behavior shift.
      iii. Insight into an opposing party's interests, concerns, Communication Styles, and Conflict Handling Modes (CHMs), for example.
6. Open-ended questions:
   a. The purpose is to seek fuller answers to draw out and explore disputant experiences, perspectives, feelings, and ideas so that the mediator will have a clearer and more well-rounded understanding. Information is gathered within a structure of open-ended questions that first explore what disputants already know.
   b. The mediator can directly or indirectly offer additional information as disputant responses dictate how to proceed.
   c. This more informative and lengthier style of response might help to avoid misunderstandings, inaccurate judgments, and possibly uninformed input from the mediator or conflict interventionist. The mediator or conflict interventionist should encourage disputants to fully engage with these questions because they beget more informative responses.

d. This style of question respects that both the mediator and disputants have expertise, experience, and insight that could be beneficial to the mediation process and the conflict's resolution. For example, the mediator might ask a disputant to explain to them some of the intricacies of the subject matter of the conflict.

7. Affirmation:
   a. Continual reminders of strengths, efforts, and past successes help to build the disputant's confidence in their decision and ability to change.
8. Mirroring:
   a. After listening, the mediator or conflict interventionist repeats or rephrases back to the disputant what they understand them to be expressing.
   b. The purpose of mirroring is to ensure correct understanding for the listener, and for a disputant to hear their own expressed thoughts presented back to them. This can assist the disputant to confirm that what they have stated actually reflects their true feelings, such as a disputant who would like to change and believes that their words relate that intent, only to find out that the opposite is in fact the case after a mirroring interaction with the mediator.
   c. Used to create empathy.
9. Identification of helpful and harmful language:
   a. Identifies what is being said against change, known in MI as *sustain talk*, and what is being said in favor of change, known in MI as *change talk*.
   b. Encourages shift, where appropriate, from sustain talk toward change talk.
10. Summarizing:
    a. Restates key points made by disputants.
    b. Provides the opportunity to clarify any misunderstandings or misconceptions, to express concerns, and ask questions disputants might have for the mediator, conflict interventionist, or one another.

DISPUTANT DECISION-MAKING PROCESS

The Transtheoretical Model of Change/Stages of Change Model[2] is a behavioral identification process that could assist a mediator or conflict interventionist in deciding how and when to apply MI techniques or mediation strategies. The ability to discern what disputants need and when they need it is a boon to the mediator in assisting parties to achieve their conflict resolution goals.

2. James O. Prochaska and Carlo O. DiClemente, *The Transtheoretical Approach*, in *Handbook of Psychotherapy Integration*, 2nd ed., 2005. (Theories are discussed in Gretchen L. Zimmerman, Cynthia G. Olsen, and Michael F. Bosworth, "A 'Stages of Change' Approach to Helping Patients Change Behavior," *American Family Physician*, 2000, https://www.aafp.org/afp/2000/0301/p1409.html#afp20000301p1409-b4.

Phases of Decision-Making

1. Precontemplation: "I'm not changing," "I don't have to change," "It's not about me."
   a. In this phase, disputant behavior is emotional with feelings of inadequacy to address the conflict and potential solution options. This can be characterized by their denial of a need to change or denial of the reality and possible severity of their current circumstances, a disinterest in changing, and doubling down on their position.
2. Contemplation: "I don't have to change, but maybe I should . . .," "Yes, but . . ."
   a. In this phase, disputants are ambivalent about the value of change as well as their ability to make changes. They are uncertain but are becoming receptive to discourse on the subject and the idea of change. They are beginning to consider change (decision-making) and all that it entails. During this early phase, the disputants' level of stress and anxiety might increase as a result of beginning to contemplate change.
3. Preparation: "I'm going to change," "I really think I can do it," "I'm trying to change."
   a. In this phase, disputants have become prepared to make a change. Their ambivalence has decreased, and they will be exhibiting more willingness to make changes. Although they might not be fully prepared to make the changes ultimately necessary to shift their position just yet, disputants will begin testing the waters. Their language and behavior indicate consideration and gradual efforts toward the sought-after shift.
4. Action: "I am changing," "I am doing it."
   a. In this phase, disputants are fully ready to make the necessary change(s) and are doing so. This might be characterized by shifting CHMs, being receptive to new information, newfound understanding of an opposing party, willingness to evaluate settlement options, or reality-based realization of potential consequences of impasse.
5. Maintenance: "I have changed," "I did it."
   a. In this phase, disputants have made the necessary changes to shift their positions. Their level of confidence might waver, however, and being aware of this possibility, the mediator should be prepared to provide support after changes have been made. Disputants might have self-doubt either immediately before or immediately after a settlement agreement has been signed.
   b. The mediator should assist the parties in designing a postmediation plan of action, especially if the mediation is Transformative or involves a settlement agreement that requires payment plans and future interaction. This plan could be critical for maintaining the changed behavior, which includes commitment to their settlement.

With strategies of MI and through the Transtheoretical Model of Change phases, a mediator or conflict interventionist should be looking for specific markers from disputants to identify their mindset, which mediation strategies might be appropriate, and which MI technique might be beneficial. These behavioral markers include:

1. Disputant willingness to change their position within the conflict.
   a. Shifting their CHM
   b. Becoming receptive to new or clarified information
   c. Understanding the position, emotions, and feelings of an opposing disputant
   d. Accepting what their settlement options are and that they will commit to a decision about them
   e. Complete understanding and acceptance of the consequences they would face should they refuse to settle in mediation and proceed with taking their case to court
2. Disputant ability to make the necessary changes.
   a. Consideration of phases of the Transtheoretical Model of Change
      i. Remember that MI techniques are strategies for the mediator to weave into the mediation process as parties work their way through the Transtheoretical Model of Change phases.
3. Disputant readiness to commit to making changes and subsequently following through with the necessary actions.
   a. A combination of change commitment phases and corresponding behavioral steps will denote to the mediator which strategies and approaches are appropriate and how to apply them.
   b. The act of changing is directly connected to disputant willingness, therefore a mediator should discuss any reservations, confusion, questions, or fears they might have about changing.
4. Mediators and conflict interventionists might seek clarity on a disputant's position within the phases of the Transtheoretical Model of Change by asking them to discuss or rate their feelings about making the specific change and how important making that change is to them at that moment. Their answers will vary at different phases, which will assist the mediator to decide how best to approach them, as approaches and strategies will need to fluctuate and be constantly adapted. Disputant needs are nothing short of a continuously moving target.
   a. Examples of scaling questions for the value of change which will also shed light on the importance a disputant has placed on the conflict itself, include:
      i. Not important
      ii. Less important than other things I want to achieve
      iii. Equally important to other needs and goals in my life
      iv. More important than most things I want to or need to achieve
      v. Most important thing in my life right now
5. Based on phase clarity, the mediator can decide which skill to apply during specific moments, as well as management techniques for the entire mediation.

It is a theoretical thermometer to gauge how to proceed that can be used many times during a mediation. Through the determination of phase position, the mediator or conflict interventionist should create a matching model of strategic approach connecting disputant needs with strategic intervention. This will be a tailor-made plan applied to intervention, strategy, approach, goals, and options.

The following discussion can provide a medium for the mediator to assist disputants to move through the Transtheoretical Model of Change phases and make headway in reaching their conflict resolution goals. Asking the parties to explain the reasons for their answers might bring about a shift in their own understanding of their relationship with the prospect of and commitment to change and could evoke new feelings and decisions in the context of their answers. A mediator should ask parties to describe what they want or need to become more comfortable with change and to make decisions that bring about that change. By initiating a conversation with the disputants focusing on their needs, they might begin to feel safer and empowered simply by virtue of engaging in the discussion, precluding any additional time or steps added to meet their needs. This change talk dialogue supports a focus on:

1. Values
   a. If a disputant is not expressing a desire to change, the mediator can guide them through a discussion of:
      i. A comparison between:
         1. Their conflict resolution goals (if they would like to settle their case or not)
         2. Their attitude toward change (how a disparity between desire to change and conflict resolution goals that require change is a hurdle that will need to be overcome)
      ii. An analysis of:
         1. How the distance between the two can be diminished
   b. Example questions a mediator might choose to ask:
      i. How important is it to you to resolve this case in mediation today?
      ii. How has this conflict affected your life?
      iii. Was your life better before this conflict?
      iv. Do you believe your life could be better after it is resolved?
      v. Do you understand that a change must occur to reach your resolution goals?
      vi. Can you identify and discuss your reservations and fears when it comes to change?
      vii. Are those reservations and fears more important to maintain than reaching a resolution to the conflict?
      viii. Can you identify what you might need to feel more comfortable with changing?
      ix. Can you provide some examples of changes you have made in your life that brought about a good outcome, or that were necessary for good to happen next?

2. Goals
   a. This portion of the conversation focuses on why the change is necessary and beneficial to achieve a disputant's desired conflict resolution outcome.
      i. Does this conflict exist in the future you see for yourself?
      ii. Are you prepared to spend more time, energy, and money on this conflict?
      iii. Has this conflict affected anyone or anything else around you?
         1. Family
         2. Friends
         3. Business
      iv. Has this conflict interfered with something you wish(ed) to accomplish in your life?
      v. What is your ideal resolution to this conflict?
         1. Do you understand what it will take to get there?
         2. Please explain.
3. Discrepancy
   a. The mediator or conflict interventionist will shine a light directly on the correlation between disputant actions and expressed goals.
      i. Are the actions you are taking, or not taking, right now supporting your conflict resolution goals?
      ii. Are the actions you are taking, or not taking, right now supporting your life goals?
   b. One strategic approach can be to invite a disputant to create a flowchart with their desired conflict end goal at the top, and their ideas for the ways to achieve that goal by filling in the spaces beginning with their present circumstance.
      i. For example:

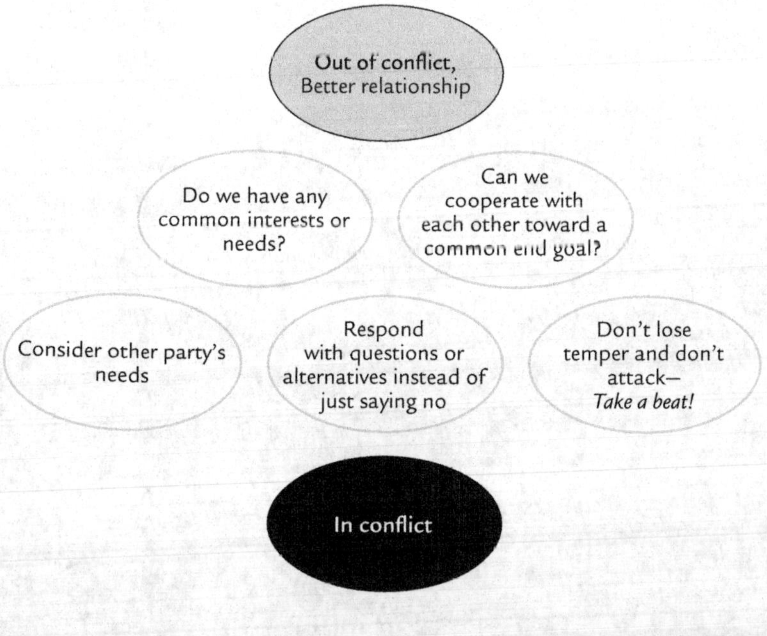

ADDITIONAL RESOURCES

1. Prochaska, J. O., C. C. DiClemente, and J. C. Norcross. "In Search of How People Change." *American Psychol* 1992, 47(9), pp. 1102–1104.
2. Miller, W. R., and S. Rollnick. *Motivational Interviewing: Preparing People to Change Addictive Behavior*. New York: Guilford, 1991, pp. 191–202.
3. MINT. Motivational Interviewing Network of Trainers. https://motivationalinterviewing.org/.
4. Miller, N. H., P. M. Smith, R. F. DeBusk, D. S. Sobel, and C. B. Taylor. "Smoking Cessation in Hospitalized Patients. Results of a Randomized Trial." *Arch Intern Med* 1997, 157(4), pp. 409-415. https://pubmed.ncbi.nlm.nih.gov/9046892/.
5. Zimmerman, G., C. Olsen, and M. F. Bosworth. "A 'Stages of Change' Approach to Helping Patients Change Behavior." *Am Fam Physician* 2000, 61(5), pp. 1409-1416.
6. Australian Government Department of Health. *Module 9: Working with Young People on AOD Issues: Learner's Workbook*. 2004. www.health.gov/au.
7. Center for Substance Abuse Treatment. *Enhancing Motivation for Change in Substance Abuse Treatment*. Rockville, MD: Substance Abuse and Mental Health Services Administration (US); 1999. Report No.: (SMA) 99-3354. https://pubmed.ncbi.nlm.nih.gov/22514841/.
8. The National Library of Medicine, National Institutes of Health. *Motivational Interviewing as a Counseling Style*. www.ncbi.nlm.nih.gov.

Index